John J. Biesle
May, 1991

I read this book in its entirety
in July 2002, Erasmus was a
true genius, multi-interested and
multi-skilled. Clarke, his grandson, read
Erasmus's books in his teens and must
have found in them nearly all his theory of
evolution — for which Charles provided
much more evidence than Erasmus had.

JJB

# DOCTOR OF REVOLUTION

*by the same author*

# Doctor of Revolution

## THE LIFE AND GENIUS OF
## ERASMUS DARWIN

by
DESMOND KING-HELE

FABER & FABER
3 Queen Square London

*First published in 1977*
*by Faber and Faber Limited*
*3 Queen Square London WC1*
*Printed in Great Britain by*
*W & J Mackay Limited Chatham*
*All rights reserved*

*British Library Cataloguing in Publication Data*

King-Hele, Desmond
Doctor of revolution.
1. Darwin, Erasmus 2. Scientists, English—Biography
I. Title
509'.2'4   QH31.D3

ISBN  0–571–10781–8

# CONTENTS

# ILLUSTRATIONS

## PLATES
*between pages 96 and 97*

## FIGURES

*Note on the transcription of manuscript letters*

Darwin usually writes 'the' as 'y$^e$'; 'and' as '&'; and 'that' as 'y$^t$'. To preserve such 'shorthand symbols' only makes the text difficult to read, so I have restored these and a few other symbols to their proper forms. Also I have used Dr, Mr and Mrs rather than D$^r$, M$^r$ and M$^{rs}$ as usually written by Darwin. But I have preserved capitalizations and mis-spellings (unless these are nonsensical or misleading).

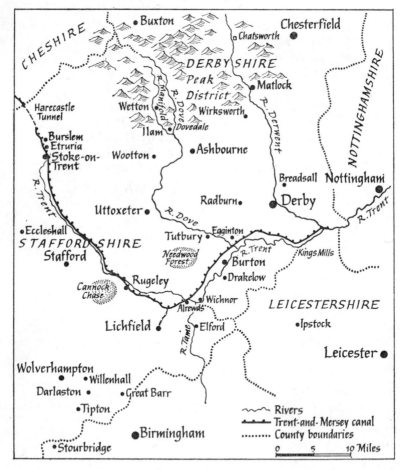

Fig. 1 Sketch map of the Darwin country

Elston, where Darwin was born, is off the map, 12 miles east-north-east
of Nottingham

ONE

# Master of Many Crafts

Erasmus Darwin, who lived from 1731 until 1802, was by profession a physician, widely acclaimed as the finest doctor of his time in England 'Within the narrow resources of 18th-century medicine, he was supreme',[1] but he refused King George III's repeated requests to become royal physician. By nature Darwin was a large and powerful-looking man (Plate 1), cheerful and healthy, and, despite a stammer, a witty and rather domineering talker. By inclination he was extremely sociable and inventive. With Matthew Boulton and William Small, he founded the Lunar Society of Birmingham, which was the chief intellectual driving force behind the Industrial Revolution in England and hence the modern technological world. Encouraged by his Lunar friends, especially James Watt and Josiah Wedgwood, he produced working inventions ranging from a speaking-machine to a horizontal windmill, and dozens of designs on paper. He won most applause, however, in a quite different sphere: his long poem *The Botanic Garden* took the literary world by storm in the early 1790s. Coleridge called him 'the first *literary* character in Europe', the Napoleon of literature, as it were.

Today Darwin earns most credit among scientists for recognizing and describing biological evolution, analysing plant nutrition and photosynthesis, and explaining the main process of cloud formation. And the literary critics honour him not so much for his poems as for his immense influence over the English Romantic poets, Wordsworth, Coleridge, Shelley and Keats.

[2]

Erasmus Darwin was born at Elston near Nottingham, the third son of an early-retired lawyer. He went to Chesterfield School and from there to Cambridge University, where he studied medicine. This was followed by two years at the Edinburgh medical school and in 1756 he qualified as a doctor. He failed to attract any patients at Nottingham, so he migrated to Lichfield, where he had the good fortune—or perhaps skill?—to cure a prominent local man whom all other doctors had condemned to death. His future career assured by this *coup de théâtre*, he settled at Lichfield: he lived there for twenty-five years, giving medical advice for a fee to the rich and freely to the poor.

At the end of 1757 Darwin married Mary Howard, and soon after took a pleasant house at the edge of the cathedral close. The marriage proved very happy, marred only by Mary's continual ill-health. They had three sons who survived infancy. The eldest, Charles, was a brilliant medical student, but he died tragically at the age of nineteen from an infection, after cutting his hand while dissecting. The second son, Erasmus, became a lawyer. The third, Robert, followed his father and was a successful doctor at Shrewsbury.

Before 1760 Erasmus became friendly with Matthew Boulton and Benjamin Franklin. Boulton was then a humble manufacturer of buckles, but by his energy and enterprise he became the leading manufacturer of England and 'the father of Birmingham'. Franklin was already famous for his electrical discoveries. In 1765 Franklin introduced to Boulton and Darwin the learned and liberal Dr William Small, recently returned from teaching in America, where Thomas Jefferson, one of his pupils, declared that Small's example 'fixed the destinies of my life'. The meetings of Darwin, Boulton and Small in the 1760s led to the monthly gatherings of friends at the time of the full moon, later characterized as the Lunar Society of Birmingham.

In the early 1760s Darwin was wildly enthusiastic about making a steam carriage with twin cylinders. Though Boulton was rightly cautious about this idea, Darwin's head of steam was not wasted: James Watt visited him in 1767 and they at once became friends. Watt was gloomy by nature and needed cheering: who better to do so than the energetic and optimistic steam-enthusiast Darwin? No wonder Watt, though usually reticent, praised Darwin so highly: 'It will be my pride, while I live, that I have enjoyed the friendship of such a man.'[2]

Another man who enjoyed that friendship was Josiah Wedgwood. In 1765 Wedgwood and James Brindley began promoting what was virtually a new transport system, the Trent-and-Mersey canal, and Darwin was one of their keenest helpers. Later Darwin designed a horizontal windmill, which was used to grind colours at Wedgwood's pottery for thirteen years, until displaced by steam. The Darwin and Wedgwood families grew up together, and Robert Darwin married Susannah Wedgwood in 1796.

One of Erasmus's friends at Edinburgh, James Keir, settled near Lichfield in 1767, and later set up an alkali factory. Keir was a pioneer of the chemical industry, and he devised a clever process for obtaining soda from salt in dilute solution.

On his daily rounds as a doctor, Darwin was bumped and joggled over the vile roads in his carriage, so it is not surprising that he was keen to construct comfortable carriages. One of his designs, specially resistant to overturning, greatly impressed Richard Edgeworth, and inspired him to become an inventor. He visited Darwin in 1766 and became a lifelong friend.

This group of friends—Boulton, Darwin, Small, Wedgwood, Watt, Keir and Edgeworth—formed the nucleus of the early Lunar Society; Joseph Priestley was a later addition to their number. 'Intellectually the most effective provincial group that has ever come together in England', C. D. Darlington has called them.[3] Individually they were among the most energetic and intellectually able men of the era, and their meetings, by some strange alchemy, channelled their talents fruitfully, producing a revolutionary forward thrust in science and technology.

Darwin also moved in a non-Lunar orbit, within the literary circle of the Cathedral Close at Lichfield, presided over by Canon Seward. Darwin was an accomplished versifier and he helped Seward's daughter Anna to success as a poet. She became known as the 'Swan of Lichfield'. There were also visits from Lichfield's 'Great Cham of Literature', Samuel Johnson, but he and Darwin did not get on well: there was not room for two heavyweight sages in one close.

During the 1760s his reputation as a doctor continued to grow, but he had no cure to offer his wife Mary, and she died in 1770, aged thirty. Her tributes to her husband were recorded by Anna Seward. In the 1770s he strengthened his ties with Benjamin Franklin and gave his approval to the American Revolution. He continued living at Lichfield, unmarried; but he had two illegitimate daughters, known as the Misses Parker, who were brought up at his home.

Then in 1778 he fell in love with the lively and beautiful Mrs Elizabeth Pole, who was thirty-one and the wife of a leading Derbyshire landowner, Colonel Sacheverel Pole of Radburn Hall. At first he could only woo her in verse; but in 1780 Colonel Pole conveniently died, and Darwin, though rather ugly, fat and nearly fifty, brushed aside more eligible rivals and married Mrs Pole in 1781. They moved to Radburn and later to Derby. The second Mrs Darwin's rare talent for creating happiness was exercised fully during the twenty-one outwardly quiet years of their marriage. They had seven children, who acknowledged their good fortune in having been brought up in such a happy atmosphere. Darwin died in 1802 at the age of seventy, of a heart attack.

[3]

In these years of his second marriage, Darwin was less active socially, and devoted much of his energy to writing books. In the 1780s he spent seven years on two lengthy translations of Linnaeus, the *System of Vegetables* and the *Families of Plants*. After that he wrote his five original books, each epoch-making in its own way. The first was his encyclopedic poem *The Botanic Garden*, which entranced the reading public and the literary pundits: 'Dr Darwin has destroyed my admiration for any poetry but his own', wrote Horace Walpole. Part II of the poem, *The Loves of the Plants*, was published first, in 1789, because it was lighter—968 rhyming couplets about the sex life of plants, nicely personified and backed by copious scientific notes. Part I, *The Economy of Vegetation*, published in 1791, is a compendium of scientific knowledge in 1224 rhyming couplets, again with lengthy notes.

Was it wrong of those readers of the 1790s to admire *The Botanic Garden*? The poem is rambling and unstructured: but Darwin's polished couplets have a lustre that time cannot tarnish, as generations of literary critics confirm.[4] To this skill in verse he added three other talents: 'a greater range of knowledge than any other man in Europe', as Coleridge put it; originality in proposing new theories and foreseeing new technology; and an amazing lightness of touch—he is forever laughing at himself. All three talents illuminate his forecast of mechanically propelled cars and aircraft:

Soon shall thy arm, UNCONQUER'D STEAM! afar
Drag the slow barge, or drive the rapid car;
Or on wide-waving wings expanded bear
The flying-chariot through the fields of air.
Fair crews triumphant, leaning from above,
Shall wave their fluttering kerchiefs as they move;
Or warrior bands alarm the gaping crowd,
And armies shrink beneath the shadowy cloud.[5]

The pictures of the plants in Part II are continuously playful. For example in *Lychnis*, where the males and females are on different plants, each female saucily peeps out when mature,

In gay undress displays her rival charms,
And calls her wondering lovers to her arms.[6]

Science so pleasantly presented was much to the taste of the leisured reading public. As L. T. C. Rolt has remarked, Darwin performed 'the astonishing feat of rendering in imaginative terms which any literate man could then appreciate the sum of human knowledge at that time. It was an achievement which was never repeated or even attempted.'[7]

His next book was quite different—a massive tome on animal life, *Zoonomia*, in two volumes totalling 1400 pages, published in 1794–6. By this time his fame as a doctor had become almost legendary, a status scarcely credible today when the mystique of the doctor has largely evaporated. His book was a great success, and was widely translated and republished. We cannot value the book so highly today, because its basic theory is wrong. But we can still admire some of Darwin's bold experimental cures, his linking of body and mind, and his pioneer work in treating mental illness humanely instead of brutally.

We can also admire the riveting chapter entitled 'of generation', where Darwin picks out the main mechanisms of what we call biological evolution, noting the changes produced in animals over many generations by selective breeding, the inheritance of mutations, the role of 'lust, hunger and security' in determining the favoured variations, and the operation of sexual selection. He suggests that 'all warm-blooded animals have arisen from one living filament', during a time span of 'millions of ages'.

In the England of the 1790s, reeling from the shock of the French Revolution, evolution—even without the initial *r*—was quite unacceptable: denying that God created species was near-treason. But Erasmus had one influential disciple, his son Robert, who generated a pro-evolutionary atmosphere in his own family and helped to prepare the mind of his son Charles for evolution.

After the massive *Zoonomia* came a slim volume of 128 pages, entitled *A Plan for the Conduct of Female Education in Boarding Schools* (1797), written for his daughters Susan and Mary Parker, who had started a school at Ashbourne in Derbyshire. He totally opposed the conventional idea that girls should become feather-brained simpering misses: he wanted to see them 'sound in body and mind', and took a significant step towards modern ideas of sexual equality.

Darwin's next book, *Phytologia* (1800), is an impressive 600-page survey of vegetable life and all that sustains it, from carbon dioxide down to manures, full of good ideas ranging from sewage farms and biological control of insects to artesian wells and designs for new drill-ploughs. Darwin does best of all on plant nutrition. He describes photosynthesis more fully than anyone had done before, specifying the essential ingredients (carbon dioxide, water and sunlight) and the end products (oxygen and sugar). He was also the first to recognize that nitrogen and phosphorus were essential plant nutrients.

His last book is another long poem, *The Temple of Nature*, published posthumously in 1803, and in my view his finest achievement. He traces the evolution of life from microscopic specks in primeval oceans through plant life, fishes, amphibia, reptiles, land animals and birds. The couplets are just as bright as in *The Botanic Garden*; but what is really astonishing is to see him calmly and correctly announcing the processes of evolution more than fifty years before *The Origin of Species* and a hundred years before the details were generally agreed. He explains the pressures shaping evolution with equal verve when he describes the struggle for existence among animals, insects, fish and plants.

Darwin's books run to one and a half million words: they show how hard he worked and how varied were his accomplishments, but they do not reveal his contributions to technology and physics. Among his Lunar Society friends he was famous for his mechanical inventions, which included new kinds of carriages, the speaking-machine, an 'electrical doubler', an office copying-machine, a wire-drawn river ferry and a canal lift, of a design proved in operation a hundred years later.

Darwin did not devote much time to what we would call scientific research, but he still managed to achieve more than most scientists today can hope for. He had five papers published in the *Philosophical Transactions* of the Royal Society, of which he became a Fellow when he was twenty-nine. Two of the papers are historic: one, in 1785, gives the first clear exposition of the principle of the artesian well; the second, in 1788, propounds the principle of adiabatic expansion, fundamental to all heat engines, and then applies it to explain the formation of clouds: 'When large districts of air are raised . . . they become so much expanded by the great diminution of pressure over them . . . that . . . the air by its expansion produces cold and devaporates.'[8]

Perhaps the most surprising of Darwin's achievements is his profound influence on the English Romantic poets. Wordsworth was nineteen and Coleridge seventeen when *The Loves of the Plants* appeared. Three years later the completed *Botanic Garden* captured Wordsworth's sympathy by its exact description of nature and fervour for the French Revolution, and it shot straight into Coleridge's subconscious: *The Ancient Mariner* and 'Kubla Khan' are riddled with verbal echoes of Darwin.

Twenty years later, when Darwin's reputation had declined, he began to fascinate Shelley and Keats. With Keats he shared a relish for 'the realm of Flora and old Pan'. Shelley was Darwin's keenest disciple and had from him the idea of infusing nature poetry with science, as in 'The Cloud', as well as admiring him for being a sceptic in religion and a radical in politics. Darwin has also been called the chief progenitor of science fiction, through his influence on Mary Shelley's *Frankenstein*, which arose from a discussion between Byron and Shelley about Darwin's ideas on the generation of life. His literary reputation remained high for many years: in the 1860s Craik's popular *History of English Literature*, though critical of Darwin, still gave him twice as much space as Shakespeare, and six times as much as Byron.

In brief, Erasmus Darwin was a giant, who achieved more in a wider range of intellectual disciplines than anyone since.

# TWO

# Learning

## 1731-1756

IF YOU wish to know where the Darwins came from, go into the little church at Elston, near Newark in Nottinghamshire, and you will find yourself confronted by sixteen memorial slabs for Darwins, ranging in time from 1654 to 1947 and occupying most of the wall area. Elston may be too small a village to have its name on the map, but you can easily mark its position, near the geographical centre of England, where the straight line from Brighton to Berwick cuts the line from Liverpool to Lowestoft. Today Elston is still much as it has always been, a typical quiet English village, set among flat and fertile fields chiefly dedicated to wheat and cattle raising.

Elston looks peaceful now, but it has more than the usual quota of skeletons from the past. On 16 June 1487, the fields between Elston and the neighbouring village of Stoke, a mile to the north, were the scene of a historic battle, which marks 'the end of an epoch':[1] the army of Henry VII defeated the forces led by the Earl of Lincoln, Richard III's successor-designate, and the pretender Lambert Simnel. This bloody finale to the Wars of the Roses was a desperate encounter,[2] and one road was renamed the Red Gutter because it flowed with blood. The slaughter has never since been equalled in a battle on English soil: seven thousand men died, leaving their bones in the Elston fields, where for centuries the ploughshare turned them out.

The digging up of bones gave Elston its second claim to fame: for it was here in 1719 that the first recognized fossil bones of a giant reptile were unearthed—the hind part of an ichthyosaurus dating from 200 million years ago, when Britain was much nearer the equator than it is today. The antiquary William Stukeley described the fossilized bones in a paper for the Royal

Society, entitled 'An Account of the Impression of the almost Entire Sceleton of a large Animal in a very hard Stone'.[3] Stukeley was able to identify sixteen vertebrae, nine ribs and eleven tail-joints: he thought the creature might be some kind of crocodile and might date back three thousand years, to the time of the Flood.

Like many English villages, Elston is surrounded by names famous in folklore, science and poetry. The lady of the manor in 1066 was the Lady Godiva, while Robin Hood's Sherwood Forest lies only a few miles to the west. Ten miles to the southeast is Sir Isaac Newton's home at Woolsthorp, where he uncovered the laws that rule the universe in his *annus mirabilis* of the plague year. And fourteen miles west of Elston lies Newstead Abbey, the boyhood home of the most famous local poet, Lord Byron.

The Darwins came to Elston in about 1680, when Erasmus's grandfather William Darwin (1655–82), who had previously lived at Cleatham, Lincolnshire, acquired Elston Hall on his marriage to Ann, daughter of Robert Waring. Their second son Robert (1682–1754), a barrister of Lincoln's Inn, inherited Elston Hall. In 1724, when he was forty-two, Robert Darwin married Elizabeth Hill, and gave up practising his profession, to live as a country gentleman at Elston Hall. Robert and Elizabeth Darwin had seven children in as many years, and Erasmus, born on 12 December 1731, was the youngest.

Robert Darwin (Plate 2A) continued studying the law after his retirement, but he seems to have taken a keener interest in archaeology, and in the early 1720s he became a member of the Spalding Gentlemen's Society. Founded in 1712, this was one of the earliest, most enduring and most distinguished of literary-antiquarian societies: it pre-dates the Society of Antiquaries of London and the list of its early members[4] includes not only Robert Darwin and William Stukeley but also Newton, Bentley, Pope and Gay, to name but a few. For Erasmus Darwin, his father's membership of the Spalding Gentlemen's Society may have provided the cue for that society of scientific gentlemen in Birmingham—the Lunar Society. The rules of the Spalding Club are reminiscent of the Lunar Society's unwritten rules.

Robert Darwin has his own little niche in history, for it was he who told Stukeley about the fossil bones, which were found in the rector's garden just across the road from Elston Hall.

Stukeley's paper for the Royal Society begins: 'Having an
Account from my friend Robert Darwin Esq, of Lincoln's Inn, a
Person of Curiosity, of an human Sceleton (as it was then
thought) impress'd in Stone. . . .'[5] So Robert Darwin figured in
the discovery of the first fossil ichthyosaur in Britain—a most
appropriate preface to the evolutionary work of his son and
great-grandson.

In the same year, 1719, Robert Darwin also won an unwanted
notoriety at Lincoln's Inn after breaking the rules by taking his
dog into Hall. When the porter tried to turn the dog out, 'the
said Mr Darwin did offer to fling a pot at the Porter's head, and
threatened to knock him down'.[6] Robert had to apologize before
a council meeting on 11 May.

Little is known about Robert apart from these momentary
glimpses of a 'person of curiosity' and a person of passion.
Although (or perhaps because) he retired from his profession so
early, he was never wealthy; still, Elston Hall (Plate 2c) provided a substantial roof over his head, so his poverty was
relative. The best picture of Robert is in a letter written by
Erasmus soon after his father's death in 1754:

> He was a man . . . of more sense than learning; of very great
> industry in the law, even after he had no business, nor expectation
> of any. He was frugal, but not covetous; very tender to his children,
> but still kept them at an awful kind of distance. He passed through
> this life with honesty and industry, and brought up seven healthy
> children to follow his example.[7]

The infant mortality rate in Nottingham in the 1730s was about
40 per cent, so it was thirty to one against all of seven children
surviving infancy, as the Darwins succeeded in doing.

Erasmus's mother Elizabeth (Plate 2B) must have contributed some of that good health. She not only survived the
hard labour of bearing seven children in seven years, but even
thrived on it, for she lived to the ripe age of ninety-five, and 'to
the last day of her life got up to feed her pigeons'. She is said
to have been a woman of strong character, capable, practical and
scholarly, who presumably had a strong impact on her children.

Further dates and details of the Darwin family may be found
in the family tree on pages 324–5. The name 'Erasmus' seems
to have derived from that of Erasmus Earle, serjeant-at-law to
Oliver Cromwell, whose daughter Anne married William
Darwin in 1653.

[2]

With three elder brothers and three elder sisters to bait him, Erasmus had an unsheltered childhood. According to his son Robert, he was 'of a bold disposition', but 'a series of bad accidents made a deep impression on his mind' and he became very cautious:

> When he was about five years old he received an accidental blow on the middle of his head from a maid-servant and ever afterwards a white lock of hair grew there. Later on, when he was fishing with his brothers, they put him into a bag with only his feet out, and being thus blinded he walked into the river, and was very nearly drowned.[8]

His eldest brother Robert said that Erasmus 'had always a dislike to much exercise and rural diversions, and it was with great difficulty that we could ever persuade him to accompany us'.[9] If their idea of 'rural diversions' was putting him in a bag, his reluctance is not surprising. But he did sometimes indulge in country pursuits, and once, in 1740, when he was eight, he went hunting with his brother John, who was a year older. The event was recorded by Robert in 'A new song in praise of two young hunters':

> One morning this winter from school J.D. came
> And him and his brother Erasmus went out to kill game
> And as it happened which was very rare
> With hounds and 2 spaniels kil'd a fine hair.

The second verse sees a complete collapse of the young author's dubious command of grammar, scansion and legibility, so we may pass to the third:

> One of the dogs catched her by the head,
> Which made Erasmus Darwin cry 'war dead war dead'.
> But John Darwin the dogs he could not hear
> Because he only cried out 'war, war, war'.[10]

In later life Robert Darwin was a meticulous writer, and he would have been shocked to know that this nearly illegible farrago has survived for us to read.

In 1741, when Erasmus was nearly ten, the two young hunters were packed off to Chesterfield School, where Robert, now seventeen, was one of the senior boys. Between 1722 and 1752 the headmaster of Chesterfield School was the Revd. William Burrow, and under his guidance 'the school became the leading establishment in the north of England',[11] with about three boys per year going on to Cambridge. After Burrow retired, the school's reputation declined. Erasmus was fortunate to have sampled Chesterfield School at its best; he remained there for nine years and seems to have enjoyed his schooldays. Among the few recorded events from his school career was another of the accidents that tempered his bold disposition: he was seriously injured when he and Lord George Cavendish were playing with gunpowder, which exploded. Another nasty accident he suffered, presumably in his schooldays, was a dose of smallpox, for in later life his face was said to bear 'the traces of a severe smallpox'.

Erasmus's eldest brother Robert, afterwards the author of *Principia Botanica*, had a taste for botany and for verse: Erasmus shared these tastes and probably learnt them from him. The two brothers corresponded in verse, and Erasmus dedicated a manuscript volume of juvenile poems to Robert, with the words, 'By whose example and encouragement my mind was directed to the study of poetry in my very early years'.[12]

Robert remembered Erasmus for other interests that remained with him throughout his life. 'He was also always fond of mechanics. I remember him when very young making an ingenious alarum for his watch; he used also to show little experiments in electricity with a rude apparatus he then invented with a bottle.'[13] Probably he liked to entertain his brothers and sisters by making sparks fly and hair stand on end, as he playfully put it in *The Botanic Garden*:

> . . . if on wax some fearless Beauty stand,
> And touch the sparkling rod with graceful hand;
> Through her fine limbs the mimic lightnings dart,
> And flames innocuous eddy round her heart;
> O'er her fair brow the kindling lustres glare,
> Blue rays diverging from her bristling hair;
> While some fond Youth the kiss ethereal sips,
> And soft fires issue from their meeting lips.[14]

There is a working model of this favourite eighteenth-century parlour trick at the Smithsonian Museum of History and Technology in Washington.

Family ties were strong among the Darwins, and Erasmus's only recorded friend at Elston outside the family is Richard Dixon. Erasmus's name, and those of his brothers William and John, appear on the back of Dixon's apprenticeship indentures,[15] dated 10 June 1747, and Dixon remained a lifelong friend.

The sharpest picture of Erasmus as a schoolboy emerges from an exchange of letters in 1748 with his sister Susannah, who seems to have been his favourite family friend. In her letter, Susannah, then eighteen, tells Erasmus rather flippantly of her abstinence at Lent:

> I come now to the chief design of my Letter, and that is to acquaint you with my Abstinence this Lent, which you will find on the other side. . . . As soon as we kill our hog I intend to take part thereof with the Family, for I'm informed by a learned Divine that Hogs Flesh is Fish, and has been so ever since the Devil entered into them and they ran into the Sea. . . .[16]

There follows her 'Diary in Lent', and a typical day is Wednesday 8 February 1748:

> A little before seven I got up; said my Prayers; worked till eight; then took a walk, came in again and eate a farthing Loaf, then dress'd me, red a Chapter in the Bible, and spun till One, then dined temperately viz: on Puddin, Bread and Cheese; spun again till Fore. . . .[17]

The sixteen-year-old Erasmus replied at length to this ill-spelt but well-spun yarn, and his letter is salted with the banter characteristic of his later years:

> . . . having had a convenient oppertunity to consult a Synod of my learned friends about your ingenious conscience . . . I must inform you we unanimously agree in the Opinion of the Learned Divine you mention, that Swine may indeed be fish but then they are a devillish sort of fish; and we can prove from the same Authority that all fish is flesh whence we affirm Porck not only to be flesh but a devillish Sort of flesh; and I would advise you for Conscience sake altogether to abstain from tasting it; as I can assure you I have done, tho' roast Pork has come to Table several Times; and for my own part have lived upon Puding, milk, and vegetables all this Lent; but don't mistake me, I don't mean I have not touch'd roast beef, mutton, veal, goose, fowl, etc for what are all these? All flesh is grass!

Erasmus's leaning towards temperance is also beginning to shine through his levity:

I fancy you forgot in Yours to inform me that your Cheek was
quite settled by your Temperance, but however I can easily suppose
it. For the temperate enjoy an ever-blooming Health free from all
the Infections and disorders luxurious mortals are subject to, the
whimsical Tribe of Phisitians cheated of their fees may sit down in
penury and Want, they may curse mankind and imprecate the Gods
and call down that parent of all Deseases, luxury, to infest Mankind,
luxury more distructive than the Sharpest Famine; tho' all the
Distempers that ever Satan inflicted upon Job hover over the
intemperate; they would play harmless round our Heads, nor dare
to touch a single Hair . . . fever banished from our Streets, limping
Gout would fly the land, and Sedentary Stone would vanish into
oblivion and death himself be slain.[18]

After this fine flourish, Erasmus comes down to earth at the end:
'Excuse Hast, supper being called, very Hungry.' In the
eighteenth century good spelling was not one of the seven
deadly virtues, and adventurous spelling was often the mark of
an adventurous mind. Erasmus, like his sister, takes full
advantage of this laxity, and even mis-spells his future profession
—which he seems to look on with some suspicion.

Erasmus realized that he was lucky to have had such good
teaching at Chesterfield. Charles Darwin refers to two letters he
wrote, one to an under-master in 1749 and one to Mr Burrow in
1750. The latter was accompanied by lengthy verses in imitation
of the Fifth Satire of Persius. These letters suggest 'a degree of
respect, gratitude, and affection for the several masters unusual
in a schoolboy'.[19]


[3]


Erasmus's eldest brother Robert had gone up to St John's
College, Cambridge, in 1743: John and Erasmus followed him
there in 1750, both matriculating on 30 June[20] and starting
residence in October. Erasmus won the Exeter scholarship at St
John's and the £16 per annum that it brought in was welcome,
because the upkeep of two sons at Cambridge was a strain on
their father's finances. They lived frugally and mended their
own clothes: 'Many years afterwards, Erasmus boasted to his
second wife that, if she cut the heel out of a stocking, he would
put a new one in without missing a stitch.'[21]

Erasmus Darwin went to Cambridge at a time when the reputation of the universities was low, and heavy drinking was rife among students and dons. Intellectually, the universities were almost moribund: they served as 'salutary bulwarks against the precipitate and desolating spirit of innovation'.[22] But it was characteristic of Darwin to make the best of outwardly unpropitious surroundings, and he emerged from his four years at Cambridge as an accomplished and knowledgeable young man. The efforts of Mr Burrow ensured that he was already well versed in the classics when he left school, and at Cambridge he gave this knowledge an attractive polish, which remained throughout his life, as we can see from the casual ease of the classical references in his poems forty years later.

At Cambridge he also became proficient in writing English verse, and he showed his skill with a 92-line poem in memory of Frederick, Prince of Wales, who died on 20 March 1751. Darwin's poem appears in the multilingual memorial miscellany rapidly compiled at Cambridge and published in May 1751 with the title *Academiae Cantabrigiensis Luctus in obitum Frederici celsissimi Walliae Principis*. A memorial volume was appropriate because Frederick, although much maligned, was a generous patron of the arts, who had tried his hand at writing poetry, songs and a play.[23] The regrets in Academia were genuine. His death may even have been a historic event, because he might not have treated the American colonies in the same way as his son George III did. Frederick deserves a better epitaph than the anonymous rhyme beginning 'Here lies Fred, who was alive and is dead', and ending 'there's no more to be said'.

Darwin certainly had more to say. He was keen to exercise his Muse, and she proves to be in good fettle:

Ye Meads enamel'd, and ye waving Woods,
    With dismal yews, and solemn cypress mourn;
Ye rising Mountains, and ensilver'd Floods,
    Repeat my sighs, and weep upon his urn.
Oft in your haunts the young Marcellus stray'd,
    There oft in thought your future glories plan'd,
Bade sacred Science lift her lawrel'd head,
    And peace extend her olive o'er the land.

Darwin then embarks on an elaborate simile comparing Frederick with a mighty cedar tree brought down by a storm. He reflects on the vanities of life and unleashes some nice images *en route*, for example:

> Oft at the fall of Kings, th' astonish'd eye
>     Views fancy'd tumults in the mid-night gleams,
> Sees glittering crests, and darting lances fly,
>     Till one thick cloud absorbs the sportive beams.

Soon after this, Neptune appears and tells us to cease mourning because the Prince may still smile on Albion from his abode in the courts of Jove.

Few undergraduates, then or now, have written more smoothly in verse. The poem rightly won its nineteen-year-old author a reputation as an accomplished man of letters; and forty-four years later, when Darwin was perhaps the most famous poet of the day, the *European Magazine* republished these early verses.[24]

The next of Erasmus's already varied accomplishments was shorthand. Darwin learnt the system of 'brachygraphy' devised by Thomas Gurney (1705–70), who was appointed official short-hand writer at the Old Bailey in 1748. Gurney wrote a manual on his technique in 1750, and the third edition (1752) includes thirty lines of verse 'To Mr Gurney, On his Book of Short-Writing' from 'E.D., Cambridge, St. John's, 14 May 1751'. The couplets are factual and concise, giving a foretaste of the style of Darwin's later poems:

> But slow the *speaking* Hand till GURNEY sprung,
> And form'd the Finger rival to the Tongue.
>     Tale-licens'd Travellers are wont to boast
> Amazing Converse in the Realms of Frost;
> Lips move unheard, each Sound in Ice entomb'd,
> Stagnate his Current, and his Wing benumb'd,
> Slumbers inactive, till a warmer Sky
> Unbinds the Glebe, and bids the Accents fly—
> Thus *Gurney's* Arts the fleeting Word congeal,
> And stay the Wanderer to repeat his Tale,
> When the quick Eye-ball thaws the letter'd Plain,
> Calls out the Sound, and wakes the dormant Strain.[25]

So, at nineteen, Darwin was already skilled in writing verse and was trying out the stylistic tricks that enliven *The Botanic Garden*. Here he elaborates a traveller's tale of words freezing as spoken, and then, just before you dismiss it as a tall story, he

thumps in its relevance to his theme. Darwin apparently wrote
several times to Gurney, and the third edition of the *Brachygraphy* has a specimen of Darwin's shorthand—the first eleven
verses of the tenth chapter of *Revelation*. Both the poem and the
specimen appear in several subsequent editions of Gurney's
manual (which had reached its fifteenth edition by 1825). In his
years at Cambridge Darwin filled six notebooks with shorthand,
and continued practising the art for some years.

Classics, verse and shorthand were semi-recreational; his
bread-and-butter study at Cambridge was medicine. Darwin
was fortunate in being able to attend lectures by four eminent
doctors, and his notes on four series of lectures have survived.
The first series was given in 1752 at King's College by Dr
George Baker (1722–1809), who later became a baronet and a
royal physician; he is best known medically for discovering that
'Devonshire colic' was due to lead poisoning, which he traced to
leaden cider vats. Darwin's shorthand notes on his lectures extend
to more than 170 pages, and cover 'the fossil and animal
kingdoms': waters, earths, metals, stones; insects, fish, birds,
quadrupeds and man—to quote some of the chapter headings in
his notebooks.[26] Darwin's second lecturer was Dr Noah
Thomas (1720–92) of St John's College, who was later knighted
after acting as royal physician. He lectured in 1753 in London,
at St Thomas's Hospital and in Cook's Court, Carey Street, on
two juicy subjects—salivation; and poisons, both 'acrimonious'
and 'narcotic'. Darwin's shorthand notes run to fifty pages.[27]

In 1752–3 Darwin attended lectures, possibly at St John's
College, by Dr William Heberden (1710–1801), later an
eminent London physician, whom Dr Johnson called 'Ultimus
Romanorum, last of our learned physicians'. Heberden is credited
with having first described angina pectoris, as well as publishing
several learned literary works. His lectures on the study of
physic covered a wide range of subjects, from chemistry to
botany, and Darwin's notes are neatly written in longhand. Four
of his fellow students apparently borrowed the notes and
recorded their ungrateful thanks on the cover: 'damn you
Darwin you have spelt a thousand words wrong, you son of a
whore.'[28] Though Darwin was erratic in his spelling, the
'thousand' is a great exaggeration. Charles Darwin tells us that
Erasmus left Cambridge during one term 'to attend Hunter's
lectures in London'. These would have been the lectures by Dr

William Hunter, possibly assisted by his brother John Hunter, who was three years older than Darwin.

[4]

Erasmus left Cambridge in the summer of 1754 without taking a B.A. degree[29] and entered the Edinburgh Medical School to complete his training as a doctor. His mode of life remained fairly frugal: the receipt for his board and lodging from 13 July to 13 October amounted to £6 12s.[30] In the 1750s the Edinburgh Medical School, founded in 1726, was pre-eminent in Britain. Most of the professors had been to Leyden as pupils of the great physician Boerhaave, who was a thoroughgoing mechanist and tried to find physical and chemical explanations for all the bodily functions.

At Edinburgh Erasmus soon met the first of the group of life-long friends who later formed the Lunar Society: this was James Keir (1735–1821), a fellow student who, in his dry Scottish style, tells us that Erasmus made quite a splash at Edinburgh: 'The classical and literary attainments which he had acquired at Cambridge gave him, when he came to Edinburgh, together with his poetical talents and ready wit, a distinguished superiority among the students there.'[31]

Keir came from a wealthy Scottish family, of Muirton, near Edinburgh.[32] His father died when he was very young and he was brought up by his mother, with help from her brother George Lind, Lord Provost of Edinburgh, whose son Dr James Lind (1736–1812) was the close friend of James Watt, and later royal physician at Windsor and the mentor of Shelley at Eton. Keir left Edinburgh without taking a degree and served in the Army for eleven years before retiring as a captain and settling near Birmingham, to become a pioneer of industrial chemistry.

Many years later, in a letter to Erasmus's son Robert in 1802, Keir remembered how mechanistic the medical teaching at Edinburgh had been, with only Dr Cullen beginning 'to throw off the Boerhaavian yoke', and he wondered how Erasmus had escaped indoctrination:

It would be curious to know (but he alone could have told us) the progress of your father's mind from the narrow Boerhaavian system, in which man was considered as an hydraulic machine whose pipes were filled with fluid susceptible of chemical fermentations, while the pipes themselves were liable to stoppages or obstructions (to which obstructions and fermentations all diseases were imputed), to the more enlarged consideration of man as a *living being*, which affects the phenomena of health and disease more than his merely mechanical and chemical properties.[33]

In his first term at Edinburgh, Erasmus received what he called 'the disagreeable news' of his father's death. (He was not trying to be pert: the use of 'disagreeable' to mean 'painful' was common in the eighteenth century.) This phrase, and the character sketch of his father already quoted, come in a letter to Dr Thomas Okes of Exeter, in which Erasmus goes on to offer some reflections on life, revealing that he was already something of a sceptic and with a mind ready to accept evolution:

> That there exists a superior ENS ENTIUM, which formed these wonderful creatures, is a mathematical demonstration. That HE influences things by a particular providence, is not so evident. The probability, according to my notion, is against it, since general laws seem sufficient for that end. Shall we say no particular providence is necessary to roll this Planet round the Sun, and yet affirm it necessary in turning up *cinque* and *quatorze*, while shaking a box of dies? or giving each his daily bread?—The light of Nature affords us not a single argument for a future state; this is the only one— that it is possible with God; since he who made us out of nothing can surely re-create us: and that he will do this is what we humbly hope.[34]

In 1755 Erasmus returned to Cambridge to take his Bachelor of Medicine degree: apparently he defended the thesis 'that the movements of the heart and arteries are immediately produced by the stimulus of the blood'.[35] Then he went back to Edinburgh for a further year. One of his friends at this time was Albert Reimarus, son of the well-known German philosopher Hermann Reimarus, who was a thoroughgoing deist, a proponent of 'natural' rather than 'revealed' religion.[36] Darwin and Keir were both influenced by the ideas of Reimarus, and twelve years later Darwin wrote to Albert Reimarus: 'Mr Keir and myself continue in the Religion you taught us, we hold you to be a great Reformer of the Church.'[37] Darwin's letters to Reimarus junior in 1755–6 include vague speculations on the resemblance between the human soul and electricity, and some useful mechanical ideas, for example a design for a rotary pump and a discussion of the advantages of using the spokes of carriage wheels as springs, an idea that is continually being re-invented.[38] Darwin also wrote a poem in honour of Reimarus taking his degree at Leyden.

Not all Darwin's activities were intellectual, however. A plausible though unsubstantiated report from an anonymous friend (or enemy?) tells us that 'in his youth Dr Darwin was fond of sacrificing to both Bacchus and Venus; but he soon discovered that he could not continue his devotions to both these deities without destroying his health and constitution. He therefore resolved to relinquish Bacchus, but his affection for Venus was retained to the last period of life.'[39] This facet of his character emerges in his happy translation of an epigram of Martial:

> Wine, women, warmth, against our lives combine,
> But what is life without warmth, women, wine.

[5]

In the summer of 1756 Erasmus completed his studies at Edinburgh and took his M.D. Replete with (unreliable) eighteenth-century medical lore, he was ready to be let loose on the public. He first tried to set up a practice on his home ground at Nottingham. As C. P. Moritz saw it twenty-five years later, Nottingham was 'the loveliest and neatest . . . of all the towns I have seen outside London'.[40] Nottingham may have been just as lovely and as neat in 1756, but it had no patients for its newest physician.

Left at a loose end, Darwin became embroiled in dispute with a London surgeon who had overcharged a poor patient sent to him by Reimarus and Darwin. Although Darwin's motive was good, his methods were devious, for he sent an anonymous letter to the surgeon, and then, in a letter to Reimarus, wrote, 'I will not say whether I am the Author or not', followed by a postscript telling Reimarus to show this second letter to the surgeon. The surgeon paid back two-thirds of the six-guinea fee, but the episode taught Darwin the salutary lesson that it is often better to be blunt and straightforward than polite and tricky.

With no patients in sight at Nottingham, Darwin decided to try elsewhere, and in November 1756 he moved to Lichfield, where his career as a doctor really began.

[6]

Before we follow Darwin to Lichfield, this early hiatus in his career is a good moment for a quick look at the parlous state of medicine in the eighteenth century, against which Darwin's achievements must be judged. The yawning gap in medical science was the failure to realize that microbes caused diseases. Fracastoro expounded the germ theory in 1543 and specified the modes of infection—by direct contact, indirectly in clothes, and through airborne germs. Sydenham, in the seventeenth century, specified sound measures for public health which half-implied a germ theory of disease. There were many pointers to the germ theory—for centuries lepers had been kept isolated; quarantine laws existed against 'contagious' diseases; and in 1721 Lady Mary Wortley Montagu introduced the Turkish custom of smallpox inoculation with live virus. But we fail to see the obvious if the obvious does not fit in with our prejudices, and people couldn't really believe in the power of microbes they couldn't see. Microbes had been observed by Leeuwenhoek in 1683, but his famous microscopic researches came to be regarded as mere curiosities, fascinating but medically irrelevant. Microscopy was neglected during the eighteenth century, and its few practitioners, such as Henry Baker, made little progress; so the cause of many infectious diseases, of septicaemia in surgery and 'puerperal fever' in childbirth, remained obscure. The consequences were often fatal.

The eighteenth century saw no discoveries worthy to set beside Harvey's in the seventeenth or Pasteur's in the nineteenth. The most influential physician of the century was Hermann Boerhaave of Leyden (1668–1738). Though Boerhaave concentrated on the hydraulics of the body, he also emphasized that patients deserved to be treated individually and not mass-medicated.

Albrecht von Haller (1708–77), a Swiss, showed how the nervous system functions and concluded that the nerves converge on the brain. He had no idea that nerve impulses were electrical, a discovery that did not come till after 1850, though we can now see how it was foreshadowed in the 1790s by Galvani, who made frogs' legs twitch when touched by different metals, and by Volta, who showed how muscles could be kept excited by electrical impulses. Even before this, however, Darwin concluded that nerve impulses were electrical, through seeing how paralytic limbs were stimulated by electric shocks.

Stephen Hales (1677-1761), an English country parson, won deserved fame for measuring blood pressure and circulation rate, but the idea of using blood pressure to help in diagnosing disease did not arrive until much later: Darwin never mentions it.

Surgery remained a painful and risky procedure throughout the eighteenth century. The failure to utilize anaesthetics in surgery now seems puzzling—surely someone could have thought of it to relieve the patients' agony? After all, opium and laudanum were often prescribed by physicians, and other anaesthetics were known to surgeons as far back as the Chinese Hua To in the second century A.D. and Hugh of Lucca in the thirteenth. The surgeons may have failed in vision over anaesthetics and hygiene, but that does not mean they were all butchers. Many were most humane, and technically some of the leading surgeons were immensely skilful. The 'lightning lithotomist' William Cheselden could complete an operation for a bladder stone in less than two minutes,[41] thus minimizing the patient's suffering; and it is said that more than 90 per cent of his patients survived. The great surgeon John Hunter was busy pioneering new operations and amassing the specimens for his famous museum, but neither he nor anyone else took heed of those rampant microbes.

The ignorance of hygiene was bad enough in surgery, but perhaps even worse in childbirth. Babies were delivered by midwives who were often unwashed and carried the germs of 'puerperal fever' from one bedside to the next. Hygiene was improved during the century, but only by chance, for aesthetic reasons. Many of England's open sewers were covered, because they were thought offensive. Army camps were fairly hygienic, because of regulations imposed by Sir John Pringle, and the prisons were improved after the efforts of John Howard. Thanks to these measures and the building of hospitals, English people were slightly healthier in 1800 than in 1700.

A few diseases lost some of their horror. The scourge of syphilis was alleviated by the mercury treatment that remained standard till after 1900. James Lind (1716–94)\* proved that plentiful fruit juices could prevent scurvy, and so saved the lives of more seamen than were lost in battle. Jenner's discovery of vaccination against smallpox came at the very end of the century, too late to be of service in Darwin's medical career.

Chemistry was at a dead end until the 1770s, imprisoned by the phlogiston theory—the belief that a burning substance gave off 'phlogiston'. The true mechanism—that the burning substance combined with oxygen—was in effect proved by Priestley in the 1770s, but he clung to the phlogiston theory and many of the Lunar Society members followed his lead. But Darwin was quick to adopt the oxygen theory and led the way in explaining the oxygenation of blood in the lungs. Another chemical advance was the recognition that gastric juices help to digest food, and that digestion is not merely mechanical, as had once been thought.

The treatment of mental illness was deplorable. Lunatics were usually chained and brutally treated, in the hope of driving out the devils that possessed them. There were some kinder doctors, however, among whom Darwin was perhaps foremost, and in 1794 the first humane lunatic asylum, the Retreat at York,[42] was founded by the Quaker William Tuke. But milder treatment did not become common until many years later.

Even the simplest clinical instruments were inefficient or little used. The thermometers were useless for taking a patient's temperature. Chest-tapping, begun in the 1760s, was slow to catch on, and the stethoscope was not invented until after 1800. So the eighteenth-century physicians had very few of the modern doctor's instruments, and had to rely unduly on the speed and strength of the pulse. Even so, they rarely used the one-minute pulse-watch invented by the Lichfield physician Sir John Floyer (1649–1734).

The chancy or useless methods of diagnosis were matched by treatments equally chancy or useless. Most patients were subjected to purgatives, emetics, bleeding and a cornucopia of herbs, from opium to cinchona bark, taken either singly or in groups. If they recovered, it was usually because their body

---

\* Not to be confused with his younger cousin, James Lind (1736–1812), the friend of Watt and Shelley.

defences overcame both the disease and the treatment. As diseases were so often fatal, rich patients would pay doctors high fees, to match the high stakes, and many fashionable physicians in London made fortunes from rich patients with strong constitutions, whose recovery could be wrongly attributed to the medication they received. Even the correct announcement of a death sentence could enhance a physician's reputation; as Belloc put it,

> They answered as they took their fees,
> 'There is no Cure for this Disease'.

Still, this is not to say that the physicians were useless. In the absence of medical science, common sense was paramount, and some of the doctors, including Darwin, were among the most perceptive and intelligent men of the day. Their advice often helped to keep patients in good health. For example, Dr John Armstrong, in his popular poem *The Art of Preserving Health* (1744), advises his readers to avoid polluted air, to eat varied food in moderate quantities, to take adequate exercise and to avoid lowering resistance by excess. No one would quarrel with that.

From the outset of his career Erasmus Darwin was determined to avoid the fate of becoming a fashionable London physician. He stayed in the Midlands and tried to help all who called on his services: he treated the poorest free, and for the others scaled his fees to the patients' wealth, as expressed by their way of life —the number of their servants and the size or splendour of their home, furniture or equipage. In practice, because of the difficulties of travel, he tended to give free treatment to the poor near his house and charged for distant calls and affluent local people. Rich or poor, Darwin knew he had a challenging future— fighting with antiquated weapons against a deadly enemy whose crack troops were invisible.

# THREE
# Lichfield
## 1757–1764

LICHFIELD HAD been a cathedral city for more than a thousand years when Erasmus Darwin arrived in November 1756. The list of bishops dates from 656, and the first cathedral was consecrated in 700, a memorial to the saintly Bishop Chad. The building of the present cathedral began in 1195, though its three splendid spires were not completed until 1330. Ever since then, these three 'ladies of the vale' have beckoned travellers from afar. For Darwin their call proved compulsive: he was to live in their shadow for nearly twenty-five years.

In the course of the eighteenth century the ancient Lichfield, 'mother of the Midlands', was gradually eclipsed by a fast-growing neighbour fifteen miles to the south—the manufacturing town of Birmingham. But in 1756 Lichfield was still much the better known of the two, for although its population was only about 3500, it was an important staging point for coaches:[1] at Lichfield the main road from London to Liverpool and Manchester crossed the road from Bristol, Bath and Birmingham to Derby, Sheffield and Leeds. The Lichfield Turnpike Trust had been set up in 1729, and so the roads around the town were slightly better kept than those in most other parts of the Midlands.

Lichfield was the home town of several famous men in the seventeenth and eighteenth centuries, including Elias Ashmole (1617–92), the scholar and founder of the Ashmolean Museum, and the eminent doctor Sir John Floyer, who was keen on cold baths and built a bath-house at Maple Hayes (afterwards the site of Darwin's botanic garden). Samuel Johnson was born in 1709 at his father's shop in the market place and educated at Lichfield's excellent grammar school, where the headmaster was

Dr John Hunter. Another of Hunter's pupils, a few years later, was David Garrick, whom Johnson befriended. Nearly twenty years before Darwin's arrival in Lichfield, Johnson and Garrick had set off together to seek fame and fortune in London, on the advice of Gilbert Walmesley, who lived at the Bishop's Palace in the close. (The bishops preferred to reside at Eccleshall Castle, rather than on the spot.)

Darwin arrived at Lichfield with a letter of introduction to Walmesley's successor as tenant of the Bishop's Palace, Dr Thomas Seward, canon residentiary of the cathedral and rector of Eyam in the Peak District. Seward (1708–90), like Darwin a graduate of St John's College, was an enterprising clergyman of literary tastes,[2] and he made the palace the centre of a literary coterie. He was well known for his edition of Beaumont and Fletcher's plays and various religious works, now forgotten. Darwin had cause to be grateful to Seward for giving him entrée into the upper stratum of local society, the key to success in his medical career.

Dr Seward had married Elizabeth Hunter, daughter of Johnson's headmaster, and they had two daughters, Anna, who was fourteen when Darwin arrived, and Sarah, two years younger. Many years later Anna wrote her *Memoirs of the Life of Dr Darwin*, amazingly prolix in style and often unreliable, but still indispensable to a biographer of Erasmus.

Darwin's medical career at Lichfield began brilliantly. One of his first patients, Anna tells us, was William Inge, 'a young gentleman of family, fortune, and consequence' who 'lay sick of a dangerous fever'. Other doctors had pronounced death sentences on him, so his mother called in the new physician: 'By a reverse and entirely novel course of treatment, Dr Darwin gave his dying patient back to existence, to health, prosperity, and all that high reputation, which Mr Inge afterwards possessed as a public magistrate.'[3]

Darwin's fame soon spread round the county, and his career was well-set, as shown by the figures of his income during these early years, from a memorandum in his own hand:[4]

1757: £192-10-6    1758: £305- 2-0  1759: £469- 4-0  1760: £544- 2-0
1761: £669-18-0    1762: £726- 7-0  1763: £639-13-0  1764: £750-13-0

These figures need to be multiplied by about twenty to bring them into line with values in the late 1970s.

[2]

Soon after his clinical success with Mr Inge, Darwin achieved a further *succès d'estime*: a scientific paper he submitted to the Royal Society in March 1757 was published in the *Philosophical Transactions* later in the year, the first of more than fifty papers by five generations of Darwins that have subsequently graced the pages of the Royal Society's journals. Darwin's paper, entitled 'Remarks on the Opinion of Henry Eeles, Esq., concerning the Ascent of Vapour', fully deserved publication, for Darwin refuted an incorrect but widely believed idea, in an easy and elegant style that spares the dignity of Mr Eeles while gently destroying his hypothesis. It is a mature and impressive paper.

This first Darwinian contribution to the *Philosophical Transactions* begins gracefully:

> Gentlemen, There is ever such a charm attendant upon novelty, that be it in philosophy, medicine, or religion, the gazing world are too often led to adore, what they ought only to admire: whilst this vehemence of enthusiasm has generally soon rendered that object contemptible, that would otherwise have long laid claim to a more sober esteem. This was once the fate of chemistry . . . and I should be sorry, if her sister electricity should share the same misfortunes. . . .[5]

Eeles contended that vapours rise only if they are electrically charged. Darwin points to various phenomena connected with clouds and steam that cast doubt on this idea, and then proceeds to his *pièce de résistance*, a conclusive experiment:

> A glass tube, open at one end, and with a bulb at the other, had its bulb, and half way from thence to the aperture of the tube, coated on the inside with gilt paper. The tube was then inverted in a glass of oil of turpentine, which was placed on a cake of wax, and the tube kept in that perpendicular situation by a silk line from the ceiling of the room. The bulb was then warmed, so that, when it became cold, the turpentine rose about half-way up the tube. A bent wire then being introduced thro' the oil into the air above, high electricity was given. The oil did not appear at all to subside: whence I conclude, the electric atmosphere flowing round the wire and coating of the tube above the oil, did not displace the air, but existed in its pores.[6]

Darwin says he performed the experiment in the hope that electricity might make the air expand and so provide a means of improving the steam engine. But he found that electricity did not affect the mechanical properties of air, thus simultaneously dashing his own hopes and demolishing Eeles's idea.

This excellent early paper of Darwin's shows he was a keen and skilful experimenter, reveals his interest in steam, and foreshadows his classic work on the formation of clouds.

[3]

The site of Darwin's first house in Lichfield is not known, but we do know that his sister Susannah acted as housekeeper for him in 1757.

Soon after arriving in Lichfield, Erasmus fell in love with a girl whose family lived near the Sewards. Her name was Mary Howard and she was seventeen. According to Anna, she was 'blooming and lovely' and had a mind of 'native strength; an awakened taste for the works of imagination; ingenuous sweetness; delicacy animated by sprightliness, and sustained by fortitude.'[7] These qualities 'made her a capable, as well as fascinating companion, even to a man of talents so illustrious.' Darwin, impelled by his 'affection for Venus' and buoyed up by his medical successes, saw no reason for delay; he and Polly, as he called her, were married on 30 December 1757.

A long letter he wrote to her six days earlier from Darlaston nicely catches the essence of Erasmus as a young man, bantering yet tender, exuberant, unconventional and confident of overcoming all obstacles. He begins with some musty recipes:

Dear Polly,
    As I was turning over some old mouldy volumes, that were laid upon a Shelf in a Closet of my Bed-chamber; one I found, after blowing the Dust from it with a Pair of Bellows, to be a Receipt Book, formerly, no doubt, belonging to some good old Lady of the Family. The Title Page (so much of it as the Rats had left) told us it was 'a Bouk off verry monny muckle vallyed Receipts bouth in Kookery and Physicks'. Upon one Page was 'To make Pye-Crust', —in another 'To make Wall-Crust',—'To make Tarts',—and at length 'To make Love'. 'This Receipt', says I, 'must be curious,

I'll send it to Miss Howard next Post, let the way of making it be what it will.'

(It was a long herbal recipe.) Then he found another prescription for making love, involving two sheep's hearts repeatedly pierced with a skewer; but the recipe was incomplete, because

> Time with his long Teeth had gnattered away the remainder of this Leaf. At the Top of the next Page, begins 'To make an honest Man'. 'This is no new dish to me', says I, 'besides it is now quite old Fashioned; I won't read it'. Then follow'd 'To make a good Wife'. 'Pshaw', continued I, 'an acquaintance of mine, a young Lady of Lichfield, knows how to make this Dish better than any other Person in the World, and she has promised to treat me with it sometime', and thus in a Pett threw doun the Book. . . .

Darwin is casual about the wedding arrangements, and scornful of both bureaucracy and gossip:

> I will certainly be with Thee on Wednesday evening, the Writings are at my House, and may be dispatched that night, and if a License takes up any Time (for I know nothing at all about these Things) I should be glad if Mr Howard would order one, and by this means, dear Polly, we may have the Ceremony over next morning at eight o'clock, before any Body in Lichfield can know almost of my being come Home. If a License is to be had the Day before, I could wish it may be put off till late in the Evening, as the Voice of Fame makes such quick Dispatch with any News in so small a Place as Lichfield.—I think this is much the best scheme, for to stay a few Days after my Return could serve no Purpose, it would only make us more watch'd and teazed by the Eye and Tongue of Impertinence. . . .

He was ready to take marriage in his stride:

> Matrimony, my dear Girl, is undoubtedly a serious affair, (if any Thing be such) because it is an affair for Life: But, as we have deliberately determin'd, do not let us be *frighted* about this Change of Life; or however, not let any breathing Creature perceive that we have either Fears or Pleasures upon this Occasion: as I am certainly convinced, that the best of Confidants (tho' experienced on a thousand other Occasions) could as easily hold a burning cinder in their Mouth as anything the least ridiculous about a new married couple! . . .[8]

Mary Howard belonged to an old Lichfield family. Her father Charles Howard, a solicitor, was a schoolfellow and friend of

Samuel Johnson, and had stood as surety at Johnson's marriage
to Mrs Porter. In 1734 Howard had married Penelope Foley:
her father, grandson of the Worcestershire merchant Thomas
Foley, had among his direct ancestors Anne Boleyn's sister and
Sir Philip Sidney's 'Stella'—Lady Penelope Devereux, sister of
the Earl of Essex. This lineage was aristocratic, but decidedly
unhealthy and also unlucky; early death was common, either
through illness or (all too often) through execution—the Earls
of Surrey (1547), Essex (1601) and Holland (1649), not to
mention Anne Boleyn, were all cut off in their prime by the
executioner. Penelope Howard herself died at forty, in 1748,
nine years before Mary married Erasmus, and only two of
Penelope's six children survived infancy. Mary, one of the two
survivors, was a martyr to pain and illness throughout her
married life and was to die at thirty. Dr T. K. With has suggested that Mary's symptoms were consistent with acute intermittent porphyria, which is hereditary:[9] the point is of interest
because of the prevalence of illness, apparently inherited, in
subsequent generations of Darwins, including the *cause célèbre* of
Mary's grandson Charles Darwin.

Soon after their marriage Darwin and Mary moved to a new
house on the western boundary of the cathedral close. Anna says
the move was in 1758 and that Darwin bought and renovated an
old half-timbered house; but the leases of the site, which are in
the Lichfield Record Office, suggest that he did not acquire the
buildings until 8 August 1760, when he paid £210 to Lady
Gresley for a forty-year lease, and that he built a new house
facing Beacon Street. Anna says the front garden contained the
moat which had once surrounded the close, and it was full of
tangled briars. Darwin cleared the undergrowth, planted lilac
and roses, and across the dell 'flung a broad bridge of shallow
steps with chinese paling, descending from his hall door to the
pavement.'[10] This handsome house (Plate 3B) still stands much
as it was in Darwin's day: the dell was filled in towards the end
of the eighteenth century and there have been some interior
changes; but the exterior brickwork and windows, the coach
house, stables and saddling room, and the cellars all appear to be
unchanged.

Settled in this pleasant home with views over fields and trees
to the west, and congenial neighbours in the close to the east,
Erasmus and Mary seem to have enjoyed what was by all

accounts a very happy married life. Their first child, a boy born on 3 September 1758, was called Charles—the traditional Howard *prénom*, borne by Mary's grandfather, father and brother. He was the first Charles Darwin in the family tree, a healthy and brilliant boy.

Just over a year later, on 11 October 1759, Mary gave birth to a second son, Erasmus, whom I shall refer to as Erasmus junior: he grew up introspective and retiring, unlike his exuberant father.

[4]

In these early years of his marriage Darwin was often away visiting patients, for he was busy establishing and extending his practice, and he accepted perhaps too many calls on his services. Still, he was at home often enough for his house to become a regular meeting place of his scientific friends.

One of those friends was John Michell (1724–93), now regarded as the most distinguished Cambridge University scientist in the century after Newton's death.[11] It was at the University that Darwin met Michell, who was Tutor of Queen's College. Michell had written a treatise on 'Artificial Magnets' in 1750, and he is known as 'the father of seismology' as a result of his *Observations on Earthquakes* (1760). He qualifies as one of the founders of modern geology through his studies of the strata of southern England; he was also influential in astronomy, skilled in Hebrew and theology, and the inventor of the torsion balance which Cavendish used to find the density of the Earth. Little wonder that Darwin referred to Michell seven years after his death as 'a man of such accurate and universal knowledge . . . whose friendship I long possessed, and whose loss I have long lamented'.[12] Darwin particularly admired Michell's technique for making artificial magnets, and in *The Botanic Garden* he tells us how

> MICHELL's hands with touch of potent charm
> The polish'd rods with powers magnetic arm. . . .
> The obedient Steel with living instinct moves,
> And veers for ever to the pole it loves.[13]

Michell leads us to the next of Darwin's friends, the famous manufacturer Matthew Boulton (Plate 4A), for Michell stayed with Boulton during his visit to Birmingham in 1757. So we may assume, though documentary evidence is lacking, that Boulton and Darwin were acquainted by 1757, probably through one of Darwin's early patients in Lichfield, Luke Robinson, a wealthy merchant whose daughter Mary was Boulton's wife. At this time Boulton was only twenty-nine, three years older than Darwin, and had not yet built the manufactory at Soho that was to bring him so much fame. Indeed, in these early years of their friendship, Boulton was going through a difficult time in his business and in his personal life too. In 1759 his wife Mary died, and, after some hesitations, and consultations with Darwin, Boulton married her sister Anne in 1760, away at Rotherhithe because the marriage was not strictly legal.

Darwin's early circle of scientific friends included the most sparkling of all, Benjamin Franklin (Plate 4B), famous for his invention of the lightning conductor and generally acclaimed as the foremost 'experimental philosopher' of the day:

Led by the phosphor-light, with daring tread
Immortal FRANKLIN sought the fiery bed
Where, nursed in night, incumbent Tempest shrouds
The seeds of Thunder in circumfluent clouds,
Besieged with iron points his airy cell,
And pierced the monster slumbering in the shell.[14]

In 1758 Franklin was touring the Midlands to visit his English relatives and to meet the Birmingham printer John Baskerville, whose fine new edition of Virgil was much admired. Franklin first visited Cambridge, where Michell gave him a letter of introduction to Boulton. There is no record of Darwin and Franklin meeting in 1758, but they probably did, because Boulton introduced Franklin to other friends and would scarcely have omitted Darwin, the author of a paper on atmospheric electricity, Franklin's speciality.

An acquaintance of different stamp was Robert Bage (1728–1801), the papermaker and novelist. His paper mill at Elford, near Lichfield, was said to produce the best paper in the country. The historian William Hutton called Bage 'one of the most amiable of men; and though barely a Christian, yet one of the best. I have known him 56 years: his friendship is an honour. . . .'[15] Sir Walter Scott was equally flattering: 'His integrity, his honour, his devotion to truth, were undeviating and incorruptible.'[16] Despite these admirable qualities, and his literary-scientific interests, Bage was never a close friend of Darwin, though they remained on good terms for nearly forty years.

Darwin's other 'philosophic Friends' cannot be identified so confidently. Possibly they included two contrasting Birmingham business-men—Samuel Garbett (1717–1803), partner in the Carron Iron Works in the 1760s, and John Baskerville (1706–75), the atheistic printer of fine Bibles, to whose Virgil Darwin subscribed in 1757. John Whitehurst (1713–88), the instrument-maker and geologist from Derby, knew Boulton in 1757 and probably met Darwin before 1760. Darwin's Edinburgh friend James Keir also made occasional visits when his Army duties allowed.

[5]

The year 1760 saw a new King, George III, come to the throne, son of the Prince Frederick whose death Darwin had marked in verse at Cambridge. At Lichfield Dr and Mrs Darwin, with their two small sons, were entertaining Darwin's scientific friends at their new house and blending into the cathedral close community, presided over by Dr and Mrs Seward, aided by the lively Anna, now eighteen years old.

For a picture of Darwin at Lichfield, we turn to Joseph Wright's portrait (Plate 3A), and Anna Seward's report:

> He was somewhat above the middle size, his form athletic, and inclined to corpulence; his limbs too heavy for exact proportion. The traces of a severe small-pox; features, and countenance, which, when they were not animated by social pleasure, were rather saturnine than sprightly; a stoop in the shoulders, and the then professional appendage, a large full-bottomed wig, gave, at that early period of life, an appearance of nearly twice the years he bore. Florid health, and the earnest of good humour, a sunny smile, on entering a room, and on first accosting his friends, rendered, in his youth, that exterior agreeable, to which beauty and symmetry had not been propitious.[17]

So far, Anna's description accords quite well with others, though there is more meaning per word in Edgeworth's blunt remark, 'He was a large man, fat and rather clumsy.' I cannot avoid quoting more of Anna Seward's descriptions, but before doing so I ought to utter four warnings : first, she was a poet not a scholar, a woman of feeling rather than of accuracy; second, her book includes some slanders on Erasmus which she had to retract; third, she was looking back through forty years of a life clouded by an unfulfilled attachment to a vicar-choral of the cathedral, John Saville, who died in the year she wrote her memoirs; and, fourth, if we accept Charles Darwin's view, she was still sore that she was never asked to be the second Mrs Darwin. So Anna was naturally a little waspish and ambivalent about her famous neighbour in the close, whom she admired and yet also sometimes detested.

Anna's comments need to be carefully weighed, because there is something of a puzzle about Darwin's demeanour towards others, both individually and in company. Dozens of his friends praised him for being kind and sympathetic to friends and patients; he had a great talent for friendship, and his friends were usually lifelong. His benevolence and his observant eye are said to have been the key to his great success as a doctor. However, Anna and a few others accused him of being domineering, ir-religious and sarcastic, both to individuals and in company, and of generally riding roughshod over people's opinions—or at least those of the writers. I am not too surprised at these seeming inconsistencies: like many of us, Darwin was something of a chameleon in adapting to his environment. In congenial surroundings, with one friend or a group, he was charming, tolerant, kindly, thoughtful and also usually the life and soul of the party : his continuous talent for friendship was so strong that this judgement must be valid. However, he could be a rougher diamond in uncongenial surroundings: a rude or malingering patient, an instance of cruelty or injustice, a casual acquaintance who contradicted him boorishly—all these could rouse him to indignation and wounding remarks.

In judging his character we should listen first to his oldest friend James Keir, writing after Darwin's death in 1802 :

> I think all those who knew him will allow that sympathy and benevolence were the most striking features. He felt very sensibly for others, and, from his knowledge of human nature, he entered into their feelings and sufferings in the different circumstances of their constitution, character, health, sickness, and prejudice. In

benevolence, he thought that almost all virtue consisted. He despised
the monkish abstinences and the hypocritical pretensions which so
often impose on the world. The communication of happiness and the
relief of misery were by him held as the only standard of moral
merit. Though he extended his humanity to every sentient being,
it was not like that of some philosophers, so diffused as to be of no
effect; but his affection was there warmest where it could be of most
service to his family and his friends, who will long remember the
constancy of his attachment and his zeal for their welfare.[18]

On one subject, his benevolence as a doctor, all reports agree.
Even Anna is quite specific, and less verbose than usual:

> Professional generosity distinguished Dr Darwin's medical practice.
> While resident in Lichfield, to the priest and lay-vicars of its
> cathedral, and their families, he always cheerfully gave his advice,
> but never took fees from any of them. Diligently, also, did he attend
> to the health of the poor in that city, and afterwards at Derby, and
> supplied their necessities by food, and all sort of charitable assist-
> ance. In each of those towns, *his* was the cheerful board of almost
> open-housed hospitality, without extravagance or parade; deeming
> ever the first unjust, the latter unmanly. Generosity, wit, and
> science, were his household gods.[19]

Another point on which all his listeners agreed was his bad
stammer. 'He stammered extremely', Anna tells us, 'but whatever he said, whether gravely or in jest, was always well worth
waiting for, though the inevitable impression it made might not
always be pleasant to individual self-love.'[20] An example is given
by his son Robert:

> A young man once asked him in, as he thought, an offensive
> manner, whether he did not find stammering very inconvenient. He
> answered, 'No, Sir, it gives me time for reflection, and saves me
> from asking impertinent questions.'[21]

If the question was asked less offensively, he often replied that
stammering helped a young doctor by drawing attention to him.
Darwin's discussion of stammering in *Zoonomia* shows that he
was well aware of its mental origin: strangely enough, he does
not offer any effective treatment, though he presumably knew
that in the 1750s Henry Baker in London was successfully curing
many speech defects.[22]

Despite his stammer Darwin was generally reckoned a
splendid talker. His son Robert thought his greatest talent lay in

his conversational powers and skill in explaining abstruse topics intelligibly. Maria Edgeworth referred to 'those powers of wit, satire and peculiar humour, which never appeared fully to the public in his works, but which gained him strong ascendancy in private society.'[23] Lady Charleville, 'who had been accustomed to the most brilliant society in London', told Robert 'that Dr Darwin was one of the most agreeable men whom she had ever met'.[24] And Coleridge called Darwin 'a wonderfully entertaining and instructive' talker. In contrast there are the rebukes of Anna Seward:

> He became, early in life, sore upon opposition, whether in argument or conduct, and always revenged it by sarcasm of very keen edge. Nor was he less impatient of the sallies of egotism and vanity, even when they were in so slight a degree, that strict politeness would rather tolerate than ridicule them.[25]

As always, Anna is expressing personal feelings, and the phrase 'early in life' suggests she may have been taking a revenge forty years deferred: in Darwin's early years at Lichfield, Anna was an uppish teenager, and he may have been too vigorous in squashing her sillier opinions. Still, he did help with her poems, as she admits: 'He became a sort of poetic preceptor to me in my early youth.'[26]

Charles Darwin answered one of Anna's charges: 'Miss Seward speaks of him as being extremely sarcastic, but of this I can find no evidence in his letters or elsewhere.'[27] This is true: he was never sarcastic in writing. But there are several examples to show that he could be wounding as well as charming in conversation. One such example, possibly of later date, is given by Charles Darwin himself:

> When he wished to make himself disagreeable for any good cause, he was well able to do so. Lady *** married a widower, and became so jealous of his former wife that she cut and spoiled her picture, which hung up in one of the rooms. The husband, fearing that his young wife was becoming insane, was greatly alarmed, and sent for Dr Darwin. When he arrived he told her in the plainest manner many unpleasant truths, amongst others that the former wife was infinitely her superior in every respect, including beauty. The poor lady was astonished at being thus treated, and could never afterwards endure his name. He told the husband if she again behaved oddly, to hint that he would be sent for. The plan succeeded perfectly, and she ever afterwards restrained herself.[28]

[6]

In 1760 Darwin's second paper in the *Philosophical Transactions* of the Royal Society was published. Entitled 'An uncommon case of an Haemoptysis', it describes a patient who was wakened nightly at 2 a.m. by the spitting of blood. Darwin argues that the lungs were 'not sufficiently sensible to push forwards the whole circulation' and that the blood accumulated and ruptured some small blood vessels. Darwin advised the patient 'to be awakened, and rise out of his bed, at one in the morning, and remain awake till three, omitting all medicines'.[29] Today the case seems fairly trivial, but the treatment did have the virtue of simplicity and Darwin claims it was completely successful.

On 9 April 1761 Darwin was elected a Fellow of the Royal Society of London. This was less of an honour than it might have been, because there was a shortage of good scientists in the mid-eighteenth century and the Royal Society was at rather a low ebb: Hooke had died in 1703, Wren in 1723, Newton himself in 1727, and Halley in 1742. The most illustrious Fellow in 1760 was Benjamin Franklin, who was really only a visitor to England, come to plead for the civil rights of the American colonists, though he stayed from 1757 to 1762. Those who sponsored Darwin as a candidate for Fellowship were Noah Thomas, John Hadley, J. L. Petit, John Ross and Charlton Wollaston. According to the certificate, all claimed to know him personally. This was true of Dr Noah Thomas, whose lectures Darwin had recorded in shorthand, and of Petit, who was familiar enough with Darwin to write in a letter to Boulton in 1762: 'I enclose this letter to Darwin who will convey it to you I hope, if he does not put it in his pockett, and forget it.'[30] Darwin did send it on, and told Boulton: 'Dr Petit desires you'll write a Paper and become Member of the R.S.' So it was probably Petit who did most to propel Darwin into the Fellowship, though Michell and Franklin may also have had a hand in it.

Becoming a Fellow of the Royal Society may not have meant much to Darwin, but for the Society it turned out to be historic: it was the start of an overlapping succession of Fellows which lasted for 201 years through five generations of Darwins. Erasmus was a Fellow from 1761 to 1802, his son Robert from 1787 to 1848, Robert's son Charles from 1839 to 1881, Charles's son Sir George Howard Darwin from 1879 to 1912, George's brothers Francis from 1882 to 1925 and Horace from 1903 to 1928; and lastly, George's son Sir Charles Galton Darwin from 1922 to 1962. This unique record of enduring family excellence is unlikely ever to be challenged: the Darwins are England's premier scientific family.

But all that lay in the unknown future: we must return to 1762, to a Darwin 'very zealous in his profession'. Although primarily a physician, he was also adept with his scalpel. In the eighteenth century it was difficult to acquire bodies for dissection, and the dastardly crime of body-snatching was rife. When the opportunity came legally, the 'zealous' Darwin seized it:

> October 23rd, 1762—The body of the Malefactor, who is order'd to be executed at Lichfield on Monday the 25th instant, will be afterwards conveyed to the House of Dr Darwin, who will begin a Course of Anatomical Lectures, at Four o'clock on Tuesday evening, and continue them every Day as long as the Body can be preserved, and shall be glad to be favoured with the Company of any who profess Medicine or Surgery, or whom the Love of Science may induce.[31]

We do not know how many were induced to attend; nor whether Mrs Darwin welcomed such a macabre lodger in her house.

Throughout his medical career Darwin was 'very zealous' in condemning alcohol, which he thought caused much of the illness he saw among the rich, such as gout, liver disease and sometimes insanity. Anna tells us 'he avowed a conviction of the pernicious effects of all vinous fluid on the youthful and healthy constitution; an absolute horror of spirits of all sorts and however diluted. . . . From strong malt liquor he totally abstained, and if he drank a glass or two of English wine, he mixed it with water.'[32] But in these early years Darwin did not fully practise what he preached: there is a fine wine cellar in his house at Lichfield; he offered Boulton a present of two bottles of wine in July 1763; and on 9 June 1769 he wrote to Boulton: 'If you see Mr Baumgartner I shall be glad of a Chest of white Florence Wine.'[33] Later Darwin became more abstemious, and even more convinced of the evils of alcohol.

With or without alcohol, Darwin's life was apparently quite happy in the early 1760s, apart from his concern over Mary's frequent spasmodic pains. On 19 November 1763 Mary gave birth to a daughter, named Elizabeth; but the baby died after four months, on 29 March 1764.

Untimely death also struck the Sewards in 1764. Anna's younger sister Sarah, now twenty, was engaged to marry Joseph Porter, Dr Johnson's stepson. But Sarah fell ill, apparently of typhus fever, and Darwin could do nothing to save her. Anna sadly notes how 'Dr D. says when the fever returned it was with a fatal change in its nature from inflammatory to putrid, and that he has very little hope of saving her.'[34]

At the end of 1764 Darwin was thirty-three and Mary twenty-four: their son Charles was six and Erasmus five. Darwin had been at Lichfield for eight years. Settled in his medical career and with no pressing need to seek new patients, he could look forward to relaxing a little.

Anna has a story, difficult to believe but too circumstantial to ignore, which certainly shows him relaxing, as well as living up to her report that if he drank wine he mixed it with water:

> Mr Sneyd, then of Bishton, and a few more gentlemen of Staffordshire, prevailed upon the Doctor to join them in an expedition by water, from Burton to Nottingham, and on to Newark. They had cold provision on board, and plenty of wine. It was midsummer; the day ardent and sultry. The noontide meal had been made, and the glass gone gayly round. It was one of those *few* instances, in which the medical votary of the Naiads transgressed his general and strict sobriety. If not absolutely intoxicated, his spirits were in a high state of vinous exhilaration. On the boat approaching Nottingham, within the distance of a few fields, he surprised his companions by stepping, without any previous notice, from the boat into the middle of the river, and swimming to shore. They saw him get upon the bank, and walk coolly over the meadows toward the town: they called to him in vain, he did not once turn his head.[35]

Nonplussed at his behaviour, Mr Sneyd and his party pursued the Doctor, Anna says, and found him in the market place standing on a tub addressing a crowd, without a trace of his usual stammer. He was lecturing his audience on the benefits of fresh air, and telling them to keep their windows open at night. Then he calmly rejoined the party, slightly damp but otherwise normal. Anna has the temerity to give Darwin's speech verbatim, as if she had tape-recorded it, though she candidly admits she only heard the story after Darwin's death—perhaps forty years after he made the speech! When asked, Mr Sneyd said something

'similar' did happen: possibly one of the party tricked Darwin
into drinking wine laced with stronger liquor.

[7]

The Industrial Revolution began to forge ahead powerfully in
the early 1760s, with the completion of Smeaton's Eddystone
Lighthouse, the building of the Carron Iron Works, the opening
of Brindley's first canal from Worsley to Manchester, and
Hargraves's invention of the spinning jenny. Boulton joined in
the general fervour: in 1761 he bought the lease of a large area
of land at Handsworth Heath on the outskirts of Birmingham,
and began building a grand new factory there, the famous Soho
works. For power Boulton intended to rely on the water mill
already on the site, with a mill pool fed by water from Hockley
Brook. Because Boulton had (as usual) overstrained his finances,
his new factory was not finished until 1766 and not profitable
until many years later. Boulton's stock reaction to financial
trouble was to expand his activities, and eventually his optimism
was rewarded: he was hailed as the 'first manufacturer of
England', and the Soho manufactory was recognized as one of
the wonders of the world.

Darwin's enthusiasm for experiments on airs, heat and
electricity had already infected Boulton; and Franklin's second
visit to Birmingham in September 1760 gave a further impetus
to both Darwin and Boulton. Scientific instruments were more
interesting to manufacture than buckles, and Boulton soon
became known for making accurate instruments, particularly
thermometers. In 1762 Dr Petit wrote to Boulton 'to desire a
few thermometers of you. I was greatly at a loss for some . . . as
I had only your Pocket one and another which I bought which I
had not any great opinion of, as it did not correspond with
yours.'[36] This was the letter sent on by Darwin, who added,
'Why won't you sell these Thermometers, for I want one also
myself.'[37] Many scientists besides Darwin wanted accurate
thermometers: their lack was seriously impeding progress in the
theory of heat.

Having acquired a Boulton thermometer, Darwin was preparing to make some bold advances in the theory of heat, as he
explained to Boulton on 1 July 1763:

As you are now become a sober plodding Man of Business, I scarcely dare trouble you to do me a Favour in the nicknachatory, alias philosophical way: I have got a most exquisitly fine Balance, and a very neat Glass Box, and have all this day been employ'd in twisting the necks of Florence-Flasks—in vain!

Now if you like Florence Wine, I begg leave to make you a present of one Bottle, or two, if the first does not answer, to drink success to Philosophy and Trade, upon condition that you will procure me one of their Necks to be twisted into a little Hook according to the copper Plate on the reverse of this Paper. It must be truly hermetically seal'd, air tight, otherwise it will not answer my End at all. . . .

I am extreemly impatient for this new Play-Thing! as I intend to fortell every Shower by it, and make great medical Discovery as far as relates to the specific Gravity of air: and from the Quantity of Vapor. Thus the specific gravity of the air should be as the Absolute Gravity (shew'd by the Barometer), and as the Heat (shew'd by Boulton's Thermometer). Now if it is not always found as these two (that is as one and inversely as the other) then the Deviations at different Times must be as the Quantity of dissolved Vapour in the air.[38]

These last two sentences are, to say the least, somewhat astonishing: Darwin states what is now usually known as the ideal gas law, that density is proportional to pressure divided by absolute temperature; and he also has a clear premonition of the law of partial pressures. Of these two fundamental gas laws, the first is usually credited to J. A. C. Charles (1787) and the second to John Dalton (1801).

Darwin seems to have been 'at the height of his invention' in 1763. Besides casually enunciating these gas laws, he was keen to put the water vapour to good practical use by improving existing steam engines, and he was busy with new designs of carriages, to make his daily rounds as a doctor more comfortable. His interests in steam and carriages combined to give birth (at least on paper) to a steam carriage. Boulton received the full flood of Darwin's enthusiasm (probably in 1763, but possibly in 1764):

As I was riding Home yesterday, I concider'd the Scheme of the fiery Chariot, and the longer I contemplated this favourite Idea, the [more] practicable it appear'd to me. I shall lay my Thoughts before you, crude and indigested as they occur'd to me . . . as by those Hints you may be led into various Trains of thinking upon this Subject, and by that means (if any Hints can assist your Genius, which without Hints is above all others I am acquainted with) be more likely to improve, or disapprove. And as I am quite mad of this Scheme, I begg you will not mention it, or shew this Paper, to . . . any Body. . . .

He goes on to discuss whether the carriage should have three or four wheels, and comes down in favour of four. He suggests a design with two cylinders operating from one boiler: 'By the management of the steam Cocks the motion may be accelerated, retarded, destroy'd, revived, instantly and easly. And if this answers in Practice as it does in theory, the Machine can not fail of Success! Eureka!'[39]

This is all very well, but what did Darwin propose for the transmission system? His design was for a beam engine, with cords from the ends of the beam winding and unwinding round a split rear axle. As his diagram shows, Fig. 2, the semi-axles

Fig. 2

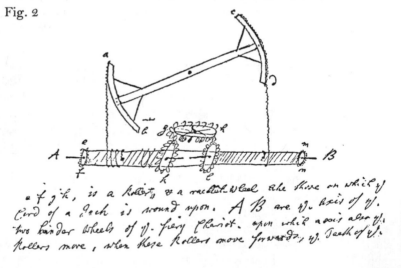

would be counter-rotating through the universal gear at the centre: each semi-axle would drive its wheel when the cord was being (forcibly) unwound by the motion of the beam, and would 'free-wheel' during the other half of the cycle, when the cord would be rewound through the forced counter-rotation of the axle. This method would propel the carriage smoothly, Darwin thought, 'without any loss of power or cumbersome weight of machinery': a similar idea has led to the design of the highly successful Daf cars, which use belts for transmission, so Darwin's design does not deserve to be dismissed as impracticable. It might have been rather jerky, and disastrously so if the timing became inaccurate, but the same criticism applies to the modern internal combustion engine.

Darwin was keen to persuade Boulton to build the vehicle:

> If you could learn the Expence of Coals of a common fire-engine, and the Weight of water it draws, some certain Estimate may be made if such a Scheme as this would answer. . . . If you think it feasible and will send me a Critique upon it, I will certainly . . . endeavour to build a Fiery Chariot; and if that answers get a Patent. If you chuse to be Partner with me in the Profit, and Expense and Trouble, let me know: as I am determined to execute it, if you approve of it.[40]

Boulton, already in debt, was not ready to chance his arm on such a futuristic project, and the enthusiastic inventor himself was too busy with his medical practice to do more than prod Boulton. So the scheme fizzled out, and the Frenchman Cugnot made the first working steam carriage, in 1769. Still, Darwin has rightly received credit for first propounding the correct principles for making steam cars.[41]

Darwin's passion for steam engines proved more rewarding than he could ever have foreseen when, a few years later, James Watt heard of his interest, visited him, became his lifelong friend and found in Boulton an ideal partner who was already half-converted to steam by Darwin's zeal.

Darwin's enthusiasm for technology led him into another ambitious project, a scheme for a twenty-mile canal from Lichfield to the River Trent. The records of this proposed canal are fragmentary and rather tantalizing. The first documents go back to 1758, when James Brindley made a survey for a canal from the Minster Pool at Lichfield to the River Trent: his estimate[42] came to £10,195. If the work had gone ahead, this would have been Brindley's first canal. Since the Minster Pool is only a hundred yards from Darwin's house, he probably met Brindley in 1758; but there is no evidence that Darwin was a sponsor of the canal at that time.

However, he was deeply involved in a new attempt to promote the canal in 1763–4. His partners in the project were John Barker, a Lichfield draper, Samuel Garbett the Birmingham merchant, and possibly Robert Bage. There are eight letters[43] about details of the project written by Darwin to Barker between December 1763 and March 1764. Concerned mainly with the letting of the mills at Alrewas and Wychnor, these letters are mostly of the type that would be replaced by telephone calls today. There is also a rough draft agreement in which 'Mr Barker and Dr D' agree to let Aldrewas Mill to Mr Woodhouse for 'the rent of £35 a year', with the tenant enjoying the benefits of the eel-fishing 'valued at £25 a year'.[44] In May 1764, Darwin, Barker and Garbett entered into an agreement with the trustees of the Lichfield Turnpike to build a bridge and carry 'a canal or ditch fourteen feet wide' under the Lichfield–Burton road at Wychnor.[45] It seems that the project collapsed during 1764, probably from lack of funds. But Darwin's hard work was not wasted: his experience proved most useful in the promotion of the Grand Trunk Canal in 1765.

# FOUR

# Forming the Lunar Circle
## 1765-1770

Between 1765 and 1768 Darwin's talent for friendship ripened into positive genius as he drew in, one by one and for different reasons, the group of lifelong friends later known as the Lunar Society of Birmingham, whose enterprise did so much to bring about the technological world we know today. At the beginning of 1765 Boulton was the only one of the future group he knew well; Small, Edgeworth, Watt and Day he had yet to meet; Wedgwood he may have met, but only casually; and his student friend Keir was still abroad on military service.

For Darwin 1765 was the Year of the Canal—the Trent-and-Mersey canal—linked with the names of Brindley and Wedgwood. James Brindley (1717–72) was already famous for such feats of hydraulic engineering as pumping out the Clifton coal mine, when he took water from the upper reaches of the River Irwell through a 600-yard tunnel, then under the Irwell by an inverted syphon, and on to the coal mine, where the water drove a wheel which pumped the mine dry, before running back into the Irwell. Brindley became known as 'the man who made water run uphill': his scheme was so good that it worked for 111 years with the waterwheel, and another fifty-seven years with a water turbine.[1]

Brindley's first canal survey was in 1758, for the twenty-mile Lichfield–Trent canal, which Darwin afterwards tried to promote. A year or so later Brindley produced plans[2] for a fifty-mile canal from Burslem to just beyond King's Mills, utilizing the route already surveyed for the Lichfield–Trent canal over the seventeen miles between Alrewas and King's Mills, and with a spur to Lichfield (shown by a broken line in Fig. 1). These plans fell into abeyance in 1759 when the Duke of Bridgewater commissioned Brindley to build the ten-mile Worsley–Manchester canal, completed in 1761, which figures in the history books as the start of the canal era in Britain. Brindley now planned to extend the Burslem–Trent canal to connect with the Mersey, to make a 'Grand Trunk Canal', so called because he foresaw that other canals would branch off it to the Severn and the Thames, to link the industrial Midlands with the ports of Liverpool, Hull, Bristol and London.

Brindley's idea appealed to an enterprising pottery manufacturer, Josiah Wedgwood of Burslem (Plate 4D). Humbly born, Wedgwood had by thrift, skill and hard work acquired a business of his own by 1759, and soon he began the experimental improvements that were to make his wares world-famous. But Wedgwood's efforts to improve his products were hampered by the problems of carrying the goods by land—to say 'by road' would be too complimentary to the rutted tracks that masqueraded as roads. The pottery was often smashed as the bone-shaking vehicles (at best) bounced over the bumps and into the pot-holes or (at worst) overturned. But if Brindley's Grand Trunk Canal materialized, Wedgwood could build a new factory beside it and send his wares cheaply and unbroken to Liverpool and to Hull for export. In 1765 Wedgwood, aided by his friend and future business partner Thomas Bentley, directed his immense energy into the project and rallied his friends in support of a parliamentary bill to sanction the new waterway.

Darwin probably first met Wedgwood about 1764, and as soon as he heard of the new canal project he threw himself into the scheme almost as keenly as Wedgwood. Darwin was already experienced in canal promotion; he urged influential patients and friends to support the idea; and he bombarded Wedgwood with ideas and advice. Wedgwood was delighted at Darwin's enthusiasm, and wrote seven long letters to Darwin between 3 April and 5 June 1765: 'I am favour'd with your last covering two papers which please me prodigiously, and I am quite charm'd with your zeal in this Public spirited scheme.'[3] There was much to discuss: as Wedgwood told Darwin, 'we shall want all the advice you can give us yourself, or procure from your Friends, respecting the model or plan for the Act of Parliament':[4] the landowners *en route* had to be judiciously canvassed; the route and the termini had to be decided; the relative merits of locks, tunnels and detours had to be assessed; the system of

charging for freight had to be settled, and the rates fixed at an
optimum level. There was much opposition to be overcome from
turnpike trusts, rival canal promoters, landowners who refused
to sell and conservatives who wanted to preserve the status quo.
On 12 December 1765 Darwin told Boulton that 'the people of
Cheshire are opposing the Navigation being brought to
Birmingham.'[5] Boulton and Samuel Garbett, Darwin's co-
promoter of the Lichfield canal, were among the supporters of
the project.

Wedgwood, Bentley, Darwin and their friends were in effect
inaugurating a new form of transport—their idea was akin to
proposing a hundred-mile motorway in, say, 1910. Any mistakes
might affect both the future of the waterways and the appearance
of the landscape for a hundred years.

Wedgwood lived at Burslem, nearly thirty miles north-west
of Lichfield, but he and Darwin met fairly often in 1765, usually
when Darwin's medical calls took him towards the Potteries: for
example, they met by chance at Uttoxeter on 27 September; and,
when Wedgwood was ill in November, Darwin went to Burslem
to treat him. Bentley was based at Liverpool, much further away,
and the lack of personal contact with him did cause one argument,
over Bentley's pamphlet about the advantages of canals. Darwin
wanted to improve the style, and his suggested amendments
certainly did so. But he expressed his views bluntly rather than
politely: 'this whole Sentence is formal and parsonic'; 'a very
garrulous Sentence, omit the last three Lines'; 'sad Language'.[6]
Writing to Bentley, Wedgwood refers to a 'long, Critical
epistle from our ingenious and poetical friend Doctor Darwin
which I doubt not . . . hath afforded you entertainment and shook
your diaphragm for you'.[7] Bentley's pride was shaken more than
his diaphragm: he was offended that anyone should criticize his
style. Darwin took Bentley's reply with good humour and the
quarrel soon spent itself. On 18 November Wedgwood wrote
again to Bentley: 'The Dr acknowledg'd he had wrote you two
or three very rude letters, and said you had drub'd him genteely
in return, which he seem'd to take very cordially and to be very
well pleas'd with his treatment'.[8]

Apart from this minor *contretemps*, the plans for the Grand
Trunk Canal went ahead with what now seems incredible
rapidity. Parliamentary approval was secured in April 1766; and
on 26 July 1766, at Bramhills near Burslem, on land owned by

his family, Wedgwood cut the first turf, which Brindley solemnly wheeled away in a barrow. Thus began the most formidable engineering project of its kind that had been attempted in England. The canal was to run south-east from the Mersey at Runcorn through the salt-rich areas of Cheshire to its summit at the 2900-yard Harecastle Tunnel, and then south-east through the Potteries to just north of Lichfield, where it would turn north-east to join the Trent south of Derby. As Wedgwood and Darwin foresaw, the canal gave new life to the industrial area of the Potteries; but it took ten years to complete, and Brindley died before it was finished.

From 1765 onwards Darwin and Wedgwood remained close friends, and Wedgwood became firmly fixed in the Lunar circle.

[2]

The shape of the Lunar circle was decided when Dr William Small arrived in Birmingham during May 1765 : he was to serve as the still centre towards whom all the more energetic members were equally attracted. Small is one of the select group of Scottish scientists born around 1730 that included Watt, Keir, Lind and Black. Small's talents matched theirs, but he is little known, because he pursued a policy of self-denial, refusing to join societies or write papers. Edgeworth referred to Small as 'a man esteemed by all who knew him, and by all who were admitted to his friendship beloved with no common enthusiasm. Dr Small formed a link which combined Mr Boulton, Mr Watt, Dr Darwin, Mr Wedgwood, Mr Day, and myself, together.'9

William Small was born in 1734 and educated at Marischal College, Aberdeen. In 1758 he became Professor of Natural Philosophy at the College of William and Mary at Williamsburg in Virginia, where he was a great success with his pupils, especially Thomas Jefferson. Few teachers have ever had so fine a tribute from so illustrious a pupil as Small received from Jefferson:

> It was my great good fortune, and what probably fixed the destinies of my life, that Dr. Wm. Small of Scotland was then professor of Mathematics, a man profound in most of the useful branches of science, with a happy talent of communication, correct and gentlemanly manners, and an enlarged and Liberal mind. He,

most happily for me, became soon attached to me and made me his daily companion when not engaged in the school; and from his conversation I got my first views of the expansion of science and of the system of things in which we are placed.[10]

Small left Virginia in 1764 after some friction at the College, and in January 1765 attended a Royal Society meeting as a guest of Franklin, who had also returned to England, in his role as 'the Voice of America'. Small heard of an opening for a physician in Birmingham, where he arrived in May with a letter of introduction to Boulton from Franklin. Boulton took to Small immediately, and in the next ten years did little without Small's help and advice. Small displaced Darwin as Boulton's chief friend and adviser, and also became Boulton's doctor. Darwin was not at all put out, however, for Small was soon his 'favourite friend'. Anna Seward, after naming Michell, Keir, Boulton and Watt, refers to 'the accomplished Dr Small' as 'above all others in Dr Darwin's personal regard'; no one has contradicted her. On 11 March 1766 Darwin in writing to Boulton referred to 'our ingenious friend Dr Small, from whom and from you, when I was last at Birmingham, I received Ideas that for many days occurred to me at the Intervals of the common Business of Life, with inexpressible Pleasure'.[11] So the Boulton-Darwin duo became the Boulton-Small-Darwin trio, with Small as the willing link between the two busy heavyweights.

Small was the right man in the right place at the right time. Accomplished, attractive, self-effacing, he was not keen on his new profession as a physician, and only too pleased to spend time talking to Boulton, Darwin, Wedgwood and (a few years later) Watt. These four were too busy in their professions to have time to organize even so informal a gathering as a Lunar meeting; but, with Small to act as invisible secretary, their invisible college flourished.

[3]

The next year, 1766, brought a new acquaintance who had none of Small's easy affability. On 11 January Jean-Jacques Rousseau landed in England, but his persecution mania made him an extremely awkward visitor and his host David Hume had great

difficulty in finding a house to suit him. Eventually the wealthy
philanthropist Richard Davenport offered Wootton Hall, near
Ashbourne; Rousseau went to live there in March 1766. There
he wrote the first five books of his *Confessions*; and there he also
met Darwin. Rousseau's prickliness was well known and he
would

> spend much of his time 'in the well-known cave upon the terrace in
> melancholy contemplation'. He disliked being interrupted, so Dr
> Darwin, who was then a stranger to him, sauntered by the cave, and
> minutely examined a plant growing in front of it. This drew forth
> Rousseau, who was interested in botany, and they conversed
> together, and afterwards corresponded during several years.[12]

This is Charles Darwin's account; but Sir Gavin de Beer says,
'Rousseau suspected the meeting had been contrived and never
let Darwin get near him again.'[13] I have found no trace of the
correspondence mentioned by Charles Darwin; but Erasmus
certainly took a keen interest in Rousseau's ideas on education
and nature study. In May 1767 Rousseau abruptly left Wootton
Hall, and Darwin never met him again.

Darwin's real new friend of 1766 was Richard Lovell Edgeworth (Plate 5A), twelve years younger. This was a friendship
that strengthened as the years passed, and when Darwin died
nearly forty years later he was in the middle of writing a letter
to Edgeworth. As Hesketh Pearson remarked, Edgeworth had
a keenly inventive mind, polished manners, natural gaiety,
facility in friendship and 'a passion for the other sex, which
brought upon him four marriages and 22 children'.[14]

Carriages rather than marriages drew Edgeworth towards
Darwin, for whom 1766 could be called the Year of the Carriage.
In the previous year, when Edgeworth was twenty-one and not
long embarked on the first of his four marriages, he saw a
travelling exhibition called 'The Microcosm'—a mechanical
contraption displaying the revolutions of the planets and a
variety of moving figures and landscapes. Darwin had seen the
Microcosm in Birmingham two years before and had mentioned
his carriage designs to the exhibitor, who now in turn told
Edgeworth. He was fascinated to hear that Darwin had designed
a carriage 'able to turn in a small compass, without danger of
oversetting'. This fired Edgeworth's imagination, and having
money in hand and nothing particular to do, he retired to his

house on Hare Hatch Common, near Reading, and constructed a
'very handsome Phaeton' on the Darwinian principle. Early in
1766 Edgeworth told the Society for the Encouragement of Arts
(now the Royal Society of Arts) about the carriage, saying that
it was Darwin's idea.

The Secretary of the Society, Dr Templeman, wrote to
Darwin, who replied on 8 March 1766 describing some of his
improvements in carriage design over the years:

> About seven or eight years ago, I observed that among other
> lesser defects in the common light Carriages that there were two
> principle ones, *First* that the foremost wheels were for the con-
> veniency of turning made too low, by which means the forepart of
> the Carriage was obliged to rise too suddenly over stones or other
> obstacles in the way; and thence continual Shocks produced, that
> injured both the Horses and the Carriage, and incommoded the
> Travellers—Besides the lesser inconvenience of increasing the
> Friction upon the Axletree. *Secondly* That in the Time of turning,
> the basis on which the Carriage rests was changed from a Parallelo-
> gram to a Triangle.

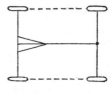

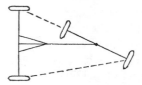

Fig. 3A                     Fig. 3B

Thus in Fig. [3A] the Carriage is a four-footed stool, in [Fig. 3B]
a three-leg'd stool. That from this Cause Carriages were most
frequently overturn'd, viz at the time of turning. And that to this
Cause was entirely owing the frequent accidents in Phaetons, where
the Body-part with the Driver were placed more forwards, that is,
upon the most hazzardous part of this three-leg'd stool in the Act of
turning.

I contrived a method of turning, which gets free of both these
inconvenience, viz, it admits the foremost wheels to be as high as
you please, those I made were four feet diameter; and the Carriage
stands on the same Basis (that is, is as safe from overturning) in the
act of turning as at other times.

I made a model about 7 or 8 years ago which is perished long
since, three years ago I made a Phaeton on this principle, and have

rode in it, I dare conjecture, above 10,000 miles and it is yet a good one, and weighs but 500 wgt.

About two years ago I made a Post Chaise on this principle, and have rode in that I dare say 10,000 miles and found no inconvenience from the new manner of turning in either of them.

Each of the foremost Wheels turns not from a Center between them but each on a Center of its own near the Knave. I can not give any drawing or description that can be at all intelligible, as the parts tho' very simple, lie in different Planes.—But if the Society will bear the Expense will direct a model to be made for them.

Otherwise Mr Greseley of Seal in Leicestershire, to whom I have now given the Phaeton, intends soon after Easter to come to London, and at my desire will shew it to the Society.[15]

This long letter, hitherto unpublished except for a few extracts, clarifies several features of Darwin's carriage designs. His main achievement was in devising a way of keeping the rectangular wheel-print pattern: he proceeded in one leap from the standard design for the front wheels of eighteenth-century carriages to the standard design for the front wheels of twentieth-century cars, and proved his design by personally road-testing it for 20,000 miles on two carriages. It is an impressive achievement; but the gap between an invention and its general use is a wide one, only to be bridged by intensive lobbying or actual manufacture by the inventor or his friends, a course of action foreign to Darwin, who had too many other interests.

Darwin did not even patent his mechanism, as he explains at the end of his letter to Dr Templeman:

I had once thoughts of applying for a Patent for making the Axletrees for this new way of turning, which are uncommon shaped Cranks and require a little accuracy in making—but I defer'd this till much experience should ascertain their being really useful.

There are some lesser conveniences in these Carriages, such as a double cross Perch much *lighter* and more *springing* than the common.

And one Shaft instead of two, by which both Horses can back the Carriage.

And Swingle-Tree Bars to draw by, which prevents the Horses from galling on their shoulders.

I believe my Carriage has fewer pieces of wood, is lighter, and will last longer than any other Carriage of the Size and Conveniences, besides its being safer from overturning, and easier to draw.[16]

Darwin's other improvements in design, mentioned here, were also well worthwhile. Until the invention of pneumatic tyres, larger front wheels provided greater comfort and easier traction, as he pointed out. His idea of a single shaft above the horses, terminating in a pivot on which the draw-bar hung, was scarcely new, because it was used by the ancient Greeks.[17] The single shaft had advantages, however, in allowing the horses to back the carriage and in giving them more freedom to turn.

Darwin's letter also gives some idea of the distances he covered on his rounds. Since he drove more than 10,000 miles in three years in the Phaeton and about 10,000 miles in the post-chaise in two of the same three years, he probably travelled about 10,000 miles per year, or about 30 miles per day.

Mr Greseley's Darwinian phaeton was apparently not taken to London for the Society of Arts to inspect, but Edgeworth showed his own phaeton to the Society, and told Darwin about it: 'The Doctor wrote me a very civil answer, and . . . invited me to his house.'[18]

So Edgeworth came to Lichfield in the summer of 1766. The doctor was out, but Mrs Darwin received Edgeworth, who had 'the pleasure of passing the evening with this most agreeable woman'.[19] Darwin was late returning, but when he did so his entry was dramatic:

> When supper was nearly finished, a loud rapping at the door announced the Doctor. There was a bustle in the hall, which made Mrs Darwin get up and go to the door. Upon her exclaiming that they were bringing in a dead man, I went to the hall: I saw some persons, directed by one whom I guessed to be Doctor Darwin, carrying a man who appeared motionless.
>
> 'He is not dead', said Doctor Darwin. 'He is only dead drunk. I found him', continued the Doctor, 'nearly suffocated in a ditch; I had him lifted into my carriage, and brought hither, that we might take care of him to-night.'
>
> Candles came, and what was the surprise of the Doctor, and of Mrs Darwin, to find that the person whom he had saved was Mrs Darwin's brother! who, for the first time in his life, as I was assured, had been intoxicated in this manner, and who would undoubtedly have perished, had it not been for Doctor Darwin's humanity.
>
> During this scene I had time to survey my new friend, Doctor Darwin. He was a large man, fat, and rather clumsy; but intelligence and benevolence were painted in his countenance: he had a con-

siderable impediment in his speech, a defect which is in general painful to others; but the Doctor repaid his auditors so well for making them wait for his wit or his knowledge, that he seldom found them impatient.[20]

Afterwards Darwin had a long talk with Edgeworth, and the next day introduced him to Anna Seward (Plate 5c), now twenty-three, and 'in the height of youth and beauty, of an enthusiastic temper, a votary of the muses, and of the most eloquent and brilliant conversation'. In the evening Mrs Darwin invited Anna and a party of her friends to dinner. Edgeworth found that Mrs Darwin 'had a little pique against Miss Seward', presumably because she was inclined to flirt with Erasmus, and, after Edgeworth had embarked on a few compliments to Anna, 'the watchful Mrs Darwin' confounded them both by 'drinking *Mrs Edgeworth's health*. Miss Seward's surprise was manifest. But [she] turned the laugh in her favor.'[21] Edgeworth enjoyed several more parties on ensuing evenings: 'How much of my future life has depended upon this visit of Lichfield!' If Edgeworth was impressed by Lichfield, Anna was impressed by Edgeworth: 'His address was gracefully spirited, and his conversation eloquent. He danced, he fenced, and winged his arrows with more than philosophic skill.'[22]

Darwin was equally impressed, and wrote at once to Boulton:

> I have got with me a mechanical Friend, Mr Edgeworth from Oxfordshire—The greatest Conjurer I ever saw—G-d send fair Weather, and pray come to my assistance, and prevail on Dr Small and Mrs Boulton to attend you, tomorrow Morning, and we will reconvoy you to Birmingham on Monday, if the D——l permit. . . .
>
> He has the principles of Nature in his palm, and moulds them as He pleases. Can take away polarity or give it to the Needle by rubbing it thrice on the palm of his Hand.
>
> And can see through two solid Oak Boards without Glasses! wonderful! astonishing! diabolical!!! Pray tell Dr Small He must come to see these Miracles.[23]

Edgeworth had shown Darwin some of the conjuring tricks he had devised for a performance at Sir Francis Delaval's house in London. Boulton and Small came to Lichfield and they liked both the conjuror and his tricks. Boulton took Edgeworth back to Birmingham and, by showing him round some factories, fired him with enthusiasm for invention: 'I would willingly join with you in a patent',[24] he wrote to Darwin soon afterwards. In the next few years Edgeworth invented a robot wooden horse (rather like a modern tank), a carriage with sails, the first semaphore telegraph system, an umbrella for covering haystacks, a turnip-cutter, and many other ingenious devices.

Edgeworth's flow of inventions won him a silver medal from the Society of Arts in 1768, and on 2 March 1769 he wrote to tell the Society about an improved Darwinian four-wheel carriage. Its main advantages, he says, are independent springing of the wheels and the Darwinian method of turning, which is explained in an appendix, copied by Edgeworth from a draft in which the drawings and some of the writing seem to be Darwin's.[25] The essence of the improved design is that the two front wheels C and D (see Fig. 4) when turned should not be parallel,

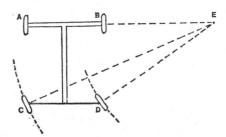

Fig. 4

as in the earlier design, but should have turning circles with the same centre (E) lying on the line of the back axle (AB), thus ensuring that the front wheels move tangential to their track instead of dragging. The Society of Arts Committee for Mechanics recommended an award for 'the application of the chains to the forepart of Mr Edgeworth's four-wheel carriage, whereby the wheels are turned on two centres',[26] and the Society duly awarded Edgeworth a gold medal. Darwin was not in the least resentful that his idea had borne golden fruit for Edgeworth. He did not seek mechanical fame himself, and was pleased at Edgeworth's success. In return Edgeworth thanked him with typical exuberance (on 16 September 1769): 'To be engaged in any thing with you would give me the greatest pleasure as I find a congeniality of disposition in us which makes me think we should agree and succeed in any scheme we should be joined in'.[27] The improved Darwinian steering, used in many cars today, is known as Ackermann steering, after Rudolf Ackermann, who re-invented it thirty years later.

[4]

If 1765 and 1766 were the Years of the Canal and the Carriage, 1767 might be called the Year of the Steam Engine, when Darwin's zeal for steam attracted the most illustrious of his close friends, James Watt (Plate 4c).

We have already seen how Darwin was hoping (in vain) to improve the steam engine in 1757 and later how he failed to persuade Boulton to make a steam carriage. In 1765 Boulton himself found he needed a steam engine; he had intended to rely on a water-wheel to power his new manufactory at Soho, until he realized (rather late) that he would be at the mercy of drought —and of anyone who took too much water from the higher reaches of the Hockley Brook. Now he wanted a steam engine to pump water back into the reservoir pool that fed the water-wheel. As there were no accepted designs, Boulton made his own engine and sent it to Franklin for comment in 1765. Darwin was impatient and wrote to Boulton on 12 December 1765:

> I am undone to know what Observations Dr Franklin supply'd you with about your Steam-Engine, besides giving you his approbation, and particularly to hear your final opinion, and Dr Small's on the important Question, whether Evaporation is at the Surface of boiling Water, or not?—or if it be at the Surface of the Vessel, exposed to the Fire, which I rather suspect—*For* if you boil Water in a Florence-Flask, you see bubbles rising from the Bottom. These are Steam, as they mount they are condensed again by the cold supernatant Fluid, and their sides clapping together make that noise call'd *Simmerring*.[28]

Darwin had still not seen the engine when he wrote again on 11 March 1766:

> Your Model of a Steam-Engine I am told gain'd so much Approbation in London that I can not but congratulate you on the mechanical Fame you have acquired by it: which, assure yourself, is as great a Pleasure to me, as it could possibly be to yourself.[29]

He was so keen to see the model that he would travel on 'the first vacant day' and 'trust to the Stars for meeting with you at Home.' The steam engine was further discussed in the summer when Boulton and Small visited Darwin to meet Edgeworth; so the embryo Lunar circle was already steam-minded.

In 1765 James Watt, instrument-maker to the University of Glasgow, twenty-nine years old, made his invention of the separate condenser to improve the efficiency of the steam engine: 'I can think of nothing else but this machine,'[30] he wrote to his friend James Lind in April 1765. Though keen on his invention, Watt had a deep-seated streak of self-doubt, and needed continual encouragement from optimistic friends. One of these was Joseph Black the chemist, who saw the advantages of Watt's design and introduced him to John Roebuck (1718–94), the leading Scottish industrialist. Roebuck had begun his career as a doctor in Birmingham, but soon, in partnership with Samuel Garbett, he had set up a sulphuric-acid works at Birmingham, followed by a larger one at Prestonpans, and then the Carron Iron works. Roebuck needed a new engine to dry out his salt mines at Bo'ness and he agreed to develop Watt's engine, taking two-thirds of the profits, if any. Meanwhile Watt took employment as a canal surveyor and engineer.

In April 1767 Watt travelled to London with the difficult task of petitioning Parliament to sanction a Forth-Clyde canal. The petition failed and Watt's opinion of the House of Commons was unflattering: 'I never saw so many wrong-headed people on all sides gathered together. . . . I believe *the Deevil* has possession of them.'[31] Roebuck had asked Watt to visit Garbett at Birmingham. He did so, and was introduced to two of Garbett's friends, Darwin and Small. It was the turning point of Watt's life: Darwin and Small took an immediate liking to him, and he to them; though Boulton was away, Watt looked over the Soho works.

Watt stayed overnight at Darwin's house, and at this very first meeting he told Darwin the secret of his new engine. From this moment Watt was fixed in the Lunar circle. The optimistic Darwin and the patient Small continually encouraged him and urged him to join forces with Boulton and settle in Birmingham. Darwin's first letter to Watt, on 18 August 1767, speaks for itself:

> Now, my dear new friend, I first hope you are well and less hypochondriacal, and that Mrs Watt and your child are well. The plan of your steam improvements I have religiously kept secret, but begin myself to see some difficulties in your execution which did not strike me when you were here. I have got another and another new hobby-horse since I saw you. I wish the Lord would send you to

pass a week with me, and Mrs Watt along with you;—a week, a
month, a year![32]

Small's first recorded letter to Watt dates from January 1768,
and he wrote almost fortnightly for the next six years, until
Watt finally settled in Birmingham.

In July 1768 Watt's friend John Robison visited Darwin when
Small was with him, and wrote enthusiastically to Watt:

> I write this principally to thank you for the favour you have done me
> in introducing me to the acquaintance of Dr darwin and Dr Small. I
> can't tell you how much I think myself obliged to you. I was quite
> charmed with the unaffected ease and Civility of darwin. . . . I met
> with no less kindness . . . from Mrs darwin. You are happy in the
> Esteem of such worthy people.[33]

In August 1768 Watt had to go to London again to apply for
a patent, and he visited Birmingham on his way back. This time
he saw not only Darwin and Small, but also Boulton, and they
liked each other so well that Watt stayed with Boulton at Soho
House for a fortnight.


[5]


Darwin's earliest friend, his student companion James Keir
(Plate 5B), now a captain in the Army, was thinking of retiring
and starting up a chemical factory. In 1767 he left the Army,
stayed first with Edgeworth, then with Darwin, and decided to
settle in the Birmingham area to be near Darwin and his friends.
On 8 November 1767 Darwin wrote to Wedgwood: 'I have the
Pleasure to introduce to your acquaintance Captain James Keir,
an old Friend of mine, a successful cultivator of both Arts and
Arms. He begs the Favour of seeing your elegant manufactory
and hopes to meet our common Friend, the Philosopher, Mr
Whitehurst at your House.'[34] Keir quickly fitted into the group,
and within a month or two he was confiding to Small his plans
for manufacturing alkali. Watt met Keir in 1768 and described
him to Dr Lind as 'a mighty chemist before the Lord, and a very
agreeable man'.[35] Everyone agreed that Keir was 'a very agreeable man', and he was to become the favourite chairman at Lunar
meetings.

So Keir entered the Lunar group, and joined Boulton and

Wedgwood as a pioneering manufacturer. Darwin seems to have tried to emulate his three manufacturing friends in the late 1760s, by joining Robert Bage and two other partners in starting an iron works. It is said that the project failed, with Bage (and presumably Darwin?) losing money—a failure that made Bage turn to novel-writing. I have not found any details of this project.[36]

Amid his many new friends, Darwin did not forget the old ones. In the letter to Boulton on 12 December 1765 Darwin mentions that Michell 'has been a day or two with me,' and Boulton himself was still in high favour, though he was a bad letter-writer. Darwin ends his long letter of 11 March 1766 with:

> I intend very shortly, if G–d permit, to pay you a visit —— 'Ay, for God's sake, come and welcom', (say you) 'any Thing but these damn'd long letters'.[37]

Darwin also had much to occupy him at home: Mary's third son was born on 30 May 1766, and was given the Christian names Robert Waring, the same as those of his uncle, Erasmus's eldest brother, who still lived at Elston and pursued his studies as a naturalist. The baby Robert proved to be the healthiest of Mary's children: he survived an experimental inoculation against measles, and lived to be eighty-two, long enough to see some of the successes of his famous son Charles.

A less fortunate baby is the subject of a letter sent to Darwin by a friend on 7 February 1767: apparently an illegitimate child was murdered by its mother. Darwin's reply is characteristic:

> I am sorry you should think it necessary to make any excuse for a Letter I this morning received from you. The Cause of Humanity needs no Apology to me. . . .
> The Women that have committed this most unnatural crime, are real objects of our greatest Pity; their education has produced in them so much Modesty, or sense of Shame, that this artificial Passion overturns the very instincts of Nature!—what struggles must there be in their minds, what agonies!—at a Time when, after the Pains of Parturition, Nature has designed them the sweet Consolation of giving Suck to a little helpless Babe, that depends on them for its hourly existence!—Hence the cause of this most horrid crime is an excess of what is really a Virtue, of the Sense of Shame, or Modesty. Such is the Condition of human Nature![38]

In happy contrast to these misfortunes, there was the brilliant promise of his eldest son Charles, who was eight years old at the beginning of 1767. Even in infancy, Erasmus tells us, Charles examined natural objects with unusual attention, 'first by his senses simply; then by tools, which were his playthings'.[39] He soon acquired accurate knowledge of science and mechanics: 'the invention and improvement of machines' occupied and amused him. Charles was also keen on examining rocks and minerals, and as soon as he was old enough he (and his father) 'descended the mines, and climbed the precipices of Derbyshire, and of some other counties, with uncommon pleasure and observation'.[40] Charles collected fossils and minerals, and in due course, through being familiar with actual substances, 'the complicate science of chemistry became not only easy, but delightful to him'. Charles had a troublesome stammer, which his parents tried to cure in 1767 by sending him to France for several months with a private tutor, thinking that if he was not allowed to speak English he might lose the stammer. (He did, but only when speaking French!) His tutor was Mr Dickenson of Blimhill in Shropshire, 'an ingenious botanist', and Charles returned from the expedition with a taste for botany as well as a command of French.

Despite Charles's progress, 1767 was not a good year for Darwin and Mary. Their fifth child, baptized William Alvey after Darwin's elder brother, was born on 27 July, but he died on 15 August and was buried at the cathedral on 18 August. Mary's health was not improved by 'the frequency of her maternal situation' (as Anna Seward neatly puts it), and her spasms were coming on more often and more severely.

Darwin's medical career was still proceeding smoothly, however—or perhaps 'roughly' would be a better word, for neither his carriage designs nor his efforts as a trustee of the Lichfield Turnpike could smooth the bumps and ruts in the public roads and the tracks leading to country houses. He took with him on his journeys a horse called Doctor, trained to follow his carriage. When the road became impassable, Darwin would get out and complete his journey on Doctor's back. Other 'optional extras' on his carriage were a hamper of food, in case he was stuck in the mud out in the country; and pen and paper, for jotting down thoughts shaken out of him on the road. Darwin's income was steadier than his carriage: the figures for 1765–7 were £800, £748 and £847.

Darwin's roles as father, doctor and Lunar recruiting sergeant still left him to play his part in the Sewards' literary circle, and help Anna with her verse-writing. The parallel between Samuel Johnson's edition of Shakespeare (published in 1765) and Dr Seward's edition of Beaumont's plays gave Darwin the cue for two scathing couplets that would not have pleased either editor:

> From Lichfield famed two giant critics come,
> Tremble, ye Poets! hear them! 'Fe, Fo, Fum!'
> By Seward's arm the mangled Beaumont bled,
> And Johnson grinds poor Shakespear's bones for bread.[41]

This was not a promising prelude to Darwin's first meeting with Johnson, probably in 1767 when Johnson stayed in Lichfield from July to October. Johnson looked on his birthplace with affection: its inhabitants were, he said, 'the most sober, decent people in England, the genteelest in proportion to their wealth, and spoke the purest English'.[42] The Bishop's Palace held special memories for him, because his benefactor Gilbert Walmesley had lived there, and he did not much relish having these memories sullied by the sight of Sewards in residence. The Sewards were no strangers to him, because Sarah Seward, who had died so tragically three years before, was to have married his stepson, but Johnson despised Dr Seward as a provincial dilettante: 'Sir, his ambition is to be a fine talker; so he goes to Buxton, and such places, where he may find companies to listen to him. . . .'[43] The Sewards returned his contempt, for they could not forget Johnson's humble origins. Mrs Seward's father Dr Hunter had been his headmaster, and Anna is probably retailing family gossip when she refers to the schoolboy Johnson as a 'huge, overgrown, mis-shapen, and probably dirty stripling'.

Meeting the Sewards was bad enough for Johnson: meeting Darwin was worse. Here, installed in his home town, was a sage more wide-ranging and knowledgeable than himself and as little inclined to yield in argument. 'Mutual and strong dislike subsisted between them', Anna tells us. 'Johnson liked only *worshippers*', and neither Darwin nor the Sewards were in 'the herd that "paged his heels", and sunk, in servile silence, under the force of his dogmas'. Opposing him was hazardous, Anna says, no doubt from bitter experience. She refers to 'his stentor lungs; that combination of wit, humour and eloquence, which "could make the *worse* appear the *better* reason"; that sarcastic contempt of his antagonist, never suppressed or even softened by the due restraints of good-breeding'.[44] Darwin, with 'his impeded utterance', had 'no chance of being heard', and he shunned Johnson. So here was one new acquaintance who did not join the Lunar group.

## [6]

In 1767 Darwin developed a keen interest in geology, through helping Wedgwood in his experiments with pottery. In 1766 Wedgwood began planning his new factory near the Grand Trunk Canal, and it was Darwin who suggested the name 'Etruria', because Wedgwood had, he thought, rediscovered 'a species of non-vitreous encaustic painting' previously known only to the ancient Etruscans. Darwin also spurred Wedgwood on in experiments to improve his pottery: though Wedgwood began experimenting earlier, it was probably Darwin who instilled in him the habit of innovation. Wedgwood was continually seeking new materials, and minerals were sent to him by Darwin, Bentley, Brindley, Whitehurst and others, including Joseph Priestley, whom Wedgwood met in 1766 when Priestley was teaching at the Warrington Academy. Darwin's admiration for Wedgwood's art comes out in *The Economy of Vegetation*:

> Charm'd by your touch, the kneaded clay refines,
> The biscuit hardens, the enamel shines;
> Each nicer mould a softer feature drinks,
> The bold Cameo speaks, the soft Intaglio thinks.    [II 307–10]

Darwin's growing taste for geology emerges in a deceptive letter to Wedgwood dated 2 July 1767. The excavations for the Harecastle Tunnel on the Grand Trunk Canal had revealed many huge fossil bones. Darwin airily identifies some of them:

> The bone seems the third vertebra of the back of a camel. The horn is larger than any modern horn I have measured, and must have been that of a Patagonian ox I believe. . . . If at your leisure you will be at the trouble to tell me the strata they shall penetrate . . . I will in return send you some mineral observations of exactly the same value (weighed nicely).

The next paragraph is just as high-spirited but more factual:

> I have lately travel'd two days journey into the bowels of the
> earth, with three most able philosophers, and have seen the
> Goddess of Minerals naked, as she lay in her inmost bowers.[45]

Probably he had explored some of the Blue John caverns near
Castleton, possibly in company with Whitehurst and the Tis-
sington brothers of Derby. Darwin was still exuberant about his
exploration when he wrote to Boulton on 29 July: 'I have been
into the Bowels of old Mother Earth, and seen Wonders and
learnt much curious Knowledge in the Regions of darkness.'[46]

Though Darwin put on an air of frivolity, he was deeply
impressed by the fossil shells and bones found in the caves, and
the experience seems to have sparked off his evolutionary ideas,
for soon afterwards (by 1770, according to Anna Seward) he
adopted the motto *E conchis omnia*, or 'everything from shells',
to go with the family arms of three scallop shells. The motto
seems innocuous until you realize its implication—that all animals
have evolved from shelly sea-creatures. Darwin was so pleased
with the motto that he had it painted on his carriage. But he
reckoned without Dr Seward. Already alert to Darwin's irreligious tendencies, Seward called his bluff with some cutting verses.
Darwin, he says,

> renounces his Creator,
> And forms all sense from senseless matter.
> Great wizard he! by magic spells
> Can all things raise from cockle shells.[47]

Pierced by his own rapier of satirical verse, Darwin could only
cry *touché*; he could not openly insult the Church on his medical
rounds, so he had to paint out the motto. According to Anna,
he was never again friendly with her father.

Darwin's expeditions to the Derbyshire caves also inspired
the picture of the Polish salt mines in *The Loves of the Plants*,
which impressed Coleridge and filtered into 'Kubla Khan':

> So, cavern'd round in vast Polandish mines,
> With crystal walls a gorgeous city shines;
> Scoop'd in the briny rock long streets extend
> Their hoary course, and glittering domes ascend.
> Down the bright steeps, emerging into day,
> Impetuous fountains burst their headlong way,
> O'er milk-white vales in ivory channels spread,
> And wondering seek their subterranean bed.    [1st ed., IV 309–16]

[7]

In 1768 the Lunar group acquired its youngest, wealthiest, most eccentric, most literary and least scientific member, Thomas Day (Plate 5D). Day's family estate, at Barehill in Berkshire, was near Edgeworth's house at Hare Hatch, and Edgeworth met Day after returning from Lichfield in 1766. They became friendly at once, and in 1768 were travelling together through Staffordshire, with Edgeworth posing as Day's servant and Day pretending to be an odd and boorish gentleman. (The pretence was scarcely needed, as Day was notorious for his bad manners and unkempt appearance.) They stopped at an inn at Eccleshall, where Edgeworth played the buffoon—he ordered the entire larder of the inn for dinner, and gave a soapbox oration on the oddities of his 'master'. These antics ended when a traveller, just arrived at the inn, asked him what he was playing at. It was Erasmus Darwin, and John Whitehurst was with him. Edgeworth had a long mechanical talk with them, which left Day speechless. But after an hour or two they turned to other subjects, 'on which Mr Day displayed so much knowledge, feeling, and eloquence, as to captivate the Doctor entirely. He invited Mr Day to Lichfield.'[48] Although so different from Darwin, and much younger, Day was to become a good friend of his in the 1770s.

Day always seems the odd man out in the Lunar circle, because he was unscientific. But he fitted in with curious ease, becoming friendly with Keir, Boulton and Wedgwood, and above all of course with Dr Small. The others probably admired him because he was such an 'original', whereas they had to conform, being business or professional men; and also because of his flowing eloquence—Edgeworth said he never knew anyone 'who in conversation reasoned so profoundly and so logically, or who stated his arguments with so much eloquence'.[49]

The fourth member of the quartet in the inn at Eccleshall, John Whitehurst (Plate 6B) was a simple, unassuming man, tall and thin, of little formal education but great natural talent. Early in his career he showed much ingenuity in designing and making clocks: he invented the time-clock on which workmen 'clock-in', and Boulton made this and many other clocks to his design. In the late 1760s Whitehurst was beginning to turn more towards geology, partly in response to Wedgwood's demands for new

minerals to try out in his pottery. By 1768 Whitehurst was well
acquainted with Boulton, Small, Darwin and Wedgwood, and
his meeting with Edgeworth and Day was, as it were, his final
step into Lunar orbit.

So by the summer of 1768 the early Lunar circle was fully
formed: Small sat at the centre, with Boulton, Darwin, Wedgwood, Watt, Keir, Edgeworth, Whitehurst and Day revolving
in interlinked orbits at various distances about him. The most
distant orbit was Watt's, for he was still in Scotland: but he kept
in touch through Small's frequent letters. Others on the fringe of
the Lunar group include Michell, who in 1767 became rector of
Thornhill in Yorkshire, a hundred miles away, and three men
pre-eminent in their professions: John Wilkinson, the ironfounder, who lived rather far away in Broseley and was not a
clubbable man; Joseph Priestley, the chemist, who was living at
Leeds (married to Wilkinson's sister); and John Baskerville,
the Birmingham printer, who was a close friend of Boulton. And
over all brooded the spirit of Franklin, their founding father, who
had been a friend of Boulton and Darwin for ten years and had
sent Small to join them.

In the late 1760s the meetings of the Lunar group were usually
in threes or fours. The semi-formal meetings at the time of the
full moon had not yet begun.

[8]

Nearly all the recruits to the Lunar circle had arrived via Darwin.
He had an insatiable talent for friendship, even though he spent
so much time on his medical rounds that his friends often found
him away if they called at his house without warning. His
friendliness is admirable; but does it imply a disenchantment
with his home life? Did he accept too many long-distance calls
to fulfil a subconscious wish to escape? Did he cultivate other
friends so assiduously because he found it dull at home and in the
Seward circle? To these questions the answer has to be that there
is no sign of domestic boredom or friction. Edgeworth found
Mrs Darwin most charming and contented; and Anna Seward,
who knew Erasmus and Mary throughout their married life,
insists that they were very happy—though Anna is ever ready to
criticize Erasmus for other faults, real or imagined. Mary's

illnesses were becoming more frequent in 1768, but there were good times too, and on 31 July 1768 Darwin wrote to Boulton: 'Mrs Darwin continues to get better.'[50]

Darwin's appetite for friendship went beyond the Lunar and Lichfield circles: in 1768 he tried to renew the links with his student friend Albert Reimarus. A visitor to Lichfield, a Mr Ferber, told Darwin that Dr Reimarus was in practice in Hamburg, so Darwin wrote a hasty letter: 'I received very great pleasure in hearing . . . that my old friend Dr Reimarus is alive and succeeds in the World.' After mentioning that Keir has left the Army 'to study Chemistry and Philosophy more at Leizure', Darwin goes on:

> For my own part I practise Medecine in Lichfield, Staffordshire, where I shall hope to hear from you. I have a good House, a pleasant Situation, a sensible Wife, and three healthful Children, and as much medical Business as I can do with Ease, and rather more. Mechanics, and Chemistry are my Hobby-horses. . . .[51]

Darwin offers an exchange of medical observations and of children—with Reimarus sending a child to Lichfield to learn English, 'and I will send you a Son in exchange . . . if such a Trafic be agreable to you'. There is no record of any reply from Reimarus, who was at this time occupied in persuading his countrymen to install lightning conductors.

In the summer of 1768 Darwin suffered a serious accident at Rugeley. He was thrown from his carriage and broke the patella of his right knee, 'an accident of irretrievable injury in the human frame', as Anna Seward put it—from bitter experience, since she suffered a similar injury in the same year. Afterwards Darwin always walked with a slight limp.

According to the Revd. R. G. Robinson, Chancellor's Vicar of Lichfield Cathedral, the accident occurred when Darwin was using a two-wheeled carriage: 'It was in the form of a garden chair, fix'd upon the axle-tree; the footboard terminated in an elastic pole, which . . . went through a ring fix'd on the saddle.'[52] Two days before the accident, Robinson dined with Sir John Every at Egginton, near Burton. The next day,

> the Doctor call'd there to see Lady Every, who was under his care in the inoculated smallpox. He took me with him to Burton in this carriage, and the horse took fright on the road at a barrow of gravel, thrown down by a labourer, employed in making the canal, called the grand trunk; and ran one of the wheels on the top of a hedge, a

yard or two. The carriage received a violent shock, which I really believe injured the axle-tree; for it broke the next day in one of the streets of Rugeley when the knee pan of the doctor was broken. He never used the carriage afterwards.[53]

So it seems that Darwin suffered this accident through using a light open two-wheeled carriage instead of his improved four-wheeled design, perhaps because the weather was set fair, or perhaps because his other carriage was under repair.

If Darwin travelled 10,000 miles a year on his medical rounds, it is not surprising that he eventually suffered this accident. It was an era when men often made their wills before going on a long journey, and the wonder is that he remained so long unscathed.

In May 1768 Josiah Wedgwood suffered an even more 'irretrievable injury in the human frame': his right leg had to be amputated above the knee. Although Darwin was not concerned in the operation, he had regretfully agreed to it, and afterwards, on 14 June 1768, we find him writing to Wedgwood to say he was sorry he could not visit his friend more often. The operation did nothing to amputate Wedgwood's immense energy: now, when he went round the factory inspecting the pottery, he would use his wooden leg to smash any pieces he thought were substandard. Wedgwood was particularly busy in 1768 because his new factory at Etruria was being built, and he was planning further ventures, including the mating of metal with clay, in collaboration with Boulton. 'This . . . is a field, to the farther end of which we shall never be able to travel',[54] he told Bentley on 15 March 1768.

Another project for Wedgwood was keeping Darwin busy. Wedgwood needed a source of power to operate a flint mill for grinding colours. Darwin proposed a horizontal windmill, with the axis vertical and the sail rotating in a horizontal plane. 'I think it is peculiarly adapted to your kind of Business, where the motion is slow and horizontal,' he told Wedgwood early in 1768. Though slightly worried that the mixture might set solid if the wind dropped for a few hours, Darwin was still confident:

I will make you the model if you require it immediately, which I can do for the expense of 3 or 4 guineas, so as to evince its Effects. The advantages are, 1. Its Power may be extended much farther than the common Wind-mill. 2. It has fewer moving Parts. 3. In your Business no Tooth and Pinion-work will be necessary. Plain

Countries are preferable to hilly ones for windmils, because the
wind acquires eddies in the latter.[55]

Darwin duly made the model, which was about three feet in
diameter, and Wedgwood came to Lichfield and inspected it on
10 March 1768. He wrote to Bentley: 'I think [the Windmill]
a very ingenious invention and have some hopes that it will
answer our expectations.'[56] Darwin estimated that the full-sized
windmill would need '68,000 bricks, 4800 ft of inch deal boards
and a shaft 30 ft long and a foot in diameter'.[57]

Finding the time and money to make a full-sized version was
a problem, and on 4 February 1769 Darwin wrote to Dr Templeman at the Society of Arts, explaining the virtues of his windmill
and enquiring whether the Society might help with a premium:

> I have lately constructed the model of an horizontal Windmill,
> which appears to have a third more Power than any vertical Wind-
> mill, whose Sail is of the same diameter, and is in other respects
> more manageable and less liable to Repair, as it has less wheel-
> work, having only an upright Shaft on the Top of which the Sail is
> fix'd, and will move three pairs of Stones.

Unless there was a chance of financial help, he says, 'I should
not chuse the Expense of sending it up'. He asks Dr Templeman's opinion, 'and must beg of you, *and in this Confidence I
write to you*, not to mention my Name, as I do not court this kind
of Reputation, as I believe it might injure me.'[58] In a postscript
to his letter Darwin says: 'The mill consists much of Brick-Work
and could not be executed in its greatest size for less than 300 £.'
The Society of Arts was unable to give Darwin financial help,
because its method was to offer a premium for particular subjects, and windmills were not among them, though the Society
did offer a prize for a horizontal windmill seventeen years later
(when Darwin's mill was already in operation).

In 1769 Darwin's windmill was not developed beyond the
model Wedgwood saw and admired. Wedgwood was keen to
have it at once, but on 15 March Darwin advised him to wait:

> I should long ago have wrote to you, but waited to learn in what
> forwardness Mr Watt's Fire-Engine was in. He has taken a
> Partner [Dr Roebuck], and I can make no conjecture how soon you
> may be accommodated by Him with a Power so much more
> convenient than that of Wind. I will make packing Boxes and send
> you my model, that you may consult the Ingenious. I am of opinion

it will be a powerful and a convenient Windmill, but would recommend steam to you if you can wait awhile.[59]

Darwin did not in fact send the model; but progress on Watt's engine was very slow, and ten years later the windmill was resuscitated, built and successfully used at Etruria.

Darwin's letter to the Society of Arts shows he was heavily shackled as an inventor: *I do not court this kind of Reputation, as I believe it might injure me.* Here, I think, is the key to Darwin's bashfulness as an inventor. He believed his medical career would be damaged if his patients got to know that he dabbled in designing carriages and windmills. So we find Darwin initiating many practicable inventions but letting others take the credit for perfecting them, as happened with Edgeworth and the carriages. It was not because Darwin couldn't be bothered to bring the design to fruition, but because he feared damaging his career. His timidity was basically reasonable, but perhaps rather overdone: fearing to publicize the diversity of his talents was Darwin's nearest approach to a neurosis.

In retrospect Darwin's medical career seems to have been a triumphant success, and quite undamaged by his diversity. But at the time when he wrote to the Society of Arts about the windmill he did have some cause for concern, because the injuries he suffered in his carriage accident in 1768 had prevented him from travelling to patients for several weeks. There was a 10 per cent drop in his income in 1768, when his earnings were £775; the deficit was more than made good by 1770, however, when his income was £956.

In 1769 Darwin's medical advice was needed again by Wedgwood, who began to see spots before the eyes. Several doctors he consulted took a serious view (to match their serious fees), and Wedgwood thought he was going blind. But Darwin said everybody at some time in life had such 'appearances before their eyes, but everybody did not *look at them*'.[60] Whitehurst suffered similarly, and Darwin told him he would soon be well again, which he was. Darwin said the same to Wedgwood, and again proved to be right.

[9]

Another and a darker cloud was gathering during 1769. 'Mrs Darwin has been long ill,' Small wrote on 7 February, and this short stark sentence says it all: Mary's health was steadily deteriorating; her spasms seized her more often and she did not recover so readily. Darwin's medications were ineffectual, and Mary died on 30 June 1770. Anna Seward, who often sat with her in the last weeks of her life, offers us a stilted account of what Mary told her:

> In the short term of my life, a great deal of happiness has been comprised. The maladies of my frame were peculiar; the pains in my head and stomach, which no medicine could eradicate, were spasmodic and violent; and required stronger measures to render them supportable while they lasted, than my constitution could sustain without injury. . . . Pain taught me the value of ease, and I enjoyed it with a glow of spirit, seldom, perhaps, felt by the habitually healthy. While Dr Darwin combated and assuaged my disease from time to time, his indulgence to all my wishes, his active desire to see me amused and happy, proved incessant. . . .
>
> Married to any other man, I do not suppose I could have lived a third part of those years which I have passed with Dr Darwin; he has prolonged my days, and he has blessed them.[61]

Mary was thirty when she died, and she left her husband with three sons to bring up, Charles, Erasmus and Robert, then aged eleven, ten and four respectively. 'My three boys have ever been docile, and affectionate', Anna reports her as saying, 'children as they are, I could trust them with important secrets, so sacred do they hold every promise they make. They scorn deceit, and falsehood of every kind, and have less selfishness than generally belongs to childhood.'[62]

Anna's report can be confirmed. Ten years later Erasmus, sadly recording the life of his son Charles in a formal style rather foreign to him, wrote:

> His ingenious mother, even to her latest hour! instilled into his breast a sympathy with the pains and with the pleasures of others, by sympathizing herself with their distress or exultation: she flattered him into a sense of honour by commending his integrity, and scorn of falsehood, before her friends . . . and as she had wisely sown no seeds of superstition in his mind, there was nothing to overshade the virtues, she had implanted.[63]

Darwin's only recorded comment on Mary's death was made twenty-one years later, when he replied with medical detachment to a query from his son Robert, who was concerned about the possibility of hereditary illness:

In respect to your mother, the following is the true history, which I shall neither aggravate nor diminish anything. Her mind was truly amiable and her person handsome, which you may perhaps in some measure remember.

She was seized with pain on the left side about the lower edge of the liver, this pain was followed in about an hour by violent convulsions, and these sometimes relieved by great doses of opium, and some wine, which induced intoxication. At other times a temporary dilirium, or what by some might be termed insanity, came on for half an hour, and then she became herself again, and the paroxysm was terminated. This disease is called hysteria by some people. I think it allied to epilepsy.

This kind of disease had several returns in the course of 4 or 6 years and she then took to drinking spirit and water to relieve the pain, and I found (when it was too late) that she had done this in great quantity, the liver became swelled, and she gradually sunk; a few days before her death, she bled at the mouth, and whenever she had a scratch, as some hepatic patients do.

All the drunken diseases are hereditary in some degree, and I believe epilepsy and insanity are produced originally by drinking. I have seen epilepsy produced so very often—one sober generation cures these dr[unkards] frequently, which one drunken one has created.

I now know many families, who had insanity in one side, and the children now old people have no symptom of it. *If it was otherwise, there would not be a family in the kingdom without epileptic gouty or insane people in it.*

I well remember when your mother fainted away in these hysteric fits (which she often did) that she told me, you, who was not then 2 or 2½ years old, run into the kitchen to call the maidservant to her assistance.

I have told everything just as I recollect it, as I think it a matter of no consequence to yourself or your brother, who both live temperate lives, keeping betwixt all extreams.[64]

The manner of Mary's death reinforced Erasmus's antipathy to alcohol, and led him towards the rather extreme views expressed in this letter. In reassuring Robert about the inheritance of drunkenness and insanity, Erasmus was both correct and humane; Robert accepted the reassurance, married and had six children. But Robert's concern about hereditary illness was also valid, for the Darwins have suffered from a hereditary debility which affected Erasmus junior, three of Robert's children and four of Charles's children.[65]

FIVE

# A Change of Life
## 1770-1775

Darwin was left a widower at the age of thirty-eight, and in the months following Mary's death he had to rearrange the threads of his life. He did so resiliently, but sadly too: there are none of his usual exuberant letters in 1770. Fortunately his elder sister Susannah was willing to keep house for him again and look after his three boys, particularly the four-year-old Robert, who became very fond of his aunt and always spoke of her in later years 'as the very pattern of an old lady, so nice looking, so gentle, kind and charitable, and passionately fond of flowers'.[1]

The loss of Mary threw Darwin more into the company of his friends in the Lunar circle: Darwin met his Lunar companions in the 1760s, was closest to them in the 1770s, and saw less of them later because of his move to Derby. During the 1770s Darwin also left his own fireside more often for the company of the Seward circle at Lichfield.

But in retrospect the most important effect of Mary's death was to turn Darwin into an author. So far he had written nothing more solid than his two Royal Society papers. With more time to spare, he now began work on a medical book, which during the next twenty years grew into his two-volume treatise on animal life, *Zoonomia*.

During the summer of 1770 Darwin had his portrait painted by Joseph Wright of Derby, who may already have been a patient, and certainly became so later. Anna Seward says the portrait is an excellent likeness. There are two versions, one in the National Portrait Gallery and the other (and better) at Darwin College, Cambridge (Plate 3A).

A new arrival at Lichfield in 1770 electrified the Seward circle and helped to divert Darwin. The newcomer was Thomas Day, who had started a curious human experiment. In the previous year he reached the age of twenty-one and decided he ought to marry. But who would suit him? He detested fashionable ladies, and wanted a wife 'simple as a mountain girl, in her dress, her diet and her manners; fearless and intrepid'. As Anna Seward admitted, 'there was no finding such a creature ready made'. Day was a keen disciple of Rousseau, and his faith in education was unbounded; so he decided to mould a girl to his own design. Armed with impressive testimonials of moral probity, and with a lawyer friend, John Bicknell, to vouch for him, he visited two orphanages: from each he was allowed to select a twelve-year-old girl to educate. He promised to apprentice one within a year and support her, and to groom the other as his wife; and if she didn't suit him, he promised to maintain her until she married. Day called the girls Sabrina and Lucretia, and took them to France to mould. But instead they moulded him, or at least led him a merry dance. Lucretia, the more fractious of the two, he apprenticed to a milliner; Sabrina he persevered with.

In his task of unique difficulty, who better than Darwin to help him? So Day came to Lichfield and rented Stowe House, only ten minutes' walk from Darwin. Sabrina favourably impressed nearly everyone she met, but she disappointed Day because she was averse to books and science, and was not stoical enough: she could not bear to have melted sealing wax dropped on her arms; and when he fired a pistol at her petticoats, she screamed, because she had neither the intelligence to realize he was using blank cartridges nor the courage that might redeem her stupidity. Darwin probably restrained him from even more outrageous experiments. Sabrina herself enjoyed being the focus of attention and gossip in the Seward circle and a privileged visitor at the palace.

Day gave up his experiment after a year and sent Sabrina to a boarding school. Later in the 1770s she came back several times to Lichfield, where she was always welcomed as a local celebrity. She was 'often the guest of Dr Darwin, and other of her friends in Lichfield', Anna tells us. Eventually Sabrina was married, happily, to John Bicknell, who had helped Day to select her from the orphanage.

In December 1770 Edgeworth arrived in Lichfield: he bubbled over with scientific ideas; he enjoyed Lichfield society; and he was captivated by Anna's beautiful companion Honora Sneyd, who had been living with the Sewards for ten years since the death of her mother, and was now nineteen. Edgeworth was so impressed that after a Lunar meeting at Darwin's house, he insisted that his friends should come to see her at the palace. Small, Keir, Darwin and others, we are told, duly trooped along and (except for Day) were unanimous in their approval of her beauty and her conversation. Edgeworth seemed unlikely to carry off Honora, since he was already married and she had another admirer, John André (whose ardent letters, as quoted by Anna, run to fourteen pages).[2] So Edgeworth sadly went home to Hare Hatch early in 1771.

But he quickly returned to Lichfield with his wife and three children, having taken over the lease of Stowe House, though Day remained as a guest. Now that Sabrina had gone, Day had himself fallen in love with Honora. Edgeworth offered to press Day's suit for him, but (as Edgeworth probably hoped) his own presence convinced Honora that she liked him better than Day. Edgeworth duly presented her with Day's proposal for marriage, which seems to have run to several thousand words; and she rejected him, not wishing to retire from the world as he required. Day became 'really ill for some days' at this rebuff and received treatment from Darwin, who first bled him (as was mandatory) and then 'administered, wisely, to that part of him which was most diseased—his mind'. After this talking-to from Darwin, Day soon recovered.

Everyone—even the sedate churchmen of the close—became infected by Edgeworth's exuberance, and during the summer of 1771 there was dancing, vaulting, leaping and archery; and in the evenings the terrace of the close rang with laughter, Anna says, 'Mr Edgeworth enlivening us by a wit, extensive as the light of the sun and active as its heat, Dr Darwin laughing with us, while we have felt the fine edge of elegant, ingenious, and what is most rare, good-humor'd irony . . . Mr Day *improving* our minds, while he delights our imaginations.'[3]

So ended the first act of the tragic-romantic comedy of the Two Gentlemen of Lichfield. Act 2 starts with the entry of Mr Sneyd, alarmed that two such lively gentlemen of leisure had designs on his daughter. He came to live at Lichfield, bringing with him four more daughters, one of whom, Elizabeth, was very like Honora. Day promptly fell in love with Elizabeth, while Edgeworth remained faithful to Honora. But Day's hopes were quickly dashed: Elizabeth rejected him, telling him he was lacking in social graces. Edgeworth and Day were now both rather desperate. Edgeworth decided to go to France, and Day went with him, to acquire those social graces. They left towards the end of 1771, taking with them Edgeworth's son Richard, a wild boy who had been educated à la Rousseau. They visited Rousseau, who approved of Richard; but they go out of Darwin's sphere until the next act of their drama.

[2]

Darwin was now seeing more of Josiah Wedgwood, whose wife was in poor health and under Darwin's care. The horizontal windmill was still a live issue: on 9 December 1770 Darwin told Wedgwood that 'Mr Watt's Fire-Engine I believe goes on, but I don't know at what rate'.[4] Darwin's scepticism about its progress was fully justified, but he still remained diffident about his own invention: in October 1771 he wrote, 'Your Windmill sleeps at my house, but shall be sent to you, if you wish it, but I should advise you to wait the Wheel Fire-Engine, which goes on slowly'.[5] Put off by the inventor's modesty, Wedgwood allowed the windmill to remain asleep for a further six years before waking it again.

On New Year's Day 1771, Darwin, Wedgwood and Boulton were due to dine with Mr Anson, the local M.P. and grandee. They apparently did not do so, but Darwin was very keen on a meeting and told Boulton: 'I shall be glad to see you Birmingham-Philosophers-and-Navigators, tho' Mr Anson is gone. You will please to acquaint me if you can and will come'.[6] The original meeting was to discuss a huge ornamental tripod: but Darwin's unusual eagerness, and his reference to 'Navigators', suggest that he was trying to interest Anson and Boulton in his latest engineering project—a plan for a narrow-gauge canal to connect Lichfield with the Grand Trunk Canal. Darwin was very keen on this canal, and his plan was extensively discussed with Wedgwood and Brindley; but no detailed account has survived, and no canal was dug.

During 1771 Darwin was working on what is perhaps the most impressive of his mechanical inventions, a speaking-machine. He first had to develop a theory of phonetics. As he explained thirty years later, in a long note to *The Temple of Nature*, he divided the sounds of speech into four classes: (1) clear continued sounds, vowels; (2) hissing sounds, sibilants; (3) semi-vocals, a mixture of (1) and (2); and (4) interrupted sounds, or consonants. He analyses the vibrations of the air which give rise to each. The vowels, for example,

> are produced by the streams of air passing from the lungs in respiration through the larynx; which is furnished with many small muscles, which by their action give a proper tension to the extremity of this tube; and the sounds, I suppose, are produced by the opening and closing of its aperture; something like the trumpet stop of an organ, as may be observed by blowing through the wind-pipe of a dead goose. . . .
>
> The hissing sounds are produced by air forcibly pushed through certain passages of the mouth without being previously rendered sonorous by the larynx; and obtain their sibilancy from their slower vibrations, occasioned by the mucous membrane, which lines those apertures or passages, being less tense than that of the larynx . . .

and so on, with much detail. He then proceeds to describe the exact formation of each sound:

> P. If the lips be pressed close together and some air be condensed in the mouth behind them, on opening the lips the mute consonant P begins a syllable. . . .

And similarly for every other sound. He found most difficulty, he says, with the vowels, especially in deciding where exactly in the mouth they were modulated.

With this theory to guide him, he embarked on the construction of his speaking-machine, which he describes as follows:

> I contrived a wooden mouth with lips of soft leather, and with a valve over the back part of it for nostrils, both which could be quickly opened or closed by the pressure of the fingers; the vocality was given by a silk ribbon about an inch long and a quarter of an inch wide stretched between two bits of smooth wood a little hollowed; so that when a gentle current of air from bellows was blown on the edge of the ribbon, it gave an agreeable tone, as it vibrated between the wooden sides, much like a human voice. This head pronounced the *p*, *b*, *m*, and the vowel *a*, with so great nicety as to deceive all who heard it unseen, when it pronounced the words *mama, papa, map,* and *pam*; and had a most plaintive tone, when

the lips were gradually closed. My other occupations prevented me from proceeding in the further construction of this machine; which might have required but thirteen movements, as shown in the above analysis, unless some variety of musical note was to be added to the vocality produced in the larynx; all of which movements might communicate with the keys of a harpsichord or forte piano, and perform the song as well as the accompaniment; or which if built in a gigantic form, might speak so loud as to command an army or instruct a crowd.[7]

Darwin's speaking-machine created a sensation whenever it was operated, and his Lunar friends were greatly impressed: after this *tour de force* Darwin's reputation as an inventor was secure. Unfortunately neither the speaking-machine nor any drawing of it has survived. The only remaining relic is a document dated 3 September 1771, witnessed by Keir and Small, in which Boulton promises to pay Darwin £1000 for a machine 'capable of pronouncing the Lord's Prayer, the Creed and Ten Commandments in the Vulgar Tongue'.[8] This contract was probably half a joke, not only because Boulton's finances were precarious, but also because the anti-Christian Darwin would not have wished to create a robot priest whose novelty might have filled empty pews.

A speaking-machine of more conventional design was installed in Darwin's house—a speaking-tube connecting his study with the kitchen. One day a local yokel who had brought a message, being left alone in the kitchen, was terrified to hear a sepulchral and authoritative voice from nowhere demand, 'I want some coals.' The man thought such a request could only come from the Devil, wishing to stoke up hell's fires: so he fled and would not come near the house again.

In the spring of 1771 Benjamin Franklin visited Darwin at Lichfield and probably heard the speaking-machine for himself. He also met Day, no doubt a novel experience even for him. Franklin must have written many letters to Darwin, but unfortunately none of them has survived.

Mary's father, Charles Howard, died in May 1771, aged sixty-four. To judge from his will, he and Darwin were not on very good terms. Howard left in trust for his grandchildren, Erasmus's sons, £1000 'and money owing me from Dr Darwin to be added to same'. As a further insult, he pointedly left Darwin ten guineas and his servant Mary Thompson ten pounds.

Twenty years afterwards Erasmus told Robert his opinion of Mr Howard:

> The late Mr Howard was never to my knowledge in the least insane, he was a drunkard both in public and private—and when he went to London he became connected with a woman and lived a deba[u]ched life in respect to drink, hence he had always the Gout of which he died but without any the least symptom of either insanity or epilepsy, but from debility of digestion and Gout as other drunkards die.[9]

This scathing denunciation of his grandfather was scarcely the best way to convince Robert of the soundness of his heredity, but it shows why Erasmus disliked his father-in-law.

Though Darwin himself had 'forsworn Bacchus', his 'affection for Venus' had grown with the years. An ascetic bachelor life was not for him, and in 1771 he was taking pleasure in the company of a lady named Miss Parker, of whom little is known except that, after her association with Darwin, she married a Mr Day. (No, it was not Thomas Day: Miss Parker played no part in the comedy of the Two Gentlemen of Lichfield.) However, she certainly played a part in the life of the Eminent Physician of Lichfield, and she bore him two daughters, Susan, born in 1772 and presumably named after his sister, and Mary, born two years later. In the easygoing way of the eighteenth century, Susan and Mary spent their childhood in Darwin's house, treated just the same as his children born in wedlock.

[3]

Apart from the successful birth of Susan, 1772 was rather an unhealthy year, and Darwin was often called on to make the thirty-mile journey to Etruria, to treat Wedgwood's wife Sally, who was dangerously ill several times. Wedgwood's letters to Bentley speak for themselves:

> When do I bring Mrs Wedgwood?—God knows. We had Dr Derwin with her yesterday. He says he is afraid her disorder will be stubborn . . . she is as complete a Cripple as you can easily imagine [30 March]. Mrs W is not yet able to dress herself [12 May].

She recovered in the summer, but not for long:

Mrs Wedgwood has had an extreme bad night, and miscarried this morning. Her situation is attended with much danger [7 September]. My Dear Sally . . . does not seem to have a drop of blood in her body . . . Doctor Derwin has left me to act as Physician in his absense [10 September].[10]

Wedgwood was worn down by the worry. On 12 October he told Bentley: 'Shewing Dr Darwin by one of my Wastcoats how much I was sunk in 9 or 10 months, he said it was wrong, and I must be very carefull of my health.'[11] On 15 October Darwin wrote, 'I would advise you to live as high as your constitution will admit of.'[12]

But soon it was Sally again: 'My poor Girl is in a very dangerous situation . . . I have sent for Dr Derwin' (2 November). 'Dr Darwin has been here and invited her to come and stay with him a few weeks, and we are to go on Sunday' (5 November). 'I brought her to [Lichfield] yesterday and we were lucky enough to find the good Doctor at home. . . . I shall return home tomorrow and leave Mrs W with her Doctor for a week or ten days' (9 November). But Darwin had other calls to honour, and Wedgwood was not always lucky: 'He is gone to Wolverhampton . . . so I must go back solo as I came, which mortifies me not a little' (1 December).

At Christmas Sally was seized with 'a sudden sickness and giddiness . . . we thought every moment would be her last.' So Darwin spent much of Christmas Day travelling to Etruria: 'I sent for her favorite Esculapius, who came here last night and he is just now left us. He says if we can preserve her thro' the cold weather to april, she will do very well, and make a perfect recovery in the summer' (26 December).[13] Fortunately Darwin's favourable diagnosis proved right: Sally lived for another forty-two years, longer than either her husband or her doctor.

So much medical detail is tedious, but it brings out, as nothing else can, the grind of Darwin's day-to-day medical career, which dominated his life for thirty years or more. The quotations apply to just one patient, Sally Wedgwood, in one year, 1772, and you must also imagine all the mud and discomfort *en route*, to savour the realities of Darwin's life.

Another important patient of 1772, whom Darwin could not save, was James Brindley—Brindley the Great, as Wedgwood often called him. His strong constitution had seen Brindley through many years of canal surveying and construction in all weathers, but in 1772 he became ill and Darwin diagnosed diabetes. The disease was advanced, and marked by an occasional discharge of blood, as Darwin recorded twenty years later in *Zoonomia*.[14] There was no cure, and Wedgwood's letters chronicle another sad story:

> Poor Mr Brindley has nearly finish'd his course in this world. . . . His disorder . . . is a Diabetes . . . though I believe no one of his Doctors found it out till Dr Derwin discover'd it in the present illness, which I fear will deprive us of a valuable friend, and the world of one of those great Genius's who seldom live to see justice done to their singular abilities, but must trust to future ages for that tribute of praise and fair fame they so greatly merit from their fellow Mortals.[15]

Brindley died the next day, 27 September 1772.

Wedgwood wrote to tell Darwin, who replied on 30 September expressing

> most sincere grief about Mr Brindley, whom I have always esteemed to be a great genius, and whose loss is truly a public one. I don't believe he has left his equal. I think the various Navigations should erect him a monument in Westminster Abbey, and hope you will at the proper time give them this hint.
> . . . And any circumstances that you recollect of his life should be wrote down, and I will some time digest them into an Eulogium. These men should not die; this Nature denies, but their Memories are above her Malice.[16]

Darwin's promise of 'an Eulogium' was handsomely fulfilled in *The Economy of Vegetation*, where he praises many scientists and inventors of the day—Franklin, Herschel, Priestley, Wedgwood and others—but reserves the longest tribute for Brindley:

> So with strong arm immortal BRINDLEY leads
> His long canals, and parts the velvet meads;
> Winding in lucid lines, the watery mass
> Mines the firm rock, or loads the deep morass,
> With rising locks a thousand hills alarms,
> Flings o'er a thousand streams its silver arms,
> Feeds the long vale, the nodding woodland laves,
> And Plenty, Arts, and Commerce freight the waves.    [III 329–36]

Darwin suggests a monument which shows Brindley 'balancing the lands', a nice phrase summing up Brindley's chief headache—

choosing routes and levels so as to equalize the volumes of earth
extracted from cuttings with those needed for embankments.

It would be wrong to think that for Darwin the year 1772 was
dominated by illness and death. These were the commonplaces of
his medical life, and 1772 was no worse than other years; it just
happens to be better documented.

[4]

Darwin developed a major new interest in 1772—chemistry,
which he began to study intensively, taking his cue from Keir.
For several years Keir had been working on a translation from
the French of Macquer's *Dictionary of Chemistry*, and his translation was published in 1771. The *Dictionary* was one of the most
important encyclopedic works of the century, and Keir's excellent
translation, with notes on recent discoveries, did much to
stimulate chemical studies in Britain. It certainly influenced
Watt and also Darwin, who began studying chemistry in
earnest: 'I rejoice exceedingly that you study chemistry so
eagerly',[17] Keir wrote, and he proceeded to list fourteen books
that Darwin should read. Keir himself found scope for his
chemical talents when he became partner and manager in a glass
manufactory at Stourbridge at the end of 1772. Further spurs to
Darwin's interest in chemistry may have come from the
enthusiasm of his son Charles, and from Wedgwood, who wanted
to obtain a better understanding of the minerals he used in his
wares, and was beginning his experiments with jasper, perhaps
his finest material.[18]

Darwin's new interest in chemistry shows his flair for embark-
ing on a subject just as it was 'taking off': 1772 was a great year
for chemistry. Lavoisier made his first experiments on combustion; and Priestley (Plate 6c) published the results of his
experiments on gases, which at a stroke more than doubled
previous knowledge, reawakened the spirit of experimental
science in Britain, and revivified the Royal Society. Darwin had
probably not yet met Priestley, who was living at Leeds, but they
knew each other by repute through their common friends
Franklin and Michell. Franklin communicated Priestley's papers
to the Royal Society, and in 1772 he sent Darwin a copy of
Priestley's pamphlet on aerated water. Though Priestley did not

join the Lunar circle until he moved to Birmingham eight years later, he was hovering on the fringe from now onwards.

Franklin visited Birmingham again in the summer of 1772, and afterwards (on 18 July) Darwin wrote him a long letter:

> I was unfortunate in not being able to go to Birmingham till a day after you left it. The apparatus you constructed with the Bladder and Tunnel I took into my Pond the next day, whilst I was bathing, and fill'd the Bladder well with unmix'd air, that rose from the muddy Bottom, and tying it up, brought it Home.[19]

But Darwin could not ignite the gas, so the experiment failed. Darwin then switches from chemistry to phonetics: 'I shall be glad at your Leizure of any Observations on the Alphabet, and particularly on the number and Formation of Vowels, as these are more intricate than the other Letters.'[20] Darwin then goes into great detail over the pronunciation of the letter W and each of the vowels, so presumably he was still improving his speaking-machine.

He was also still riding his hobby-horse of carriage design, and on 31 December 1772 Wedgwood commented on a new carriage made by Mr Butler, a Lichfield coachmaker, at Darwin's suggestion. The carriage had

> *Patent spring wheels*, every spoke being a spring, by which means the *Vis inertia* of all sudden obstructions it meets with upon the road are overcome without any Jolt to the rider, or what is more with perfect ease to the poor Horses. Another advantage these carriages have over the common ones is their *stillness*, and as every spoke in the wheel is in the form of *the line of beauty*, I am told they have a most elegant appearance.[21]

Darwin had first proposed the idea in a letter to Reimarus sixteen years before, and the delay can probably be attributed to the difficulty and expense of making such spokes.

Darwin's design is described in detail in British Patent No. 1026 (A.D. 1772), authorized on 17 February 1773, though the patentee is, needless to say, the coachmaker James Butler rather than Darwin himself. According to the patent, 'the springs which serve instead of spokes are made of steel' and are in the form of a gently curved S. The spokes are made 'with square feet' which 'are strongly screwed into the nave'. The feet of the other ends are made lengthways and with two holes to receive the ends of the bolts that come through the iron hoop confining

the rim. Such S-shaped spring-spokes are continually being re-
invented even today: British Patent 1292928, filed in 1973, is
remarkably similar to Butler's patent of 1773. The main dis-
advantage of spring-spokes seems to be that the rim inevitably
becomes non-circular, which does not make for a comfortable
ride.

[5]

The next act in the tragi-comedy of Edgeworth and Day is now
upon us. In the early months of 1772, when they were in
France, Day tortured himself for up to eight hours a day with
exercises and dancing lessons, so that he might qualify for
Elizabeth Sneyd's approval. Edgeworth, never idle for long, was
trying to divert the course of the River Rhone so that the city of
Lyons could be enlarged. His wife came to join him, but she
returned to England in the autumn with Day, while Edgeworth
continued his Herculean engineering task, supervising armies of
workmen laden with baskets of rubble.

Day's return to Lichfield, apparently late in 1772, was far
from triumphant: Elizabeth decided she liked him better as a
boor than as a fop, so he was rejected again, and went off to
wander unhappily in Europe.

Edgeworth returned to England in March 1773, as his wife
was expecting a baby. But the baby was born prematurely; com-
plications set in, and Mrs Edgeworth died before her husband
arrived. She left him with four children: a son Richard, eight,
bold and unruly as a result of that education à la Rousseau; a
studious daughter Maria, six; Emmeline, four; and the baby
Anna, who was later to marry Thomas Beddoes.

Before long, in March or April, Edgeworth called at Darwin's
house. The doctor was out, but his sister welcomed Edgeworth:
she was about to go to tea with the Sneyds, so he went with her
and, to cut a short story shorter, Edgeworth was married to
Honora Sneyd in Lichfield Cathedral by Canon Seward in July.
Anna was most upset at losing her best friend Honora. But the
newly-weds were very happy, and they went off to Edgeworth's
estate in Ireland for the next three years.

The unhappy Day made several visits to the Birmingham area
in 1773 and 1774, and to the Lunar circle he proved the old

adage about a friend in need when he lent money to Boulton, Small and Keir. There had been a general collapse of credit in Britain in 1772, and Day's generous loan to Boulton, £2200 in 1772, later increased[22] to £3000, probably saved Boulton from bankruptcy and made possible the development of Watt's engine in 1774. Day kept away from Lichfield to avoid meeting Elizabeth Sneyd, and consequently saw Small more often than Darwin. Amazingly, Small succeeded in sorting out his personal affairs: Miss Esther Milnes from Wakefield would, he thought, tolerate Day's eccentricities and make an excellent wife for him. At first Day objected that Esther was too wealthy, to which Small replied, 'My friend, what prevents you from despising the fortune and taking the lady?' Some years later Day did marry Esther, and she became quite devoted to him.

Darwin's enthusiasm was often diverted into new paths by the interests of his Lunar friends, and Day inspired one of those changes. When Day read the story of a Negro slave who escaped, married a white servant and then shot himself, all his Rousseauistic ideas of the Noble Savage were aroused. With his friend John Bicknell, he wrote a poem, *The Dying Negro*, which was published in 1773. It proved popular, going through four editions and identifying Day with the nascent anti-slavery campaign. Its effect on Darwin was all the more important for being subconscious: he and Day were often linked as the most literary of the Lunar circle; so the idea of writing a popular poem himself was injected into Darwin's mind. And when *The Loves of the Plants* was published sixteen years later, attacks on slavery were its strongest 'political' feature.

So far Darwin's life had not been much affected by political events in the world at large. His medical practice and the Seven Years' War began in the same year, but never interacted, and after the war British politics became narrow and inbred, dominated by the sound of intriguing politicians and shuffling ministries—presided over by such uninspiring characters as Grenville, Rockingham, Grafton and North, or occasionally by Chatham.

But 1773 and 1774 brought events of real importance: the American Revolution began, with the Boston Tea Party in December 1773, and the first Congress of the colonies in September 1774. The Lunar circle's father-figure, Benjamin Franklin, was still in England in 1774, acting virtually as

1  Erasmus Darwin,
   from a
   portrait-bust
   by William Coffee

2A  Robert Darwin (1682–1754), Erasmus's father
2B  Elizabeth Darwin (1702–1797), Erasmus's mother

2C  Elston Hall, where Erasmus was born and spent his childhood

3A Erasmus Darwin, aged 38, by Joseph Wright

3B Darwin House, Lichfield, where Erasmus lived from 1760 to 1781

4A Matthew Boulton

4B Benjamin Franklin

4C James Watt

4D Josiah Wedgwood

5A R. L. Edgeworth

5B James Keir

5C Anna Seward

5D Thomas Day

6A Brooke Boothby

6B John Whitehurst

6C Joseph Priestley

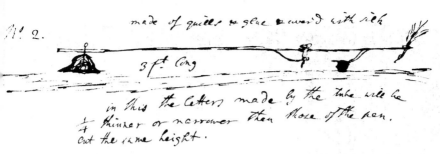

*N.º 2.*

*made of quills & glue covered with silk*

*3 f.t long*

*in this the letters made by the tube will be ¼ thinner or narrower then those of the pen. but the same height.*

7A One of Darwin's 'bigraphers': the words written by the
quill pen on the right are reproduced by the quill in the middle.
From Commonplace Book, 1777

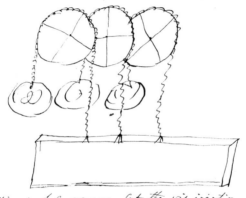

*nothing is to be overcome but the vis inertiæ & friction, as the water box is always the same weight, whether the boat is in it or not, since the boat whether full or empty will delude just as much water as it's own weight.*

*Perhaps levers like fire engine beams, would be preferable to wheels? perhaps the best ballence would be another trough full of water, as they might both of them be let dry if necessary occasionally.*

7B Some of Darwin's sketches for a canal lift,
from his Commonplace Book, 1777

8A Elizabeth Pole, who became Darwin's
second wife in 1781

8B Elizabeth Pole with a frisky dog, said
by family tradition to be Erasmus, being
led a dance

9A Radburn Hall, where Erasmus lived from 1781 to 1783

9B The house in Full Street, Derby,
where Erasmus lived from 1783 to 1802,
before its demolition in 1933

9C Breadsall Priory, where Erasmus died in 1802

10A Ferry across the Derwent linking the Darwins' garden with their orchard, from a drawing by their son Francis, who is the child in the boat, with his mother and Dewhurst Bilsborrow

10B Dr Erasmus Darwin (*right*) playing chess with his second son Erasmu

so well, (which I mind much more.)

Why will not you live at Derby? I want *learning* from you of various kinds, & would give you in exchange *chearfulness* which by some parts of your letter, you seem to want. — & of which I have generally a pretty steady supply.

Why the D—e do you talk of your mental faculties decaying, have not you more mechanical invention, accuracy, & *execution* than any other person alive? — besides an *inexhaustible fund* of wit, when you please to call for it? (so misers talk of their poverty, that their companions may contradict them.) your headachs & asthma would recieve permanent relief from warm bathing I dare say. — but perhaps you are too indolent to try it' use? — or have some theory against it?

Page of a letter from Erasmus to James Watt, 19 January 1790. See p. 204

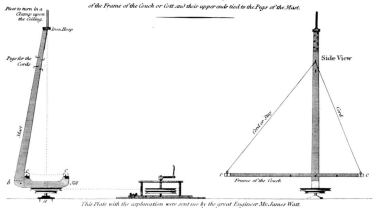

*The length of the Mast must be suited to the height of the Ceiling.—The angle at b must be secured by a Plate of Iron screwed on the outside.—*
*The cast Iron Cup (a) for the bottom Pivot may have three spikes to fix it to the Floor:— The whole of the Wood-work may be made of Oak or*
*Elm.—The frame of the Couch (cc) is not fixed to the Sill, but the latter has two projecting Iron Pegs, which go into holes in the Frame, so*
*that the centre of motion may be changed at pleasure.—When not in use, the Frame may be lifted off the Sill, and set up paralel to the Mast, in*
*a corner of the room.—There are four Cords or Stays, one fastned to each corner*
*of the Frame of the Couch or Cott, and their upper ends tied to the Pegs of the Mast.*

*This Plate with the explanation were sent me by the great Engineer Mr. James Watt.*

12A 'Rotative couch' designed by Watt to try out Darwin's
ideas on the effect of centrifugation

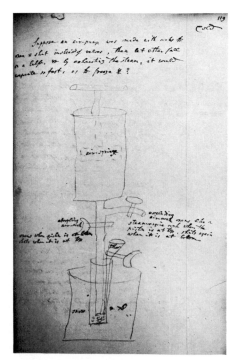

12B Apparatus for experiments on
the cooling of air, from Commonplace
Book, 1784

American ambassador: King George III was to call him the evil genius behind the Revolution, and Lord North branded him as 'the great fomenter of the opposition in America'. Darwin usually suppressed his own political opinions to avoid offending patients, but now he came out strongly in favour of Franklin and the American colonists. From this time onwards he can safely be labelled a radical in politics, though he did not publicize the fact to his conservative patients. Most of the Lunar circle supported the Americans, Darwin and Day being the most fervent; but Boulton, as a conservative and captain of industry, deplored the trade boycott imposed by the colonists. Franklin's friendship with Boulton seems to have ended about 1774, but his correspondence with Darwin and Whitehurst continued.

Franklin was also the leading scientist of the day and Darwin's next letter to him, on 24 January 1774, is to Franklin as scientist, not Franklin the American:

> I have inclosed a medico-philosophical Paper which I should take it as a Favour if you will communicate to the royal Society, if you think it worthy a place in their Volume, otherwise must desire you to return it to the Writer.
>
> I have another very curious paper containing Experiments on the Colours seen in the closed Eye after having gazed some Time on luminous objects, which is not quite transcribed, but which I will also send you, if you think it is likely to be acceptable to the Society at this Time, but will otherwise let it lie by me another year. I hope you continue to enjoy your Health and that I shall sometime again have the pleasure of seeing you in Staffordshire, and am, dear Sir
>
> your affectionate Friend,
>
> Eras. Darwin.[23]

The 'very curious paper' on colours in the closed eye did not see the light of day for many years, but Franklin communicated the medical paper to the Royal Society: it was read at their meeting on 24 March 1774 and was printed in the *Philosophical Transactions* later in the year.

In this paper, entitled 'Experiments on Animal Fluids in the exhausted Receiver',[24] Darwin examines the idea that 'elastic vapours' are dissolved in the blood and other body fluids. He describes various experiments conducted for him by Mr Young of Shiffnall, Mr Warltire, 'who gives very accurate lectures in natural philosophy', and Mr Webster of Montrose. The experiments consisted mainly in taking blood, or fluids from the gall bladder and urinary bladder, from sheep and swine at slaughter, and placing the fluids in a vacuum pump, or 'exhausted receiver'. The results of the experiments were conflicting, and so are Darwin's conclusions: indeed at the end, as if to cover up the inadequacies, he adds some comments about curing deafness by putting a cupping glass over the ear and lowering the pressure. The method worked on one out of three patients and is always worth trying, he concludes.

All in all, this is Darwin's worst scientific paper: he tried to get others to do the work, though he must have regretted this when the results conflicted; and after their efforts he felt bound to 'write it up'. Unlike his earlier papers, the manuscript is not in his writing. No wonder he was diffident in offering the paper to Franklin. Perhaps he hoped Franklin would send it back; if so, he was out of luck.

## [6]

Back at Lichfield, Darwin's life was running smoothly. He continued his liaison with Miss Parker, and their second child Mary was born in 1774. Darwin's three sons were now aged between eight and sixteen, and he would occasionally help them with their homework. The teacher who asked Charles to write verses about a visiting fair received the following mild rebuke:

Good sir you bid us to my sorrow
Write verses on the Fair tomorrow.
Now I suspect the subject scarce is
Of Consequence enough for verses.[25]

Charles continued to show brilliant promise in scientific subjects and he entered Oxford University in October 1774, when he was sixteen.

At the beginning of the year James Watt was still in Scotland, continuing his work as a canal surveyor and engineer. Developing his steam engine at Roebuck's works at Kinneil had proved frustrating, chiefly because the moving parts could not be machined accurately enough. Boulton had tried to take over the engine in 1769, but without success. In 1773 Roebuck was caught in the general collapse of credit and became bankrupt. He owed £1200 to Boulton and his partner Fothergill, and, since the trustees of the Roebuck estate attached no value to Watt's rusting steam engine, Boulton was able to acquire it in August. Watt was still reluctant to move south, despite continued pleas from Small and his own dislike of the Scottish weather, which made his canal surveys so arduous. Then, in September 1773, Watt's wife Margaret died in childbirth. 'I am heartsick of this country', he wrote to Small, and in May 1774, to the delight of Boulton, Small and Darwin, he at last moved to Birmingham.[26]

And so began one of the most illustrious partnerships in the history of technology. The genial optimist Matthew Boulton, owner of the finest metal works in the world and the indulgent employer of nearly a thousand workmen, was the perfect foil for the gloomy self-doubting James Watt, one of the greatest engineers of all time, who hated dealing with workmen and accounts. After two years of work, and the essential assistance of the ironfounder John Wilkinson, the Boulton-and-Watt engine was to begin its career in the world, and do more than any other single invention to bring about the modern technological era, though it was more than ten years before the engine brought any profit to Boulton.

Darwin was very pleased to have Watt close at hand: through all the lean years he had never lost faith in Watt's engine, and now, with Boulton's energy to push it on, Darwin was confident of early success. This is another example of Darwin helping his friends in their scientific interests: he had turned to geology because of Wedgwood's need for minerals, and to chemistry because of Keir's translation of Macquer; now the arrival of Watt revived his interest in the mechanical and chemical properties of steam and water vapour.

In 1774 Small, Boulton and Darwin were mainly concerned with getting Watt established and happy at Birmingham, so that he would stay. They succeeded, though not without a few scares. Early in 1775 Watt was offered a post in Russia at £1000 a year. On 29 March Darwin reacted with typical verve:

> Lord, how frightened I was when I heard a Russian bear had laid hold of you with his great paw, and was dragging you to Russia! Pray don't go if you can help it. Russia is like the den of Cacus: you see the footsteps of many beasts going thither, but of few returning. I hope your fire engines will keep you here.[27]

Fortunately the fire engines proved more powerful than the bear, and Watt remained.

At the beginning of 1775, with Watt settled, the Lunar circle was complete. As Schofield has pointed out, its expertise was wide. On mathematics and astronomy Small was pre-eminent; on industrial technology Boulton and Wedgwood; on engineering and invention Watt (and the now absent Edgeworth); on instrumentation Whitehurst; on chemistry Keir; on literary questions Day; while Darwin was the master of many of these and other crafts, from medicine to meteorology.

[7]

But the Lunar circle sustained a grievous loss in February 1775. Dr Small had never enjoyed good health: possibly he suffered from malaria contracted in Williamsburg. He was now much worse, and early in February Boulton said he had lost hope of recovery. Small died on 25 February. Boulton wrote to Watt, then in London: 'The last scene is just closed; the curtain is fallen, and I have this evening bid adieu to our once good and virtuous friend for ever and for ever.'[28] The buoyant Boulton was thoroughly depressed, and, in a strange reversal of roles, Watt had to cheer him: 'Come, my dear Sir, and immerse yourself in this sea of business as soon as possible, and do not add to the griefs of your friends by giving way to the tide of sorrow.'[29]

Small, the hub of the Lunar wheel, was unobtrusive but essential, and the tributes to him were many and sincere. Boulton wrote: 'His virtues were more and his foibles fewer (for vices he had none) than in any man I ever knew.'[30] Keir said that 'he had, I think, the greatest variety, as well as the greatest accuracy of knowledge, that I have ever met in any man'.[31] Day wrote a high-flown elegy ending:

O gentle bosom! O unsullied mind!
O friend to truth, to virtue, and mankind!
Thy dear remains we trust to this sad shrine,
Secure to feel no second loss like thine![32]

Darwin paid tribute to Small in an unpublished section of a letter to the Royal Society two years later, when he referred to 'my ever to be lamented friend Doctor Small of Birmingham, whose strength of reasoning, quickness of Invention, patience of investigation, and, what is above them all, whose benevolence of

Heart, have scarcely left an equal, not a superior, in these sub-
lunary realms!'[33] Darwin wrote a rather abstract elegy for
engraving on a vase in Boulton's garden. Here is the last verse:

> Cold Contemplation leans her aching head,
>   On human woe her steady eye she turns,
> Waves her meek hand, and sighs for Science dead,
>   For Science, Virtue, and for SMALL she mourns.[34]

Later in the year Small received a different kind of tribute,
from Thomas Jefferson, who did not know of his death. In May
Jefferson honoured the teacher who had shaped the destinies of
his life by sending a present of six dozen bottles of Madeira: 'I
hope you will find it as fine as it came to me genuine from the
island and has been kept in my own cellar eight years'.[35]

Without Small, the Lunar circle he had shaped was in danger
of falling apart, unless semi-formal arrangements for meeting
were made. The meetings at the time of the full moon began
soon after the death of Small, a memorial to his talent for
friendly cooperation which had held the group together. Schofield sets the first Lunar Society meeting on Sunday 31 December
1775.

[8]

The death of Small left an opening for a physician who might
take over his practice, preferably a man of Lunar mind. Again
Darwin took the initiative. His chosen recruit was Dr William
Withering, a young doctor with interests in chemistry and
botany as well as medicine, whom Darwin had known for ten
years. Withering's uncle Dr Brooke Hector (son of Dr George
Hector, who delivered Samuel Johnson) was in practice in
Lichfield, and the young Withering stayed with his uncle in the
summers during his medical course at Edinburgh. Darwin wrote
to Withering on 25 February 1775:

> I am this moment returned from a melancholy scene, the death of
> a friend who was most dear to me, Dr Small of Birmingham. . . .
> A person at Birmingham desired I would acquaint you with Dr
> Small's death as soon as I could, but would not permit his name to
> be mentioned. . . . Now it occurred to me that if you should choose
> that situation your philosophical Taste would gain you the friend-
> ship of Mr Boulton, which would operate all that for you which it did

for Dr Small. I saw by Dr Small's papers that he had gain'd about £500 a year at an average taking the whole time he had been at Birmingham, and above £600 on the last years. Now as this was chiefly in the town, without the Expense and Fatigue of Travelling and Horsekeeping, and without being troubled with visiting the people, for he lived quite a recluse, studious life, it appears to me a very eligible situation.[36]

This letter shows Darwin at his most resilient. Though grieved at the death of Small, he got on at once with what needed to be done. The letter also reveals, obliquely, how Boulton and Dr Ash, Small's partner, were ready to accept his choice of a man they had never met. Another point of interest is the contrast between Small's sedentary practice and the toilsome travel of Darwin's. Since Darwin could have taken a less exacting practice had he wished, he must have preferred his own strenuous life. Darwin's choice of Withering as Small's successor was discerning, for, although then quite unknown, Withering was to become one of the most famous of provincial physicians, a rival to Darwin himself.

By the end of March 1775, Withering had agreed to leave his post as physician to the Infirmary at Stafford, and to take on Small's practice. But he did not fit too well into the Lunar Group: he was rather prickly and reserved, and lacked the exuberance of Darwin, Boulton, Wedgwood or Edgeworth, the eloquence of Day, or the tact of Keir.

Withering was completing a book on British botany, based on his own extensive collection of botanical specimens. In May 1775 Darwin wrote to him suggesting that the title of his botanical book should be short and snappy—Darwin proposed 'The scientific Herbal', 'Linnean Herbal' or 'English Botany'— and added, 'We'll settle all this at Mr Boulton's with the assistance of Mr Keir and Mr Watt'.[37] Withering was not keen to take their advice and, as if to defy Darwin, he adopted a title that runs to twenty-four lines on the title page. Probably Darwin's remark that 'we'll settle all this . . .', though well-meant, was too patronizing for Withering to stomach. So he turned against Darwin, though Darwin may not have realized it. Withering was guilty of the common fault of being sullen and ungrateful towards an influential friend who was trying to help. And Darwin was at fault for tending to treat Withering as if he were still a medical student on holiday at Lichfield.

Withering's book was duly published in 1776 under a title
beginning *A Botanical Arrangement of all the Vegetables naturally
growing in Great Britain* . . . Later editions became quite
famous, but this first edition was 'little more than a translation
from Linnaeus of such genera and species of plants as are
indigenous to Great Britain'. The book's most curious feature
was the bowdlerization of some of the sexual terms, so that they
would not give offence to ladies. Withering changed 'stamen' to
'chive', and 'pistil' to 'pointal'. Such mealy-mouthedness irritated
Darwin and may have provoked him to sarcasm strong enough
to germinate the seeds of animosity already sown between
Withering and himself.

Although Darwin was interested in botany before 1775,
Withering's book seems to have spurred him on: from now
onwards botany was a major theme in Darwin's life, rather than
a fringe interest. And Withering's bowdlerization of the sexual
terms may have alerted Darwin to the idea that vegetable
naughtiness might appeal to the reading public, as he was to
prove with *The Loves of the Plants*.

In taking up botany seriously about 1775, Darwin was again
responding quickly to a new trend: the vogue for botany that
grew in strength through the 1780s was one reason for the
success of his *Loves of the Plants*. The creator of this botanical
band-wagon was Carl Linnaeus (1707–78), whose encyclopedic
works classifying plants, such as the *Genera Plantarum*, went
through many editions between 1740 and 1770, and were
universally welcomed for bringing order out of chaos in the
vegetable world. In Britain the interest in botany was stimulated
by the voyage of Captain Cook in the *Endeavour*, completed in
1771. The wealthy young botanist Joseph Banks, with Daniel
Solander and artists to help him, had sailed with Cook and
brought back a huge hoard of 1300 hitherto unknown exotic
species. Unfortunately Banks's elaborate plans for publication of
the beautiful drawings of the plants never came to fruition,[38] but
botany became fashionable, the Royal Botanic Garden at Kew
was founded, natural history societies were formed in all parts of
Britain, and naturalists such as Gilbert White (1720–93) found
themselves in tune with the times, instead of being regarded as
eccentrics.

Darwin's newly heightened interest in botany revived his
pleasure in writing verse. In a letter of 21 November 1775 to

Joseph Cradock, who had been a patient of his in the 1760s, Darwin thanks Cradock for the gift of his *Village Memoirs* and says:

> What shall I send you in return for these? I who have for twenty years neglected the Muses, and cultivated medicine alone with all my industry! . . . I lately interceded with a Derbyshire lady to desist from lopping a grove of trees, which has occasioned me . . . to try again the long neglected art of verse-making, which I shall enclose to amuse you, promising, at the same time, never to write another verse as long as I live, but to apply my time to finishing a work on some branches of medicine, which I intend for posthumous publication.[39]

In 1775 Darwin had no intention of writing *The Botanic Garden*. But he must already have had a yearning to do so: renouncing verse so passionately, and promising 'never to touch another drop', was like confessing to an addiction which he would one day succumb to.

# SIX

# Climacteric Years
# 1776-1780

IN 1776 DARWIN began writing down his ideas—mainly inventive, medical or scientific—in a Commonplace Book, a massive volume of three hundred outsize pages. During the next ten years he filled about two hundred of them with his slightly untidy but (for a doctor) surprisingly legible writing. The Commonplace Book (which is preserved in the Darwin museum at Down House) shows that in the critical years from 1776 to 1780 his mind was still running strongly on medicine and invention, though outward events might have suggested that other subjects, such as botany, grief and frustrated love, would be prominent.

During these years his sister Susannah continued to keep house for him; Miss Parker may still have been keeping open house for him too, but there were no further children. Darwin was pleased with the progress of his sons. In 1776 Robert was ten years old, and thriving. Erasmus junior was seventeen, and too timid and studious to please his father entirely; but he was most intelligent and had already won the friendship of Thomas Day. It was the eldest son, Charles, now eighteen, who was his father's favourite, because he was so exceptionally talented. To his interests in mechanics, geology and chemistry he had now added biology. Charles only stayed a year at Christ Church, Oxford. He didn't like the place because he thought that 'vigour of the mind languished in the pursuit of classical elegance', and he transferred 'to the robuster exercise of the medical schools of Edinburgh'[1] in the autumn of 1775.

Being so keen on geology, Charles probably helped in building up the museum which the apothecary Richard Greene established at Lichfield in the 1770s. This contained fossils, including ammonites and probably ichthyosaurs, and a wide range of minerals—ores, crystals, marbles and so on.[2] Darwin and other members of the Lunar group helped Greene with the collection, which greatly impressed Dr Johnson: 'Sir, I should as soon have thought of building a man-of-war, as of collecting such a museum.'[3]

In March 1776 Johnson brought Boswell to Lichfield. They first visited Birmingham, to meet Johnson's old school friend Mr Hector, and he took Boswell to see the Soho works, where Boulton showed Boswell round. 'I shall never forget Mr Boulton's expression to me: "I sell here, Sir, what all the world desires to have—POWER". He had about seven hundred people at work. I contemplated him as an *iron chieftain*, and he seemed to be a father to his tribe.'[4] Johnson and Boswell then made for Lichfield, where Johnson defended the natives against Boswell's charge of idleness: 'Sir, we are a city of philosophers, we work with our heads, and make the boobies of Birmingham work for us with their hands.' Boswell was impressed by Greene's museum and by Canon Seward, 'an ingenious and literary man', but he didn't meet Darwin.

Richard and Honora Edgeworth returned from Ireland in 1776 and visited Lichfield. Darwin was pleased to welcome them, but when they called on Anna Seward, she took it very badly: 'I had not the least expectation of such an event. Good God! I exclaimed, and sunk back in my chair more dead than alive. . . . A violent flood of tears relieved me. . . . It was an hour before my aunt could prevail upon me to go down.'[5] Anna cannot bring herself to describe the 'heart-rending scene' when they actually met. It is all long ago now, and we may scoff at such overdone feeling; but this was the penalty for over-cultivating sensibility as a shelter against the roughness of the age.

Darwin made many friends in the 1760s but few in the 1770s, and foremost among those few was Brooke Boothby (1744–1824), heir to a baronetcy, who after travelling widely in Europe in his twenties had now settled near Lichfield. Boothby was a humane and accomplished man of literary tastes, a confidant of Rousseau, and a welcome addition to the Lichfield literary circle, but not keen enough about science and technology to qualify for the Lunar Society. He was a man of ease rather than a man of industry, as Joseph Wright neatly implied with his famous reclining portrait (Plate 6A). Boothby admired Darwin's kindness to his patients, and in one of his poems refers to Darwin,

> whose ever-open door
> Draws, like Bethesda's pool, the suffering poor;
> Where some fit cure the wretched all obtain,
> Relieved at once from poverty and pain. [6]

Darwin and Wedgwood met frequently during 1776. Both were beginning to be exercised by the problem of educating their children. Erasmus had seen his eldest son Charles turn against classics and the moribund routine of Oxford, and had willingly agreed to transfer him to Edinburgh. Schools in England were for turning out gentlemen with classical attainments, and were not really suitable for budding doctors, like Charles and his youngest brother Robert, or future captains of industry, as Wedgwood hoped his sons would be.

Another topic of discussion between Wedgwood and Darwin was David Williams's Chapel, just opened near Cavendish Square. The chapel was based on a proposal of Franklin's for a chapel where morality would be taught without any mention of religious faith: Wedgwood, Bentley, Banks and Solander were among the sponsors. Wedgwood was offhand about religion, but he wanted to publicize the chapel, and in May 1776 he told Bentley of Darwin's suggestions on how to do so, 'to hire some Parsons to abuse it in the Papers—To call upon the Government for immediate help, and advise the burning of them (Parson and Congregation) altogether.—To lay the disturbances in America, and any other Public disasters which may happen at their Door—and he offers his service if you should be at a loss for an abuser of this new Sect.'[7]

The Lunar Society meetings seem to have been held regularly during 1776. Darwin attended the meeting on Sunday 4 February, but Keir did not, and Boulton wrote to him: 'Pray where were you at the last full moon? . . . I saw Darwin yesterday at Lichfield. He desires to know if you will come to Soho on Sunday, the 3rd March. . . .'[8] After that, the next meeting was apparently on 30 March, also at Soho, and Boulton refers to a meeting on 28 July with 'Keir, Darwin, Charles [Darwin] and Withering'.[9] There was another in August, when Whitehurst was present.

This was a notable year for Boulton and Watt, and for the

history of technology: the first of Watt's engines, with a cylinder of diameter 50 inches and stroke 7 feet, began work. Aris's *Birmingham Gazette* records that on 8 March 1776 'a Steam Engine constructed upon Mr Watt's new Principles was set to work at Bloomfield Colliery, near Dudley, in the presence of . . . a Number of Scientific Gentlemen whose Curiosity was excited to see the first Movements of so singular and so powerful a Machine; and whose Expectations were fully gratified by the Excellence of its performance.' (It emptied the engine pit, which stood fifty-seven feet deep in water, in less than an hour.) As the *Gazette* notes, 'the Iron Foundry parts (which are unparalleled for truth) were executed by Mr Wilkinson'; and a second engine was erected for Wilkinson's blast furnace at Broseley. Boulton was pleased at Soho's growing fame, which attracted visitors from all over the world. One of his guests at Soho House during 1776 was the Empress Catherine the Great of Russia.

Darwin was probably among the Scientific Gentlemen who watched the début of Watt's engine, but most of his energy continued to go into his medical duties. In 1776 his Commonplace Book includes fourteen pages of case notes on scarlet fever, gangrenous sore throat, drunkenness, headache from diseased teeth, dropsy, ulcers, carbuncles of the eyelid, polypus of the nose, worms, smallpox and lockjaw, the last two of which he treated with opium. Most of these case histories are of little interest now, but some of Darwin's incidental remarks are arresting. For example, he notes that witches often floated when subjected to trial by ordeal. He attributes this to the fact that hypochondriacs and hysterics have bad digestion, so that 'the stomach and bowels become distended with air'.

There is also a startling case history, probably from 1776, and certainly not intended for publication: 'Mrs ———— was asthmatic and dropsical, but did not appear near her end. She took four draughts of the decoction of Foxglove. . . . She vomitted two or three times, and then purged twice and died upon the close-stool.'[10] This looks rather like murder from an overdose of drugs, but such accidents were inevitable in the cut and thrust of eighteenth-century medicine. The question was, 'Did the doctor learn from his mistakes?', and with Darwin the answer was usually 'yes'.

At the beginning of the Commonplace Book is a system of

indexing devised by Darwin's son Charles. The first letter and the first subsequent vowel are used to break the words into groups, so that aardvark and anaconda would both creep into the first group, anteater would appear in the second, alligator in the third, axolotl in the fourth and ayu in the fifth. The method certainly has some advantages over normal indexing.

[2]

It was not long before Darwin broke his promise to Mr Cradock by lapsing into verse with his 'Address to the Swilcar Oak', published in 1776. The cue came from an acquaintance of Darwin's, Francis Mundy of Markeaton near Derby, who had written a pleasant topographical poem about the Needwood Forest, an area of primeval woodland a few miles north of Lichfield. Mundy's poem appealed to the Lichfield literary circle and probably had some influence on Darwin's own later verse. Mundy led his readers into the forest seductively:

> What green-rob'd Nymph, all loose her hair,
> With buskin'd leg, and bosom bare,
> Steps lightly down the turfy glades,
> And beckons tow'rd yon opening shades?[11]

Darwin accepted Munday's invitation, but, surprisingly, ignored the Nymph and looked at the ancient Swilcar Oak instead:

> Hail, stately oak, whose wrinkled trunk hath stood
> Age after age, the Sov'reign of this wood;
> You, who have seen a thousand springs unfold
> Their ravell'd buds, and dip their flowers in gold;
> Ten thousand times yon moon relight her horn.
> And that bright eye of evening gild the morn.[12]

—with three more verses in similar vein.

'The Swilcar Oak' had a curious publication history. It first appeared as a tailpiece to Mundy's poem, signed E.D., in company with three other short poems, signed A.S., B.B. and E.D.Jun. The Lichfield literary circle in full cry? Not so, it would seem. Anna says that Darwin wrote three of the poems himself: 'To the best he put his son's initials; to the second best his own; and to the worst mine. Not a syllable of any of the three did I see, or hear of, till I saw them in print. . . . I did not like this manoeuvre, and reproached him with it. He laught it off in a manner peculiar to himself.'[13] So 'The Swilcar Oak' began life as a second best. Twenty years later Darwin revised it, making it smoother but less vigorous. (He might better have revised the best of the three poems—except that he had resigned authorship of it to his son.) The revised 'Swilcar Oak' was printed in 1800 in the *European Magazine* and in *Phytologia*. It next appeared, with a few alterations, in 1873 in the *Quarterly Review*, where it is said to have referred to a tree at Holland House and to have been written by Samuel Rogers.[14] Perhaps some Victorian was punishing Darwin: he had thrown away the authorship of two of his poems, so wouldn't it be poetic justice to deprive him of the third as well?

[3]

Darwin's interest in nature, after this first flowering on paper, soon flowered in the field as well: he started work on a botanic garden about a mile west of Lichfield, near Abnalls. Anna Seward tells the story in her inimitable manner:

> About the year 1777, Dr Darwin purchased a little, wild, umbrageous valley, a mile from Lichfield, amongst the only rocks which neighbour that city so nearly. It was irriguous from various springs, and swampy from their plenitude. A mossy fountain, of the purest and coldest water imaginable, had, near a century back, induced the inhabitants of Lichfield to build a cold bath in the bosom of the vale. *That*, till the doctor took it into his possession, was the only mark of human industry which could be found in the tangled and sequestered scene.[15]

Today the bath still exists and is still the only mark of human industry in the little valley. The bath is about fifteen feet square, and the water is still perfectly clear and cold, as Anna says, and about three feet deep. An inscription nearby reads: 'This stone marks the site of the Ancient Bathhouse purchased by Dr ERASMUS DARWIN of Lichfield and his son ERASMUS DARWIN the younger from Thomas Weld of Lulworth Castle, Dorset, Esq. in the 20th year of the reign of KING GEORGE III . . .' (This is two years later than indicated by Anna—possibly just legal delay.) The bath-house was built in the previous century by Sir John Floyer. To judge from Anna's description, the little valley with the bath-house at its head was probably the site of Darwin's botanic garden. It is about ten feet deep and a hundred yards long with a plashy stream running down it from west to east, about a hundred yards south of Abnalls Lane. Today nearly all the signs of Darwin's garden have gone: the valley lies in a field used as pasture, and only a few gnarled oaks survive to mark the site that Darwin once beautified. 'In some parts he widened the brook into small lakes, that mirrored the valley; in others, he taught it to wind between shrubby margins.'[16] There was a fountain too, where Darwin inscribed a 'Speech of a Water Nymph' to warn off those incapable of savouring the scene—those immune to the charms of 'the meek flower of bashful dye' and 'the soft, murmuring rill'.

Darwin kept Anna away from his garden until the landscaping and planting were completed. Then, after inviting her to see it, he was called away on an urgent case; so she came alone. 'She took her tablets and pencil, and, seated on a flower-bank, in the midst of that luxuriant retreat, wrote the following lines':

> O, come not here, ye Proud, whose breasts infold
> Th' insatiate wish of glory, or of gold . . .
> But, thou! whose mind the well-attemper'd ray
> Of Taste, and Virtue, lights with purer day . . .
> For thee my borders nurse the glowing wreath,
> My fountains murmur, and my zephyrs breathe. . . .
> Thus spoke the Genius as he stept along,
> And bade these lawns to Peace and Truth belong;
> Down the steep slopes he led, with modest skill,
> The grassy pathway and the vagrant rill. . . .[17]

When Anna showed him the poem, he seemed pleased and said: 'I shall send it to the periodical publications; but it ought to form the exordium of a great work. The Linnaean System is unexplored poetic ground, and an happy subject for the muse. It affords fine scope for poetic landscape; it suggests meta-morphoses of the Ovidian kind, though reversed. Ovid made men and women into flowers, plants, and trees. You should make flowers, plants, and trees, into men and women. I . . . will write the notes, which must be scientific; and you shall write the verse.' Anna replied that the plan was 'not strictly proper for a female pen'; but 'she felt how eminently it was adapted to the efflorescence of his own fancy'.[18]

Darwin sent Anna's verses to the *Gentleman's Magazine*, where they were printed with her name;[19] and he began writing a poem about the Linnaean system—in 1779 according to Anna, earlier according to Edgeworth. Darwin also proved true to his idea that Anna's verses would make a good start to his poem: they appear without acknowledgement at the beginning of *The Botanic Garden*, somewhat altered and interwoven with eighteen lines of Darwin's. This reprinting of verses he had already had printed with her name was intended as a compliment, but Anna took it as an insult. Though Darwin's action was cavalier, Anna was rather cheeky in complaining, because the best lines in some of her poems were written by Darwin, and because she is equally cavalier in altering poems by Darwin quoted in her *Memoirs*.

We can find another starting point for *The Botanic Garden* in Darwin's Commonplace Book in 1778, when he wrote:

> Linneus might certainly be translated into English without losing his sexual terms, or other metaphors, and yet avoiding any indecent idea. Thus, Classes: 1, One male (beau); 2, two males, etc.; 13, many males; 14, two masters (lords); 15, four masters . . . 20, male-coquetts ['male ladies' and 'viragoes' crossed out] . . . 23, polygamies ['cuckoldoms' and 'many marriages' crossed out]; 24, clandestine marriages.[20]

Many of these names are preserved in the poem published eleven years later.

Besides cultivating his botanic garden, Darwin also started a Botanical Society at Lichfield. Though grand-sounding, it consisted only of himself, Brooke Boothby, and Joseph Jackson, a proctor in the cathedral who admired Boothby, and 'worshipped and *aped* Dr Darwin'. Unfortunately 'no recruits flocked to his botanical standard . . . the original triumvirate received no augmentation'.[21] But the Society is important because it induced Darwin to start on the translations from Linnaeus, which were published in its name, though Darwin did most of the work, with some help from Boothby, and Jackson acting as 'a useful drudge'.[22]

[4]

Other threads in Darwin's intellectual life also show up in his

Commonplace Book. Although only a few of the entries are dated exactly, most of them can plausibly be placed to within a year or two. In 1777 and 1778 we find the usual mixture of medicine and invention. One of the case histories records the successful use of electrotherapy on Mr Saville, probably Anna Seward's *inamoroso*, and it was reproduced with a few additions in *Zoonomia*:

> Mr S., a gentleman between 40 and 50 years of age, had had the jaundice about six weeks, without pain, sickness, or fever; and had taken emetics, cathartics, mercurials, bitters, chalybeates, essential oil, and ether, without apparent advantage. On a supposition that the obstruction of the bile might be owing to the paralysis or torpid action of the common bile-duct, and the stimulants taken into the stomach seeming to have no effect, I directed half a score smart electric shocks from a coated bottle, which held about a quart, to be passed through the liver, and along the course of the common gall-duct, as near as could be guessed, and on that very day the stools became yellow; he continued the electric shocks a few days more, and his skin gradually became clear.[23]

The medical use of electricity was not unknown in the eighteenth century, but this certainly ranks among Darwin's experimental treatments—a successful experiment too, apparently.

Other case histories are less impressive, for example the following case of pleurisy:

> Mr Jauncey was blooded nine times, he then became feeble, with obscure hiccup for a day and twitching of the corners of his mouth into a kind of risus sardonicus.[24]

After such treatment his laugh might well be sardonic: it is a wonder he could laugh at all. However, he did recover in about ten days.

If the treatment of Mr Jauncey seems a trifle callous, Darwin makes up for it with many touches of kindness: 'I have this day (Dec. 25—78) seen a Mrs Riley of Stafford, who has a diseased digestion, and perpetual sickness.'[25] How many doctors today would care to drive sixty miles on Christmas Day over muddy rutted 'roads' in an unheated bone-shaking carriage, to see a patient with a bad digestion?

Some of the medical entries are in the form of short notes rather than case histories. For example: 'In diabetes the quantity of sugar to be obtained from the urine is quite astonishing.' 'Dilute an acquired taste and it ceases to be agreeable, hence a test of acquired taste.'[26] One of his remarks, 'The placenta serves the place of an organ of respiration, similar to the gills of fish',[27] foreshadows his idea of evolution through fish to reptiles and mammals. Darwin was also already groping towards the idea of the essential role of sugar in plant and animal nutriment. 'It seems that as the farinaceous matter in the grain of barley or peas is converted into sugar during germination for the nourishment of the young embryo, so by digestion the saccharine process is carried on for the nourishment of the animal.'[28]

Other medical entries, running to about fifteen pages, dwell on asthma, ulcers, worms, consumption, epilepsy, menstruation, sleep, tears, pain, hydrophobia, vertigo, angina and mumps, which provokes the following curious queries: 'Mr S died of a sore throat, which retreated and fell on the brain. Mr P had a sore throat ceased suddenly and he became stupid but recover'd. I suppose both these might be a Mumps originally?'[29]

These medical entries in the Commonplace Book rub shoulders rather roughly with the mechanical inventions, of which there are dozens in 1777 and 1778. Either Darwin was the world's fastest inventor, or, more likely, he is recording a backlog from previous years.

The most massive of the inventions of 1777–8 is the canal lift. If a canal has to climb a hill, a flight of locks is needed; this delays traffic, may be difficult to build, and allows water to escape from the upper stretches of the canal whenever the flight is used. Darwin saw the merits of the lift, which avoids these troubles and is especially suitable for linking a canal with a river passing beneath it. He describes his design (Plate 7B) as follows:

> Let a wooden box be constructed so large as to receive a loaded boat. Let the box be join'd [to] the end of the upper canal and then the boat is admitted, and the doors of admission secured again. Then the box with the boat in it, being balanced on wheels, or levers, is let down, and becomes part of the inferior lock.

His idea is that the box should hang from chains which run over pulleys and have counterweights to balance the weight of the box. The key to success is, as he notes, the fact that

> nothing is to be overcome but the vis inertiae and friction, as the

water box is always the same weight, whether the boat is in it or not, since the boat whether full or empty will detrude [displace] just as much water as its own weight.[30]

Darwin at first proposed a metal counterweight, but then he saw the advantages of having a second box identical with the first. This doubles the possible capacity of the lift; and when repairs are needed, both caissons can be emptied of water simultaneously without upsetting the balance.

The first actual canal lift was built about ten years later, in Saxony, and was counterbalanced by weights. In 1792 a lock with a submerged caisson was patented by Robert Weldon of Lichfield, and one of these began operating at Combe Hay in Somerset in 1798. In 1800 James Fussell's 'patent balance lock', very like Darwin's lift, was installed on the Dorset and Somerset canal. The large Anderton lift near Northwich in Cheshire, opened in 1875, was similar in design to Darwin's. This lift, which still operates in modified form, raises boats some fifty feet from the Weaver Navigation Canal to the Grand Trunk Canal— the very canal Darwin had been associated with. Many large lifts have since been built in other European countries and the U.S.A.[31]

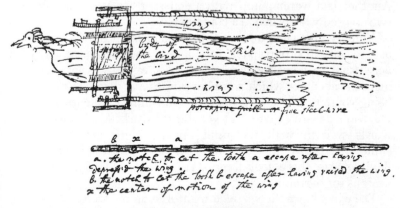

Fig. 5 Artificial bird (1777)

The most advanced of the inventions in the Commonplace Book is an artificial bird with flapping wings, Fig. 5, which Darwin explains as follows:

Let a watch-spring be fix[ed] with one end to a frame and the other wrap'd round an axis; at each end of the axis let a wheel be put with teeth of such form and situation that they shall move a wing, like a bat's wing, or like a ladies fan, one tooth carrying it downwards, another carrying it towards the body, another carrying it upwards, and a fourth outwards again from the body. N.B. One edge of the wing is to be fasten'd to the body and the other to a kind of fan-stick made of a porcupine quill. The tail of feathers spread out and lying obliquely to the action of the wings, or rather to its intended track in the air.

Then, a few pages later, comes the excellent idea of replacing the watch-spring by a compressed-air bottle, the very method often used for actuating the control surfaces of modern guided missiles:

> But the simpler way, and better, would be to have a copper globe fill'd with condensed air, and the tube to make the longest feather in the tail of the bird.[32]

So Darwin succeeded in overcoming the main bugbear of early aircraft designers—the lack of power. But I fear his feathery flapper would have been aerodynamically unstable.

In contrast to this exotic bird, many of Darwin's inventions are quite mundane. One of these is a lever-type machine for weighing people, rather like the modern physician's scales. Another is a water pump with a constant stream, basically just two cogged wheels inside a container.

Equally mundane, but more important because of its practical use, is Darwin's 'bigrapher' for copying documents. In his day it was usual to copy by hand, and he saw the advantages of a mechanical copier which would duplicate any document as it was being written. Though rather large and clumsy, like its inventor, Darwin's design (Plate 7A) apparently worked quite well. The words written with the quill on the right are reproduced simultaneously by the tube in the middle, which is attached to a flexible arm three feet long. (He also produced three other designs for bigraphers.)

Darwin's bigrapher proved fruitful in an unexpected way, for his success provoked Watt to invent a better method: 'I have fallen on a way of copying writing chemically, which beats your bigrapher hollow,'[33] Watt wrote triumphantly in 1779. Watt's chemical process remained the standard office copying method for nearly a hundred years, though now displaced by the electrostatic Xerox methods.

This brings us back to Darwin again, for he was a keen

inventor of electrostatic generators. His 'electrical doubler' was quite famous in its time, and Fig. 6 shows a sketch of it in his Commonplace Book, slightly touched up. The central disc, apparently of glass with a metal sheet imbedded in it, was given an initial charge. The two outer discs are 'movable brass plates which being mounted on cranked levers, could be made to approach or recede from the central plate by turning the winch'.[34] As the plates approach the central one, charges are induced on them which apparently pass to a Leyden jar via the conductor $w$. Then the plates are withdrawn and earthed via $e$ and $z$. The mechanism is not very clear in the sketch, but apparently the design worked.

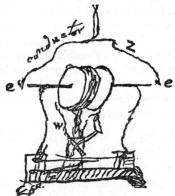

Fig. 6 Electrostatic doubler (1778)

Afterwards Darwin made several improvements in his electrical doubler and then handed it over to his friend Abraham Bennet (1750–99), curate of Wirksworth and inventor of the gold-leaf electroscope. Bennet tells us: 'Dr Darwin . . . made the first attempt with two plates moving between two others by a lever, so as to bring them exactly to the same position in each operation. This contrivance he soon improved by another instrument in which the plates stood vertically and moved by rack work in a direction exactly parallel to each other.'[35] Bennet also says that he kept a diary of atmospheric electricity 'at the request of my friend Dr Darwin, who hoped some important atmospheric discoveries might be made thereby'.

This is a reminder that the weather was the most enduring of all Darwin's scientific interests because, like carriage design, it affected him daily in his travels through the muddy Midlands, over vile roads or rutted tracks, which were impassable to carriages after heavy rain. He had to decide whether to take his horse Doctor with him or not, and to weigh the chance of being stranded, stuck in the mud miles from anywhere, against the chance of a patient dying if he didn't try to make the journey. Darwin made two meteorological 'inventions', which are trivial mechanically but significant for the thought behind them.

The first meteorological gadget is a machine to measure the net flow of air from north to south; it exists only as a rough sketch and was probably never made. He describes it as follows:

> A machine to measure the quantity of air passing from N. to S. and from S. to N. is not impossible to construct. Let there be a tube about six inches diameter and a foot or $\frac{1}{2}$ a yard long, placed exactly in the meridian on a chimny with a windmill sail in the center of it, having a crank which at every revolution should strike against the extremity of a rod which might come down into a garret and be made to register the number of revolutions of the fly [i.e., rotor] for a month or two together one way, and to unwind again when the wind blew in the contrary direction.[36]

In the diagram drawn by Darwin, Fig. 7, the tube is more slender than he implies in his description. The line of circles at the bottom of the diagram represents reduction gearing, the rotation of the cog-wheel furthest to the left being perhaps 100,000 times slower than that of the primary wheel on the right—rather like a household electricity meter today.

The machine is interesting because it reveals Darwin's intuitive grasp of what mathematicians now call the continuity equation, one of the fundamental equations on which computer weather forecasting rests. His machine might be worth adding to the regular armoury of modern meteorological instruments.

The second gadget is even simpler, and still more significant. To help with his personal weather forecasting service, he installed in his house a weathercock with an extended spindle which came through to the ceiling of his study where it operated a pointer, so that he could monitor the changes in wind from the comfort of his armchair. This was not really an 'invention': a similar device was installed in the tower of the winds at Athens, built in the first century B.C.[37] But Darwin's decision to install this device in his study marks three important advances in meteorology—which no one had the wit to see, and which have

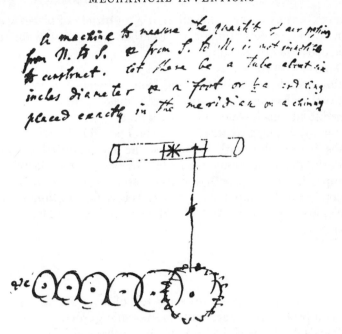

Fig. 7 North-south air machine (1778)

gradually been rediscovered during the twentieth century. First, Darwin recognized the importance of cold and warm fronts. He wrote in his Commonplace Book, near the diagram of the north-south airflow gauge:

> Certain it is that in change of the wind from N.E. to S.W. the air becomes instantly warm, before it can have moved half over this island: and on the contrary when it changes from S.W. to N.E. it becomes instantly cold before it has blown more than an hour or two, so that the change of the direction of the wind evidently changes its tendency to absorb or to give out heat.[38]

This early hint remained unknown to meteorologists, and it was not until the 1920s that they finally realized the great importance of fronts, which today tend to dominate the weather charts.

Darwin's second achievement was to appreciate that these sudden changes of wind required an instrument with a sharp time-resolution to detect them. In contrast meteorologists tended to be satisfied, until quite recently, with intermittent data, often six-hourly; even today, the computer models operate primarily with data at fixed time intervals, whereas the exact time of changes in wind direction at a multitude of places would be a stronger determinant of weather patterns—if the data could conveniently be collected.

Darwin's third achievement was to seize on the virtues of continuous telemetry—observing from a distance in comfort. In contrast, subsequent meteorologists made rather a fetish of intermittent on-the-spot observation, as if, perhaps by some puritan mystique, a weather-beaten and possibly frozen observer makes better observations because he has endured hardship. Recently the continuous telemetry pioneered by Darwin has triumphed, and now the British forecasters sit in comfort in their air-conditioned computer complex, receiving continuous telemetry, greater in quantity and better in quality than Darwin ever dreamt of.

[5]

In 1777 Darwin was forty-five and full of invention and energy. It was a productive year, with the botanic garden taking shape (if Anna's dating is right), the many mechanical inventions, the usual medical rounds and many meetings with his Lunar friends. Four letters from Darwin to Boulton in 1777 have survived in manuscript,[39] but they are mostly orders, for items ranging from 'square and round cylinders in brass' to the framing of some Kauffman prints. The Lunar meetings probably petered out late in 1777, to Darwin's disappointment, as Keir told Boulton: 'I had a letter yesterday from Dr Darwin in which he says he longs for a little philosophical laughing—Therefore when you are at leisure some full Moon Sunday, I hope you will indulge the Dr . . .'[40] On 4 February 1778 Darwin wrote himself to rouse Boulton:

> Not having heard of you for so many moons has induced me to think you are dead—pray send me word that I may begin your epitaph— If you are still alive, I design to visit you next Sunday but one.[41]

It was only in a Lunar sense that Darwin had not heard of Boulton, for three weeks earlier he had sent Boulton a long letter with some verses of Miss Rogers which he had 'polish'd, japan'd and handed up'.

Soon, on 5 April 1778, it was Darwin who had to send apologies:

I am sorry the infernal Divinities, who visit mankind with diseases, and are therefore at perpetual war with doctors, should have prevented my seeing all you great men at Soho today—Lord! What inventions, what wit, what rhetoric, metaphysical, mechanical, and pyrotecnical, will be on the wing, bandy'd like a shuttlecock from one to another of your troop of philosophers! While poor I, I by myself I, imprizon'd in a post chaise, am joggled, and jostled, and bump'd, and bruised along the King's high road, to make war upon a pox or a fever![42]

Darwin goes on to complain that the prints by Mrs Kauffman have still not been sent, and in another letter on 21 April he threatens to 'come over to Soho' and 'carry them off by force and arms'.[43]

[6]

For Darwin, 1778 was a year of crisis. One of his patients in 1777 was Milly Pole, the three-year-old daughter of Colonel Pole and his wife Elizabeth, of Radburn Hall, near Derby. It was a difficult case: 'Miss Milly Pole about 3 years old from a very healthy lively beautiful child lost her spirits and flesh, without fever, or tumid belly, or any apparent cause. . . . Her hands and feet are almost always cold, and what is strange they appear of a florid red.' Darwin brought her to Lichfield for treatment:

Oct:       She take opium 2/3 of a grain thrice a day.
Nov. 16 :  She has now taken a grain of opium thrice a day for a
           month.[44]

Darwin handed out opium with what now seems horrifying nonchalance, but of course he was unaware of the chemical addiction which it produces. Opium or no, Milly recovered and in March he reports her to be thriving. Soon after, probably about April, all three of the Pole children became ill, 'injured by a dangerous quantity of the cicuta, injudiciously administered in the hooping cough', as Anna remembered it. 'Mrs Pole brought them to the house of Dr Darwin, in Lichfield, remaining with them there a few weeks, till, by his art, the poison was expelled from their constitutions, and their health restored.'[45]

While restoring her children to health at his house, Darwin fell in love with Elizabeth Pole. She was by all accounts a most remarkable woman, not only beautiful (see Plate 8A) but also

witty, carefree and unconventional. Elizabeth was the illegitimate daughter of the second Earl of Portmore, and, in looks as
well as temperament, she resembled her grandmother Catherine
Sedley, who was the mistress of King James II before she
married the first Earl of Portmore. Elizabeth was brought up at
Farnham by Mrs Mainwaring, who remained a close friend in
later life. When Darwin first met her, Elizabeth was thirty, and,
as even the jealous Anna Seward admitted, 'in the full bloom of
her youth and beauty. Agreeable features; the glow of health; a
fascinating smile; a fine form, tall and graceful; playful sprightliness of manners; a benevolent heart, and maternal affection . . .
contributed to inspire Dr Darwin's admiration, and to secure his
esteem.'46

Elizabeth's husband, Colonel Edward Sacheverel Pole, was
head of one of the leading families of Derbyshire and nearly
thirty years older than his wife. According to Whitehurst, the
Colonel served in Germany under Prince Ferdinand, fought in
eleven battles and was left for dead in the field in three of them.
At the Battle of Minden he was shot through the head, the ball
going in at his left eye and coming out at the back of his head.
Darwin's attentions to the wife of so intrepid a military hero
seemed likely to be fruitless, or dangerous.

Darwin expressed his frustrated love by commissioning
Boulton to make a tea-vase as a present for Elizabeth. Boulton
received the order in a vigorous conversational poem which
nicely catches Darwin's exuberance:

> Friend Bolton, take these ingots fine
> From rich Potosi's sparkling mine;
> With your nice art a tea-vase mould,
> Your art, more valu'd than the gold.
> With orient pearl, in letters white,
> Around it, 'To the Fairest', write;
> And, where proud Radburn's turrets rise,
> To bright Eliza send the prize.

Darwin specifies the decorations in detail:

> I'll have no bending serpents kiss
> The foaming wave, and seem to hiss;
> No sprawling dragons gape with ire,
> And snort out steam, and vomit fire;
> No Naiads weep; no sphinxes stare;
> No tail-hung dolphins swim in air.

Let leaves of myrtle round the rim,
With rose-buds twisting, shade the brim . . .[47]


[7]


Falling in love with Elizabeth Pole was perhaps the most delightful event of Darwin's life, but it was immediately followed by the deepest tragedy. His eldest son Charles was enjoying a brilliant undergraduate career at the Edinburgh Medical School. In March 1778 he won the first gold medal of the newly established Aesculapian Society of Edinburgh for his essay on the best ways of distinguishing between pus and mucus. Although the subject set by the Society now seems misjudged, Charles attacks it keenly and successfully. He greatly impressed his teacher, Dr Andrew Duncan, and helped him in his public dispensary: Charles 'undertook the care, and attended with diligence all the sick poor of the parish of Waterleith, and supplied them with the necessary medicines'.[48]

At the end of April, Charles cut his finger while dissecting the brain of a child who had died of 'hydrocephalus internus', and on the same evening was seized with a severe headache, followed the next day by 'delirium, petechiae, haemmorrhage, paralysis of the bladder and other circumstances of extreme debility'. Erasmus was summoned to Edinburgh, and for a few days after he arrived had hopes that Charles might recover. But it was not to be, and he died on 15 May 1778, four months before his twentieth birthday. Dr Duncan wrote a 23-page elegiac poem commemorating his achievements,[49] and Charles was buried in the Duncan family vault, with an inscription composed by his father which begins: 'Possessed of uncommon Abilities and Activity, he had acquired Knowledge in every Department of Medical and Philosophical Science, much beyond his Years. . . .' While at Edinburgh, Erasmus met the great geologist James Hutton, and on 3 July he wrote to give Hutton the wording for the inscription; he also promised to send Hutton 'coal full of vegetable seeds'.[50]

The memory of Charles's energy and talents remained strong for many years. His namesake (and nephew) Charles Darwin said that 'the venerable professor [Duncan] spoke to me about him with the warmest affection forty-seven years after his death, when I was a young medical student in Edinburgh.'[51]

The death of Charles distressed Erasmus more than any other event in his life, and cast a gloom over the next year or two, deepening the sadness of his apparently hopeless love for Elizabeth Pole.

[8]

As usual, Darwin had plenty of medical work to distract him from his personal problems, and Anna Seward[52] has given a full account of one case, that of the Countess of Northesk. In the summer of 1778 Lady Northesk stopped overnight at a Lichfield inn, on her way home to Scotland to die, after the most eminent physicians of London and Bath had told her there was no hope for her. The innkeeper advised her to 'send for *our* Doctor, he is so famous'. Darwin invited her to stay at his house and asked Anna to visit her frequently. Anna found her lying on a couch in the parlour 'drawing with difficulty that breath which seemed often on the point of final evaporation. She was thin, even to transparency; her cheeks suffused at times with a flush, beautiful, though hectic.'

But 'her great and friendly physician' had a look which seemed to say, 'You shall not die thus prematurely, if my efforts can prevent it'. Darwin first suggested a blood transfusion: Lady Northesk agreed, and Anna gallantly offered herself as a donor; but after 'consulting his pillow' Darwin told them he had decided it was too dangerous. Instead he put Lady Northesk on a diet of milk, vegetables and fruit. Within three weeks she was cured and went back to Scotland with a feeling of 'grateful veneration towards her physician, whose rescuing skill had saved her from the grave'.[53] If the cure seems a trifle simple, at least it succeeded: Lady Northesk remained well, until she died by setting her clothes alight some years later.

Though 1778 was a traumatic year for Darwin, it was happier for others in the Lunar group. One of them accomplished a feat he had so often attempted in vain before: Thomas Day was at last married to Esther Milnes in August. 'They are good people and I hope will not sacrifice real solid happiness to whim and caprice,' Wedgwood remarked.[54] His hope was at least partially fulfilled, for Esther was content to live as Day wished, secluded and far from the taint of society.

Another of Darwin's friends, John Whitehurst, had moved away from the Lunar circle when he accepted the post of 'Stamper of the Money Weights' in London in 1775; his most famous book *The Formation of the Earth* was published in 1778, and Darwin was to find it very useful in his own studies of geology.

With the departure of Lady Northesk, Darwin had more time to brood over Charles's death and his own attentions to Elizabeth Pole, which he exposed in plaintive verse:

> Dim, distant towers! whose ample roof protects
>   All that my beating bosom holds so dear,
> Far shining lake! whose silver wave reflects
>   Of Nature's fairest forms, the form most fair;
>
> Groves, where at noon the sleeping Beauty lies;
>   Lawns, where at eve her graceful footsteps rove;
> For ye full oft have heard my secret sighs,
>   And caught unseen, the tear of hopeless love;
>
> Farewell! a long farewell!—your shades among
>   No more these eyes shall drink Eliza's charms;
> No more these ears the music of her tongue!—
>   O! doom'd for ever to another's arms![55]

These three verses (and there are more) are the nearest Darwin came to self-pity in all his writings; he did not entirely escape the heightened sensibility which caused Anna Seward such agonies.

Darwin luxuriated in misfortune again in the autumn of 1778, when Elizabeth was taken ill of a violent fever. Darwin was called to Radburn to treat her, but was pointedly not invited to stay the night, which he expected would be critical in the disease. According to Anna, he passed the night beneath a tree outside Elizabeth's room, and occupied the gloomy hours by writing a poem paraphrasing Petrarch's sonnet about the death of Laura:

> Dread Dream, that, hovering in the midnight air,
> Clasp'd, with thy dusky wing, my aching head,
> While, to Imagination's startled ear,
> Toll'd the slow bell, for bright Eliza dead. . . .[56]

The rest of this miserable poem is an elegy for Eliza, as badly written as you might expect if Darwin really did compose it out there under the tree.

Fortunately Elizabeth survived the crisis and Darwin celebrated her recovery with an 'Ode to the River Derwent', a cheerful landscape-poem of eight quatrains. The first four innocently trace the course of the Derwent from its source in the Peak country past the lawns of Chatsworth and the gorge of Matlock to its full strength at Derby. There Darwin asks the river to pause:

> But when proud Derby's glittering vanes you view,
> And her gay meads your sparkling currents drink;
> Should Bright Eliza press the Morning Dew,
> And bend her graceful footsteps to your brink,
>
> Stop, gentle wave, in circling Eddies play,
> And, as your scaly squadrons gaze around,
> Quick let your Nymphs with Pencil fine pourtray
> Her Angel Footsteps on your painted ground.
>
> With playful Malice, from her kindling cheeks
> Steal the warm Blush, and dye your passing stream,
> Mock the sweet Roseat Dimples when she speaks,
> And when she turns her Eye, reflect its Beam.

These verses show how Darwin was beginning to develop a rare delicacy of touch in verse. Large and clumsy in person, he was deft and charming in his persona as poet. He learnt from Anna's sensibility, but he was normally so down-to-earth that he never took this heightened feeling seriously, and was able to use it with designedly comic effect, turning the minnows into 'scaly squadrons'. The comic exaggeration continues in the final verse:

> And tell her, Derwent, as you murmur by,
> How in these wilds with hopeless Love I burn,
> Teach your soft gales and echoing caves to sigh,
> And mix my briny sorrows in your Urn.[57]

These verses to Elizabeth Pole need to be quoted at length because of the light they throw on Erasmus. As Charles Darwin aptly remarked, 'The love of woman is a very different affair from friendship, and my grandfather seems to have been capable of the most ardent love of this kind. This is seen in his many MS verses addressed to her before their marriage.'[58]

[9]

'The philosopher in love', as Anna called him, was still also pursuing his scientific interests, and in 1778 one of these was blind spots, the subject of his paper 'A New Case in Squinting' published in the *Philosophical Transactions* of the Royal Society. The subject is a five-year-old boy, Master Sandford, who looked at every object with only one eye (the one furthest from the object) by turning his head so that the image fell on the blind spot in the retina of the nearer eye. Darwin believed the habit was caused by his wearing, as a baby, a nightcap which had appendages at each side visible only to the opposite eye. Darwin's proposed cure was to fit a large false nose like the gnomon of a sundial, which would force the boy to view with the near eye. This treatment was not persevered with—presumably it was too unsightly—and when Darwin saw the boy again six years later he found the habit more fixed. He made experiments which showed that Master Sandford had blind spots four times larger than normal:

> Two circular papers, each of 4 inches diameter, were stuck against the wall, their centres being exactly at 8 inches distance from each other. On closing one eye, and viewing the central spot of these papers with the eye farthest from it, and then retreating 26 inches from it, the other paper became invisible. This experiment was made on 5 people, of various ages, from 10 years old to 40; and the paper disappeared to them all at about this distance, or an inch or 2 more or less; but to Master Sandford the paper disappeared at about 13 inches distance from the wall.[59]

This experiment is quite simple, but it does show how Darwin would take a great deal of trouble to elucidate a puzzling case, even though in this instance he believed the gnomon would eventually effect a cure.

In the autumn of 1778 Darwin was busy with his latest invention, a polygrapher, or machine for making multiple copies of drawings or documents. He persevered with this machine at the request of one of his few London acquaintances, Charles Greville, a politician with scientific interests. 'I can assure you at my few vacant hours I have incessantly labour'd at the completion of the Polygrapher in its triple capacity',[60] Darwin wrote to Greville on 12 December 1778. In two further letters to Greville in May and June 1779 he explains how the machine can be used to record facial profiles, discusses whether to patent and market it, sends a twelve-page instruction manual on its uses, and remarks that 'it performs all its functions pretty well'. This was another major invention, fully engineered and practicable, though no one took it up commercially.

In the first of these letters to Greville, Darwin says he is sorry to hear that war is likely—'I hate war!' He goes on: 'What an empire would this have been if Lord Chatham's idea had been followed.' But perhaps the American Revolution was all for the best, he says, because 'Britain would have enslaved mankind, as ancient Rome, and have been at length enslaved themselves'. Realizing that a politician might not like such far-sighted remarks, Darwin ends his letter with: 'I never talked so much politicks in my life before.'[61]

The manuscript of this letter of 12 December 1778 exists in two identical versions: Darwin wrote it with the polygrapher, to show Greville how well the machine performed. The demonstration was most impressive. The copy is better than a modern Xerox print, because the same types of paper and ink are used for the original and the copy, so that it is difficult to tell which is which. This is probably the earliest manuscript of which a perfect mechanical copy exists.

Another of Darwin's inventions, the horizontal windmill, having languished for nearly ten years in limbo, or more probably in the cellar, was brought out, dusted off and perfected in 1779, with the help of Edgeworth and Watt. Early in 1779 Edgeworth had to go to Ireland to settle a lawsuit. This was his first separation from Honora and on his return he found her 'weak, flushed, feverish'. They quickly decided to go to Lichfield. 'Here I consulted my friend, Doctor Darwin, from whose manner I soon perceived that he thought Honora's illness more serious than I had in the least suspected'. Darwin had known Honora as a child, and had always thought she had a tendency to consumption.

The Edgeworths moved into Mr Sneyd's house at Lichfield for the summer. 'Doctor Darwin shewed the most earnest attention to his patient. At times he thought the disease, which came on slowly, might be averted before it had taken root in her constitution, and at others he spoke with so much reserve as to alarm her most sanguine friends.' Edgeworth continues:

I had the utmost reliance on the skill and attention of Doctor Darwin. His enemies, for merit must excite envy, always hinted that he was inclined to try experiments upon such patients, as were disposed to any chronic disease. I had frequent opportunity of knowing this to be false; and, in the treatment of Mrs Edgeworth, he never, without the entire concurrence of her friends, followed any suggestion, even of his own comprehensive and sagacious mind, that was out of the usual line of practice; on the contrary, it was always in the most cautious, I may almost say the most timid manner, that he proposed anything, which he thought beyond the established limits.[62]

Edgeworth encouraged Darwin to finalize his windmill design, and Wedgwood came to discuss it in July. Soon Darwin was busy on further experiments with a model windmill, recorded in his Commonplace Book under the date 6 August 1779. First he tried a naked windmill sail six inches in diameter with the axis horizontal (as in a normal windmill): this turned 875 times in 84 seconds. Then he put it in a square box with the axis vertical, 'an aperture 6 inches high and two sides taken off so as to present one corner to the wind'. Two tries gave 820 revolutions only. Then 'with a board added under the arm to represent the earth', it turned 804 times. 'I think one may safely conclude that air loses nothing in being reflected by unmoved bodies.' He then added wings 'above and below so as to stand diagonally from the corners'. This is not very clear, but the number of rotations increased to '1044–1035'. Then 'a board was added under the arm to represent the friction of the Earth', and 1053 turns were obtained. Finally a cover, 6 inches square, was put on top: this gave 970–965 turns. Darwin concludes, 'N.B. I made all these experiments with great accuracy, such as was quite satisfactory to myself.'[63]

These experiments show that Darwin was prepared to put in more hard work on his windmill, even though he must have spent much effort on it ten years before. Darwin was far-sighted in investigating the ground effect—recently exploited in hovercraft—but there is no sign that he allowed for scale effects: this is not surprising since the Reynolds number now so familiar in wind-tunnel experiments was not defined until the 1890s.

Edgeworth helped Darwin to finish the design, and wrote to Wedgwood on 20 August 1779: 'by several ingeneous contrivances which the Dr proposed and which I subjected to the test of Experience this species of Machinery may be made to exceed any other horizontal wind-mill in the proportion of four to one or perhaps in a yet higher ratio.'[64]

Darwin's windmill was soon installed at Etruria and gave good service in grinding colours for thirteen years, when it was displaced by steam. No detailed drawing survives of the windmill as built for Wedgwood, but it was probably similar to the horizontal windmill Darwin describes in *Phytologia*, though this

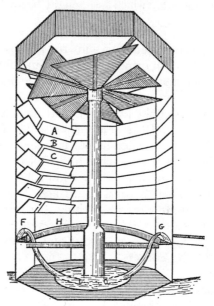

Fig. 8  Horizontal windmill

design (Fig. 8) was for use as a pump to drain morasses or irrigate land a few feet above the water table:

> It consists of a windmill sail placed horizontally like that of a smoak-jack, surrounded by an octagon tower. . . . [The pillars at the 8 corners] are connected together by oblique horizontal boards A, B, C . . . at an angle of about 45° . . . ; the wind as it strikes against any of them, from whatever quarter it comes, is bent upwards and then strikes against the horizontal wind-sail. . . .
>
> At the bottom of the shaft of the wind-sail is placed a centrifugal pump with two arms at F, G. . . .
>
> H is a circular trough to receive the streams of water from F and G, to convey them where required.   (*Phytologia*, Plate VII)

[10]

The windmill was not the only innovation of 1779, for this was
the year when Darwin and Wedgwood began the novel course
of education for their sons, Robert Darwin (who was twelve),
John Wedgwood (twelve) and Josiah junior (nine). The first
sign of action is in February, when Wedgwood engaged John
Warltire to instruct the boys: they 'took the infection very
kindly'. Warltire was one of the most famous of the itinerant
eighteenth-century lecturers on science, highly accomplished
men who partly made up for the absence of science teaching in
schools by giving weekly lectures.

Later in the year Wedgwood decided to remove his three
boys John, Joss and Tom from school at Bolton, where they had
become ill, and to teach them at home. 'I had some talk with Dr
Darwin upon my plan,' Wedgwood wrote to Bentley on 8
November 1779. 'He approv'd of the idea, and said he thought it
a very idle waste of time for any boys intended for trade to learn
latin, as they seldom learnt it to any tolerable degree of perfection, or retain'd what they learnt. Besides they did not want it,
and the time would be much better bestowed in making themselves perfect in french and accounts.'[65]

In November the boys all came to Lichfield, where Darwin
engaged a French prisoner named Potet to teach the language,
and wrote to Wedgwood early in December: 'Your little boys
are very good, and learn french and drawing with avidity—and
I hope you will let them stay, till we write you word we are tired
of them.'[66] The French that Joss learnt in three weeks at
Lichfield so impressed Wedgwood that he engaged Potet for a
year. On 19 December he wrote telling Bentley of his Etruscan
school, and the curriculum—drawing, riding, gardening, fossil-
ing or experimenting, Latin, French, accounts.

In the autumn of 1779 Darwin was also kept busy attending
Wedgwood's youngest daughter, the one-year-old Mary Anne.
She suffered alarming convulsions and paralysis, and Darwin
prescribed electrical treatment: 'Doctor Darwin . . . order'd our
little girl to be electrified two or three times a day on the side
affected, and to be continued for some weeks. We are willing to
flatter our selves that she has received some benefit from
electricity already, as she begins to move her arm and leg a

little.' But a month later the attacks recurred, and Darwin resorted to opium again. Wedgwood reports him as saying: 'All the boasted nostrums only take up time, and as the disease is often of short duration they have gain'd credit which they do not deserve—If they contain opium, they will often relieve; but the common ones are only *animal charcoal*.'[67] Mary Anne recovered, though she remained rather unhealthy.

In the late 1770s Wedgwood was adding another famous article to his repertoire—the portrait medallion.[68] He made more than a thousand of these cameos—the portrait of an age, frozen in enamel. Among the first so to be immortalized was Erasmus Darwin: his medallion, based on the Wright portrait, was produced early in 1780.

Darwin seems to have been quite keen on electrical treatment in the 1770s. On 11 July 1779 his Commonplace Book records the treatment of 'Mrs Stubs', possibly the consort of George Stubbs the painter, who was a close associate of Wedgwood and painted for him a portrait of Erasmus in enamel.[69] Mrs Stubs had a sore throat and 'the greatest number of rotten teeth in the highest degree of decay, that I ever saw in one mouth. I have advised her teeth to be drawn and 10 or 20 electric shocks from a pint or quart phial to be passed through the sore part twice a day for a month.'[70]

For once Darwin records some ailments of his own in the Commonplace Book:

> Aug. 10 1779 . . . this morning about three I waked with much pain, and tumour, and redness about the joint of the toe. I bled immediately to about 10 or 12 ounces, my pulse was not much quicken'd nor much hard. about 4 I took calomel gr. vi. at six this operated, at seven I was very faint, and had a slight chillness and 3 or 4 more stools. At 8 I put aether repeatedly on the tumid and red part, and kept it from evaporating by a piece of oil'd silk, the pain became less. At 9 set out for Burton, with difficulty got into the chaise. At 11 was easier, went on to Aston. . . . About Mar 10 1780 I had a similar fit of less violence . . . and then totally left off all spirituous potation. April 27 1780. Having abstained about six weeks from all spirituous potation, I had another slight attack of the gout.[71]

So it seems that Darwin did not give up alcohol until 1780. Before that he frowned on alcohol but did sometimes drink it, though probably only in the form of table wines, having renounced hard liquor in his early twenties. Abstaining from alcohol kept Darwin free of gout for the next seven years.[72]

[11]

The years 1779–80 were splendidly productive in inventions: only the windmill and polygrapher were practical engineered articles; but three others, though mere sketches, are impressive because they are a century or two ahead of their time. The first sketch shows high-pressure steam directed towards the blades of a multi-bladed turbine wheel, very like the Parsons steam turbine which came into use about a century later. This is elaborated in another drawing which shows the boiler.

Even more advanced is a very rough sketch, without explanation, of what appears to be a rocket motor with hydrogen and oxygen as propellants, though diluted by ordinary air. He shows the hydrogen and oxygen stored in separate containers and being fed into a cylindrical combustion chamber with an exit nozzle at one end, rather like the propellant feed and combustion chamber of a modern rocket. Tsiolkovskii (1903) is usually credited with the idea of the hydrogen-oxygen rocket, and it came into operational use in the late 1960s, in the upper stages of the Saturn rockets that propelled the Apollo spacecraft on their journeys to the moon.

Another idea in the Commonplace Book is two hundred years early—the multi-lens or multi-mirror telescope: 'Suppose twenty glasses, either lenses or concave specula, are so placed as to throw all their images of a certain object on to one focus— there will then be one image with 20 times the brightness that one lens or speculum could produce.'[73] Once the diameter of a telescope mirror exceeds about fifty inches, the cost and difficulty of making it increase enormously as its size increases: that is why the 200-inch telescope at Mount Palomar remained the world's largest for so many years. Darwin's multi-mirror idea is excellent, and the only problem—how to position the mirrors accurately—has now been solved by the use of lasers. The Darwinian design has reached fruition in the shape of a telescope with six mirrors each seventy-two inches in diameter at the Mount Hopkins observatory in Arizona that came into use in 1977.

A fourth invention in the Commonplace Book, dated 13 July 1780, is a most complicated machine for automatically mapping any estate over which the machine was wheeled.[74] Even Darwin doubted whether it would work, and, as far as I know, it never has; but again he was two hundred years ahead of his time with this idea for automated mapping.

[12]

1780 was a year when death brought great changes to Darwin and two of his friends. In the early months of the year Honora Edgeworth was steadily sinking, as Darwin had feared, and she died on 1 May, having enjoyed seven happy years married to Edgeworth. He called her 'the most beloved as a wife, a sister, and a friend, of any person I have ever known'. Before she died, Honora advised her husband to marry her sister, Elizabeth, but at first she and Edgeworth thought they were unsuited to each other. Since Elizabeth was beginning to show symptoms suspiciously like Honora's, Darwin recommended sea-bathing, and in the summer the Sneyds went to Scarborough, taking Edgeworth with them. Acting with his usual rapidity, he married Elizabeth Sneyd on 25 December 1780, after an acrimonious public debate in the Birmingham newspapers between Edgeworth and the Bishop of Lichfield. The Bishop thwarted Edgeworth's first attempt to marry Elizabeth by forbidding any clergyman in his diocese to marry a man to his deceased wife's sister.

Wedgwood continued his private school in 1780 and Darwin made a two-day visit to him early in May. Darwin told him of Honora's death and also asked him to write to Bentley in London, to try to find a publisher for a poem of Anna's, possibly her elegy on Captain Cook.

For the Lunar Society 1780 was a good year. In the previous year Boulton and Watt had been away in Cornwall a great deal, arranging for installation of their engines at the tin mines; Keir acted as manager at Soho in their absence. But in 1780 Boulton and Watt were in Birmingham more often, and, with Edgeworth also at hand, Lunar meetings were probably more regular. In 1780 Keir set up the Tipton Chemical Works, where he began by making lead oxides for sale to glass makers and was soon to develop his process for making soda from salt.

But the event of the year for the Lunar Society was the arrival in Birmingham of one of the greatest experimental chemists of all time, Joseph Priestley. He was appointed minister at the New Meeting House and he came to live in Birmingham in October 1780. The group soon organized a subscription to allow him to start a chemical laboratory, and for the next decade his researches dominated the proceedings: the day of meeting was changed to Monday because he was occupied on Sundays with his religious (some said irreligious) duties.

But 1780 was also the year of the first real Lunar quarrel, between Withering and Darwin. It arose when Darwin published the prize essay and medical dissertation of his son Charles, with a nine-page biographical memoir.[75] The dissertation, on 'retrograde motions of the absorbent vessels', includes an account of five cases treated with digitalis (foxglove): these may have been written by Charles, but seem more likely to have been added by Erasmus. Whoever wrote it, this was the first published account of the therapeutic use of digitalis in heart disease. Withering was furious, because he regarded the discovery as his, and Darwin was naturally even more furious that Withering should attack his dead son, who could not answer back. Since foxglove was a traditional 'country remedy' known even in antiquity and mentioned by Pliny, neither Darwin nor Withering deserves credit for 'discovering' it. Darwin probably did use it, rather unscientifically, in the 1760s when Withering was still a student; but Withering rightly receives credit for scientifically assessing the proper doses, and his *Account of the Foxglove* (1785) remains a classic. After this dispute Withering and Darwin were never friendly again, though they attended Lunar meetings together.

Charles's prize essay was worth publishing: it was an impressive and ingenious performance for its time, though of little interest now. The foreword is a 'covering letter' from Erasmus to Dr Andrew Duncan, 'whose friendship was so dear to the departed Author; and by whose example and incitement he pursued the study of medicine with such uncommon ardor and success.' Darwin refers to his son as 'a youth, who might have been, had Heaven assented, an ornament to medicine, to philosophy, and to mankind!'

In the summer of 1780 Darwin himself was still getting nowhere with Elizabeth Pole, but he was recovering his former *joie de vivre*. In November he wrote a letter on behalf of his Persian cat, Snow Grimalkin, to Anna's tabby, Miss Po Felina. Anna quotes the letter in full, but with dozens of editorial alterations which blunt its bite. Here are some connected excerpts from the original manuscript:

> Dear Miss Pussy,
>     As I sat the other day carelessly basking myself in the sun in my parlour window, and saw you in the opposit window washing your beautiful round face, and elegant brinded ears with your velvet paw; and whisking about with graceful sinuosity your meandring tail; the treacherous porcupine, Cupid, concealing himself behind your tabby beauties, shot one of his too well-aim'd quills, and pierced, Oh cruel fate! my fluttering heart. . . .
>     Many a serenade have I sung under your window, and with the sound of my shrill voice made the whole neighbourhood re-echo, through all its winding lanes and dirty alleys,—all heard me, but my cruel fair one! . . .

Instead you sleep, he says,

> lulled on the lap of your fair mistress and dip with her permission your white whiskers in delicious cream! . . . Permit me this very afternoon to lay at your divine feet the head of an enormous rat, who has even now stain'd my paws with his gore.

He then asks Pussy to sing the following song, and 'I will bring a band of catgut, and catcall, to accompany your mellifluous voice in the chorus':

> Cats I scorn who, sleek and fat,
> Shiver at a Norway-rat . . .
> Rough and hardy, bold and free,
> Be the cat that's made for me.
> He whose nervous paw can take
> My Lady's lapdog by the neck . . . .
>     Deign, most adorable heart, to pur your assent to this request, and believe me with most profound respect your true admirer
>                     Snow Grimalkin[76]

Anna's answer is intolerably long and precious. The tenor of it is that Po Felina could never marry so ferocious a creature, and she gently reproaches him:

O, should cat of Darwin prove
Foe to pity, foe to love!
Cat, that listens day by day,
To mercy's mild and honied lay,
Too surely would the dire disgrace
More deeply brand our future race. [77]

Anna was also busy on more serious poems in 1780: so far her verses had appeared only in periodicals; now her elegy on Captain Cook was about to be published, and it set her on the road to the fame she was to enjoy in the late 1780s. But Edgeworth told Walter Scott it was not entirely her own work:

> Miss Seward's ode to Captain Cook stands deservedly high in the public opinion. Now, to my certain knowledge, most of the passages, which have been selected in the various reviews of that work, were written by Dr Darwin. Indeed they bear such strong internal marks of the Doctor's style of composition that they may easily be distinguished by any reader who will take the trouble to select them. I remember them distinctly to have been his, and to have read them aloud before Miss Seward and Doctor Darwin, in presence of Sir Brooke Boothby, who will corroborate my assertion. [78]

So here is another instance of Darwin allowing someone else to receive the kudos for his work. Certainly the elegy on Cook often reads like Darwin, for example:

> Now the warm solstice o'er the shining bay,
> Darts from the north its mild meridian ray. . . . [79]

[13]

On 26 November 1780 Wedgwood's partner and great friend, Thomas Bentley, died in London, aged fifty. It was a serious blow to Wedgwood, for they had achieved a rare rapport; Wedgwood entirely relied on his friend to handle the business in London. Wedgwood went to London at once, but Darwin was out when he passed through Lichfield and he left a letter, to which Darwin replied on 29 November:

> Your letter communicating to me the death of your friend, and I beg I may call him mine Mr Bentley, gives me very great concern; and a train of very melancholy ideas succeeds in my mind, unconnected indeed with your loss, but which still at times casts a shadow

over me, which nothing but exertion in business or in acquiring knowledge can remove. This exertion I must recommend to you, as it for a time dispossesses the disagreeable ideas of our loss; and gradually their impression or effect upon us becomes thus weakened, till the traces are scarcely perceptible, and a scar only is left, which reminds us of the past pain of the united wound. . . .[80]

Darwin commends to Wedgwood the letter of Sulpicius to Cicero on the loss of his daughter: 'I think it contains everything which could be said upon the subject.' He concludes glumly by saying, 'I am rather in a situation to demand than to administer consolation.'[81]

This is the gloomiest of Darwin's letters, but we do not have far to look for a possible reason: Colonel Pole, thirty-one years after being 'stormed at by shot and shell' at Minden, died at the age of sixty-three on 27 November 1780, one day after Bentley. Darwin may have gone to Radburn on 28 November, when Wedgwood found him away from home. If so, the visit would not have been a happy one: Darwin would have felt the family grief and he probably also thought Elizabeth would now be snatched from him by some wealthy and dashing young bachelor. But instead the death of Colonel Pole was to open a new chapter in Darwin's own life.

SEVEN

# Radburn

## 1781-1783

THE NEWS of Colonel Pole's death sent the close at Lichfield into a ferment of gossip. Darwin was forty-nine, and rather unattractive to the eye, for he had never been handsome and now he was lame and growing rather fat. Would his attentions to Elizabeth prove to be the pursuit of the unwilling by the unwieldy? Elizabeth had been left £600 per annum by her husband, and her children were also 'amply portioned'; so Darwin soon saw her surrounded by rivals younger, richer and better-looking than himself. Anna followed the state of play with keen interest:

> Mrs Pole . . . had much vivacity and sportive humor, with very engaging frankness of temper and manners. Early in her widowhood she was rallied in a large company upon Dr Darwin's passion for her, and was asked what she would do with her captive philosopher. 'He is not very fond of churches, I believe, and if he would go there for my sake, I shall scarcely follow him. He is too old for me.'— 'Nay, madam, what are fifteen years on the right side?' She replied, with an arch smile, 'I have had so *much* of that right side!'[1]

This remark 'was thought inauspicious to the Doctor's hopes'. What chances would he have against the 'young fox-hunting esquires' and 'dashing militaries' who crowded round her? People thought she was 'playing with the old dog' (Plate 8B). But, against all the odds,

> she took Dr Darwin for her husband. Darwin, never handsome, or personally graceful, with extremely impeded utterance; with hard features on a rough surface; older much in appearance than in reality; lame and clumsy!—and this, when half the wealthy youth of Derbyshire were said to have disputed the prize with him.[2]

But Elizabeth imposed one condition: she had taken a dislike to Lichfield (or possibly just to Anna Seward and her clique?), and 'nothing would induce her to live there'. Darwin was bound to Lichfield by many ties—his medical practice, his botanic garden, his Lunar Society friends and twenty-four years of living there. 'But the philosopher was too much in love to hesitate one moment.'[3] He married Elizabeth Pole on 6 March 1781 and went to live with her at Radburn Hall, four miles west of Derby and twenty miles north-east of Lichfield.

Radburn Hall (Plate 9A) still stands much as it was then, an impressive red-brick mansion with a huge flight of steps up to the door and a triangular monumental frieze across the top of the main front. Built in 1730, it stands in a park of about six hundred acres, at one corner of which lie the church and hamlet of Radbourne (as it is now known). The church has been associated with the Pole family for nearly seven hundred years, and the Chandos-Poles still live at the Hall. (Elizabeth's son Sacheverel Pole took the surname Chandos-Pole in 1807.) Though so near industrial Derby, Radbourne is still rural and peaceful.

Here, in 1781, there is every reason to suppose that Darwin passed his happiest summer for many a year, but of course happiness leaves no written records to identify itself.

When she married Darwin, Elizabeth already had quite a family, comprising her son Sacheverel (eleven) and daughters Elizabeth (ten) and Milly (six); there was also the twenty-four-year-old Edward Pole, Colonel Pole's illegitimate son, who later became rector of Radburn. To these four Erasmus added his daughters Susan and Mary Parker, now aged eight and six respectively, and his son Robert (fourteen). Erasmus junior, now twenty-one and studying law, probably stayed in Lichfield; but he moved to Derby in 1782.

About six weeks after their marriage, Erasmus and Elizabeth travelled to the south of England and made a round of visits. Thomas Day came specially to London to meet them, but unfortunately missed them. Darwin wrote on 16 May 1781 to tell Day about Elizabeth: 'Mrs Darwin and I had long been acquainted with each other; she is possessed of much inoffensive vivacity, with a clear and distinct understanding, and great active benevolence; like myself, she loves the country and retirement, and makes me as happy as my nature is capable of.' Elizabeth, having read this, added: 'Mrs Darwin . . . thinks the Doctor has done her great injustice, as he has left out a principal part of her character, that is, that she loves and esteems her husband.'[4]

## [2]

Darwin's departure to the depths of Derbyshire was a blow to the Lunar Society, for he often provided the fireworks at their meetings by proposing new and outrageous ideas, or tearing old ones to pieces. Fortunately they found new combustible material—Priestley's experiments. But Darwin had a hand in suggesting some of these too.

The first Lunar meeting of 1781 was in January, before Darwin left Lichfield. The invitation came from Watt:

> I beg that you would impress on your memory the idea that you promised to dine with sundry men of learning at my house on Monday next. . . . For your encouragement, there is a new book to cut up; and it is to be determined whether or not heat is a compound of phlogiston and empyreal air, and whether a mirror can reflect the heat of the fire.[5]

Unfortunately Darwin had to tell Watt he could not come:

> You know there is a perpetual war carried on between the devil and all holy men. Sometimes one prevails in an odd skirmish or so, and sometimes the other. Now, you must know this said devil has played me a slippery trick, and, I fear, prevented me from coming to join the holy men at your house, by sending the measles with peripneumony amongst nine beautiful children of Lord Paget's. For I must suppose it is a work of the devil! Surely the Lord could never think of amusing himself by setting nine innocent little animals to cough their hearts up? Pray ask your learned society if this partial evil contributes to any public good? . . . Pray inquire of your philosophers, and rescue me from Manichaeism.

This is typical Lunar banter, which Darwin could reel off so fluently.

But the remainder of Darwin's letter, still flippant in tone, is serious, and indeed historic, for it marks the beginning of the celebrated 'water controversy' which convulsed the scientific world in the 1780s. This is what Darwin said to Watt on 6 January 1781: 'As to material philosophy, I can tell you some secrets in return for yours; viz, that . . . water is composed of aqueous gas, which is displaced from its earth by oil of vitriol.'[6]

In 1781 nearly everyone interested in chemistry believed in the phlogiston theory. Though we now know that, when a substance burns, it combines with oxygen and becomes heavier, the phlogistians believed that a burning substance gave off an elusive effluvium called phlogiston, and they explained the weight increase by supposing that 'fire' had weight. In England most of the chemists, including Priestley and his Lunar friends Watt and Keir, continued to believe in phlogiston until after 1790, though it had already been attacked during the 1770s in France by Lavoisier, who arrived at the correct theory for combustion (but did not succeed in convincing the phlogistians). Water remained a mystery to both groups, however, and was generally considered to be a 'simple element' which could not be decomposed. Darwin's letter was the spark that changed the situation.

The 'secret' which Darwin told Watt now looks like three secrets in one. First, he was saying that water is not an element, but can be decomposed; second, that one of its components is a gas; third, that the gas is hydrogen, generated when sulphuric acid (oil of vitriol) acts on a metal (though 'earth' is more often a mineral). Hydrogen ('inflammable air') had been discovered by Cavendish fifteen years before.

At the time no one realized that Darwin's speculations were correct, and he himself never claimed any credit for the idea. After his letter was discussed at the Lunar meeting, Priestley was soon busy with the hazardous process of using an electric spark to explode a mixture of hydrogen and air in a glass vessel. He found that the glass 'became dewy'—because of the water formed, though he didn't realize this. John Warltire (who was trying to find whether heat had weight) made similar experiments, with copper vessels on Priestley's advice: he found that 'smoke' (actually steam) was expelled after the explosion. Priestley and Warltire told Henry Cavendish of their results later in 1781: he repeated and elaborated their experiments, and showed that 'all the inflammable air and about one fifth of the common air are turned into pure water'. Although his results were widely known in 1783, Cavendish did not publish them until 1784, and his phlogistic explanation of the reaction was unhelpful.

In June 1783 Charles Blagden, Secretary of the Royal Society, visited Lavoisier and told him of Cavendish's results. Lavoisier at once repeated the experiments and, without mentioning Cavendish, reported to the French Academy that the combustion of inflammable air with oxygen yielded pure water. In November 1783 Lavoisier presented a paper showing that water 'is not really an element but can be decomposed and recombined', and soon afterwards he identified the components as the gases oxygen and 'inflammable air', thus fully elucidating Darwin's secret.

Meanwhile Watt himself, the recipient of Darwin's secret, had not been idle: he had spent his life working with water vapour, and took a fatherly interest in its composition. Early in 1783 he told the Lunar Society his conclusion that 'water is pure air [oxygen] deprived of part of its latent heat and united to phlogiston', and on 26 April Watt wrote a letter to Priestley for communication to the Royal Society, which was seen by Blagden before he visited Lavoisier, but was not then read to the Society.

These are the ingredients of the water controversy, which roused strong feelings for many years. We can easily see why: Lavoisier stepped in at the end and gave the right explanation, but only because he was told by Blagden of Cavendish's results and Watt's hypothesis, facts which he rather perfidiously failed to acknowledge. Watt was the first to produce a semi-correct hypothesis, publicized at the Lunar meeting and written down. Cavendish's explanation was unsatisfactory, but his experiments were crucial and correct; he only made them, however, because he was told about those of Priestley and Warltire. And Priestley began his experiments in response to Darwin's letter to Watt. So Darwin started the chain of events that led to the discovery of the composition of water, and also, in a sense, ended it by teasing his Lunar friends out of their phlogistic rut. He ignored the clouds of phlogiston smoke hanging over the battleground and casually presented the modern view in skittish verse a few years later:

> Nymphs! Your bright squadrons watch with chemic eyes
> The cold-elastic vapours, as they rise;
> With playful force arrest them as they pass,
> And to *pure* AIR betroth the *flaming* GAS . . .
> Whence rills and rivers owe their secret birth,
> And Ocean's hundred arms infold the earth.[7]

[3]

The water controversy has lured us forward, but now we go back to Darwin at Radburn in the autumn of 1781. His second marriage quite altered his way of life: he became much more studious and domesticated, and the social life in the Lunar and Lichfield circles was a thing of the past. The change was drastic, but there are three obvious reasons for it. First, he wanted to be with Elizabeth as much as possible, for he was a man who needed to be married, and he enjoyed the change after ten years as a widower. Second, they were very much 'out in the wilds' at Radburn, too far from Lichfield and Birmingham to join in their social circles; Derby was mainly an industrial town, where Darwin had no close friends. Third, he was now, at the age of fifty, feeling an impulsion to distil the experience of his life into books. The 1760s and 1770s brought out his sociable side, the 1780s and 1790s his scholarly qualities.

The first of his scholarly projects had already been started— the translations from Linnaeus by the Lichfield Botanical Society. Darwin could not count on receiving much help from the other members of the society, Brooke Boothby and Joseph Jackson; so it would not have been surprising if he had conveniently forgotten this daunting task when he left Lichfield. But Darwin was determined to go ahead with the project, and to do the job as thoroughly and perfectly as he could.

'Operation Linnaeus' was in full swing by the autumn of 1781, as Darwin vigorously set about enlisting the advice and interest of as many British botanists as possible. He began by preparing some specimen pages of the translation, and in September he sent these to forty of the country's leading botanists, including the most eminent of all, Sir Joseph Banks, who had just begun his forty-two years as President of the Royal Society. In the first of six letters to Banks, on 13 September 1781, Darwin asks permission to dedicate the work to Banks and solicits comments: 'your opinion will much encourage or retard the progress of the work'.[8] Darwin wrote another very long letter to Banks on 29 September. By then Darwin had received favourable comments from several of the forty botanists, of whom Mr Lightfoot recommended translating Murray's edition of the *Regnum Vegetabilium*, rather than the *Genera Plantarum* as Darwin had intended. Another of the botanists, Mr Crowe of Norwich, encouraged Darwin to try borrowing books from Banks—'his noble spirit would *give* anything'.[9] Darwin then tells Banks about the niceties of the translation: he thinks the English words can be more precise and expressive than the Latin, for example, 'bristle pointed' is better than *cuspidatum*, and 'scollop'd' is better than *repandum*. In the next paragraph Darwin discusses at length whether 'eggshape' should be changed to 'eggshaped', and other similar minutiae, on which he says he will consult Dr Johnson.[10] This is a new Darwin, serious, unbantering, all intent on detail.

Banks made an encouraging reply and, taking the hint from the flattering remark included in Darwin's letter, offered to lend books. Darwin replied on 24 October 1781, thanking him and saying that the Society has translated Elmgren's *Termini*—a list of botanical terms—'which we think of prefixing to the first number'.[11] He then asks to borrow various books, including 'a Murray', which is the one they have decided to translate. Darwin tells Banks he intends to publish the translation in monthly parts and hopes to have one out by Christmas. On 1 November he wrote again, sending Banks the translation of the *Termini* for comment,[12] and on 2 December Darwin approached the book-seller Thomas Cadell: 'Our design is to publish it in monthly numbers, 112 pages in a number, at 2/- each with a few prints.'[13] The whole work will run to about 2500 pages, Darwin estimates. On 23 February 1782 he wrote to ask Banks for the loan of a second copy of Murray and several other botanical books: 'Your known liberality of sentiment, and desire of encouraging every kind of science, is my excuse for asking these favours.'[14] Darwin wrote to Banks again on 17 March returning one of the books, regretting the difficulty of obtaining others, and explaining how he had 'contrived to inspect the absorbent system of the Picris with a colour'd liquor'.[15]

These letters to Banks, though dull after the Lunar banter, are revealing for that very reason. They show a scholarly Darwin, beavering away at Linnaean translation, and being sensibly practical in canvassing botanical opinion before starting on the translation. The letters also reveal Banks's generosity in lending valuable and perhaps irreplaceable books from his private library to assist Darwin's project.

In the end the translation apparently came out in four parts, between 1782 and 1785, and was then published as a two-volume book (with the date 1783) under a lengthy title which may be abbreviated to *A System of Vegetables, according to their classes, orders* . . . translated from the *Systema Vegetabilium* of Linneus by a Botanical Society at Lichfield. Darwin was very shy of personal fame, and, just as he had let Edgeworth take the gold medal for his carriage, so now he credited the book to 'a Botanical Society at Lichfield' rather than 'a hard-working doctor at Radburn'. One swallow may not make a summer, but in this instance one Darwin nearly made a Society.

The *System of Vegetables* is a massive work and is, very appropriately, dedicated to Banks, whose voyage with Cook is praised: 'The rare and excellent example you have given, so honourable to science, by forgoing the more brilliant advantages of birth and fortune, to seek for knowledge through difficulties and dangers, at a period of life when the allurements of pleasure are least resistable . . . justly entitles you to the pre-eminence you enjoy in the philosophical world.'[16] There are grateful acknowledgements to thirty-three botanists for their suggestions, and to Dr Johnson, but Withering receives short shrift: 'Dr Withering has given a *Flora Anglica* under the title of *Botanical Arrangements* . . . but has intirely omitted the sexual distinctions, which are essential to the philosophy of the system; and has . . . rendered many parts of his work unintelligible to the latin Botanist.' Darwin's own plan is straightforward: 'We propose to give a literal and accurate translation of the *Systema Vegetabilium* of LINNEUS, which unfolds and describes the whole of his ingenious and elaborate system of vegetation.'[17] Darwin's main problem was to decide whether to translate the Latin names or merely Anglicize them. Today his compromise seems sensible: he kept semi-Latin names for calyx, corol, stamen, pistil and pericarp.

The main text of the book begins with a table defining 674 botanic terms; then, after two alphabetical catalogues of plants, one of English and one of Latin names, come eleven plates executed by the Lichfield artist Edward Stringer. Plate I shows sixty-six forms of leaf, from orbicular, roundish, and egg'd to scollop'd, tooth'd, saw'd—to name but six. The other plates deal in equal detail with the forms of stems, roots, flowers, foliation and the twenty-four classes of the Linnaean system.

After about a hundred pages of these preliminaries we reach

page 1, and the catalogue of plants, 1444 of them in all, divided among the twenty-four classes. The detailed descriptions begin on page 51, with

> 1. CANNA. *Corol.* 6-parted, erect; lip 2-parted, revolute. *Style* lanced, growing to the corol. *Calyx* 3-leaved. . . .

The varieties are then listed. And so it goes on, through the remainder of Volume I and up to page 838 in Volume II, the final entry being *Mucor*, or mould, of which the last variety is *septicus*, unctuous yellow and putrescent. Two more indexes, of genuine and trivial names, bring us to page 897.

Including the preliminary material, *The System of Vegetables* runs to a thousand pages: it is the complete answer to anyone who accuses Darwin of dabbling in too many fields, without much depth. This work of massive scholarship gave him the highest scientific qualifications for his frivolous rehandling of the subject in *The Loves of the Plants*. The translation also pleased the reviewers: the 22-page notice in the *Monthly Review* says its publication 'is a matter of too much consequence in the annals of natural history to be passed over in silence. We therefore congratulate the Lichfield Society, upon the completion of this first part of their labours—labours, arduous, as they appear to be successful.'[18]

[4]

This botanic bonanza did not much affect the ordinary run of life for Darwin at Radburn in 1782. His Commonplace Book records the arrival of the first of his children by Elizabeth, a son Edward: '1782 Jan 31. Mrs Darwin was brought to bed in the morning— the child had a violent purging all the next night.'[19] The purging was brought on through the baby being suckled by a woman of the parish, a practice Darwin normally opposed; but on this occasion he no doubt gave way to Elizabeth's wishes. There is a long account of the treatment of the baby, and his mother, who was also ill. Both were soon well again and Edward, named after Elizabeth's late husband, Edward Sacheverel Pole, grew into quite a healthy though rather overweight young man, who made his career in the Army.

Darwin's first autumn at Radburn convinced him that such an

isolated house was not at all convenient for an active doctor. He had a long journey to nearly every patient, and travelling to and from Radburn was difficult in bad weather, both for him and for the messengers who came to summon him. His house at Lichfield had been on the main road from London to Lancashire, in a town that was a centre of transport, with seventy inns to serve the coaching trade. Radburn was at the other extreme, right out in the country, and even today to be reached only by narrow country roads. So Darwin soon began looking for a house in Derby. The result of the house-hunting emerges from a flood of Lunar banter in a letter to Boulton on 27 January 1782:

> Whether you are dead and breathing inflammable air below; or dephogisticated air above; or whether you continue to crawl upon this miry globe, measuring its surface with your legs instead of compasses, and boring long galleries, as you pass along, through its dense heterogeneous atmosphere. . . .
>
> Now a second purport of this letter is to tell you, that I have bought a large house at Derby, and if it be not inconvenient to you, should be glad if you could repay me the £200 you have of mine. As I shall want money to compleat this purchase.[20]

Boulton was not keen to repay the money and on 26 December 1782 Darwin wrote that he had furnished the house 'which has rather distress'd me for money'.[21] Darwin may have lived in the new house at times in the winter of 1782–3, but the whole family did not make the move until the autumn of 1783, presumably because Elizabeth was reluctant to abandon Radburn; and the return of Darwin's money was delayed even longer, because Boulton was reluctant to pay up.

Darwin's separation from his Lunar friends brought changes. He remained on the best of terms with Boulton, Watt and Keir, but some of the old intimacy faded. Whitehurst had been away in London for more than five years; Priestley he never knew well because he left Lichfield soon after Priestley arrived in Birmingham; and Withering's presence he was glad to miss.

One member had now moved right out of Lunar orbit to lead the simple life—Thomas Day. With his wife Esther, Day had returned to nature, as he always intended, to make a barren plot of land bring forth fruit. He had thought of standing for Parliament in the election at the end of 1780; but to have angled for —or bought—a seat would have compromised his integrity. Darwin wrote jestingly to him on 16 May 1781:

Pray, my good friend, why did not you contribute to the *benevolent*
designs of Providence by *buying* a seat in Parliament? Mankind will
not be *served* without being first *pleased* or tickled. They take the
present pleasure of *getting drunk* with their candidate, as an *earnest*
or proof, that he will contribute to their *future good*; as some men
think the goodness of the Lord to us mortals in this world, his
temporary goodness, is a proof of his future and eternal goodness to us.

Now you wrap up your talent in a *napkin*, and instead of speaking
in the assembly of the nation, and pleading the cause of America and
Africa, you are sowing turnips, in which every farmer can equal or
excel you.[22]

Darwin's last remark was truer than he knew, for Day had
bought Anningsley House at Ottershaw, with two hundred un-
productive acres on the edge of the Surrey heathland near
Woking: 'The soil I have taken in hand, I am convinced, is one
of the most completely barren in England.'[23] After some hesitation, Day finally settled at Anningsley in 1782, and there he
lived until his untimely death seven years later. Darwin
remained on the friendliest of terms with Day: 'I know the
general benevolence of your heart, and your friendly disposition
to me from innumerable instances,'[24] he wrote in 1781. Darwin
and Day probably never met again, but they kept in touch
through Erasmus junior, who visited Day quite often. In his
isolation at Ottershaw, Day found his other friends dropping
away one by one until, apart from the Darwins, he had only
two, Edgeworth and Keir.

Edgeworth remained in London in 1781 after his marriage to
Elizabeth Sneyd, joining in the scientific-literary group that
included Sir Joseph Banks, John Hunter, Sir William Hamilton
and others. In 1782 Edgeworth and Elizabeth left to settle in
Ireland. Distance did nothing to diminish the friendship between Darwin and Edgeworth, and they cooked up several
inventive new schemes by correspondence: the nineteen letters
from Edgeworth to Darwin between 1785 and 1800 that have
survived in manuscript are probably less than half the total.

Darwin's removal to Derbyshire also took him further away
from Wedgwood at Etruria. But again distance was no bar: after
the death of Bentley, Darwin became Wedgwood's closest
friend, and throughout the 1780s there was constant to-and-fro-
ing among their families. Wedgwood was experimenting with
pyrometers to measure high temperatures, and he consulted

Darwin and his other 'chemical friends' about the design of the instruments. One of Darwin's letters to Wedgwood at this time (17 October 1782) shows his continuing sympathy for the American colonists: 'I hope Dr Franklin will live to see peace, to see America recline under her own vine and fig-tree, turning her swords into plough-shares.'[25]

At about the time when Darwin left Lichfield, a new member joined the Lunar Society, Samuel Galton (1753–1832), a Quaker gun-maker with a taste for science. Darwin became quite friendly with the Galton family in the 1780s, not because of the Lunar connection but because Galton's wife needed frequent medical aid and he was wealthy enough not to be deterred by the high charges Darwin made for long medical journeys.

Another relatively new friend, James Hutton the geologist, rarely met Darwin because he lived in Edinburgh. But they kept up a correspondence of Lunar timbre, to judge from a letter in the early 1780s from Hutton, who quizzically discusses the absolute zero of temperature, the connection between light and heat, the temperature of hell and whether the soul can feel it without sense organs.[26]

Darwin made little effort to keep his friendships at Lichfield in good repair. Anna felt the slight, and she retaliated in a letter by describing him as 'that large mass of genius and sarcasm'.

Though he did not regret the loss of Anna's company, Darwin did miss the stimulus of the Lunar meetings, as he told Boulton on 26 December 1782: 'I am here cut off from the milk of science, which flows in such redundant streams from your learned lunations; which, I can assure you, is a very great regret to me. . . . Pray if you think of it, make my devoirs to the learned Insane of your society'.[27]

[5]

Darwin's inventiveness, lacking that Lunar spur, waned in the years 1781–3, and his Commonplace Book has fewer entries. One detailed design, dated 'Radburn, July 13 1781', is a 'steam wheel': this is not a turbine, but rather a pressure-pump. It is a closed container of water into which high-pressure steam is led. The pressure drives the water up a pipe with a valve into a higher open vessel, from which runs a pipe leading to a water-wheel. After turning the wheel, the water drops back into the closed container. The steam pipe has a tap and presumably the operation is intermittent. The device seems a practicable (though probably inefficient) way of obtaining mechanical power from steam on a small scale.

There are two sketches in the Commonplace Book embodying bright ideas for automation in the garden. The first of these is a mini-plough to make trenches for potato planting. The second and more interesting is a 'melonometer, or brazen gardener', an ingenious device for opening the windows of a hotbed frame when the sun shines. The design is basically a see-saw, with four-inch copper globes joined underneath by a long pivoted horizontal tube. One globe is filled with hydrogen and the other with mercury (with a vacuum above the mercury in the top half of the globe). When the sun shines on the globes, the hydrogen expands and pushes the mercury along the tube and up into its globe, thereby overbalancing the see-saw and providing by its weight enough force to open the window. As the hydrogen cools, the process reverses. It is a pity that Darwin never persuaded the world of the advantages of this and similar inventions, for the financial losses due to lack of automation in horticulture have been huge over the centuries, and could have been greatly reduced by simple devices like the melonometer.

In contrast to these useful inventions are several that are trivial or frivolous. There is a 'factitious spider', designed to startle the innocent by moving around on a salver, under the influence of hidden rotating magnets. Still on the 'party game' level, though far more complicated, is a machine for moving chessmen, which occupies two full pages in the Commonplace Book. More practical, though trivial mechanically, is a telescopic candlestick (dated 1 November 1781).

As these examples show, Darwin's designs were becoming more homely: the theme of domestic convenience flows at its strongest in his design for a water closet of modern cut, though rather more automated. Darwin's design has a cistern which is normally kept filled, the water level being regulated by a float-valve. From the cistern, a pipe normally kept closed by a valve takes the water to the basin. The valve is opened, thus flushing the basin, by closing the cover of the basin, and the valve is shut again by the visitor opening the door to leave the room. So Darwin introduces a greater degree of automation than exists in

modern designs. At the bottom of the basin is another valve
(with pivot and counterweight), which swings open under the
weight of the flushing water. Darwin thus fails to include the
modern water-trap, but as if to anticipate this omission, he
writes across the drawing: 'There should be no valve at bottom
but a stink trap.'

[6]

In the wider world of invention, 1783 saw the beginning of a
new era that fired Darwin's imagination—the first hot-air
balloon flights by the Montgolfier brothers. Darwin must have
wondered why he never thought of hot-air balloons himself; he
didn't, but he quickly seized on the possibilities, for he had been
stuck in the mud as much as any man of his time, and the prospect
of mud-free aerial navigation appealed to him immensely. In
*The Loves of the Plants*, which he was now writing, he hailed the
'intrepid' aeronauts:

> So on the shoreless air the intrepid Gaul
> Launch'd the vast concave of his buoyant ball.—
> Journeying on high, the silken castle glides
> Bright as a meteor through the azure tides. . . .
> Silent with upturn'd eyes unbreathing crowds
> Pursue the floating wonder to the clouds. . . .

The 'calm Philosopher' aloft, breathing 'purer gales',

> Sees at his feet the forky lightnings glow,
> And hears innocuous thunders roar below.

Then Darwin lets his enthusiasm run away with him and
specifies, presciently if prematurely, the interplanetary space
flights of the 1970s:

> Rise, great MONGOLFIER! urge thy venturous flight
> High o'er the Moon's pale ice-reflected light;
> High o'er the pearly Star, whose beamy horn
> Hangs in the east, gay harbinger of morn;
> Leave the red eye of Mars on rapid wing,
> Jove's silver guards, and Saturn's crystal ring;
> Leave the fair beams, which, issuing from afar,
> Play with new lustres round the Georgian star. . . .[28]

The 'Georgian star' is the planet Uranus, discovered by William Herschel in 1781 and unlikely to be visited by a space probe before 1981. Though Darwin made no practical advances in ballooning, his ideas ranged from interplanetary fantasies to the earthy suggestion that Edgeworth should use balloons to carry manure up the hills on his muddy estate. Darwin's enthusiasm for balloons was not wasted: it opened his mind to the possibilities of air travel, and led to the lines in *The Botanic Garden* about the flying chariot (already quoted in Chapter 1), which had a great public influence in preparing the way for aeronautics.

[7]

In 1783 Darwin used up some of his still superabundant energy by starting the Philosophical Society of Derby, as he told Boulton on 4 March:

> We have established an infant philosophical Society at Derby, but do not presume to compare it to you well-grown gigantic philosophers at Birmingham. . . . I wish you would bring a party of your Society and hold one Moon at our house. N.B. our Society intend to eclipse the Moon on the 18 of this month, pray don't you counteract our conjurations. I beg to be remember'd to all the Insane at your next meeting.[29]

Susannah Wedgwood wrote to her father on 13 March that 'the Philosophical Club goes on with great spirit, all the ingenious gentlemen in the town belong to it, they meet every saturday night at each others houses'.[30] At one meeting, where non-scientific ladies were present, 'Doctor D——— with his usual politeness made it very agreeable to them by shewing several entertaining experiments adapted to the capacities of young women; one was roasting a tube, which turned round itself.'[31] The initial enthusiasm may have evaporated, however: Darwin told Boulton there were seven members in March, who met weekly, but we hear little more about the Society until sixteen months later, when Darwin gave his inaugural address as president.

Back at Radburn, Elizabeth was expecting the birth of their second child, and on 18 April they had to cancel a visit from the

Wedgwoods, 'as Mrs is confined to her room, though not yet brought to bed, and expects every hour, and the Dr is obliged to go to Ipstoc in Leicestershire early tomorrow morning unless prevented by Mrs Darwin'.[32] The child, Violetta, was born on 23 April 1783 at Radburn Hall. She was the most talented of their children and also the healthiest, 'a joyous and unconventional girl'[33] who married Galton's son Tertius and lived to be ninety.

The Darwins spent the summer at Radburn. Darwin scoffed at the superstition that flaming apparitions in the sky foretell the fall of kings, but his own departure from Radburn was preceded by one of the most spectacular fireballs of the decade, at 9.30 p.m. on 18 August 1783. Shining more brightly than the full moon, it streaked along a line from Edinburgh to Lincoln to Margate, and was observed from the Shetlands in the north to Paris in the south. The many observations sent to the Royal Society were put together by Blagden,[34] who established the track of the fireball and deduced that its height was about fifty-eight miles over England and its speed about twenty miles per second. Darwin reported his own observations in an unpublished letter to the Royal Society:

> At Radbourn-Hall about four miles west from Derby I . . . observed the meteor pass from north-west to north-east, and give out numerous large sparks just before it was conceal'd by the cornice of the corner of the house. This part of the cornice I accurately attended to, and also to the height of my eye against the window-frame: and on the next morning found a line drawn from these two points lay, as nearly as could be easily measured, at an angle of forty-five degrees.
>
> As the four corners of this house lie within a few degrees to the four cardinal points of the compass, the line, along which I look'd, would intersect the course of the meteor, as described by Dr Blagden, nearly as it pass'd over Lincoln; where it was probably vertical. . . . Lincoln is . . . from Radbourn . . . about 58 miles in a straight line; which must have been nearly the height of the meteor in that part of its course; which well coincides with the other estimations mention'd in Dr Blagden's ingenious paper on this subject.[35]

As we would expect, Darwin had the presence of mind to make an accurate observation, which provides useful independent confirmation of Blagden's findings.

Darwin was as busy as ever on his medical work in 1783, as shown by the remark about being 'obliged to go to Ipstoc in Leicestershire', and in September he wrote a careful account of a contagious and deadly disease of horned cattle which was rife in the neighbourhood. This was published in the Derby *Weekly Entertainer* for 29 September 1783. Darwin's advice was to kill and bury any infected cattle when they began to be ill—the same 'slaughter policy' that is followed today for foot-and-mouth disease. Uninfected cattle should not be 'blooded and purged' as was usual, he says: 'Blood-letting and purging are of the worst consequence; and on the contrary, whatever contributes to encrease their strength, makes them less liable to infection.' Good advice: yet, despite this insight into what now seems the obvious, Darwin did not oppose the universal practice of bleeding, purging and weakening human patients.

In the autumn of 1783 the Darwins left Radburn, as planned, and moved into their house in Derby.

# EIGHT

# Derby
## 1784-1787

ABANDONING THE spacious acres of Radburn for the confinement of a town house in Derby was probably a wrench for Elizabeth, but for Erasmus there were compensations. The move helped him in his medical practice and brought him the 'social-scientific' life that fired his inventiveness. At their new home, in Full Street, they still enjoyed a touch of rurality because they had a large garden running down to the river Derwent, which carries nearly all the water from the Peak District and is about a hundred feet wide at Derby. On the far side of the river was an orchard, which Darwin acquired within a few years. Full Street was so called not because it was filled with houses, but because it had been the home of fullers—the textile workers who scoured and cleansed cloth and removed grease, and therefore needed plenty of water. Darwin's house (Plate 9B) was demolished in 1933; its site can be located by going to the police station entrance and walking a hundred yards up Full Street. There is a plaque to Erasmus on the Exeter Bridge nearby.

Derby in the 1780s was a thriving town of about nine thousand inhabitants, owing its prosperity largely to the manufacture of porcelain (Royal Crown Derby), silk and other textiles, with the Derwent providing ample power for the silk mill which amazed visitors and was said to work seventy thousand yards of thread for every revolution of the water-wheel. The famous names of Derby were the Lombes, who had established the silk mill; the Strutts, who manufactured textiles in their mill upstream at Belper, and were allied with Richard Arkwright, whose factory was further upstream at Matlock; William Duesbury, the manufacturer of Crown Derby porcelain; and Joseph Wright the painter, whom Darwin had known since 1770.

The surname Darwin, in the common alternative form
Derwin, probably derives from Derwent, so it was a curious
coincidence that Erasmus should come to live beside the river.
He had shown a liking for it in his Ode five years before:

Derwent, what scenes thy wandering waves behold!
As bursting from their hundred springs they stray,
And down these Vales, in thundering Torrents roll'd,
Seek to the shining East their mazy way![1]

In the poem, he had imagined Eliza might 'bend her graceful
footsteps to your brink': now she would really do so.

## [2]

Though there was plenty of water in the Derwent, Darwin had
to improve the water supply to the house before his family could
move in, as he explains in a paper sent to the Royal Society on 16
July 1784 and published in the *Philosophical Transactions* in 1785:

I send you an account of an artificial spring of water, which I
produced last summer near the side of the river Darwent in Derby.

Near my house was an old well, about one hundred yards from
the river, and about four yards deep, which had been many years
disused on account of the badness of the water. . . . The mouth of
this well was about four feet above the surface of the river; and
the ground, through which it was sunk, consisted of a black, loose,
moist earth, which appeared to have been very lately a morass, and
is now covered with houses built upon piles. At the bottom was
found a bed of red marl, and the spring, which was so strong as to
give up many hogsheads in a day, oozed from between the morass
and the marl. . . .

Having observed that a very copious spring, called Saint Alkmund's well, rose out of the ground about half a mile higher on the
same side of the Darwent, the level of which I knew by the height
of the intervening weir to be about four or five feet above the ground
about my well; and having observed that the higher lands, at the
distance of a mile or two behind these wells, consisted of red marl
like that in the well; I concluded that, if I should bore through this
stratum of marl, I might probably gain a water similar to that of
St. Alkmund's well, and hoped that at the same time it might rise
above the surface of my old well to the level of St. Alkmund's.

With this intent a pump was first put down for the purpose of
more easily keeping dry the bottom of the old well, and a hole about
two and a half inches diameter was then bored about thirteen yards

below the bottom of the well, till some sand was brought up by the auger. A wooden pipe, which was previously cut in a conical form at one end, and armed with an iron ring at the other, was driven into the top of this hole, and stood up about two yards from the bottom of the well, and being surrounded with well-rammed clay, the new water ascended in a small stream through the wooden pipe.

Our next operation was to build a wall of clay against the morassy sides of the well, with a wall of well-bricks internally, up to the top of it. This completely stopped out every drop of the old water; and, on taking out the plug which had been put in the wooden pipe, the new water in two or three days rose up to the top, and flowed over the edges of the well.[2]

Here we see Darwin at his best, solving a pressing practical problem by a bold idea and decisive engineering work which proved the speculation to be correct. His account of the operation could have been as dull as the ditch-water he was faced with; instead his narrative is as clear and flowing as the water he discovered, though he gives all necessary details.

Darwin continues by explaining how, 'for the agreeable purpose of procuring the water at all times quite cold and fresh', he directed 'a pipe of lead, about eight yards long, and three-quarters of an inch diameter' to be fixed in the well so that the water rose up above the rim of the well and provided a stream of water for use in the house. 'The new water has now flowed about twelve months,' he says, giving about twice the original flow of a pure water like that in St Alkmund's well.

Not content with boring through the strata to obtain clear water, Darwin also bores through the strata of ignorance to give the first clear exposition of the principle of the artesian well. First he points out that geological strata are often tilted. 'Many mountains bear incontestable marks of their having been forcibly raised by some power beneath them':

> . . . whoever will inspect, with the eye of a philosopher, the lime-mountain at Breedon, on the edge of Leicestershire, will not hesitate a moment in pronouncing that it has been forcibly elevated by some power beneath it; for it is of a conical form, with the apex cut off, and the strata which compose the central parts of it, and which are found nearly horizontal in the plain, are raised almost perpendicularly, and placed upon their edges, while those on each side decline like the surface of the hill; so that this mountain may well be represented by a bur made by forcing a bodkin through several parallel sheets of paper.

From the bodkin-and-bur model he deduces that the strata lying uppermost near a mountain peak are generally lowest in the contiguous plains. The waters of cold springs on mountains slide between two impervious strata and then

> descend till they find or make themselves an outlet, and will in consequence rise to a level with the part of the mountain where they originated. And hence, if by piercing the earth you gain a spring between the second and third, or third and fourth stratum, it must generally happen that the water from the lowest stratum will rise the highest, if confined in pipes, because it comes originally from a higher part of the country in its vicinity.[3]

He expects that such artesian springs will become stronger as they make themselves a wider channel through soluble materials, and that these older stronger springs will also be purer, since at first they were 'loaded with the soluble impurities of the strata through which they transuded'.

Darwin ends with a plea for the wider use of artesian wells for supplying water to houses, and for irrigation. He does not use the name 'artesian', which was not coined until the 1830s when a well in the Artois region of France gave its name to the breed. It would be more logical to refer to 'darwinian wells'; but custom and long usage have a habit of prevailing over logic.

Darwin's paper, entitled simply 'An account of an artificial spring of water', is a splendid contribution to science. His explanation of the artesian well is among the cleanest and clearest-cut of scientific discoveries—and one of the few to spring directly from a household problem. Darwin's discovery has also been of immense practical value: half of southern England relies on artesian wells for its water supply. Many older wells were artesian, of course, but by chance rather than design: Darwin explained their *raison d'être*.

His own well was commemorated by an iron plaque fixed to the garden wall (and now in the Derby Museum).

[3]

The move to Derby was a new beginning for Erasmus, and 1784 was a busy year: to start with, the Derby Philosophical Society had to be carefully nurtured. Darwin was the president and leading spirit, and his move into Derby allowed him to fire the members with some of his own enthusiasm—including his enthusiasm for balloons. On 17 January 1784 Darwin told Boulton, 'We sent your Society an air-balloon, which was calculated to have fallen in your garden at Soho; but the wicked wind carried to Sir Edward Littleton's.'[4]

On 18 July the members of the Derby Philosophical Society gathered at Darwin's house to hear his presidential address. He spoke about the avenues by which science advances, citing the senses of touch and of vision as leading to the development of arithmetic, geometry and the science of motion. The invention of the alphabet was a crucial advance because it allowed discoveries to be transmitted; and the invention of printing, 'like the Giant with a hundred hands', greatly accelerated the diffusion of knowledge. The printed scientific word has, he says, 'strangled the monstrous births of superstitious ignorance; and scatter'd among the great mass of mankind the happy contagion of science and of truth'.[5] This last phrase sounds strangely over-optimistic today, a relic from a more innocent age. But our sceptical response does not tarnish Darwin's bright and unbounded faith in the power 'of science and of truth'.

Darwin was keen that the Derby Philosophical Society should help in the enlightenment by building up a library, 'which may hold our Society together'. Perhaps, too, 'by our own publications we may add something to the common Heap of knowledge; which I prophesy will never cease to accumulate, so long as the human footstep is seen upon the Earth.'[6] Darwin's emphasis on establishing a library was both natural and admirable: natural because he had found it difficult to obtain books himself; and admirable because the lack of libraries was a serious handicap to scholarship which he did well to combat.

His efforts were successful, and the Society flourished. At its first full session, on 7 August 1784, the Society adopted a printed set of 'Laws or Regulations'[7] covering the dates of meetings and the circulation of books. The meetings were to be at the King's-Head Inn on the first Saturday of every month a t6 p.m., a president and secretary being chosen by majority vote at the two 'annual meetings' in April and October. The entry fee was one guinea and the subscription one guinea a year, with a fine of one shilling for each absence from a meeting ('half-a-crown' for annual meetings).

This income was for purchasing 'books of natural history and philosophy' to be suggested by members and ordered by the president at every meeting, if approved by the members present. The books were to be circulated to members, each being allowed a fortnight's loan (for an octavo volume) and being fined at a rate of 'Two-pence a Day' on overdue loans. The system worked well. A manuscript 'Catalogue and Charging Ledger' for 1786–9 shows the dates of receipt and return by the members of more than a hundred books, while a cash book records the fines for overdue books and absence. In 1786, for example, Darwin was absent on 4 August and 1 September, for which he was fined two shillings, and his fines for overdue books totalled nine shillings.[8] These rules served the Society well for more than fifty years: a set of its rules in 1835 is almost identical,[9] and by then the catalogue of books ran to nearly 1200 volumes.

Though the Derby Philosophical Society was very much Darwin's baby, this Society was not a one-man band but a genuine orchestra. The most helpful member was William Strutt, son of the wealthy manufacturer Jedediah Strutt. There were ten other local members, including Erasmus junior, Robert French, Revd. C. S. Hope and 'Mr Hadley, surgeon'. The fourteen original 'non-resident members' included Brooke Boothby of Ashbourne, Joseph Jackson of Lichfield and Mr Strutt the elder; Robert Bage joined in 1788. The society never became as important as the Manchester Literary and Philosophical Society, of which Darwin was made an honorary member in 1784; but the Derby Society endured for over seventy years, organizing lectures and meetings until 1857, when it was merged with the Derby Museum and Library.[10]

When Darwin moved into Derby there was no clinic for the relief of the sick poor. In 1784 he drew up a circular, relying on fears of smallpox to stimulate a public subscription:

> As the smallpox has already made great ravages in Derby, showing much malignity even at its commencement; and as it is now three years since it was last epidemic in this town, there is great reason to fear that it will become very fatal in the approaching spring, particularly amongst the poor, who want both the knowledge and the assistance necessary for the preservation of their children.[11]

He proposed forming a society (financed by subscriptions of one guinea per annum), so that a room could be hired as a dispensary, where the doctors of the town could give their services free. To disarm criticism, he suggested the prescriptions should be taken in due order to all the town's apothecaries. Finally Darwin expressed the hope that this dispensary 'may prove to be the foundation stone of a future infirmary'. The dispensary, and Darwin's 'Derby Health Service' apparently did materialize soon afterwards, but I have not found any further details and I suspect that Darwin did not receive the support he hoped for.

## [4]

By 1784 Darwin had written much of his poem *The Loves of the Plants*, at least as a first draft, and he began to wonder about publishing it. He was very apprehensive, because physicians who ventured into verse, such as Armstrong and Akenside, usually suffered setbacks in their medical careers.

Still, Darwin did send his poem to the radical publisher Joseph Johnson (1738–1809). Johnson's reply, sent on to Darwin by Henry Fuseli, provoked an unusually cautious letter from Darwin to Johnson on 23 May 1784. After expressing his confidence in Johnson, he states his conditions:

1. I would not have my name affix'd to this work on any account, as I think it would be injurious to me in my medical practice, as it has been to all other physicians who have published poetry.
2. I would not wish to part with the entire copy-right. . . .
I would propose . . . that we publish one edition consisting of 500 copies, at our joint equal expense, and equal profits, and afterwards, if you think proper, to publish another edition of 500 copies. . . .
The above refers to the work only, which you have seen, call'd the *second part* of the botanical garden; for I would not yet bind myself to publish the first part, which I believe will consist of but 400 lines, but which will have 3 or 4 times the quantity of notes, and those of more learned, and newer matter, but half of which are not yet done.[12]

The 'first part' mentioned by Darwin, which grew into *The Economy of Vegetation*, was probably not yet started (apart from the notes), because it eventually ran to 2448 lines, rather than the 400 he predicted. *The Economy of Vegetation* is more mature in style than *The Loves of the Plants*: so the 1784 draft of the latter was probably not very different from the completed poem, and we may conclude that *The Loves of the Plants* was written mainly between 1779 and 1784, as light relief during Darwin's hard labour on the translations from Linnaeus.

Darwin's letter to Joseph Johnson continues:

> If you accept of these proposals, you will please to acquaint Mr Fuseli, who is so kind as to promise some ornament for the work. . . . Also pray send me any *general or particular criticisms* which may have occur'd to you—and particularly if you think it too long, and would wish any part to be omitted, as I am unacquainted with what is like to make a book sell.[13]

Finally, Darwin offers to have the book printed at Lichfield, so that he could correct the press himself. This suggestion was eventually adopted, but the negotiations with Johnson dragged on for three years.

[5]

The move to Derby brought Darwin some new friends, such as William Strutt and other members of the Derby Philosophical Society, and Joseph Wright, who lived nearby. But nobody in Derby could compete with his old Lunar friends.

Boulton had still not repaid the money he owed Darwin, but they continued on good terms. In March 1783 Boulton paid £30 interest, but Darwin had to half-apologize for having bothered him for the principal—'I supposed the income from your Engins would have render'd it not inconvenient to you to return it.'[14] On 17 January 1784 Darwin ventured to ask again: 'If it be not very inconvenient to you to pay me the 200 £ (as you seem'd to say when I had the pleasure of seeing you), it would be very acceptable to me at this time, as I have a sum of money to pay, to compleat a purchase I made here some time ago.'[15] Darwin was not the only friend who found Boulton unwilling to pay up: in 1781 Thomas Day asked him to repay his debt of £1000, but for two years Boulton failed to reply to Day's letters. By 1785 Day was reduced to sarcasm: 'I have been employed in the un-entertaining ceremonial of soliciting for three years what it appears to me I have so good a right to.'[16] In the end he got the money, but his friendship with Boulton was over. Boulton apparently treated the money borrowed from his friends as part of his working capital, rather than a loan to be repaid: the genial

'first manufacturer of England' appears in a new and unflattering
light.

With Wedgwood there were no such problems, and his
friendship with Darwin was growing more scientific because of
Wedgwood's work on pyrometers. In March 1784 Darwin
wrote a long scientific letter to answer Wedgwood's suggestion
that water vapour froze more easily than water. Darwin rightly
challenged this idea but sent an account of Wedgwood's observations to his son Robert, who was now a medical student at
Edinburgh and could ask the opinion of Dr Black. Darwin then
discusses the melting or freezing of ice, snow and water, and
neatly states the property of latent heat of fusion, discovered by
Black in the 1760s: 'Thus ice in freezing gives out heat suddenly,
and in thawing gives out cold suddenly.' This long chemical
letter has a social ending: 'When shall we meet? Our little boy
[Edward] has got the ague, and will not take bark, and Mrs
Darwin is therefore unwilling to leave him, and begs to defer her
journey to Etruria till later in the season. Pray come this way to
London or from London.'17

Darwin wanted Wedgwood to do the visiting, because he
knew very well that Elizabeth was pregnant and that 'later in the
season' would be very late indeed. The baby, born on 24 August
1784, was their second daughter, Emma. As a child she suffered
measles and scarlet fever at the same time, and afterwards she
never enjoyed really good health. But she was remembered by
one of her nieces as 'very beautiful and agreeable'. And what of
her beautiful and agreeable mother, who had now given birth for
three years in succession? Elizabeth was far from being exhausted by 'the frequency of her maternal situation': she cruised
through life and all its problems with an unruffled exuberance,
and it was probably she who finally persuaded the bashful author
Erasmus to 'publish and be damned'. Even the critical Anna
Seward had no fault to find with Elizabeth after three years of
marriage: 'She makes her ponderous spouse a very attached, and
indeed devoted wife.'18

Darwin still visited Lichfield when called by patients of long
standing, and sometimes he looked in on Anna. Now forty-two,
she had won acclaim as a poet for her elegy on Captain Cook
(1781) and her 'Monody' on John André, the former admirer of
Honora Sneyd, who became a hero of the hour in 1780 when he
was shot as a spy by the Americans. In 1784 Anna added to her

reputation with *Louisa*, a poetical novel. She continued to care for her ageing father, sighed after John Saville, and greatly enjoyed being the 'Swan of Lichfield'.

One of Darwin's visits to Anna was in December 1784, and on 23 December Anna wrote to Hayley:

> Dr Darwin called here the other morning. We walked to Mr Saville's garden, accompanied by its owner. Talking about some rare and beautiful plants, Dr Darwin turned to me and asked if I had seen the CALMIA. On my saying *no*, he continued, 'it is a flower of such exquisite beauty, that would make you waste the summer's day in examining it:—you would forget the hour of dinner; all your senses would be absorbed in *one*; you would be all *eye*'. I smiled and asked him to describe it: 'What in the first place was its colour?' 'Precisely that of a seraph's plume'. We laughed, as he intended we should, at the *accuracy* of the description. He told us afterwards he had heard much of the flower but not seen it.[19]

The close at Lichfield has a timeless quality and Darwin probably enjoyed revisiting this haven of stability. But there was one former visitor to the close who would not be there again: Samuel Johnson died on 13 December 1784, after a last visit to Lichfield in July.

[6]

Darwin's mechanical inventiveness, dormant at Radburn, returned at full pressure in 1784. His was no cloistered talent: he needed a social stimulus to spur him to invention. Now he had three spurs: first, he had to secure a pure water supply; second, he had committed himself to starting the Derby Philosophical Society; and third, he had met the Derbyshire textile manufacturers, the Strutts and Arkwright. There are thirty-one full pages in the Commonplace Book belonging to 1784, and thirteen of those pages are devoted to an entirely new interest, spinning machines for use in textile manufacture, with many detailed drawings of what he thought would be improvements in design.

It was fifteen years since Richard Arkwright had patented a 'water-frame' for spinning cotton with rollers powered by water. Joining forces with two other manufacturers, Jedediah Strutt of Derby and Samuel Need of Nottingham, Arkwright had built his fine factory, employing three hundred workers, in the gorge of the Derwent near Matlock,

... where Derwent guides his dusky floods
Through vaulted mountains, and a night of woods.[20]

Arkwright's factory, which is still in business, is seen by historians as the 'take-off point' of the Industrial Revolution. Darwin was fascinated by Arkwright's machinery, and on 26 January 1785 he told Boulton that many improvements had recently been made, 'all which I am master of, and could make more improvements myself'.[21] His mastery is apparent in a detailed note on the subject in *The Loves of the Plants*:

> The cotton-wool is first picked from the pods and seeds by women. It is then carded by *cylindrical cards*, which move against each other, with different velocities. It is taken from these by an *iron-hand* or comb, which has a motion similar to that of scratching, and takes the wool off the cards longitudinally in respect to the fibres or staple, producing a continued line loosely cohering called the *Rove* or *Roving*. This Rove, yet very loosely twisted, is then received or drawn into a *whirling canister*, and is rolled by the centrifugal force in spiral lines within it; being yet too tender for the spindle. It is then passed between *two pairs of rollers*; the second pair moving faster than the first elongate the thread with greater equality, than can be done by the hand; and is then twisted on spoles or bobbins.

Or, if you prefer it versified:

> First with nice eye emerging Naiads cull
> From leathery pods the vegetable wool;
> With wiry teeth *revolving cards* release
> The tangled knots, and smooth the ravell'd fleece;
> Next moves the *iron-hand* with fingers fine,
> Combs the wide card, and forms the eternal line;
> Slow, with soft lips, the *whirling Can* acquires
> The tender skeins, and wraps in rising spires;
> With quicken'd pace *successive rollers* move,
> And these retain, and those extend the *rove*;
> Then fly the spoles, the rapid axles glow,
> And slowly circumvolves the labouring wheel below.[22]

It is easy to write off these lines as 'forced versification', but F. D. Klingender has offered a more fruitful comment, emphasizing the 'tension between content and form, and the engaging charm which is the outcome of that tension',[23] with mischievous transformations between machinery, plants and elemental forces

and, above all, the burning faith in the new technology that
animates Darwin. Such lines were an easy target for parody, 'for
where the faith is lacking, the form becomes ridiculous',[24] and in
*The Loves of the Triangles* Canning and his co-authors parodied
Darwin by describing a roasting spit:

> The spiral *grooves* in smooth meanders flow,
> Drags the long *chain*, the polish'd axles glow,
> While slowly circumvolves the piece of beef below.[25]

Though Darwin's verse is open to parody, his prose description of the cotton spinning is not, and he foresees the development of industrial Lancashire in the nineteenth century when he
predicts that 'the clothing of this small seed [cotton] will
become the principal clothing of mankind. Though animal wool
and silk may be preferable in colder climates, as they are more
imperfect conductors of heat, and are thence a warmer clothing.'[26]

Arkwright's patent was being legally challenged, and he
sought and obtained Darwin's support. What is more, Darwin
asked Boulton and Watt to help, and to be more friendly
towards Arkwright. Darwin wrote to Boulton on 26 January
1785: 'I believe some shyness has existed between you and Mr
Arkwright, but is it not your interest to assist him with your
evidence on his trial? Which also may make good humour
between you, and you make fire-engines for cotton-works in
future.'[27] After some grumbling, Watt agreed to help, and both
Watt and Darwin went to the trouble of travelling to London to
appear as witnesses for Arkwright at the Court of Common
Pleas on 17 February 1785. Arkwright won the verdict; but,
because of a conflict with an earlier decision, the case was
brought before the King's Bench in June, when Watt and
Darwin again travelled to London and testified that the specifica-
tions in the patent were adequate to reconstruct the water-frame.
The verdict went against Arkwright, probably because of doubts
about the originality of the patent. Arkwright was furious, and
there was a good deal of further lobbying for new parliamentary
bills on cotton and wool-spinning: Wedgwood, Arkwright,
Watt and Banks were all involved, but there is no mention of
Darwin, who had probably had more than enough of this con-
tentious, exhausting and irrelevant business, which occupied
him too long in 1785.

[7]

As well as the thirteen pages on spinning machines, the Commonplace Book for 1784 has ten on meteorology. These reveal some
of the ideas about vapours, heat and cold that led to Darwin's
discovery of the main mode of cloud formation. Seven years
before, in 1777, he had written in his Commonplace Book: 'Now
if air be suddenly rarefy'd without the addition of heat, as in
going into an exhausted receiver, or by being pump'd out of it,
cold is produced.'[28] And there is a marginal note: 'Rarefy'd air
attracts heat, condensed air gives it out.' Now, in 1784, he was
making some careful experiments on measuring the drop in
temperature when air is allowed to rush into a vacuum, and
Plate 12B shows the apparatus he used. This was work in
progress towards his classic paper on clouds.

The other meteorological entries for 1784 range widely.
Darwin first discusses atmospheric circulation, suggesting that
hot air rises above the tropics and comes down again at higher
latitudes (an idea that had previously been proposed by Hadley).
There are three pages of discussion on winds and the advantages
of weather control, which served as a draft for the notes to *The
Botanic Garden*, and some tentative discussion of the formation
of eddies near mountains.

In December 1784 Darwin began an 'occasional journal' in the
Commonplace Book, a kind of weather diary with speculations
added. Darwin was over-optimistic in thinking he might be able
to comprehend the vagaries of the weather by intelligent analysis
of his own observations, but he was not to know that our weather
is of a complexity that often baffles even the forecasters of today,
heavily armed with computers and worldwide data. Darwin's
daily entries in his weather diary, like his stocking-frame
designs and plant dictionaries, show him once again working
with the 'nitty-gritty' of the subject he is studying, and again
give the lie to those who have accused him of mere dabbling.

Apart from the spinning and meteorology, the Commonplace
Book for 1784 includes the usual mixture of subjects: medical
notes on melancholia and gastric juices; a design for a machine
to convert circular to reciprocating motion; and a discussion on
the possibility of exploding hydrogen with oxygen to provide
propulsion—the germ of the internal combustion engine, in a

form which is now attracting attention as a promising future
pollution-free engine.

In 1785 the Commonplace Book was not opened so often, and
systematic entries cease early in 1786, though there are occasional remarks written in later, including a number of poems
probably composed some years earlier. The main themes for
1785 are the weather diary and many mechanical designs. These
include another water pump, a machine for sewing silk, three
designs for wooden bridges, a mercury clock (governed by
mercury dripping through an orifice) and a number of designs
for oil lamps, one condemned with 'This is very bad and will not
succeed'—whereupon he promptly draws another. There are also
a few medical entries, including comments on milk in mothers
suffering from jaundice, and an attempt to electrocute parasitic
worms: 'Now he had 20 smart electric shocks passed from the
region of the stomach . . .'[29]

[8]

Arkwright's patent was not the only controversy of 1785: there
was a further skirmish with Withering. Though five years had
now passed, Withering's attack on Darwin's dead son still
rankled as deeply as ever. Darwin probably heard that Withering was at work on a book about the foxglove treatment, and, as
if to show he was not to be intimidated, Darwin wrote to Cadell
on 13 January 1785 asking whether any more copies of his son's
essay and thesis had been sold, 'since if you have disposed of
those I could send you another hundred of them'.[30]

Darwin also wrote a paper entitled 'An Account of the successful Use of Foxglove in some Dropsies, and the Pulmonary
Consumption', and on 14 January 1785 he sent it to the College
of Physicians in London. It was read on 16 March, and published
in the *Medical Transactions* later in the year. The paper, which
runs to thirty pages and does not mention Withering, reports
twenty further cases of dropsy treated with the decoction of
digitalis, prepared by boiling four ounces of fresh green leaves of
foxglove from two pints of water to one pint, and adding to the
strained fluid two ounces of vinous spirit. Darwin claims success
in most of the cases he cites. The medicament did not succeed,
however, with pulmonary consumption, asthma or melancholia.

Darwin concludes: 'Several patients do I now with pain recollect, whom I in vain endeavoured to relieve with squills, emetic tartar, and drastic purges; and who, I am confident, might have been long preserved by the cautious exhibition of *digitalis*.'[31]

After Darwin's paper there is a twenty-page appendix by the eminent physician Sir George Baker, who describes an unsuccessful treatment by digitalis, and mentions that its use may have been known to Pliny. The paper ends with a plaintive footnote: 'While the last pages of this volume were in the press Dr Withering published a large number of cases.' This was Withering's *Account of the Foxglove*, published in the summer of 1785, which inevitably superseded Darwin's paper.

Withering was a neurotic and quarrelsome man, and he was probably nettled by Darwin's paper. So he launched a venomous flank attack. The very favourable review of the Lichfield Society's translation of Linnaeus in the *Monthly Review* for June and July 1785 was written by Dr Samuel Goodenough, a distinguished botanist. In the twenty-two pages of the review he makes one comment on Withering's 'overstrained notions of delicacy'. It was enough. Withering seized the chance to send in a libellous six-page letter to the editor, beginning with a false accusation: 'I either must suppose the reviewer to be in the secret counsels of the Lich Society, or that the Article was written by the Society itself.'[32] Withering then makes a series of almost paranoiac complaints about the Lichfield Society stealing his system of accentuation, upsetting a friend of his who had also intended to translate the *Systema Vegetabilium*, and using his advice without acknowledgement—though in fact the Society (i.e., Darwin) had rejected Withering's bowdlerization of the sexual terms. The editor, Bentley's friend Ralph Griffiths, politely rejected Withering's accusations and assured him that the reviewer was 'indeed a most respectable man'.[33]

Dr Goodenough in his review offered the Lichfield Society 'our warmest wishes for their success' in future publications. Darwin (probably unaware of Withering's letter) responded by starting work on the translation of Linnaeus's *Genera Plantarum*. On 17 August he wrote to Charles Blagden, Secretary of the Royal Society, asking his help in procuring the latest edition, 'as the Lichfield Society intend shortly to publish a translation of the genera plantarum, encouraged by the favourable reception of their translation of the systema vegetabilium.'[34] Presumably

Darwin did obtain the new edition soon after, and he was able to complete the translation within a year or so.


[9]

The problems of Arkwright and Withering created only minor ripples for Darwin, and the real flavour of his life in 1785 is better captured in a bantering letter (dated 18 March) to his boyhood friend at Elston, Richard Dixon. Darwin had advised him to slim, and his letter begins jokily:

> My dear Friend,
>     I am glad you find yourself better by losing 7£—You may say with the Irishman 'you have gained a loss'—but I should not advise you to sink yourself any further.[35]

Darwin then recommends Dixon to get false teeth, preferably 'made of *ivory* instead of the bone of the *seahorse*'. He says he gave the same advice to his brother at Elston (presumably John), 'but I believe he thought it a sin and would not at all listen to me about it'. He also tells Dixon about Mrs Day (*née* Parker), the mother of his daughters Susan and Mary: 'She is got into her new house at No. 21 Prospect Row, Birmingham and has a good-tempered man for her husband and is very happy I believe.'[36] So Dixon knew Miss Parker: possibly she came from Elston. Dixon seems to have been a radical and an unbeliever: Darwin addresses his letter 'Richard Dixon, Citizen', and ends it with: 'Adieu. God bless you if it be possible.' Three months later, on 16 June, when Darwin was in London to give evidence at the King's Bench hearing, he wrote to Dixon suggesting they should meet in London.[37]

Domestically, the year was quieter than usual in one respect, because Elizabeth did not give birth. But it was a close call, for her next child was born on 17 January 1786. On the previous day Elizabeth had fainted when a murderer's bone fell near as she was passing a gibbet. The shock may have speeded the birth, but fortunately the gibbet cast no shadow over the long and adventurous life of the new baby, a second son, Francis. He was to become the best known of Darwin's sons—Sir Francis Sacheverel Darwin, a doctor and an intrepid traveller, who had much in common with his nephew Sir Francis Galton.

Time was not standing still for the growing brood of Darwins and Poles. In 1786 Darwin's daughter Susan Parker was fourteen and Mary was twelve, while Elizabeth's daughters Elizabeth and Milly Pole were sixteen and twelve respectively. Her son Sacheverel, seventeen, was in his last year at Harrow. Then there were the four young Darwins, Edward (four), Violetta (three), Emma (two) and the baby Francis. All in all, there can scarcely have been a dull moment, and at times chaos probably reigned supreme in that full house in Full Street.

Darwin's son Robert fell in with his father's wish that he should become a doctor, though he was not enthusiastic at the idea. He entered the Edinburgh Medical School in 1783, when he was seventeen, and in 1785 Anna Seward reported him to be 'grown to an uncommon height, gay and blooming as a morn of summer'.[38]

Robert's elder brother, Erasmus junior, not nearly so 'gay and blooming', was now twenty-six and working as a solicitor in Derby. He and his father had never quite been on the same wavelength, and the fault lay with his father: it was the one social failure of his life. Apparently Darwin was domineering to the three sons of his first marriage, as was not unusual at that time. But Erasmus junior had his own inner direction, intellectually, and he reacted badly to the pressure, becoming very shy and withdrawn. His father, a man of 'unaffected ease and civility' socially, famous for his sympathy to patients and to friends, and his wide experience of human nature, somehow failed to feel sympathy with his talented but slightly neurotic son, and tried to jolly him out of his shell by force, instead of allowing a natural break-out. While in his teens at Lichfield, the young Erasmus had shown most interest in genealogy, statistics and coin-collecting, and had expressed a wish to become a parson. These were all unworldly pursuits, and his father discouraged them. It is a pity he had the same name as his father—a perpetual reminder that he did not possess the omnitalent attached to the name. Eventually Erasmus junior followed his grandfather and at least one of his uncles in becoming a lawyer. He was not keen on his profession, but he seems to have been reasonably contented. One of his friends was Thomas Day, who was still living retired from the world at Ottershaw: during the 1780s Erasmus junior made a number of long visits to Day at home and also travelled with him several times.

Erasmus senior did not visit Day, nor was he seeing much of his other Lunar friends, apart from Wedgwood (and the brief visit to London with Watt in 1785). But Darwin did write to them, especially to Edgeworth, who was hard at work on his Irish estates and as full of ideas as ever. When Edgeworth was unwell in 1786, Darwin wrote a long and humorous letter against 'vinous potation', because he suspected Edgeworth had fallen in with Irish customs and had been drinking too freely. The letter was burnt, but Maria Edgeworth remembered that he ended it: 'Farewell, my dear friend. God keep you from whiskey —if he can.'[39] The suspicion was groundless, because Edgeworth was famous in Ireland for his temperance. Edgeworth turned the tables by asking Darwin to explain why the Irish, nearly all of whom 'drink intemperately of whiskey-punch', usually live to a ripe age. His reply is not known.

The meetings of the Derby Philosophical Society continued regularly at the King's-Head Inn, though 'vinous potation' was presumably forbidden. Darwin presided at nearly every meeting, but he gave less attention to the Society in 1786–7 because he was working to complete the translation *The Families of Plants*, the final fling of the Lichfield Botanical Society.

At home, Elizabeth was pregnant again in 1787, and the Darwins' third son, John, was born on 5 September. John was one of the non-exuberant Darwins, like his half-brother Erasmus junior, and he became a clergyman, like his uncle John.

Darwin himself remained unimpressed by his great fame as a doctor and continued hard at work as a general practitioner, rather than resting on his laurels or becoming a fashionable doctor in London. In 1787 he was elected to the Medical Society of London, an honour he politely acknowledged in a note dated 22 December. Though such recognition by the medical Establishment was not unwelcome, Darwin valued more the gratitude of the sick poor whom he attended, which on one occasion saved him from robbery by a highwayman, as Charles Darwin recorded:

As the doctor was riding at night on the road to Nottingham a man on horseback passed him, to whom he said good night. As the man soon slackened his pace, Dr. Darwin was forced to pass him, and again spoke, but neither time did the man give any answer. A few nights afterwards a traveller was robbed at nearly the same spot by a man who, from the description, appeared to be the same. It is added that my grandfather out of curiosity visited the robber in prison, who owned that he had intended to rob him, but added: 'I thought it was you, and when you spoke I was sure of it. You saved my life many years ago, and nothing could make me rob you.'[40]

Darwin continued to keep in touch with local medical problems through the dispensary. His own health remained good, but he had another touch of gout in November 1787, severe enough to earn a note in the Commonplace Book now so rarely opened:

Nov. 13 1787, after eating much salt ham, and drinking near a pint of beer, contrary to my custome, having many years totally abstain'd from spirituous drink, I felt a debility at night, and next day had a little gout. The next more, still more on the third. Took 6 grains of calomel, and had but one restless night. The top of the foot, and right toe swell'd considerably.[41]

## [10]

Darwin's years of work on the translations from Linnaeus came to fruition in 1787 with the publication of another two thick volumes, *The Families of Plants, with their natural characters . . .* translated from the last edition of the *Genera Plantarum*. As before, the authorship is attributed to 'a Botanical Society at Lichfield', but Darwin's two sleeping helpers are unlikely to have done more than comment on the text and check the proofs.

Again Darwin's aim is accurate translation, but he found great difficulty in deciding how far to Anglicize the terms and refers to 'the general difficulty of the undertaking, in which almost a new language was to be formed'. As in the earlier book, Darwin chooses to retain the semi-Latin names calyx, corol, and so on, and his choice of 'stamen' and 'pistil' has prevailed over the 'chive' and 'pointal' preferred by Withering. In the preface Darwin criticizes Withering for coining 'uncouth' English botanical names and writes Withering off as a 'pseudo-botanist'.

In *The Families of Plants* the main catalogue runs to 751 pages, but various prefaces and indexes bring the total to near 1000. The format of the main text is best indicated by one of the shortest examples:

13. CALLITRICHE (Fine Hair) . . . Stargrass
    CAL:   none
    COR:   *Petals* two, incurved, pointed, channel'd, opposite

STAM: *Filament* one, long, recurved. *Anther* simple
PIST: *Germ* roundish. *Styles* two, capillary, recurved.
*Stigmas* acute
PER: *Capsule*, roundish, quadrangular, compressed, two-cell'd
SEEDS: solitary, oblong. . . .[42]

And so on, through another 1400 plants.

Little more needs to be said about *The Families of Plants*, except that it shows Darwin's immense capacity for hard work. Even a quick skimming through the pages is fairly exhausting, and I doubt whether anyone in the past century has actually read the book right through. This would be a suitably Mikado-ish punishment for the superficial critics who have dared to call Darwin superficial.

Not so obviously superficial are the many historians who have compared Erasmus Darwin with his grandson Charles and concluded that Erasmus was 'speculative' and Charles 'factual'. 'Charles's virtue, sadly lacking in Erasmus, was a passion for facts'[43] is a typical recent quotation. Superficially the contrast seems acceptable: but anyone who takes the trouble to spend a few hours browsing through the four thick volumes of *The System of Vegetables* and *The Families of Plants* will emerge with a different view. Erasmus also had 'a passion for facts', as Charles Darwin himself remarked: 'From my earliest days I had the strongest desire to collect objects of natural history, and this was certainly innate or spontaneous, being probably inherited from my grandfather. . . .'[44]

By a strange coincidence, 1787 also saw the publication of the *Principia Botanica* written by Robert Darwin, Erasmus's elder brother, an admirable textbook giving 'a concise and easy introduction to the sexual botany of Linnaeus', as the subtitle says. Erasmus recommends his brother's book in the preface to *The Families of Plants*. Rarely if ever can two brothers have produced independently two such weighty and similar botanical tomes in the same year. It is a stunningly effective proof of the passion for scientific classification that ran through the Darwin family in this and later generations.

Darwin summarizes the publication history of his translations from Linnaeus in a letter to Benjamin Franklin on 29 May 1787:

Since I had the pleasure of seeing you, I have removed from Lichfield to Derby, and have superintended a publication of a translation of the botanical works of Linneus, viz. The System of Vegetables in two volumes octavo and the Genera or Families of Plants in 2 vol octavo also. I did this with design to propagate the knowlege of Botany. They are sold to the booksellers at 14/- the System of Vegetables—the Genera will be finished in a month, and will be sold to the booksellers at 12/- I believe. . . . If I thought 20 sets of each were likely to be sold I would send them at 10/- a set of each, that is 20/- for the four volumes . . . as I think they would not be worth reprinting in America, and perhaps 20 sets would be as many as would find purchasers.[45]

## [11]

Returning from *The Families of Plants* to the families of Darwin, we find him giving most attention to his son Robert, who completed his medical studies at Edinburgh in 1786, and in the autumn set up as a doctor in Shrewsbury, though he was only twenty. Erasmus had prepared the ground by writing to his friends in Birmingham asking them to recommend Robert to their friends in the Shrewsbury area, but Robert himself deserves the credit for his success—he had more than fifty patients within six months. Although never really happy as a doctor, Robert was most sympathetic and observant, and extremely successful throughout his sixty years of practice in Shrewsbury. With his own earnings augmented by money from the Wedgwoods via his wife Susannah, Robert left enough money to allow his son Charles to live as a man of private means.

Though nobody called him brilliant, Robert completed his course at Edinburgh and obtained the degree of Doctor of Medicine at the University of Leyden before he was twenty, with a thesis on ocular spectra. The thesis, with appropriate alterations, was published as a thirty-page paper, 'New experiments on the Ocular Spectra of Light' by Robert W. Darwin, in the *Philosophical Transactions* of the Royal Society.[46] The subject of the paper is the image left on the retina after gazing intently at a coloured pattern. For example, if you stare at a circular yellow patch for about a minute, and then cover your eyes, you will see a violet after-image of the same size and shape; if the original is red, the after-image is green; if the original is blue, the after-image is orange.

Robert's paper, recording a long series of experiments on the subject, is dated 1 November 1785 (when Robert was just nineteen); it is well written, in a mature style rather like that of Erasmus. Was Erasmus operating under a filial pseudonym? The suspicion deepens when we find that Robert never wrote another scientific paper: his son Charles, who revered him, says that his father did not have a scientific mind. Of the paper on ocular spectra Charles says: 'I believe he was largely aided in writing it by his father.'[47] Twelve years earlier Erasmus had told Benjamin Franklin about a paper describing 'Experiments on the Colours seen in the closed Eye after having gazed some time on luminous objects'.[48] Presumably Erasmus kept this paper, because he had thought of more experiments, and then, when Robert had to choose a subject for his thesis, took the paper out of the cupboard, helped Robert with the further experiments and the writing up, and let Robert have the credit of being the author. The situation is rather piquant: Erasmus's self-effacement is evident again, but this time coupled with a touch of ruthlessness in pushing his son forward, even at the expense of 'bending the rules'. We can safely treat the paper as being by Erasmus and Robert Darwin jointly, with the inspiration coming from Erasmus.

This paper on ocular spectra is the first systematic investigation of after-images, and it was praised by the chief subsequent workers on the subject, Goethe, Helmholtz and Young. The Darwins' paper also contains what is apparently the first published description of the colour-top, a disc painted with different colours in different sectors: when spun rapidly, it produces one colour, which depends on the individual colours and their proportions on the disc. The Darwins describe how they removed the red sector and found that the spinning disc looked green. The invention of the colour-top is usually attributed to Thomas Young, who showed it in lectures during 1801–2, published in 1807. Yet here it is in 1787, and Samuel Galton had written a paper about it in 1782 (published in 1799). Most probably, Darwin had the idea from Galton[49]—unless Darwin thought of it himself in 1775 and self-effacingly told Galton in 1782.

Soon after the paper on ocular spectra was published, Erasmus decided it would be a good idea to have Robert elected a Fellow of the Royal Society. Erasmus himself had been a Fellow for more than twenty-five years, and Edgeworth, Keir, Boulton, Watt and Wedgwood had all become Fellows between 1781 and 1785. Darwin approached Wedgwood first, on 8 May 1787:

> When I want anything to be done, I look out for a man who has the most business of his own; for if I can prevail on him to undertake it, it is sure to be done soon and well! Hence I apply to you, who have more to do of your own than any other man I have the pleasure to be acquainted with. My son, Dr Robert Waring Darwin, of Shrewsbury, I wish to be a member of the Royal Society, as it would be a feather in his cap, and might encourage him in philosophical pursuits; and I flatter myself he will make an useful member of that ingenious society.[50]

On 21 May, when writing to Jonas Dryander the botanist, Erasmus said much the same, that Fellowship 'might add new Spirit to his industry in philosophical pursuits'.[51] Darwin did not expect his son to be able to walk into the Society without any achievements to display: the paper on ocular spectra was recommendation enough, he thought, as indeed it was by the standards of the 1780s—or would have been if Robert had done the work himself.

As usual, Darwin's efforts were successful. Robert was proposed for election at the age of twenty-one, on 15 November 1787, and his certificate[52] carries an impressive list of eleven signatures, the first four being 'Charles Greville, Josiah Wedgwood, James Watt, Matthew Boulton'. Erasmus himself tactfully refrained from signing the certificate. Robert was duly elected F.R.S. three months later, but he did little for the Royal Society during his subsequent sixty years of Fellowship—except for nurturing his son Charles.

[12]

In the wider world the year 1787 was quiet, the calm before the storm of the French Revolution, the year of Mozart's *Don Giovanni* and *Eine Kleine Nachtmusik*, that swansong of the classical polite society of the eighteenth century. In England the young William Pitt was Prime Minister, but for Darwin the elderly Benjamin Franklin in America was the statesman most worthy of respect. Darwin wrote to Franklin on 29 May 1787, addressing his letter as usual to 'Doctor Franklin, America', and he begins with a flourish:

> Whilst I am writing to a Philosopher and a Friend, I can scarcely forget that I am also writing to the greatest Statesman of the present, or perhaps of any century, who spread the happy contagion of Liberty among his countrymen; and . . . deliver'd them from the house of bondage, and the scourge of oppression.[53]

Darwin never indulged in idle flattery; this was his genuine opinion, and it is quite defensible. Franklin was perhaps foremost among the founding fathers of what is today the world's most powerful state, and no other statesman since can claim so great an achievement. Darwin's letter was written four days after the beginning of the Philadelphia Convention which was to produce the Constitution of the United States. Although eighty, Franklin attended the exhausting debates through the scorching summer months and was instrumental in framing, and persuading the delegates to accept, the Constitution which has now stood the test of time for two hundred years.

'I can with difficulty descend to plain prose, after these sublime ideas', Darwin continues, 'to thank you for your kindness to my son Robert Darwin in France.' Then he tells Franklin about electrical experiments made by his friend Abraham Bennet, curate of Wirksworth, who 'has found out a method of doubling the smallest conceivable quantity of either plus, or minus electricity, till it becomes perceptible to a common electrometer, or increases to a spark'. Darwin explains how Bennet samples atmospheric electricity and doubles it up until it is detectable with the gold-leaf electroscope, Bennet's best-known invention (used in every school physics laboratory), which figures in *The Economy of Vegetation*:

> You bid gold-leaves, in crystal lantherns held,
> Approach attracted, and recede repel'd. [I 345-6]

Among the 'philosophical news' Darwin conveys to Franklin is Herschel's discovery of 'three Volcanoes in the Moon', the bright areas in the dark part of the moon which were the source of Coleridge's 'bright star within the nether tip' of the moon in *The Ancient Mariner* and are now closely studied under the jargon-name of 'transient lunar phenomena'.[54]

After describing the translations from Linnaeus, Darwin ends this his last letter to Franklin with gentle courtesy:

A Line from you at your leizure, only to acquaint me that you continue to possess a tollerable share of health would be very acceptable to, dear Sir with true esteem

your most obed. ser. E. Darwin.[55]

It is a charming conclusion to Darwin's correspondence with the man who 'snatched the lightning from the heavens and their sceptre from tyrants'. Franklin died three years later.

# NINE

# Fame as a Poet
## 1788-1790

DARWIN WAS very doubtful whether to publish his poem *The Loves of the Plants*, so he sent a copy of the manuscript to his oldest and most judicious friend James Keir, who replied on 1 September 1787: 'I return with this your exquisite Poem. . . . I am confirmed in the opinion I always had, that you would have been the first Poet of the kingdom if you had not suppressed your talent.'[1] Everyone Darwin consulted was in favour of publication, so he reluctantly agreed. On 21 February 1788 he wrote to Robert: 'I am printing the 'Loves of the Plants', which I shall not put my name to, tho' it will be known to many. But the addition of my name would seem as if I thought it a work of consequence.'[2]

The reasons for his caution are plain enough: it *was* a frivolous poem, not 'a work of consequence'. He felt that he was on to a certain loser: he would gain nothing if it failed; and if it was a splendid success, he might be written off as a superficial versifier by readers ignorant of the scholarly *System of Vegetables* and *Families of Plants*. His fears were, in the long term, well founded. The reading public creates its own single image of a writer, based on the writer's most popular work: multiple images are bewildering and unacceptable. So Darwin was to be type-cast as a writer of comic-sounding rhyming couplets.

[2]

In 1788 Darwin's image was still scholarly and scientific: his classic paper on adiabatic expansion and the formation of clouds was published in the *Philosophical Transactions* of the Royal Society. The full title is 'Frigorific Experiments on the mechanical Expansion of Air, explaining the Cause of the great Degree of Cold on the Summits of high Mountains, the sudden Condensation of aerial Vapour, and of the perpetual Mutability of atmospheric Heat'.[3]

In this paper Darwin takes two separate steps forward in science, the first in physics, the second in meteorology. First, he recognizes and correctly describes the principle of the adiabatic expansion of a gas; second, he applies the principle to explain how clouds are formed.

A gas expands 'adiabatically' when it is allowed to expand into a region of lower pressure in the absence of any external sources of heat. A familiar example is air let out of a tyre: under pressure inside the tyre the air is generally rather hotter than the ambient air, but it feels cool when it is allowed to escape. Examples of this cooling had often been noted before, but Darwin was the first to propound it as a principle, as Cardwell has shown in his history of thermodynamics in the eighteenth century.[4]

Darwin plunges straight into the subject at the beginning of his paper:

> Having often revolved in my mind the great degree of cold producible by the well known experiments on evaporation; in which, by the expansion of a few drops of ether into vapour, a thermometer may be sunk much below the freezing point; and recollecting at the same time the great quantity of heat which is necessary to evaporate or convert into steam a few ounces of boiling water; I was led to suspect that elastic fluids, when they were mechanically expanded, would attract or absorb heat from the bodies in their vicinity.[5]

He tried several experiments. In the first (with Hutton and Edgeworth to help) he charged an air gun, left it for half an hour to take up room temperature, and then discharged it on to the bulb of a thermometer, which showed a decrease of 2°. The experiment was repeated many times with the same result. Later he placed the thermometer bulb in the exit jet and repeatedly obtained a decrease of about 5°. The second experiment, made with the help of Mr Warltire and 'my very ingenious friend Mr Forester French', extends and confirms the first. In the third experiment Darwin tapped the high-pressure air in the principal pipe of the waterworks that supplied Derby: the escaping air made a thermometer held in it fall by 4°. His fourth piece of evidence is a version of the fountain of Hiero in Hungary.

In this machine the air, in a large vessel, is compressed by a column of water 260 feet high; a stop-cock is then opened, and as the air issues out with great vehemence, and, in consequence of its previous condensation, becomes immediately much expanded, the moisture it contained is not only precipitated, as in the exhausted receiver above-mentioned, but falls down in a shower of snow, with icicles, adhering to the nosel of the cock.

Darwin's use of 'condensation' to mean 'compression' is quite correct, and he coins the word 'devaporate' to describe the formation of liquid droplets from vapour—logically, since it is the opposite of 'evaporate'. Unfortunately, 'condense' has now come to mean the same as Darwin's 'devaporate' ('water was condensing on the walls') yet still retains the meaning 'make denser' (when we condense milk or verbose sentences). In our confusion we should at least salute Darwin's clarity, and it would be better still if we adopted his word 'devaporate'.

Having established that air cools when allowed to expand from a condition of higher pressure to lower, Darwin proceeds to apply the principle to the atmosphere:

When large districts of air from the lower parts of the atmosphere are raised two or three miles high, they become so much expanded by the great diminution of the pressure over them, and thence become so cold, that hail or snow is produced from the precipitated vapour, if they contain any: and as there is, in these high provinces of the atmosphere, nothing else for the expanded air to acquire heat from, after the precipitation of its vapour, the same degree of cold continues, till the air, on descending to the earth, acquires again its former state of condensation and of warmth.

The next section of Darwin's paper is entitled 'The devaporation of aerial moisture'—that is, the formation of clouds:

As heat appears to be the principal cause of evaporation . . . the privation of heat may be esteemed the principal cause of devaporation. . . . When the barometer sinks (from whatever cause not yet understood this may happen), the lower stratum of air becomes expanded by its elasticity, being released from a part of the superincumbent pressure, and, in consequence of its expansion, robs the vapour which it contains of its heat; whence that vapour becomes condensed, and is precipitated in showers.

(Yes, he has nodded, and used 'condensed' to mean 'devaporated' in the last sentence.)

Darwin points out that 'the deduction of a small quantity of heat' can devaporate a whole 'cloud or province of vapour', as happens at the start of thunderstorms, when 'a small black cloud at first appears', and 'in a few minutes the whole heaven is covered with condensing vapour'.

Forward-looking as ever, Darwin concludes his paper with some over-optimistic remarks about the chances of weather control:

> . . . if it should ever be in the power of human ingenuity to govern the course of the winds, which probably depends on some very small causes; by always keeping the under currents of air from the S.W. and the upper currents from the N.E. I suppose the produce and comfort of this part of the world would be doubled at least to its inhabitants, and the discovery would thence be of greater utility than any that has yet occurred in the annals of mankind.[6]

I have quoted Darwin's paper at perhaps excessive length, because it marks his finest achievement in physical science, and because, although of fundamental importance, it receives no mention in the standard histories of science and was unknown to most meteorologists until recently.

[3]

At home Darwin had to contend with a few clouds which cast shadows on his large and growing family. Erasmus junior was quietly pursuing his legal career, but Robert's medical career at Shrewsbury was not all plain sailing: in October 1788 he had a head-on collision with Dr Withering. One of Robert's patients at Wellington, Mrs Houlston, was seen by Withering, who reversed the treatment Robert had prescribed the previous evening, and, although he knew Robert was in the town, did not consult him. Withering wrote to say that he had taken a different view of the case, and thought there was no point in discussing it, since he had no time to spare 'either for the purpose of idle ceremony or useless altercation'.[7] This pointed insult was followed by an exchange of letters which grew increasingly intemperate.

Erasmus was furious that Withering, not content with having attacked his dead son Charles, was now trying to wreck Robert's career. He encouraged Robert to retaliate by publicizing Withering's unfortunate habit of congratulating patients on their recovery the day before they died. This happened in 1781 with Mrs Gresley of Tamworth, in 1785 with Mr Inge of Lichfield (Darwin's early patient) and in 1787 with Mr Francis of Birmingham. On 16 December 1788 Erasmus wrote to Dr Johnstone of Birmingham saying that Robert intended to ask Withering: 'Did not you by the solemn quackery of large serious promises of a cure get the management of this patient [Mr Francis] into your own hands, and did not you, Sir on the night before he died congratulate his son on his perfect recovery?'[8] On 18 January 1789 Darwin wrote to Boulton asking him to confirm that he had said, 'Dr Withering had congratulated Mr Francis of the Moat at Birmingham on the perfect recovery of his father on the day before he died'.[9] But Boulton did not wish to be involved.

In his letter to Johnstone, Darwin also says he had recently 'dined at the Hotel with the philosophical (or lunar) society, and was sorry to see no physician there but Dr Withering. How does this happen? when philosophers are liberal-minded and agreeable; and there are so many ingenious of the faculty at Birmingham.'[10] Apparently Dr Johnstone gave Darwin's letter to Withering, who publicized it. But Darwin was unabashed. It was 'simply a letter of inquiry', he told Boulton on 12 March 1789, 'and Dr W. by shewing it only published his own disgrace. I think Dr Robert Darwin has given him a dressing He will not soon forget.'[11] This 'dressing' took the form of a 45-page pamphlet issued in February 1789 and entitled *Appeal to the Faculty Concerning the case of Mrs Houlston*, in which Robert printed the texts of the seven letters between Withering and himself. The rights and wrongs of this unedifying medical dispute are now impossible to judge, but Robert was right to show he would not be browbeaten.

Fortunately no such problems afflicted the younger children. But Darwin was beginning to be exercised by the need to decide on the future careers of Susan and Mary Parker, who were sixteen and fourteen respectively at the end of 1788. Although they had so far been brought up like his other children, he accepted the convention that they should seek employment, perhaps as governesses, rather than be allowed to lead a genteel unemployed life waiting for a husband, the future to be expected for Elizabeth's daughters Elizabeth and Milly.

At the end of 1788, Erasmus and Elizabeth had five children, Edward (six), Violetta (five), Emma (four), Francis (two) and John (one). Their sixth child, Henry, born on 10 April 1789, died when he was twelve months old: he was their only child to die as a baby. Three months after his death the last of Elizabeth's children, Harriot, was born on 5 July 1790. She grew to be a beautiful girl, like her sister Emma; she started a school at Derby but gave it up when she married at the age of twenty-one.[12] Elizabeth must have been glad to rest from her labours: she had given birth to eleven children, seven of them during her nine years married to Darwin. She was now forty-three, but she was far from exhausted and had another forty-two years of exuberant living ahead.

Erasmus's brothers and sisters were surviving the perils of eighteenth-century life surprisingly well. Though all six were older than Erasmus, only one had so far died—William, in 1783, at the age of fifty-seven. But in April 1789 the sister who had always been closest to Erasmus, Susannah, died aged sixty. After helping Erasmus as housekeeper and fostermother to Robert in the 1770s, Susannah went to live with her sister Ann at Sleaford during the 1780s. She was buried at Elston, and there is a memorial tablet in the church.

Darwin's old friend John Whitehurst died in 1788 at the age of seventy-five, but another absent friend, Edgeworth, was as lively as ever, and apt to send 'short scrawling letters full of questions, which take up one line, and expect me to send you dissertations in return',[13] as Darwin playfully complained on 20 February 1788. The dissertation in this letter describes Darwin's hothouse, which 'has a fire 4 months in a year only . . . is about 82 ft long and 9 ft wide . . . produces abundance of kidney-beans. cucumbers, Melons, and Grapes'. He then gives a diagram showing a lean-to design against a wall twelve feet high, with details of the positions of the hearths, chimneys and plants—though still protesting that he 'cannot write a volume for you to light tapers with'.

The rest of the letter is a series of mixed-up answers to Edgeworth's many questions:

> Mr [Sacheverel] Pole is at Cambridge. Miss Pole at Derby goes to London with Mrs and Miss Wedgewood for some weeks. Miss M. Pole at Cambden-House. Erasmus is indifferent well, and writes law-parchments. Keir makes soap and dictionaries, and such things.[14]

This last cryptic remark is expanded elsewhere in the letter: 'Mr
Keir amuses his vacant hours by mixing oil and alcaline salts
together, to preserve his Majesty's subjects clean and sweet—
and pays 1000 Guineas every six weeks to an animal call'd an
Exciseman.' Of himself Darwin says, 'I drink water *only*, and am
always well'; and of his family, 'We have five young creatures,
3 male, and two female, all tall (and hansome as Mrs Darwin
thinks) the boys strong, the girls less so.' The parting shot is,
'You put fewer words in a line than a lawyer, and fewer lines in
a page. God mend you.'

At about this time, or perhaps earlier, Edgeworth sent
Darwin a 'hygrometer', an ingenious device which crept along a
shelf at a rate dependent on the changes in humidity of the air. A
note to *The Loves of the Plants* (p. 99) describes this wooden
automaton, made by 'that very ingenious Mechanic Philosopher
Mr Edgeworth':

> . . . its back consisted of soft Fir-wood, about an inch square and four
> feet long, made of pieces cut the cross way in respect to the fibres
> of the wood, and glued together; it had two feet before, and two
> behind, which supported the back horizontally; but were placed
> with the extremities, which were armed with sharp points of iron,
> bending backwards. Hence in moist weather the back lengthened
> and the two foremost feet were pushed forwards; in dry weather the
> hinder feet were drawn after; as the obliquity of the points of the
> feet prevented it from receding. And thus in a month or two it
> walked across the room which it inhabited.

Darwin was not to be outdone, and he designed an equally
ingenious device for creeping across a river—a cable-controlled
ferry across the river at the end of his garden, to allow his family
to visit the orchard on the far side. Plate 10A shows a sketch of
the ferry in operation in 1789, drawn later by Francis Darwin,
the child in the boat. Though the winding mechanism is not at
all clear, the ferry seems to have worked well and is another of
Darwin's engineered inventions. Presumably the wires lay on
the river bed when the ferry was not in use.

Darwin's old hobby-horse of carriage design was now much
less frisky, and he confined himself to making minor improvements to the interior, if we believe the critical eye of the ten-
year-old Mary Anne Galton. Darwin made a deep and unfavourable impression on her, and sixty years later, when she
wrote her memoirs, her dislike had not abated. In later life Mary

Anne (Mrs SchimmelPenninck) was a notorious mischief-maker
—'she broke off *eleven* marriages', according to her nephew Sir
Francis Galton. She was also deeply religious and quite unreliable. But her caricature of Darwin is so vivid that it demands
quotation, despite its exaggerations and inconsistencies:

> It was in the autumn of 1788 that the celebrated Dr Darwin first
> came to see my mother. It was in the latter part of the morning that
> a carriage drove up to our door. . . . The front of the carriage within
> was occupied by a receptacle for writing-paper and pencils, likewise
> for a knife, fork and spoon; on one side was a pile of books reaching
> from the floor to nearly the front window of the carriage; on the
> other, a hamper containing fruit and sweetmeats, cream and sugar,
> the greater part of which, however, was demolished during the time
> the carriage traversed the forty miles which separated Derby from
> Barr. We all hastened to the parlour window to see Dr Darwin, of
> whom we had heard so much, and whom I was prepared to honour
> and venerate, in no common degree, as the restorer of my mother's
> health. What then was my astonishment at beholding him as he
> slowly got out of the carriage! His figure was vast and massive, his
> head was almost buried on his shoulders, and he wore a scratch wig,
> as it was then called, tied up in a little bob-tail behind. A habit of
> stammering made the closest attention necessary, in order to under-
> stand what he said. Meanwhile, amidst all this, the doctor's eye was
> deeply sagacious, the most so I think of any eye I remember ever
> to have seen; and I can conceive that no patient consulted Dr
> Darwin who, so far as intelligence was concerned, was not inspired
> with confidence in beholding him; his observation was most keen;
> he constantly detected disease, from his sagacious observation of
> symptoms apparently so slight as to be unobserved by other doctors.
> His horror of fermented liquors, and his belief in the advantages both
> of eating largely, and eating an almost immeasurable abundance of
> sweet things, was well known to all his friends; and we had on this
> occasion, as indeed was the custom whenever he came, a luncheon-
> table set out with hothouse fruits, and West India sweetmeats,
> clotted cream, Stilton cheese, etc. When the whole party were
> settled at table and I had lost the fear that the doctor would speak to
> me, and when, by dint of attention, I could manage to understand
> what he said, I was astonished at his wit, his anecdotes, and most
> entertaining conversation.[15]

These visits to the Galtons enabled Darwin to catch up with
the latest Lunar news, but he must have found it frustrating to
have to visit Birmingham on the days when his patients chose to
be ill, rather than on the days of Lunar meetings. Still, he tried

to keep up his Lunar links. Writing to Watt on 18 November 1788, he says: 'I have some design, if not prevented, of coming to see the next Lunar Meeting—pray acquaint me, whether yourself and Mr Boulton and Dr Priestley are likely to attend it and likewise, what day it will be celebrated upon.' Darwin's friendship with Watt remained close and unclouded throughout his life, and in this letter he shows a tender concern about Watt's health, prescribing Balsam of Canada for his stomach complaint and telling him to 'remember the philosophical experiment Monsr. Rabelais determined to try upon himself for the good of the Public—which was "to try how long an ingenious and agreable man might last, if taken good care of".'[16] Watt took this advice and 'lasted' until well into his eighties, outliving Darwin by seventeen years.

## [4]

In 1788 one of the burning issues of the day was slavery and the slave trade, on which so many British owners of West Indian sugar estates waxed wealthy. The Society for the Abolition of the Slave Trade was campaigning vigorously, led by Wilberforce and Clarkson, but was not to secure any success in the House of Commons for nearly twenty years because the planters' lobby was so strong. But John Newton's book *Thoughts on the Slave Trade* was well received in the country, and there was widespread feeling against slavery. At Birmingham, Priestley, Boulton and Garbett were among those joining in resolutions against the slave trade.

Wedgwood and Darwin went further, by putting their talents into the anti-slavery movement. Wedgwood made the famous medallion of a

... poor fetter'd SLAVE on bended knee
From Britain's sons imploring to be free.[17]

The medallion carried the words 'Am I not a man and a brother'; Darwin included it among the illustrations to *The Botanic Garden*, with the couplet above to go with it. The anti-slavery campaign brought Darwin and Wedgwood closer than ever, and Darwin was always on the alert for propaganda. In February 1789 he told Wedgwood he had been reading Defoe's *Colonel*

*Jacque,* and he suggests reprinting in a journal Defoe's account of the generous spirit of the slaves. On 13 April 1789 he wrote to Wedgwood:

> I have just heard that there are muzzles or gags made at Birmingham for the slaves in our islands. If this be true, and such an instrument could be exhibited by a speaker in the House of Commons, it might have a great effect. Could not one of their long whips or wire tails be also procured and exhibited? But an instrument of torture of our own manufacture would have a greater effect, I dare say.[18]

Darwin felt so strongly about slavery that he made a last-minute addition to *The Loves of the Plants*:

> E'en now in Afric's groves with hideous yell
> Fierce SLAVERY stalks, and slips the dogs of hell;
> From vale to vale the gathering cries rebound,
> And sable nations tremble at the sound   [III 441–4]*

He appeals to Parliament to abolish the trade:

> YE BANDS OF SENATORS! whose suffrage sways
> Britannia's realms, whom either Ind obeys;
> Who right the injured, and reward the brave,
> Stretch your strong arm, for ye have power to save! ...
> Hear him, ye Senates! hear this truth sublime,
> 'HE, WHO ALLOWS OPPRESSION, SHARES THE CRIME.'
>    [III 445–8, 455–6]


[5]


Now at last we come to the event that brought Darwin instant fame as a poet, at the age of fifty-seven: the publication of *The Loves of the Plants* in April 1789. Although his name was not on the title page, it was widely known that he was the author. He was surprised at the poem's success, and not altogether pleased, because of his fear that it would damage his reputation as a serious author.

*The Loves of the Plants* began as a mere versification of Linnaean botany, a didactic poem promising to be deadly dull. Darwin then baked the stodgy mass with plenty of bicarbonate, to produce the lightest of confections; but the instructional theme

---

* Canto and line numbers (in the third edition) are given in brackets after each quotation from *The Loves of the Plants.*

is still there. His aim, he says, is 'to inlist Imagination under the banner of Science', and to induce readers of poetry 'to cultivate the knowledge of Botany . . . that delightful science' by explaining the Linnaean system:

> Linneus has divided the vegetable world into 24 Classes; these Classes into about 120 Orders; these Orders contain about 2000 Families, or Genera; and these Families about 20,000 Species; besides the innumerable Varieties, which the accidents of climate or cultivation have added to these Species.
>
> The Classes are distinguished from each other in this ingenious system, by the number, situation, adhesion, or reciprocal proportion of the males in each flower.

Darwin goes through the twenty-four classes, with English translations: Class 1, *Monandria*, one male, i.e., one stamen per flower; Class 2, *Diandria*, two males; and so on down to Class 13, *Polyandria*, many males; then through other more complex systems, such as Class 17, *Diadelphia*, two brotherhoods (with many stamens united into two companies), down to *Cryptogamia*, clandestine marriage (plants whose flowers are not discernible). He then discusses the Orders, based on the number of females or pistils, and gives diagrams of several examples for each of the twenty-four classes. In the poem the number of males or females is given in italics, for example, '*two* gentle shepherds', and the word *secret* indicates clandestine marriage.

*The Loves of the Plants* was published by Joseph Johnson and printed at Lichfield by John Jackson. Though plagued by misprints and mis-spellings, the book is beautifully printed and laid out, with the verses in very large type (fifteen point) and the footnotes much smaller. The attractive layout, recaptured in the recent Scolar Press reprint of *The Botanic Garden*, contributed to the success of the poem.

So far there is nothing to suggest a best seller, and the first hint comes in the Proem, where Darwin almost defines television, and certainly sees its potential popular appeal:

> Gentle reader!
> Lo, here a CAMERA OBSCURA is presented to thy view, in which are lights and shades dancing on a whited canvas, and magnified into apparent life!—if thou art perfectly at leisure for such trivial amusement, walk in, and view the wonders of my INCHANTED GARDEN.

Whereas Ovid transmuted men and women into trees and flowers, 'I have undertaken by similar art to restore some of them to their original animality'. His descriptions of the flowers should, he says, be looked on as 'diverse little pictures suspended over the chimney of a Lady's dressing-room, *connected only by a slight festoon of ribbons*'.

So the glittering pageant of vegetable sex-life begins, with Darwin keen to tell us

> What Beaux and Beauties crowd the gaudy groves,
> And woo and win their vegetable Loves.   [I 9–10]

These two lines epitomize the whole poem—not only its subject but also its ironical humour. Darwin wallows in irony as he gives intimate details of the sex-life of the humanized vegetables. His curious catalogue of plant behaviour pokes fun at the humans, even if they are too thick to see it. The catalogue begins with *Canna*, or Indian reed, which bears a crimson flower housing one male and one female; so the male virtuously 'plights his nuptial vow' to the solitary female. Next is *Callitriche*, Stargrass, in which one male enjoys two females—

> Thy love, CALLITRICHE, *two* Virgins share,
> Smit with thy starry eye and radiant hair.   [I 45–6]

In *Collinsonia* on the other hand, two males woo one female, who obligingly satisfies them both, while in *Meadia*, American cowslip, '*five* suppliant beaux' attend the 'laughing belle', who

> bows with wanton air,
> Rolls her dark eye, and waves her golden hair.   [I 63–4]

And so the catalogue goes on, often charming, often ridiculous, sometimes witty, sometimes pedestrian, always accurate in its essentials and fanciful in its embellishments, and with footnotes of about the same length as the verses.

Darwin's personalization of the plants was not a gimmick: he was fully committed to the idea that plants feel, though much less keenly than animals. That is why he liked insectivorous, climbing and sensitive plants, which seem 'almost human'. He is particularly keen on two insectivorous plants, *Silene* (catchfly) and *Drosera* (sundew). In each flower of *Silene* three females lie in wait for the insects:

Haste, glittering nations, tenants of the air,
Oh, steer from hence your viewless course afar!
If with soft words, sweet blushes, nods, and smiles,
The *three* dread Syrens lure you to their toils,
Limed by their art in vain you point your stings,
In vain the efforts of your whirring wings!   [I 143–8]

The tiny *Drosera* fascinated Erasmus, as it was to fascinate his grandson Charles, who said: 'I care more about *Drosera* than the origin of all the species in the world.'[19] Erasmus gives the plant a royal fanfare:

Queen of the marsh, imperial DROSERA treads
Rush-fringed banks, and moss-embroider'd beds;
Redundant folds of glossy silk surround
Her slender waist, and trail upon the ground.   [I 231–4]

Two of the five plates in *The Loves of the Plants* are of insectivorous plants, *Dionaea muscipula* (Venus flytrap) with leaves which close 'like the teeth of a spring rat-trap', and *Apocynum androsoemifolium*, 'a kind of dog's bane'. Darwin's note on the latter refers to observations at Elston by his brother Robert, 'who show'd me the plant in flower, July 2d 1788, with a fly thus held fast by the end of its proboscis' (p. 182). Darwin was also attracted by the sensitive plant, mimosa, which shrinks from the touch:

Weak with nice sense, the chaste MIMOSA stands,
From each rude touch withdraws her timid hands . . .
Shuts her sweet eye-lids to approaching night,
And hails with freshen'd charms the rising light.
Veil'd, with gay decency and modest pride,
Slow to the mosque she moves, an eastern bride.
[I 301–2, 307–10]

*The Loves of the Plants* has four cantos, each of over four hundred lines, separated by three interludes, in which Darwin has imaginary conversations with his bookseller. In the first interlude, when asked the difference between poetry and prose, Darwin replies (pp. 47–8):

Next to the measure of the language, the principal distinction appears to me to consist in this: that Poetry admits of but few words expressive of very abstracted ideas, whereas Prose abounds with them. And as our ideas derived from visible objects are more

distinct than those derived from the objects of our other senses, the
words expressive of these ideas belonging to vision make up the
principal part of poetic language. That is, the Poet writes principally
to the eye, the Prose-writer uses more abstracted terms.

Darwin goes on to discuss, rather inconclusively, the relations
between art and poetry.

In the second canto the digressions begin to dominate, and the
catalogue of plants recedes into the background. The first plant,
the Carline thistle, whose plumes drift far in the wind, leads on
to the Montgolfiers in their balloon; flax and cotton provide the
cue for the digression about Arkwright's cotton mills; and
Papyra provokes a digression about writing.

*Menispermum*, or Indian berry, which intoxicates fish, lures
Darwin into his most ludicrous vignette, St Anthony preaching
to the fishes:

> 'To Man's dull ear', He cry'd, 'I call in vain,
> Hear me, ye scaly tenants of the main!'

The 'scaly tenants' duly gather round in 'twinkling squadrons':

> Then kneel'd the hoary Seer, to heaven address'd
> His fiery eyes, and smote his sounding breast;
> 'Bless ye the Lord', with thundering voice he cry'd,
> 'Bless ye the Lord!' the bending shores reply'd;
> The winds and waters caught the sacred word,
> And mingling echoes shouted 'Bless the Lord!'
> The listening shoals the quick contagion feel,
> Pant on the floods, inebriate with their zeal,
> Ope their wide jaws, and bow their slimy heads,
> And dash with frantic fins their foamy beds.    [II  249–50, 257–66]

Venerating the relics of saints was one of the superstitious facets
of Christianity that Darwin most disliked, so his burlesque on St
Anthony is no surprise.

*Papaver*, poppy, evokes a chilling picture of opium addiction,
turning people into death-like lethargy, then rousing them again:

> And now the Sorceress bares her shrivel'd hand,
> And circles thrice in air her ebon wand . . .
> —She waves her wand again!—fresh horrors seize
> Their stiffening limbs, their vital currents freeze;
> By each cold nymph her marble lover lies,
> And iron slumbers seal their glassy eyes.    [II  277–8, 287–90]

The plant cinchona, Peruvian bark, was one of the eighteenth-century doctor's favourite medicines, and from the restoring of health it is a short step to benevolence, which leads to John Howard and his toil in the prisons. When the Spirits of the Good first saw Howard, they

> Mistook a Mortal for an Angel-Guest,
> And ask'd what Seraph-foot the earth imprest.   [II 469–70]

In the second interlude the poet and bookseller discuss the nature of similes and the distinction between the tragic and horrid. This is a prelude to the rather horrid Canto III, in which *Circaea*, Enchanter's Nightshade, is first to darken the scene:

> Pale shoot the stars across the troubled night,
> The tim'rous moon withholds her conscious light;
> Shrill scream the famish'd bats, and shivering owls,
> And loud and long the dog of midnight howls!   [III 11–14]

Two 'imps obscene' arrive to unbar the 'ponderous portals' of a church:

> As through the colour'd glass the moon-beam falls,
> Huge shapeless spectres quiver on the walls;
> Low murmurs creep along the hollow ground,
> And to each step the pealing ailes resound.   [III 23–6]

It is an impressive picture, which Keats remembered in the *Eve of St Agnes*.
'Seductive Vitis', the Vine, then proffers her alcoholic poison:

> 'Drink deep', she carols, as she waves in air
> The mantling goblet, 'and forget your care'. . . .
> Fell Gout peeps grinning through the flimsy scene,
> And bloated Dropsy pants behind unseen.   [III 363–4, 367–8]

Darwin suggests in a note that the fire Prometheus stole was really fiery spirits, the 'vulture perpetually gnawing his liver' being 'so apt an allegory for the effects of drinking spirituous liquors'.

Darwin next refers to cassia and other American plants whose seeds are carried by the Gulf Stream to the Norwegian coast, 'frequently in so recent a state as to vegetate, when properly taken care of'—

> Soft breathes the gale, the current gently moves,
> And bears to Norway's coasts her infant-loves.   [III 419–20]

In the third interlude Darwin explains to the bookseller the close resemblance between painting and poetry—or at least Darwinian poetry, in which the appeal is mainly to the eye. Asked to compare music and poetry, Darwin points to the similarities between metre and musical tempo, and dissects various verses into crotchets and quavers.

Pleasantry is the dominant theme of the final canto: the 'tuneful Goddess' plays 'softer chords' and 'sweeter tones'. The oat, in the form of the oaten reed, the first musical instrument, sounds with such a 'silver tongue' that all nature listens:

> From ozier bowers the brooding Halcyons peep,
> The Swans pursuing cleave the glassy deep,
> On hovering wings the wondering Reed-larks play,
> And silent Bitterns listen to the lay.   [IV 95–8]

This delightful image so impressed Shelley that he copied it in his *Epipsychidion*.

In the plant *Trapa*, which grows partly under water and partly above, four males dance round the single female:

> Above, below, they wheel, retreat, advance,
> In air and ocean weave the mazy dance;
> Bow their quick heads, and point their diamond eyes,
> And twinkle to the sun with ever-changing dyes.   [IV 213–20]

Take a quick step sideways in this fishy-comic dance and you arrive at Lewis Carroll's lobster quadrille.

In the mobile plant *Hedysarum gyrans* ten males admire one female:

> Clasp'd round her ivory neck with studs of gold
> Flows her thin vest in many a gauzy fold;
> O'er her light limbs the dim transparence plays,
> And the fair form, it seems to hide, betrays.   [IV 341–4]

For his final fling Darwin chooses the plant *Adonis*, with many males and females living together in one flower. He shows them going to the shrine of 'licentious Hymen', attended by 'light Joys on twinkling feet', while 'exulting Cupids' pepper them with 'promiscuous arrows'. Darwin compared them with the society of the Areoi on the island of Tahiti, 'about 100 males and females who form one promiscuous marriage':

Thus where pleased VENUS, in the southern main,
Sheds all her smiles on Otaheite's plain,
Wide o'er the isle her silken net she draws,
And the Loves laugh at all but Nature's laws.   [IV 487–90]

It is a happy finale, and subtly subversive too.

## [6]

Today we may either admire *The Loves of the Plants* as novel and
lively humorous verse or write it off as a rather tedious didactic
poem in the tradition of Baker's *The Universe*, Brooke's *Universal
Beauty* and Mallet's *The Excursion*. But in 1789 the poem
delighted everyone, young and old, male and female. The reviews were glowing, and so was Horace Walpole, usually a
difficult man to please: 'You will agree with me that the author
is a great poet. . . . I send you the most delicious poem upon
earth . . . all is the most lovely poetry. . . . The *Botanic Garden*,
the *Arabian Nights* and King's Chapel are above all rules.'[20]
William Cowper in his eight-page review says the poetry is 'of
a very superior cast', and commends Darwin for showing 'so
much versatility of genius that we could not but admire the grace
and ease, and the playfulness of fancy.'[21] Edgeworth was even
more enthusiastic when he wrote on 14 April 1790: 'I have felt
such continued, such increasing admiration in reading the Loves
of the Plants, that I dare not express any of my Enthusiasm, lest
you should suspect me of that tendency to Exaggeration, which
you used to charge me with. . . . It has silenced for ever the
complaints of poets, who lament that Homer, Milton, Shakespeare and a few Classics had left nothing new to describe.'[22]

Anna Seward might be expected to find fault with *The Loves of
the Plants*: but no, she praises it, and her hundred-page analysis
is the best full critique that has been written. The poem is very
frolicsome, she says, and its sexiness is acceptable because 'the
sexual nature of plants' has been proved, and 'the female form is
always attractive from the poetic pencil of Darwin'. She hands
out many bouquets: 'Creative imagination, the high and
peculiar province of the genuine Poet, has few more beautiful
creations.' But her close criticism of the verse is often severe,
and she tears to pieces some individual lines and images. She

sums up the poem as 'a brilliant little world of Genius and its creations',[23] and in a letter she says: 'Surely his genius is strong, glowing and original; his numbers grand, rich and harmonious.'[24] According to Anna, the second part of *The Botanic Garden* was published first because it would be more congenial to the superficial reader, while still strong enough 'to entertain and charm the enlightened and judicious few'.[25] The former, 'not liking to possess the poem incomplete' would later buy Part I, while the 'judicious few' would buy it because it was better than Part II.

## [7]

*The Loves of the Plants* was not Darwin's only publication in 1789: he contributed a twenty-page essay on the waters of Buxton and Matlock to Pilkington's *View of the Present State of Derbyshire*. Darwin believes that the warmth of the springs at Buxton and Matlock is due not to chemical action, as was often suggested, but to heat deep in the Earth. He gives several reasons for this correct opinion: the heat has been constant for centuries; when cold springs dry up, these hot ones do not and hence have deep sources; the limestone has many perpendicular clefts; volcanoes prove the existence of 'central fires'. In October 1780 he went with Edgeworth, he says, for 'the opening of two of the springs of Matlock about 200 yards above their usual place of appearance. We found them both at these new openings about one degree of heat, or somewhat more, warmer than at the places of their usual exit.'[26]

Darwin discusses vapours condensing and sliding between strata, as in his paper on the artesian well, and says his own well has continued to flow for five years, increasing 'in quantity and perhaps in purity'. Darwin emphasizes that the Derbyshire caverns are very ancient, but he did not appreciate that they were formed by water erosion: he thought they were caused by the Earth opening its jaws and failing to shut them exactly.

Darwin's interest in geology in the late 1780s was accompanied by a quickening of his interest in chemistry, a result of his conversion to the new French heresy of oxygen. Darwin's strength of mind appears very clearly in his rejection of phlogiston. His oldest friend, James Keir, a 'mighty chemist' and a pioneer of the chemical industry, was deeply committed to the phlogiston theory; and so was his illustrious friend James Watt. Above all, Joseph Priestley, whom Darwin rightly respected as the greatest experimental chemist of the day, was rigidly phlogistic to the end of his life. Darwin was a sociable man, not a hermit, and a doctor, not a chemist; so the psychological pressure on him to continue believing in phlogiston could scarcely have been greater. If he changed, he would be regarded as 'deserting to the enemy camp' by three respected friends who knew more about chemistry than he did. But Darwin had little hesitation: all through his life his letters show that for him the pursuit of scientific truth was paramount. If friendships suffered as a result, that was a setback to be cheerfully borne, and minimized by diplomatic banter.

Darwin's abandonment of phlogiston was a gradual process, which began with a few doubts in the early 1780s and was complete by 1788, as is shown by his spirited letter to Watt on 18 November:

> Pray read the 40 first pages of the Introduction to Fourcroy's Elements, and tell me if the facts are in general true—if they be, the theory holds them nicely together.
>
> When steam is passed through red hot iron scrapings, if the water be not decomposed, whence comes the vital air, which united to the iron?—does the water vanish, or is it annihilated? Pray explain this experiment.

Although Darwin makes his own view plain enough, he tactfully admits that the question may not be settled:

> I shall wait with patience to see this great dispute decided, which involves so great a part of the theory of chemistry—and thank the Lord, that chemical Faith is not propagated by fire and sword. At present I am inclined to the heterodox side of this question.[27]

Darwin was just as tactful to Keir, whose devotion to phlogiston was stronger than Watt's. When Darwin read the preface of Keir's dictionary of chemistry in 1789, he politely commented: 'You have successfully combated the new nomenclature, and strangled him in the cradle before he has learnt to speak.'[28]

It would be tedious to go over these long-forgotten arguments, and fortunately Keir himself provides a ready-made summary in a letter to Darwin on 15 March 1790: 'I am much obliged to you for your advice to me to be converted to the true faith in chemistry. . . . You are such an infidel in religion that you cannot believe in transubstantiation, yet you can believe that apples and pears, hay and oats, bread and wine, sugar, oil, and vinegar, are nothing but water and charcoal, and that it is a great improvement in language to call all these things by one word, oxyde hydro-carbonneux.'[29] There is a real sting in the tail here, and it is Keir who is stung, for he defines quite accurately—though only for the purpose of ridicule—what are now known as carbohydrates. Indeed Keir might easily have written 'carbohydrate' (first used in 1869, according to the *O.E.D.*) instead of 'oxyde hydro-carbonneux'.

Darwin's early conversion to 'the true faith in chemistry' allowed him to adopt the new chemistry in *The Economy of Vegetation* and greatly enhanced the appeal of the poem. If it had been written ten years earlier it would have been phlogisticated, and less acceptable today.

## [8]

Darwin's multiple interests, and his loyalty to old friends, come out in his letters of 1789–90 to Wedgwood, Boulton, Watt, Keir and Edgeworth. There were probably also some letters to Hutton, but none has survived: Darwin refers to Hutton twelve times in *The Economy of Vegetation*.

Darwin's first letter to Wedgwood, on 22 February 1789, accompanies a pre-publication copy of *The Loves of the Plants* 'of which I am the *supposed*, not the *avow'd* author. After you have read the page on the Slave-trade 117 and the eulogy on Mr Howard's Humanity in visiting prisons p. 80—I do not insist on your reading any more.'[30] But Darwin does ask Wedgwood to help 'to get it reviewed early; as that I am told may influence the sale of it'. In his reply (7 March) Wedgwood offers 'a thousand thanks for the pleasure and instruction I am receiving in the perusal of these beautiful and charming Cantos'.[31]

One of Wedgwood's many projects, in which Darwin helped, was to take some clay brought back from Botany Bay by Sir Joseph Banks and use it to make medallions of Hope attended by Peace, Art and Labour at Sydney Cove, 'to show the inhabitants what their materials would do, and to encourage their industry',

as Darwin put it.[32] The medallion was to appear in a book about
Botany Bay, and in June Darwin sent Wedgwood some lines of
verse to go with the cameo. On 28 June Wedgwood wrote to say
how much he admired the verses, and we can still admire them
today for their prophetic vision of modern Sydney, including the
bridge:

> *There* shall broad streets their stately walls extend,
> The circus widen, and the crescent bend. . . .
> *There* the proud arch, Colossus-like, bestride
> Yon glittering streams, and bound the chafing tide;
> Embellish'd villas crown the landscape-scene,
> Farms wave with gold, and orchards blush between.—
> *There* shall tall spires, and dome-capt towers ascend,
> And piers and quays their massy structures blend. . . .[33]

Darwin wanted to add an extra couplet,

> Here future Newtons shall explore the skies,
> Here future Priestleys, future Wedgewoods rise.[34]

But Wedgwood scotched this idea by saying that 'Wedgewoods'
should be changed to 'Darwins'.

Wedgwood was very pleased with the verses about pottery
written for *The Economy of Vegetation*, and called Darwin a
'powerful *magician*, who can work wonders,—who can liquefy
the granite, and still harder flint, into the softest poetic
numbers'.[35] A second edition of *The Loves of the Plants* was being
prepared, to meet the demand, and Wedgwood's next letter, in
mid-July, shows how much trouble he took over the engravings,
particularly the Cupid at the end of the Proem, which is much
better than Stringer's rather ugly figure in the first edition.
Then Wedgwood changes gear and turns to the events of 14
July: 'I know you will rejoice with me in the glorious revolution
which has taken place in France. The politicians tell me that as a
manufacturer I shall be ruined if France has her liberty, but I am
willing to take my chance in that respect, nor do I yet see that
the happiness of one nation includes in it the misery of its next
neighbour.'[36]

In October 1789, after three years of trials, Wedgwood at last
succeeded in making his first perfect copy of the Portland Vase.
It was immediately sent to Derby for Darwin to see, with strict
injunctions that he should show it to no one outside his family.
But he could not resist the temptation: 'I have disobeyed you,

and shown your vase to two or three, but they were philosophers, not cognoscenti. How can I possess such a jewel, and not
communicate the pleasure to a few Derby philosophers?'[37]
Darwin had his own ideas about the meaning of the figures on
the vase, and soon Wedgwood was thanking him 'for a page of
charming poetry, and many pages of very ingenious and learned
notes, which I have read over and over with great pleasure, and
could not do so without much improvement'.[38] Darwin believed
the figures on the Vase represent a ritual of death and rebirth
deriving from the Eleusinian mysteries, and he expounds this
view in convincing detail in his note, printed in *The Economy of
Vegetation*, with engravings of the Vase. Many explanations of
the scenes on the vase have been suggested, but Darwin's is still
regarded as the best.[39] His note goes with a tribute in verse to
Wedgwood:

> Whether, O Friend of Art! your gems derive
> Fine forms from Greece, and fabled Gods revive;
> Or bid from modern life the Portrait breathe,
> And bind round Honour's brow the laurel wreath;
> Buoyant shall sail, with Fame's historic page,
> Each fair medallion o'er the wrecks of age.    [II 341–6]

Although Wedgwood was now his closest friend, Darwin's
thirty-year-old friendship with Boulton was still flourishing, and
four of his letters to Boulton in 1789 have survived. The first, on
18 January, is mainly about Robert's dispute with Withering, but
Darwin also says: 'I often lament being at so great a distance
from you—your fire-engine for coining money gave me great
pleasure for a week after I saw it—and the centrifugal way of
regulating the fire.'[40] His next letter (12 March) is even more
friendly: 'I was much obliged to you for your kind letter from
London, which breath'd the true spirit of our long and antient
friendship; which I dare say will not cease on either side, till the
earthy tenement of our minds becomes decomposed.'[41]

The other two letters (22 October and 31 December 1789)
ask Boulton for information on the fire engines and coining
machines Darwin so much admired. Boulton's reply was the
basis of a long note in Canto I of *The Economy of Vegetation*:

> Mr Boulton has lately constructed at Soho near Birmingham, a most
> magnificent apparatus for Coining, which has cost him some
> thousand pounds; the whole machinery is moved by an improved

steam-engine, which rolls the copper for half-pence finer than copper has before been rolled for the purpose of making money.[42]

The excellence of the workmanship and the power of the machinery 'must totally prevent clandestine imitation'. Boulton deserved the country's thanks, Darwin says, not only for at last providing Britain with a secure currency, but also for abolishing at a stroke the crime of counterfeiting and saving 'many lives from the hand of the executioner'. It is characteristic of Darwin that he should seize on this humane by-product of Boulton's work.

Darwin versifies the coining machine with his usual enthusiasm:

> With iron lips his rapid rollers seize
> The lengthening bars, in thin expansion squeeze;
> Descending screws with ponderous fly-wheels wound
> The tawny plates, the new medallions round;
> Hard dyes of steel the cupreous circles cramp,
> And with quick fall his massy hammers stamp.
> The Harp, the Lily and the Lion join,
> And GEORGE and BRITAIN guard the sterling coin.[43]

If it had to be said in verse, could it have been done better? But these verses, like those on the cotton mills, need all Darwin's burning faith to hold them together.

Darwin wrote to Watt on a similar quest on 20 November 1789, saying he would include a note on steam engines in *The Economy of Vegetation* 'if you will at a leisure hour tell me what the world may know about your *improvements* of the steam-engine'.[44] Watt replied on 24 November: 'I know not how steam-engines come among the plants; I cannot find them in the Systema Naturae, by which I should conclude that they are neither plants, animals, nor fossils.'[45] Despite these doubts, he sent an account of his work, which Darwin utilized in his long note on the history of steam engines in *The Economy of Vegetation*.

There is also a short footnote on steam engines in the poem. After explaining how Watt and Boulton advanced the design, Darwin looks to the future:

> There is reason to believe it may in time be applied to the rowing of barges, and the moving of carriages along the road. As the specific levity of air is too great for the support of great burthens by balloons, there seems no probable method of flying conveniently

but by the power of steam, or some other explosive material;
which another half century may probably discover. [46]

Darwin's prophecy was right, though the internal combustion
engine took a whole century rather than a half century to
develop. This note is near the lines about flight quoted in
Chapter 1. Darwin foresees other uses for the 'Giant-Power' of
the steam engine, in providing piped water supplies and in
driving grinding-mills:

> Here high in air the rising stream He pours
> To clay-built cisterns, or to lead-lined towers;
> Fresh through a thousand pipes the wave distils,
> And thirsty cities drink the exuberant rills.—
> There the vast mill-stone with inebriate whirl
> On trembling floors his forceful fingers twirl,
> Whose flinty teeth the golden harvests grind,
> Feast without blood! and nourish human-kind. [47]

Darwin's next letter to Watt, on 19 January 1790, is
characteristic in its mixture of banter and sympathy:

> For my part I court not fame, I write for money; I am offer'd
> £600 for this work, but have not sold it. I have some medico-
> philosophical works in MS which I think to print sometime, but
> fear they may engage me in controversy (which I should not much
> mind) and that they will not pay so well (which I mind much
> more). [48]

This may suggest that Darwin really did write for money; but
Edgeworth says he had often heard Darwin say so, but never
thought of believing him. It seems that Darwin was ashamed of
parading himself as an author: he thought it somehow indecent,
so he diverted suspicions that he was enjoying it by saying he
wrote for money. If he had really been writing for money, he
would have cashed in on *The Botanic Garden* by writing another
poem, whereas in fact he plodded on with *Zoonomia*, already
twenty years in the making.

Darwin continues his letter to Watt (Plate 11) in a warmer
tone:

> Why will not you live at Derby? I want *learning* from you of
> various kinds, and would give you in exchange *chearfulness,* which
> by some parts of your letter, you seem to want—and of which I have
> generally a pretty steady supply.

Why the d——l do you talk of your mental faculties decaying, have not you more mechanical invention, accuracy, and execution than any other person alive?—besides an inexhaustible fund of wit, when you please to call for it? So Misers talk of their poverty that their companions may contradict them.

Your headachs and asthma would recieve permanent relief from warm bathing I dare say—but perhaps you are too indolent to try its use?—or have some theory against it?

What I said about your steam-engine, I believed; I said it was the most ingenious of human inventions, can you tell me of one more ingenious? I can think of none unless you will accept the Jew's harp, which is a combination of wind and wire instruments—or the partridge-call, which is a combination of the drum and fiddle.

Seriously, I do think the inventor of a wheel for a carriage had wonderful luck, or wonderful genius. The bow and arrow is also a curious invention, which the people of New South Wales, a continent of 2000 miles square, had not discover'd.

Do you not congratulate your grandchildren on the dawn of universal liberty? I feel myself becoming all french both in chemistry and politics. Adieu....[49]

This is the latter half of a friend and half of a psychologist. Darwin knew Watt's temperament to a nicety. While sympathizing with his debilities, real or imagined, Darwin lifts him from the trough by judicious praise and banter.

Edgeworth was also in need of sympathy in 1790: his daughter Honora had died of consumption, like her mother ten years before. Honora was just fifteen, a girl of outstanding talent and beauty, according to Maria and all who knew her. She had written a story called 'Rivuletta' not long before her death, and Edgeworth sent a copy to Darwin, who replied on 24 April:

I much condole with you on your late loss, I know how to feel for your misfortune! The paper you sent me is a prodigy, written by so young a person with such elegance of imagination. Nil admirari may be a means to escape misery, but not to procure happyness—there is not much to be had in this world, we *expect* too much—I have had my loss also!—the letter of Sulpitius to Cicero ... is fine eloquence but comes not to the heart, it tugs but does not draw the arrow—pains and diseases of the mind are only cured by forgetfulness; Reason but skins the wound, which is perpetually liable to fester again.[50]

Edgeworth also sent Darwin his enthusiastic comments on *The Loves of the Plants*, and a second walking hygrometer, which

Darwin called 'brazen wheels'. 'I will sometime make a shelf for your animal to walk upon, but not till I repair my study, which wants a new roof . . . but I prefer *long-back* for a race; and would wager him against *brazen-wheels* for a cool hundred.' Edgeworth's praise of *The Loves of the Plants*, Darwin says,

> is very flattering to me indeed—it was your early approbation that contributed to encourage me to go on with the poem, which I have now sold to Johnson. . . . I got £100 by the first edition of this 2nd part, and have sold the copyright of it for £300 more, and the copyright of the first part, which will be published in two or three months for £400—in all £800.[51]

Darwin says he purposely gave *The Loves of the Plants* 'a little air of burlesque to shelter myself under'.

## [9]

Sadly, there was now one Lunar friend whom Darwin would see no more: Thomas Day. During the 1780s Day remained in seclusion at Anningsley House, farming his land near Ottershaw and in other parts of Surrey. Even so, he became famous, as the author of the children's book *Sandford and Merton*, of which Volumes I, II and III were published in 1783, 1786 and 1789 respectively. One of the precepts in the book was that 'even the fiercest beasts are capable of being softened by gratitude and moved by humanity'. Fortified by this belief, Day rode a horse that was only half broken-in when he went to join his wife and mother at Barehill in Berkshire on 28 September 1789. Near Barehill the horse shied at a man winnowing corn. Day was thrown head-first onto the stony road and died immediately.

At the time of this tragic accident Day was only forty-one, and he had not yet achieved the great things expected of him by his friends. Whether he would ever have made much of a mark in politics remains an open question. Day's great achievement was literary, and 'great' is the right word: for a century after his death *Sandford and Merton* probably had 'a larger number of readers than any other work of the period'.[52] Although Day and his book have now faded from remembrance, the distinction of having written the most-read book of a century sets him on a pinnacle that only two or three other authors have ever scaled.

Darwin and Day had probably not met during the 1780s, but the bonds between them remained strong. The only reference to Day's death in Darwin's extant letters is a polite note in a letter to Robert: 'I much lament the death of Mr Day. . . . He was dear to me by many names . . . as friend, philosopher, scholar, and honest man.'[53] Often linked in life, particularly for their originality, Darwin and Day were linked in death in a macabre manner: both had their tombs burnt by suffragettes in 1914.

Day's wife Esther was shattered by his death. Erasmus junior helped her with the legal formalities; Keir tried to assist her too, and wrote a circumspect *Life* of Day. But Esther remained inconsolable, and she died within three years.

## [10]

At about the time of Day's accident, or possibly a little earlier, Darwin made the acquaintance of a lively young man, Dr Thomas Beddoes. Born in 1760 in Shropshire, Beddoes studied languages, chemistry and botany at Oxford, and went on to qualify in medicine, first in London and then in 1784 at Edinburgh, where he may have met Robert Darwin. His acquaintance with Erasmus began soon after he became lecturer in chemistry at Oxford University in 1788. Nearly thirty years younger than Darwin, Beddoes was a live wire, a disciple, a correspondent and a friend, in that order. He helped Darwin to keep in touch with new ideas, made useful criticisms of his books, and also praised and publicized them.

Darwin's correspondence with Beddoes begins about 1790. The first letter is from Beddoes, regretting that they did not exchange Derbyshire and Shropshire fossils 'when I had the pleasure of seeing you at Shifnal'. In reply, Darwin offers to send a hundredweight of fossils, invites Beddoes to Derby and asks some questions about magnetism, coal and sandstone; but Beddoes was rather bashful in replying. In his next letter Darwin says he has sent the fossils and has a paper written 'a year or two ago' about coal and the tar spring at Coalbrook-Dale, 'which I intend for the Royal Society'. If Beddoes would make an analysis of the tar, Darwin would add it to his paper, 'where it would hang like a diamond in an Ethiop's ear'.[54] Darwin says bluntly that he thinks coal 'was *not* formed beneath the sea, because there are no marine shells in it, in general, or in the strata above it'. Beddoes, whose perception was not always equal to his energy, opposed this view; and he did not like being asked so many questions. To which Darwin replied brusquely: 'You say a man can only expose himself by asking or answering questions. I think he may show his ignorance by doing neither, when he corresponds with ingenious men.'[55]

One young doctor—his son Robert—had no hesitation in asking questions. On 19 April 1789 Erasmus gave him some good advice:

> I am sorry to hear you say you have many enemies, and one enemy often does much harm. The best way, when any little slander is told one, is never to make any piquant or angry answer; as the person who tells you what another says against you, always tells them in return what you say of them. I used to make it a rule always to receive all such information very coolly, and never to say anything biting against them which could go back again; and by these means many who were once adverse to me, in time became friendly. Dr Small always went and drank tea with those who he heard had spoken against him.[56]

When Robert asked his father to recommend a young man who wanted to start as an apothecary in Lichfield, he replied: 'I cannot give any letters of recommendation to Lichfield, as I am and have been from their infancy acquainted with all the apothecaries there; and as such letters must be directed to some of their patients, they would both feel and resent it.' To make up for this refusal, Erasmus goes to great trouble in the rest of the letter (dated 17 December 1790) to explain how the apothecary might succeed: 'I should advise your friend to use at first all means to get acquainted with the people of all ranks. At first a parcel of blue and red glasses at the windows might gain part of the retail business on market days, and thus get acquaintance with that class of people. . . .'[57] There follow several pages of practical and painstaking advice, a good example of the patient 'benevolence' for which Darwin was famous.

For Erasmus himself, 1790 was a busy year: he was hard at work on *The Economy of Vegetation*, Part I of *The Botanic Garden*. With Part II already published and a great public demand for Part I, he was writing under strong pressure.

# TEN

# The Botanic Garden Complete
## 1791–1793

Darwin thought he had finished *The Economy of Vegetation* at the beginning of 1791: on 5 January he told his son Robert, 'My next book will come out in May'; and on 31 March, writing to thank Edward Jerningham for his poem *Il Latte*, which urged mothers to nurse their children, Darwin says: 'In my next poem, which is now printing. and I suppose will be out in 6 or 8 weeks, I shall borrow something from your Il Latte, but not without acknowledgements. I hope you will continue to write. I think I have exhausted my stock.'[1] Darwin can scarcely be blamed for feeling exhausted after writing a poem of 2500 lines with notes running to 100,000 words, but his guess that it would be 'out in 6 or 8 weeks' was wildly over-optimistic: it was more than a year, because Wedgwood condemned the first engravings of the Portland Vase (by Bartolozzi) and new engravings had to be made by 'Mr Johnson's engraver'—William Blake.[2]

Though the publication of *The Economy of Vegetation* dragged on through 1791, the third edition of *The Loves of the Plants* came out more quickly. This is the edition usually bound up with the first edition of *The Economy of Vegetation* to form the complete *Botanic Garden*. So the *third* edition of *The Loves of the Plants* is, to everyone's confusion, part of the *first* edition of *The Botanic Garden*.

In this third edition of *The Loves of the Plants* many of the misprints, mis-spellings and misnumberings of the first edition are corrected, and many new ones introduced; Darwin also added more verses—thirty-four lines in Canto I, four in Canto II, and sixty-eight in Canto III. In Canto IV he adds nearly a hundred lines, and includes a potent newcomer, Cannabis. Darwin notes that a cannabis plant grown from seed sown on 4 June in England reached a height of fourteen feet seven inches by October, with a stem seven inches in circumference. Darwin was ahead of his time (and of ours) in seizing on these extraordinary growth rates. If cannabis were not banned in Britain, its cultivation and use for papermaking might greatly reduce the huge U.K. timber import bill and postpone the destruction of the world's forests.[3]

Darwin's labours on *The Botanic Garden* did not exhaust his capacity for light verse. In the summer of 1791 there was a lavish archery meeting at Drakelow, Staffordshire, the seat of Sir Nigel Gresley. The winner was Miss Susan Sneyd, and Darwin wrote a poem to celebrate her skill:

> With careless eye she view'd the central ring,
> Stretched her white arms, and drew the silken string!
> Mute wonder gaz'd the brazen studs betwixt;
> Full in the boss the flying arrow fix'd!
> Admiring circles greet the victor fair,
> And shouts of triumph rend the breezy air. . . .[4]

A more prosaic career was being planned for another Susan, Darwin's daughter Susan Parker, now eighteen, and her sister Mary, who was sixteen. They went to stay with Darwin's 'dear old friend' Richard Dixon early in 1791, and on 30 March he wrote to Dixon:

> I have often experienced the readiness with which you serve your friends; as to these girls, they ought to esteem you as a father. . . .
> Your goodness to them requires that I should tell you my whole design about them. I think to leave them when I die (N.B. that is not till the next century) the value of £500 a piece, part in money and part in annuities—which last I design to prevent their coming to absolute poverty in case of unhappy marriage. If they marry with my approbation I shall give them 2 or 300£ a piece at the marriage and an annuity of the value of the remainder at my death. By this sum and some employment as Lady's Maid or teacher of work they may be happier than my other girls who will have not much more than double or treble that sum and brought up in more genteel life, for I think happiness consists much in being *well* in one's situation in life—and not in that situation being higher or lower.[5]

Darwin's plans were practical and kindly, and in fact he did much more for Susan and Mary than he outlined here.

Elizabeth's son Sacheverel, Colonel Pole's son and heir, completed his course at Cambridge in 1790, and in 1791 he married

and went to live at Radburn Hall. He became High Sheriff of
Derbyshire for 1793–4, an office held by his father twenty-seven
years before.

Sacheverel's departure eased the overcrowding in the house,
but with six children aged between one and nine, Erasmus could
not expect an atmosphere of scholarly calm. In his later years he
usually woke early, and probably did much of his writing in the
comparative peace of the early morning. His health remained
good, but he was now fifty-nine and occasionally he began to feel
it, to judge from the letter to Robert on 5 January 1791: 'I have
lately taken to drink two glasses of home-made wine with water
at my dinner, instead of water alone, as I found myself growing
weak about two months ago; but am recovered and only now feel
the approaches of old age.'[6]

His daughters Violetta and Emma were aged seven and six
at the beginning of 1791 and a favourite playmate was Penelope,
the five-year-old daughter of Sir Brooke Boothby (who had now
succeeded to his father's title). In March Penelope fell ill.
Darwin was unable to save her, but he did manage to divert her
father from suicide, as Boothby recalled in a sonnet:

> When the last efforts of thy art had fail'd,
> And all my thoughts were wedded to the tomb,
> Thy mild philosophy repell'd the gloom,
> And bade me bear the ills on life entail'd.[7]

On Penelope's death, Boothby's wife left him—hence the inscription on Penelope's monument in Ashbourne Church: 'The
unfortunate parents ventured their all on this frail bark, and the
wreck was total.' The epitaph proved true, for the accomplished
and elegant Boothby was soon to sink in financial ruin. He spent
his last years (after Darwin's death) sadly wandering in Europe.

[2]

The year 1791 was also disastrous for the Lunar Society at
Birmingham. Priestley's house, library and laboratory were
destroyed during the savage Birmingham riots in July: Priestley
was driven away and eventually emigrated to America. The
pretext for the riots was provided by the Revolutionary Society

(formed to commemorate the English Revolution of 1688), which held a dinner on 14 July to celebrate Bastille Day. Priestley was a member of the Society, but did not attend the dinner. Keir agreed to be chairman, 'never conceiving that a peaceable meeting for the purpose of rejoicing that 26 millions of our fellow-creatures were rescued from despotism, and made as free and happy as we Britons are, could be misinterpreted as being offensive to a government, whose greatest boast is liberty'.[8]

The riots began that evening. They were started by professional ruffians, who directed and egged on the riotous populace, and were paid either by local authorities or by the government.[9] The violence was aimed at dissenters: the Old and New Meeting Houses were destroyed, along with Priestley's house and all his goods, apparatus and papers. The same fate befell William Hutton, another dissenter who for many years had as a magistrate devoted two days a week (unpaid) to settling quarrels; and even Dr Withering had his house ransacked. The magistrates refused to act until the rioting became more general and not just directed against dissenters. Cries of 'No philosophers—Church and King for ever' were heard during the riots, and the Lunar members were naturally alarmed: Boulton and Watt armed their workmen to defend Soho. The Government refused an inquiry into the riots, but the victims were paid compensation: Hutton received £5390 and Priestley £2502.[10]

For the Lunar Society 'the wreck was total', or very nearly so; for Darwin, the Birmingham riots were a clear smoke signal. Britain's brief flirtation with the French Revolution was over, and soon it was to be 'Church and King for ever' and to hell with Liberty. From now onwards Darwin became much more cautious in publishing radical opinions, though it was too late to tone down the enthusiasm for the French Revolution expressed in *The Economy of Vegetation*.

After the Birmingham riots Darwin persuaded the Derby Philosophical Society to send a sympathetic 'address' to Priestley, dated 3 September 1791:

> We condole with yourself and with the scientific world on the loss of your valuable library, your experimental apparatus, and your more valuable manuscripts. . . . Almost all great minds in all ages of the world, who have endeavoured to benefit mankind, have been persecuted by them. . . . Your enemies, unable to conquer your arguments by reason, have had recourse to violence; they have

halloo'd upon you the dogs of unfeeling ignorance, and of frantic fanaticism.[11]

The Society then suggested that, to avoid further danger, Priestley should 'leave the unfruitful fields of polemical theology, and cultivate that philosophy, of which you may be called the father; and which . . . will . . . overturn the empire of superstition'. The only clergyman in the Derby Philosophical Society, the Revd. C. S. Hope, complained to the newspapers that not enough members were present at the meeting when this message was sent. Darwin had him thrown out: the Society, having heard Mr Hope's explanation, resolved that 'he be desired to withdraw his name from the list of the Society'.[12]

In reply, Priestley said he was not discouraged, and was resuming his chemical pursuits. 'Excuse me, however, if I still join theological to philosophical studies, and if I consider the former as greatly superior in importance to mankind to the latter.' Darwin and Priestley were poles apart in their valuations of theology.

## [3]

*The Economy of Vegetation*, dated 1791 but probably not published until June 1792, served as the solid base for Darwin's reputation as a poet. Far stronger than the frivolous *Loves of the Plants*, the new poem was a selective encyclopedia of science, expressed in verse but backed up by extensive 'notes', often essays of several pages, and quite long enough to have been published as a separate book. The poem is in four cantos, their ostensible subjects being Fire (I), Earth (II), Water (III) and Air (IV). Darwin speaks through the lips of the Goddess of Botany, who addresses in turn the Nymphs (or Salamanders) of Fire, the Gnomes of Earth, the Nymphs of Water and the Sylphs of Air. Darwin says these Rosicrucian personages provide suitable machinery, because 'they were originally the names of hieroglyphic figures representing the elements', and the frontispiece, by Fuseli, shows the Goddess being 'attired by the elements'. For us, the exclamations 'Nymphs!' or 'Gnomes!' at the beginnings of paragraphs are rather distracting. But you soon learn to ignore them and to treat the poem as narrative.

In Canto I, after the fifty lines largely stolen from Anna Seward, we meet the Goddess gliding down in her flowery car to make a graceful landing:

> Light from her airy seat the Goddess bounds,
> And steps celestial press the pansied grounds.   [I 67–8]*

The gnomes, sylphs and nymphs gather to welcome her. First, she calls on the nymphs of fire—

> From each nice pore of ocean, earth, and air,
> With eye of flame the sparkling hosts repair.   [I 85–6]

The scene is now set for the creation of the universe, which Darwin presents with splendid aplomb:

> NYMPHS OF PRIMEVAL FIRE! your vestal train
> Hung with gold-tresses o'er the vast inane,
> Pierced with your silver shafts the throne of Night,
> And charm'd young Nature's opening eyes with light;
> When LOVE DIVINE, with brooding wings unfurl'd,
> Called from the rude abyss the living world.
> —'LET THERE BE LIGHT!' proclaim'd the ALMIGHTY LORD,
> Astonish'd Chaos heard the potent word;—
> Through all his realms the kindling Ether runs,
> And the mass starts into a million suns;
> Earths round each sun with quick explosions burst,
> And second planets issue from the first;
> Bend, as they journey with projectile force,
> In bright ellipses their reluctant course;
> Orbs wheel in orbs, round centres centres roll,
> And form, self-balanced, one revolving Whole.   [I 97–112]

It is a heady concoction, as Horace Walpole's enthusiasm shows: 'The twelve verses that by miracle describe and comprehend the creation of the Universe out of chaos, are in my opinion the most sublime passage in any author, or in any of the few languages with which I am acquainted.'¹³ Anna Seward, no less intoxicated, thought the passage 'of excellence yet unequalled in its kind, and never to be excelled in the grandeur of its conceptions'.¹⁴ Darwin's lines are certainly fine, even if a few phrases are borrowed from *Paradise Lost*; and there is matter in them as well as art, for he is propounding, with uncanny fore-

---

* Canto and line numbers in the first edition of *The Economy of Vegetation* are given after quotations.

sight, what is now the fashionable 'big bang' theory of cosmogony, as he explains in a footnote:

> It may be objected, that if the stars had been projected from a Chaos by explosions, that they must have returned again into it from the known laws of gravitation; this however would not happen, if the whole of Chaos, like grains of gunpowder, was exploded at the same time, and dispersed through infinite space at once, or in quick succession, in every possible direction.
>
> [I 105, note]

Darwin believes the stars threw out their planets, which in turn ejected moons, very early in the development of the universe. He suggests that there are perhaps a million suns (that is, stars) with planets; and hence that there are a large number of habitable and probably inhabited worlds, a heresy slipped in behind his reference to 'the Almighty Lord'. Again Darwin shows his prophetic flair by adopting an idea that is now accepted as orthodox science.

Confining himself to Earth, Darwin rolls his eye rapidly round the sky, seeing shooting stars, lightning and rainbows:

> ETHEREAL POWERS! you chase the shooting stars,
> Or yoke the vollied lightnings to your cars,
> Cling round the aërial bow with prisms bright,
> And pleased untwist the sevenfold threads of light.  [I 115–18]

After visiting the outermost atmosphere of hydrogen—

> Where lighter gases, circumfused on high,
> Form the vast concave of exterior sky—

the Ethereal Powers turn up as fireballs and auroral streamers:

> Ride, with broad eye and scintillating hair,
> The rapid Fire-ball through the midnight air;
> Dart from the North on pale electric streams,
> Fringing Night's sable robe with transient beams.
>
> [I 123–4, 127–30]

For our further illumination Darwin offers us volcanoes, phosphoric light, glow-worms, and gunpowder, and he peps up the catalogue with amusing erotic episodes from classical mythology. For Darwin, fire's finest product is the steam engine, and he details its uses in pumping piped water, in driving mills, such as Boulton's coining machine, and possibly in air travel (as quoted on pages 204, 203 and 17). Electricity arrives again, in the form of the highly charged beauty (page 24), and Darwin refers to Franklin, whose 'bold arm' invades 'the lowering sky' to 'seize the tiptoe lightnings ere they fly'. After mentioning the bright idea of navigating icebergs into tropical waters to reduce extremes of temperature, he sends off the Nymphs of Fire in a display of fireworks:

> Red rockets rise, loud cracks are heard on high,
> And showers of stars rush headlong from the sky.    [I  595–6]

The second canto is addressed to the Gnomes of Earth, whose first task was to create our planet:

> . . . high in ether, with explosion dire,
> From the deep craters of his realms of fire,
> The whirling Sun this ponderous planet hurl'd,
> And gave the astonish'd void another world.    [II  13–16]

Darwin's idea that the Earth was ejected from the sun became quite popular in the 1930s, but has now been largely abandoned in favour of the belief that the Earth condensed out of a cloud of smaller particles round the sun.

At first the Earth was mostly ocean, Darwin believes, thus giving himself an excuse to discover—or uncover—Venus rising from the sea:

> The bright drops, rolling from her lifted arms,
> In slow meanders wander o'er her charms,
> Seek round her snowy neck their lucid track,
> Pearl her white shoulders, gem her ivory back,
> Round her fine waist and swelling bosom swim,
> And star with glittering brine each crystal limb.    [II  59–64]

To have gone further would have outraged conventional taste, so Darwin fades out the pleasantry.

To revive our attention, we have the moon's explosive birth:

> GNOMES! how you shriek'd! when through the troubled air
> Roar'd the fierce din of elemental war;
> When rose the continents, and sunk the main,
> And Earth's huge sphere exploding burst in twain.—
> GNOMES! how you gazed! when from her wounded side
> Where now the South-Sea heaves its waste of tide,
> Rose on swift wheels the MOON's refulgent car,
> Circling the solar orb, a sister-star,

Dimpled with vales, with shining hills emboss'd,
And roll'd round Earth her airless realms of frost.   [II 73–82]

The idea that the moon originated by fission from the Earth is generally known as the 'Darwinian theory', not because of Erasmus, but because his great-grandson Sir George Darwin gave the idea a coherent mathematical basis.[15] The theory has been violently attacked and stoutly defended in the past twenty years: the question of the moon's origin remains unsettled.

Then Darwin explains how limestone forms from sea shells, and salt deposits arise by evaporation. Salts of iron ooze from morasses to form iron ores, he says, from which come 'adamantine steel', basis of the magnet, 'the plowshare and the sword'. Via acids, precious stones and clay, Darwin reaches pottery, with the lines about Wedgwood and the Portland Vase (page 202). Flashing past coal and jet to amber, and then to electricity again, Darwin lets himself be diverted into praising 'immortal Franklin', who inspired the American Revolution by combating the 'Tyrant-Power' until

The patriot-flame with quick contagion ran,
Hill lighted hill, and man electrised man;
Her heroes slain awhile Columbia mourn'd,
And crown'd with laurels Liberty return'd.   [II 367–70]

In France meanwhile, 'the Giant-form' of Liberty had long

Inglorious slept, unconscious of his chains;
Round his large limbs were wound a thousand strings
By the weak hands of Confessors and Kings. . . .
—Touch'd by the patriot-flame, he rent amazed
The flimsy bonds, and round and round him gazed.
[II 378–80, 385–6]

If Darwin had known how these lines would damage his reputation in the repression of the later 1790s he might have toned down his praise; or he might have scorned to do so.

Tin, copper, zinc and lead receive only one line each, but the Spanish conquest of Mexico and Peru for the sake of their mineral wealth infuriates Darwin:

Heavens! on my sight what sanguine colours blaze!
Spain's deathless shame! the crimes of modern days!
When Avarice, shrouded in Religion's robe,
Sail'd to the West, and slaughter'd half the globe;

> While Superstition, stalking by his side,
> Mock'd the loud groans, and lap'd the bloody tide.    [II 413–18]

This leads to a further onslaught on the British slave trade. He asks Britannia to note

> How AFRIC's coasts thy craftier sons invade
> With murder, rapine, theft,—and call it Trade!
> —The SLAVE, in chains, on supplicating knee,
> Spreads his wide arms, and lifts his eyes to Thee;
> With hunger pale, with wounds and toil oppress'd,
> 'ARE WE NOT BRETHREN?' sorrow choaks the rest;—
> —AIR! bear to heaven upon thy azure flood
> Their innocent cries!—EARTH! cover not their blood!
>
> [II 423–30]

Nowhere else in the poem does Darwin become so emotional and spluttering. He asks the gnomes to help in bringing 'Heaven's dread justice' to smite

> in crimes o'ergrown
> The blood-nursed Tyrant on his purple throne.    [II 431–2]

The example he gives is the army of Cambyses being buried in the sand while crossing the desert. This is Darwin at his most vigorous, dealing out seven of his favourite 'double-hammer blows' with repeated words:

> Onward resistless rolls the infuriate surge,
> Clouds follow clouds, and mountains mountains urge;
> Wave over wave the driving desert swims,
> Bursts o'er their heads, inhumes their struggling limbs;
> Man mounts on man, on camels camels rush,
> Hosts march o'er hosts, and nations nations crush,—
> Wheeling in air the wingèd islands fall,
> And one great earthy Ocean covers all!    [II 487–94]

The third canto belongs to the 'aquatic Nymphs', who

> lead with viewless march
> The wingèd vapours up the aërial arch,

and then lead them down again, as rivers, to the sea, an endless cycle that Darwin likens to the circulation of the blood. The nymphs ride the tides and play in fishy realms, chasing the shark, guarding the Mermaid and feeding

> ... the live petals of her insect-flowers,
> Her shell-wrack gardens, and her sea-fan bowers.    [III 81–2]

They control all kinds of waters, rivers under Alpine snows, Icelandic geysers, the warm springs of Buxton, and the cascades of Chatsworth. The nymphs are well versed in the new chemistry, and they make pure Air (oxygen) combine with flaming gas (hydrogen) to manufacture water (see page 143). These sportive nymphs beautify 'Britannia's isle' with 'lucid cataracts' or guide their 'liquid silver' through 'peopled vales'. After smiling on Brindley's cradle (see page 92), the nymphs preside over water pumps, drain swamps, and irrigate the land:

> Wide o'er the shining vales, and trickling hills,
> Spread the bright treasure in a thousand rills.   [III 519–20]

In the final canto we meet the Sylphs of Air, who

> With soft susurrant voice alternate sweep
> Earth's green pavilions and encircling deep,   [IV 19–20]

making the plants exude oxygen and the sea breezes blow. In sourer mood the sylphs bring fogs, the sirocco, simoom and tornado. These patron saints of atmospheric science taught Torricelli and Boyle about 'the spring and pressure of the viewless air', and helped in devising barometers that

> Weigh the long column of the incumbent skies,
> And with the changeful moment fall and rise.   [IV 133–4]

Darwin asks the sylphs to help Priestley in his researches on airs,

> To his charm'd eye in gay undress appear,
> Or pour your secrets on his raptured ear.   [IV 169–70]

The 'sage' Priestley's discovery of oxygen will allow air to be supplied for long journeys by submarine, Darwin thinks:

> Led by the Sage, Lo! Britain's sons shall guide
> Huge SEA-BALLOONS beneath the tossing tide;
> The diving castles, roof'd with spheric glass,
> Ribb'd with strong oak, and barr'd with bolts of brass,
> Buoy'd with pure air shall endless tracks pursue,
> And PRIESTLEY's hand the vital flood renew. . . .   [IV 195–200]

Darwin foresees the submarines travelling not only through the warm waves of the tropics, but also

> Beneath the shadowy ice-isles of the Pole.

What he so confidently foresaw in 1790 was at last accomplished by the U.S.S. *Nautilus* in 1958.

Then at last, in the final two hundred lines, Darwin proves that the poem's title is not just a joke by giving quite an economical summary of vegetation, asking the sylphs to tend the seeds, sap and stamens, and providing elegant drawings of two plants. Darwin praises the new Botanic Garden at Kew, where

> Delighted Thames through tropic umbrage glides,

and the Botanic Goddess asks the sylphs to

> Bring my rich Balms from Mecca's hallow'd glades,
> Sweet flowers, that glitter in Arabia's shades;
> Fruits, whose fair forms in bright succession glow
> Gilding the Banks of Arno, or of Po . . .
> Each spicy rind, which sultry India boasts,
> Scenting the night-air round her breezy coasts.
>
> [IV 595–8, 601–2]

Loaded with these delicacies, the Goddess makes off into the upper atmosphere again.

## [4]

*The Economy of Vegetation* is much more than a poem. The footnotes alone are longer than the verses, and the Additional Notes are longer still: they run to 120 pages of small type—about 70,000 words. These notes are not just stodgily factual: they include many speculations, often dazzling, sometimes far-seeing, sometimes misdirected. Because *The Botanic Garden* was so popular, the notes were very widely read. Even the more trivial items, such as Note VIII on Memnon's lyre and Note IX on luminous insects, entered the conscious or subconscious memory of Wordsworth and Coleridge, as we shall see later. Two of the longer notes, on the Portland Vase and the history of the steam engine, had a wider appeal.

The notes on vegetation run to twenty pages and show that Darwin's theme is the 'economy of nature', and not just the economy of vegetation:

> . . . since animals are sustained by these vegetable productions, it would seem that the sugar-making process carried on in vegetable vessels was the great source of life to all organized beings. . . . It would seem that roots fixed in the earth, and leaves innumerable

waving in the air were necessary for the decomposition of water, and the conversion of it into saccharine matter, which would have been not only cumbrous but totally incompatible with the loco-motion of animal bodies. [Notes, pp. 111–12]

Darwin wonders whether 'our improved chemistry' may one day discover how to make sugar from 'fossile or aerial matter', there-by making food 'as plentiful as water'. *Our* improved chemistry *can* now make protein-rich food from fossil hydrocarbons, but for most of the world the age of plenty remains remote.

The most influential of the notes were those on geology. Darwin's geology is modern in spirit and usually correct in principle, though sometimes wrong in detail and in emphasis. The occurrence of hot springs and volcanoes convinces him that the Earth is very hot at great depths, and he believes that 'the central parts of the earth'—what is now called the 'core'—'consist of a fluid mass and that part of this mass is iron', the remainder being molten lava. The iron in the core creates the Earth's magnetic field, he thinks. Coming nearer the surface, Darwin notes 'that many of the highest mountains of the world consist of limestone replete with shells' and 'bear the marks of having been lifted up by subterraneous fires'. The limestone strata, he says, 'consist of the accumulated exuviae of shell-fish, the animals perished age after age but their shells remained, and in progression of time produced the amazing quantities of lime-stone which almost cover the earth' (Notes, p. 32).

All this is important and essentially correct geology: Darwin has steered a clever middle course through the great geological controversy of his day, between the Neptunists, who thought the deposition of strata beneath the sea was all-important, and the Vulcanists, who believed in the supremacy of volcanic or plutonic events. Darwin acknowledges that water and fire are the 'two great agents in producing the various changes which the terraqueous globe has undergone'; but he believes some geolo-gists 'have perhaps ascribed too much to one of these great agents of nature, and some to the other' (Notes, p. 49). Darwin was a personal friend of three of the century's best geologists, Hutton, Michell and Whitehurst, and he had taken a keen practical interest in rocks and fossils since his visits to the Peak District in the 1760s: so his skill in making 'the best of both worlds' is not too surprising.

Darwin continues with notes on morasses, iron, flint, clays, enamel and coal. There is no need to pursue him too far into the morasses, which, he correctly explains, form from decaying vegetation. His note on coal has a modern ring. Its formation from buried forests he accepts as proved, as 'evinced from the vegetable matters frequently found' in the coal; and he concentrates instead on 'a fountain of fossil tar, or petroleum' found associated with a seam of coal in the gorge of the Severn at Coalbrookdale 'about a mile and a half below the celebrated iron-bridge' (Notes, p. 60). 'From ten to fifteen barrels a day' of this petroleum, 'each barrel containing 32 gallons, were at first collected in a day', but later the rate decreased. The petroleum is, he thinks, 'distilled' out of the coal by the effects of heat and pressure down the ages. Although this North Severn oilfield proved a dud by North Sea oil standards, Darwin's interest in it shows he was alert to the possibility of extracting petroleum, more than sixty years before the first oil well bored in the U.S.A.

Darwin summarizes his views in a lengthy 'geological recapitulation', having fourteen numbered paragraphs and accompanied by a speculative section of the Earth (not to scale), shown as Fig. 9. He begins:

> 1. The earth was projected along with the other primary planets from the sun. . . .

The Earth acquired its spheroidal shape as a result of rotation, he says; and, as it cooled, its 'attendant vapours' were condensed to form the oceans.

> 3. The masses or mountains of granite, porphery, basalt, and stones of similar structure, were a part of the original nucleus of the earth; or consist of volcanic productions since formed.
> 4. On this nucleus of granite and basaltes, thus covered by the ocean, were formed the calcareous beds of limestone, marble, chalk, spar, from the exuviae of marine animals; with the flints, or chertz, which accompany them. And were stratified by their having been formed at different and very distant periods of time.
> 5. The whole terraqueous globe was burst by central fires. . . . [Notes, p. 65]

These convulsions raised islands and continents of granite and limestone, and ejected the moon, he believes. On some parts of the continents extensive morasses formed 'from the recrements of vegetables and of land animals', from which 'were produced

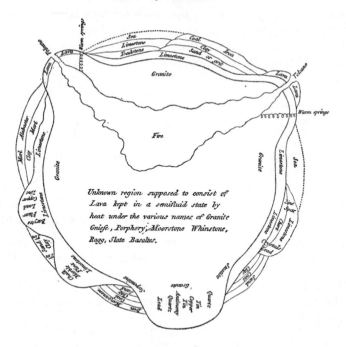

Fig. 9 Darwin's diagrammatic section of the earth

clay, marle, sandstone, coal, iron', again all stratified by being 'formed at different and very distant periods of time', and subsequently disturbed by earthquakes.

Because of the great fame of his book, Darwin's recapitulation was one of the best-known current accounts of geology, and his middle course between the extremes of vulcanism and sedimentation was helpful in muting the fanaticisms and allowing geology to advance. His picture is not altogether correct, of course. The idea of central fires 'bursting' the Earth and ejecting the moon is certainly too dramatic; but lesser cataclysms may have occurred, even though they do not figure in orthodox modern theories (which tend to under-dramatize Earth-history). Darwin correctly identifies the mode of formation of granites, limestones and coal, hundreds of millions of years ago, but he has no inkling of the Ice Age which, only ten thousand years before, had moulded the Derbyshire scenery.

[5]

Darwin's notes on the atmosphere were less influential, but more important in the long run, than those on geology. He took a far-seeing, space-age view of the complete atmosphere, and some of his speculations were not confirmed until the 1960s. Darwin divided the atmosphere into three strata, as shown in Fig. 10:

> There seem to be three concentric strata of our incumbent atmosphere; in which, or between them, are produced four kinds of meteors; lightning, shooting stars, fire-balls, and northern lights. First, the lower region of air . . . which may extend from one to three or four miles high. In this region the common lightning is produced. . . .
>
> The second region of the atmosphere I suppose to be that which has too little tenacity to support condensed vapour or clouds; but which yet contains invisible vapour, or water in aerial solution. . . . In this stratum it seems probable that the meteors called shooting stars are produced; and that they consist of electric sparks, or lightning, passing from one region to another of these invisible fields of aero-aqueous solution. . . .
>
> The second region or stratum of air terminates I suppose where the twilight ceases to be refracted, that is, where the air is 3000 times rarer than at the surface of the earth; and where it seems probable that the common air ends, and is surrounded by an atmosphere of inflammable gas tenfold rarer than itself. In this region I believe fire-balls sometimes to pass, and at other times the northern lights to exist. One of these fire-balls . . . was estimated to be between 60 and 70 miles high, and to travel 1000 miles at the rate of about 20 miles in a second.    [Notes, pp. 1–2]

In the associated footnotes to the poem (I 123 and I 126) Darwin refers to inflammable air by Lavoisier's name, 'hydrogene', and he defines the height where his third stratum begins. He says that 'between 40 and 50 miles' height, the air is '4000 to 10,000 times' more rarefied than at the Earth's surface. This implies that it is 3000 times rarer at a height of about 37 miles. According to current atmospheric models the height where the density decreases to $\frac{1}{3000}$ of the sea-level value is 36 miles, so Darwin's model of density was amazingly accurate (largely because he followed Halley's correct analysis of air density a century before).[16]

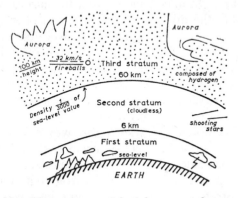

10 Three-tier model of the atmosphere,
as proposed by Darwin in 1791

Darwin's first stratum corresponds to what is now called the troposphere, and his second, nearly cloudless region corresponds to the stratosphere. Darwin was right, and for the right reasons, in believing that there would be an outermost atmosphere of hydrogen, now often called the 'hydrogen exosphere', but he placed its base far too low: hydrogen does not become dominant until a height of about 300 miles, when the sun is quiet.[17] Two intermediate layers now recognized, the mesosphere (30–60 miles) and the thermosphere (60–300 miles) do not appear in Darwin's model. His error of omission is, however, far less serious than that of orthodox scientists early in the twentieth century, who made the error of omitting hydrogen altogether, thinking it had escaped from the Earth.

Darwin suggests that shooting stars are 'electric sparks, or lightning', and that the brilliant fireballs are initiated by electrical discharges which make the hydrogen in the outermost region combine violently with oxygen. Darwin's explanation is very reasonable, but completely wrong; the meteors are fluffy particles from outer space burning up, and the fireballs are larger and more solid lumps of space debris. This idea was too radical even for the radical Darwin, and he never thought of it, though the speed he quotes (twenty miles per second) shows that the object (if substantial rather than electrical) was on a hyperbolic orbit relative to the Earth, and was therefore a visitor from space. The idea of meteorites coming from space, familiar to the ancients, was revived in 1794 by Chladni.[18]

Darwin was right in concluding that the aurora was electrical and belonged to the third region of the atmosphere, above forty miles. But his views on the atmosphere were unknown to most aeronomists, and therefore unheeded. So when the International Polar Year of 1882 was planned, the stations for photographing the aurora were sited on the assumption that it was five miles high, and the results were almost useless—except to show that the height was more than sixty miles.[19]

Darwin also notes Priestley's discovery that 'the electric shock taken through inflammable air was red', and suggests that this might 'bear analogy' to the red colours seen in the aurora, thus confirming the existence of hydrogen in the outermost atmosphere. Strangely enough, Darwin's idea was used in the early twentieth century to try to prove there was no hydrogen: but the argument ended in Darwin's favour in 1951, when hydrogen lines were identified in an aurora. Now hydrogen is an accepted resident of the exosphere.

The aurora, produced by high-energy charged particles in the upper atmosphere, has a less brilliant cousin, the night airglow— caused by the flashes of light from atoms in the high atmosphere as they return to normal after having been raised to an excited state by the sunshine during the day. The textbooks tell us that the night airglow was not discovered until 1909, so why mention it now? Because Darwin correctly specified its existence and its mechanism:

> The light of the evening, at the same distance from noon, is much greater, as I have repeatedly observed, than the light of the morning; this is owing, I suppose, to the phosphorescent quality of almost all bodies, in a greater or less degree, which thus absorb light during the sun-shine, and continue to emit it again for some time afterwards, though not in such quantity as to produce apparent scintillations.[20]

The night airglow often emits more light than all the stars combined, and is plainly visible to astronauts in orbit. Everyone on the ground can also 'see' it on a starry night, but the glow is very difficult to identify with the eye—most observers would say it is impossible. Did Darwin really observe it? There are two points in his favour. First, he lived at a time when artificial lighting was weak or non-existent. Second, he was supreme as an observer: his great success as a doctor depended mainly on his ability to observe and recognize the smallest deviations from normality in a patient's appearance. So possibly he did sense the airglow. If not, his correct analysis is even more astonishing!

The longest of Darwin's notes (eight thousand words) is on the more mundane atmospheric topic of winds. 'The theory of winds is yet very imperfect', he begins; and unfortunately he does little to improve it. Today meteorologists treat winds simply as the outcome of solar heating and pressure systems, and still cannot always predict them correctly. Darwin set himself a much more difficult—indeed impossibly difficult—task, because he believed that the creation and destruction of gases by chemical action (for example, photosynthesis or forest fires) was a primary generator of wind. This belief was strengthened because he could not otherwise explain the 'disappearance' of $\frac{1}{15}$ of the atmosphere when the barometer falls from 30·5 to 28·5 inches. So he had to imagine 'a great and sudden absorption of air', probably in the polar regions, and he wastes a good deal of energy barking up this wrong tree. He finishes the note with a weather journal for part of 1785 (Notes, p. 92).

Though much of his essay on winds is nugatory, Darwin does formulate one important concept, the idea that 'vertical spiral eddies', or 'great cylinders of air rolling on the surface of the earth', are created when air flows over a coast with a line of mountains behind (Notes, p. 84). This phenomenon is now well established, and important because it is a prime source of gravity waves, which, it has been suggested, may dominate the world's weather.

Though he failed to produce a valid theory of winds, Darwin's achievements in atmospheric science were many and fundamental: he discovered the main mode of cloud formation, noted the sharp change in wind direction at fronts, designed some ingenious and automated instruments, proposed the three-stratum atmospheric model with an outermost layer of hydrogen, explained the aurora and recognized the airglow. Yet Darwin's name does not appear among the seventy-four pioneers of meteorology whose achieve-

ments are outlined in Napier Shaw's *Meteorology in History*. So
fickle is fame that meteorologists seem to know him, if at all, as
the author of some weather verses, 'Signs of Rain', printed on
the jacket of Inwards's *Weather Lore*; and the final irony is that
these verses were actually written by Jenner.[21]

## [6]

With the complete *Botanic Garden* published, Darwin was for a
few years the most famous poet of the day in England. The
reviewers were enthusiastic. 'The verse has afforded delight to
all who delight in verse; and the notes instruction to all philosophical enquirers . . .', wrote William Cowper in his seven-page
notice in the *Analytical Review*.[22] Cowper's friend William
Hayley admired the poem too, and they wrote their 'Lines
Addressed to Dr Darwin':

> Two poets (poets by report
>     Not oft so well agree)
> Sweet Harmonist of Flora's court!
>     Conspire to honour thee. . . .[23]

This flattering poem has five more verses in similar vein: Hayley
sent it to Darwin, who replied on 15 July 1792. He thanked
them courteously and returned the compliment, saying he had
studied *their* poems 'with great delight and improvement'.[24]
Cowper further signalled his debt to Darwin with his poem 'The
Yardley Oak', written in 1792, which has several resemblances
to *The Botanic Garden*.[25]

A younger and more famous disciple declared himself in 1793,
with a poem in Darwinian couplets entitled *Descriptive Sketches*.
The author was the twenty-three-year-old William Wordsworth, and he follows a number of Darwin's stylistic tricks and
subjects, including lines on Memnon's lyre, to which Wordsworth adds a note saying that the lyre 'is reported to have
emitted melancholy or cheerful tones, as it was touched by the
sun's evening or morning rays'. This obviously derives from
Darwin's note, where the lyre is said 'to have saluted the rising
sun with chearful tones, and the setting sun with melancholy
ones'.[26] So Wordsworth was among Darwin's earliest admirers;
and, to Darwin's credit, he was already among Wordsworth's.[27]

Darwin's fame left him unmarked. He was still shy of being an author, and pretended he wrote for money. His casual attitude to literary fame emerges in a letter to his 'dear old friend' Richard Dixon on 25 October 1792:

> I go on as usual to practice physic, and to write books—I sold a work called 'The Botanic Garden' for 900£ to Johnson the bookseller near St Paul's, it is a poem; perhaps you may borrow it from some circulating library; it is in two parts and sold for 1-13-0.

'I sold a work called 'The Botanic Garden' . . . it is a poem': Horace Walpole would have been amazed to read this understatement of the year, but it shows how quite unimpressed Darwin was by his success.

This letter to Dixon reveals a Darwin as exuberant as ever. Dixon had suffered a slight stroke which left his mouth drawn down on one side. Darwin says he ought to come to Derby to visit his cousin Sumner: 'She expects an annual kiss from you at least—whether your mouth is drawn on one side or not—you must mind on which side you approach lest you should kiss her ear.' Darwin starts talking of his own health but is soon sidetracked into banter:

> The worst thing I find now is this d———n'd old age, which creeps slily upon one, like moss upon a tree, and wrinkles one all over like a baked pear—but I see by your letter that your juvenility will never fail you; you'l laugh on to the last, like Pope Alexander, who died laughing, on seeing his tame monkey steal to bed side, and put on the holy Tiara, the triple crown, which denotes him king of kings. Now Mr Pain says that he thinks a monkey or a bear, or a goose may govern a kingdom as well, and at a much less expense than any being in Christendom, whether idiot or madman or in his royal senses.[28]

Darwin addresses the letter to 'Richard Dixon Citizen' and ends it with 'adieu dear Citizen from thy affectionate equal'. There is only one sentence about the French Revolution in the letter, but it shows where Darwin stands: 'The success of the French against a confederacy of kings gives me great pleasure and I hope they will preserve their liberty, and spread the holy flame of freedom over Europe.'[29]

Darwin's new fame as a poet brought a flow of visitors to Derby in the 1790s: among them was one of the heroes of the poem, William Herschel, perhaps the greatest of observational astronomers. Herschel called in July 1792, and he records that Darwin 'shewed me a curious specimen of lead confined like a nucleus in a shell of iron ore'.[30] So Darwin's eye was still alert for geological curiosities.

Another welcome visitor in 1792 was Edgeworth, who arrived in February and stayed for nearly three weeks. Maria says the Darwins 'were extremely kind, and pressed him very much to take a house in or near Derby for the summer'.[31]

Edgeworth had returned to England in the summer of 1791 for two years; he stayed at Clifton, Bristol, so that one of his sons could 'take the waters' there for his health. Edgeworth visited his old friends—Darwin, Watt, Keir and Wedgwood—and made two new ones, William Strutt and Dr Beddoes. Strutt, besides being Darwin's deputy in the Derby Philosophical Society, made some mechanical inventions of his own, which would have appealed to Edgeworth. Beddoes moved to Clifton in 1792 after being forced to resign from his post at Oxford because he had published a pamphlet praising the French Revolution and attacking the Church. By 1793 he was becoming fixed in what remained of the Lunar circle, being on good terms with Darwin, Keir and Edgeworth, and (soon) with Watt as well. Beddoes was a demon for work, and he was publishing a stream of pamphlets on medical, political and religious topics, not to mention a poem, *Alexander's Feast*, in imitation of Darwin. He always sent the pamphlets to Darwin, who was usually able to find some favourable comments to send in reply.

[7]

Darwin himself was still going strong on his medical rounds, but in 1792 and 1793 he was working even harder putting the finishing touches to his massive medical treatise *Zoonomia*. 'His continued zeal in his profession' at the age of sixty emerges in a letter to his son Robert written on 13 April 1792:

> In medicine I am sure unless one reads the work of others, one is liable perpetually to copy one's own prescriptions, and methods of treatment; till one's whole practice is but an imitation of one's self . . . and the apothecaries say the doctor has but 4 or 6 prescriptions to cure all diseases.

Reasoning thus, I am determined to read all the new medical journals which come out, and other medical publications.[32]

On completing the draft of *Zoonomia*, he asked Keir to read it, and as usual received good advice: 'I have much availed myself of your observations, and have corrected my work accordingly',[33] Darwin wrote on 17 January 1793. He adopted Keir's suggestion of publishing *Zoonomia* in two volumes, at separate times.

When Robert urged his father to think about retiring, he replied:

It is a dangerous experiment, and generally ends either in drunkenness or hypochondriacism. Thus I reason, one must do something (so country squires fox-hunt), otherwise one grows weary of life, and becomes a prey to ennui. Therefore one may as well do something advantageous to oneself and friends or to mankind, as employ oneself in cards or other things equally insignificant.[34]

Despite his advancing age, Darwin would often go on long journeys to see special patients, though he charged high fees as a protest against the discomfort of the journey. In 1793 he went to Margate to treat Mary Anne Galton (who was later to libel him in her memoirs), and charged her father a hundred guineas —which he could well afford out of the profits of his arms manufacturing.

Another lengthy medical journey, probably made at about this time, was to Newmarket, to attend his old schoolfellow Lord George Cavendish, who was godfather to his daughter Emma. Darwin stayed at a hotel in Newmarket and during the night was woken by a man at his bedside, who said he had not dared to speak in the daytime: 'I have never forgotten your kindness to my mother in her bad illness, but have not been able to show you my gratitude before. I now tell you to bet largely on a certain horse (naming one), and not on the favourite, whom I am to ride, and who we have settled is not to win.'[35] Charles Darwin says he traced this story 'through four distinct channels to my grandfather, whose veracity has never been doubted by any one who knew him'. The next day Erasmus saw in the newspaper that 'to the astonishment of everyone, the favourite had not won the race'.[36]

Darwin continued to receive formal recognition as well as informal confidences from jockeys. In 1792 he became one of the first Fellows of the Linnaean Society, and on 12 September he wrote to the president, J. E. Smith, proposing Boothby and 'Dr Johnson of this town' as Fellows. In 1793 Darwin was elected a member of the American Philosophical Society, and in a letter to Professor B. S. Barton on 3 July he sent his 'thanks for the great honor the society has confer'd upon me'.[37]

[8]

In the autumn of 1793 Darwin became concerned over the health of Tom Wedgwood, Josiah's youngest son, now twenty-two. Darwin, who had of course known and treated Tom from his earliest years, recognized his exceptional brilliance, and the danger that it would be blighted by disease more imaginary than real. This fear was fully justified, and Tom Wedgwood is a classic example of genius *manqué*, with only a few unfinished achievements (such as the invention of photography) as a re-minder of what he might have done.

Eleven long medical letters from Darwin to Tom Wedgwood between 1793 and 1797 are preserved in the Wedgwood Archives at the University of Keele. The letters show Darwin's immense patience and kindness: he quite soon decided that Tom's problems were mainly mental rather than physical, but he continued writing long and comforting letters in the hope that they might help Tom get back on an even keel and overcome his chronic hypochondria.

In the first of the letters, dated 15 November 1793, Darwin has to quieten Tom's fear that he has an eye disease. Darwin explains that Tom's symptoms are not at all like 'a beginning gutta serena or a beginning cataract', and are more likely to be a side effect of another malady, possibly intestinal worms, which afflicted Tom as a child and might not have been eradicated. Darwin suggests that Tom should visit Harrogate to drink the waters, and also recommends various saline potions thought to be specific against ascarides (as he usually calls the worms). Darwin believes the eye problems, and the headaches Tom was suffering, to be 'more troublesome than dangerous'.[38] On 30 November Darwin wrote to recommend a stronger 'salinic purge', which sounds horrible and is intended to produce '4 or 6 stools a day'. The next letter is only a week later, on 6 December. Apparently the salinic solution gave Tom a terrible thirst, and Darwin hastily countermands his previous orders: 'You will please either to dilute it, or take gruel or barley water between the doses. I rather think you possibly take too much of it, as 5 or 6 stools will be sufficient, instead of 8 or 10.' It is easy to be critical, but Darwin was doing his best, within the resources available to him and the treatments acceptable to his patient. Still, all this purging was enough to produce a psychological conviction of illness in a patient so sensitive as Tom.

Within a month Darwin was writing again, and this time he gave up his medications, recommending normal food in good quantities and an end to the purging. He continues:

> That lassitude or want of spirits you complain of may in some measure be owing to want of employment, you should find out something to teaze you a little—a wife,—or a law-suit—or some such thing. I think Virgil said that Jupiter found it necessary to send Care amongst mankind, to prevent them from feeling less evils. . . .
>
> You will see, that I do not esteem your complaints dangerous, but that they are, what you well express, owing to nervous debility, and that time and occupation will cure you.[39]

Darwin thought, rightly, that the best hope of curing Tom was to get him working and persuade him he was not ill. But the problem was not to be solved so simply, and Darwin had not heard the last of it.

# ELEVEN

# Zoonomia
## 1794–1797

For a long time Darwin had been dissatisfied with conventional education, and he had it in mind to set up his daughters Susan and Mary Parker in a school of their own, where some of his ideas on education might be tried out. They prepared for this role by acting as governesses in 'polite households' and as assistant teachers.

Their chance came in the autumn of 1793, when Darwin's old friend Sir Brooke Boothby offered him a house at Ashbourne, fifteen miles north-west of Derby. The site was ideal. Ashbourne, only four miles from Dovedale, is the gateway to the Peak District and is sheltered from the north by the hills. The house itself was on dry sandy soil at the eastern edge of the town, adjoining Boothby's estate. Darwin bought the house for £550 on 7 December 1793: previously it had been a pub, The Nag's Head, and he probably chuckled at the idea of converting it into a ladies' seminary. Darwin also bought an acre of grounds (for £100) and a pew in Ashbourne Church (for £5).[1]

The school opened during 1794, and in his will on 4 December 1794 Darwin made over the property to the Misses Parker.[2] At first the pupils were mainly children of Darwin's friends, and his own children: Violetta was now eleven and she went there for several years. But soon the full complement of thirty pupils was reached, and the school won a high reputation. Susan Parker remained in charge for more than twenty years,[3] until her marriage in 1817: Mary then took over, retiring in the late 1820s. The building, 58 St John Street, still stands at the corner of Park Road.

When Susan and Mary set up school, they asked their father for guidance, and he wrote down his ideas for their benefit. They followed his advice, and found it good: his manuscript was in great demand, and three years later he was persuaded to publish it as a little book, *A Plan for the Conduct of Female Education in Boarding Schools*. We may appropriately look at it now, since it was circulated from 1794 onwards.

In this book, the most delicate and charming of his prose publications, Darwin is on his best behaviour, for he had to avoid scandalizing the parents of prospective pupils. He still manages to be quite radical, however, and his book has earned a distinctive place in the history of girls' education in England.[4] Darwin was totally opposed to the idea that girls were meant to be weak and empty-headed, and he went a long way towards modern ideas on sexual equality.

He begins unconventionally, with the accent on physical education:

> The advantages of a good education consist in uniting health and agility of body with cheerfulness and activity of mind . . . and in the acquirement of the rudiments of such arts and sciences as may amuse ourselves, or gain us the esteem of others.    [p. 10]

Generally, 'the female character should possess the mild and retiring virtues rather than the bold and dazzling ones'; but there are exceptions, as when 'the inactivity, folly or death of a husband' calls for energy of mind.

> Hence if to softness of manners, complacency of countenance, gentle unhurried motion, with a voice clear and yet tender, the charms which enchant all hearts! can be superadded internal strength and activity of mind, capable to transact the business or combat the evils of life; with a due sense of moral and religious obligation; all is obtained which education can supply; the female character becomes complete, excites our love, and commands our admiration.    [p. 11]

After these generalities Darwin gets down to detail, in thirty-nine sections on specific topics. He thinks music and dancing are overdone, and states his objections to Latin and Greek: modern languages, like French and Italian, are easier to learn and much more useful. He condemns the 'illiterate men' who ridicule well-informed women, and he wants young ladies to learn scientific subjects, especially botany, chemistry and mineralogy: they should do practical work too, and visit factories like the cotton mills on the Derwent.

He thinks girls should study shorthand, though he might not

have been too pleased at the over-development of this practice in the twentieth century. From his own experience he has two criticisms of shorthand: first, those who master it when young are 'liable not afterwards to spell our language correctly'; and, second, the volumes of shorthand notes he wrote as a student 'I now find difficult to decypher'.

After the academic subjects, Darwin turns to the tricky question of morals. He makes only guarded references to religion and specifies a secular morality based on compassion:

> A sympathy with the pains and pleasures of others is the foundation of all our social virtues. 'Do as you would be done by' is a precept which descended from heaven. . . . The lady who possesses this christian virtue of compassion cannot but be a good daughter, a good wife, and a good mother, that is, an amiable character in every department of life. . . . This compassion, or sympathy with the pains of others, ought also to extend to the brute creation, as far as our necessities will admit. . . . To destroy even insects wantonly shows an unreflecting mind, or a depraved heart.    [pp. 46–8]

To give this injunction more bite, he tells the story of a young man who saw his girl friend take 'two or three steps out of her way on the gravel walk to tread upon an insect'. Thereafter her image was associated with 'active cruelty', and ceased to be agreeable, so that 'he relinquished his design of courtship'. Darwin also commends fortitude: the girls should aim for a 'serene strength of mind, which faces unavoidable danger with open eyes'.

The most influential part of the book was that on exercise and air. Most school pupils are too sedentary, he says, 'which impairs their strength, makes their countenances pale and bloated, and lays the foundation of many diseases'. Some hours each day should be devoted to bodily exercises, such as 'playing at ball, at shuttlecock, swinging as they sit on a cord or a cushion, and dancing'. He would also recommend 'skating on the ice in winter, swimming in summer, funambulation, or dancing on the straight rope'; but these are 'not allowed to ladies by the fashion of this age and country' (p. 70).

Their health also depends on the purity of the air they breathe, Darwin says, and he insists on good ventilation in crowded rooms: he suggests sawing off an inch from the top of every door and fixing a two-inch tin plate at 45°. Darwin also wants to let a breath of fresh air into bedrooms: 'during the summer months a window should be kept a few inches open during the night as well as the day' (p. 72). This was quite a radical suggestion, because bedrooms were usually sealed, to keep out the 'noxious vapours of the night'.

Darwin has a chapter on 'Care of the shape', as 'delicate young ladies are very liable to become awry at many boarding schools'. He advises that their stays should be symmetrical or (preferably) done away with. The shape thus cared for should be clothed as gracefully as fashion permits. And grace is achieved by 'lines flowing in easy curves', such as 'a sash descending from one shoulder to the opposite hip, or a Grecian veil thrown back and winding carelessly down behind' (p. 83).

As amusements, Darwin recommends the sports previously mentioned, plus embroidery, drawing, music and chess, but not card-playing. When youthful play becomes destructive and rebuke is needed, Darwin is against harsh punishment. He thinks refractory children should be governed by the teacher's superiority of mind.

Darwin knows all about childish ailments. Stammering is 'a disease of the mind, and not of the organs of speech'. Nail-biting and face-twitching occur when children become fidgety through being confined too long in the schoolroom; once started, the habits are very difficult to eradicate. Darwin discusses diet at some length, recommending fresh milk, ripe fruit, fruit pies, butter and sugar, but not too much salt or spice.

Darwin's *Female Education* is rich in uncommon common sense and well ahead of its time. Most of his suggested reforms in the curriculum are now generally accepted, for example, the inclusion of science, modern languages and adequate physical exercise. In retrospect the most important feature of the book is Darwin's determined stand against the nearly universal belief that women were intended to be feeble and feather-brained: here we see him taking an early and courageous step along the path to sexual equality. But he did more than merely propose ideas: he had the enterprise to put them into practice—most effectively, too, because many of the leading families in the Midlands sent their children to the Ashbourne school. At the same time he gave his daughters satisfying careers.

[2]

For Darwin the great event of 1794 was the publication of Volume I of *Zoonomia, or the Laws of Organic Life,* which he had been working on for more than twenty years. This volume alone runs to more than 200,000 words, has 586 quarto pages and weighs four pounds. As the subtitle implies, Darwin was trying to classify animal life, in the hope of bringing its exuberant chaos into some kind of order, 'to reduce the facts belonging to ANIMAL LIFE into classes, orders, genera, and species; and, by comparing them with each other, to unravel the theory of diseases' (I 1).* His aim was supremely ambitious, and, with the advantage of hindsight, we can see that he was not destined to be the Linnaeus of medicine, and was doomed to splendid failure. But we have to applaud the attempt, which shows Darwin's immense confidence and wide mental grasp. He was confident that the complex operations of nature would soon yield to human scrutiny, and felt that his own mind was capable of grasping and analysing that complexity. Although the classification in *Zoonomia* is fallacious, the 55-page chapter on 'Generation' does unveil the 'laws of organic life', by specifying the processes of what we now call biological evolution. Darwin can scarcely be said to fail when he successfully propounds the fundamental law of biology.

He begins by dividing all bodily action into four classes, Irritation, Sensation, Volition and Association, which he explains most concisely in the preface to Volume II:

> The sensorium possesses four distinct powers, or faculties. . . . These are the faculties of producing fibrous motions in consequence of irritation, which is excited by external bodies; in consequence of sensation, which is excited by pleasure or pain; in consequence of volition, which is excited by desire or aversion; and in consequence of association, which is excited by other fibrous motions.   [II v]

This is about as clear as mud, and the circumlocution is in stark contrast to the direct style of Darwin's letters; he is being forced to muddy the usual clarity of his mind. Still, it is only fair to add that he does assign each disease to its appropriate class with an air of certainty.

* Volume and page numbers refer to the 1796 edition of *Zoonomia* (2nd ed. of Vol. I, 1st ed. of Vol. II).

Some examples may clear the mud a little. 'Irritation' is response to external stimuli, for example, the effect of drinking alcohol; and drunkenness would be a 'disease of irritation'. 'Sensation' is the most unsatisfactory class, because it seems to cover almost everything: the 'diseases of sensation' range from sneezing to cancer, and from smallpox to dreams. But Darwin's category of 'Volition' is a good one, and the diseases of volition are what would today be called mental illness, plus Darwinian extras such as anger, sleep and credulity. The class of 'Association' has some validity, since it covers conditions which are basically side effects, for instance, vomiting or fever.

The detailed treatment of diseases is deferred to Volume II, and Volume I of *Zoonomia* is devoted to forty general essays on a wide range of biological subjects, including instinct, sleep, reverie, vertigo, drunkenness, circulation, saliva, the stomach, the liver, temperaments, and digestion, to quote just the shortest. As an aperitif, here is a taste of his tirade against alcohol:

> In drunken people it generally happens that the secretory vessels of the liver become first paralytic, and a torpor with consequent gall-stones or schirrus of this viscus is induced with concomitant jaundice; otherwise it becomes inflamed . . . and produces the gout, or the rosy eruption of the face, or some other leprous eruption on the head, or arms, or legs. . . . Mark what happens to a man who drinks a quart of wine or of ale, if he has not been habituated to it. He loses the use both of his limbs and of his understanding! He becomes a temporary idiot, and has a temporary stroke of the palsy! And though he slowly recovers after some hours, is it not reasonable to conclude that a perpetual repetition of so powerful a poison must at length permanently affect him? [I 250–1]

Darwin has twenty pages on sleep and dreams, most of it quite acceptable today. He believes dreams enable us to 'let off steam' and are not just a 'waste of sensorial power'. He suggests that the daily periodicity of sleep may stem from solar and lunar tides in the atmosphere, which were overrated in his day. Still, his alertness to 'the periods of diseases' foreshadows the recent revival of interest in circadian rhythms as a result of space flight and the 'jet-lag' problems of travellers between different time zones.

One of Darwin's successes is his chapter on oxygenation of the blood, where he cuts through the fog of phlogiston to a correct picture:

It appears that the basis of atmospherical air, called oxygene, is
received by the blood through the membranes of the lungs; and that
by this addition the colour of the blood is changed from a dark to a
light red.   [I 476]

The same process occurs in the gills of fish, he says, and in the
placenta.

Another of Darwin's successes is his prediction of the future
importance of electricity, at a time when it was thought of only
as a toy. The modern era in electricity began in 1800 with the
invention of the Voltaic cell: Volta found that two different
metals (such as lead and zinc), when dipped in a conducting
solution, generate an electric current in a wire attached to the
dry ends. Darwin was writing before 1800, but he sensed the
importance of Volta's earlier experiments, remarking that if
pieces of lead and silver, touching outside the mouth, are applied
to different parts of the tongue, an 'acidulous taste is perceived,
as of a fluid like a stream of electricity passing from one of them
to the other' (I 120). He thinks this 'deserves further investigation, as it may acquaint us with new properties of matter'—
which it certainly has.

More shocking to his contemporaries was Darwin's analysis
of beauty, which he traces to the infant's perception of the form
of the mother's breast:

> Hence at our maturer years, when any object of vision is presented
> to us, which by its waving or spiral lines bears any similitude to the
> form of the female bosom . . . we feel a general glow of delight,
> which seems to influence all our senses. . . . This animal attraction
> is love . . . the purest source of human felicity, the cordial drop in
> the otherwise vapid cup of life.   [I 146–7]

Even today these ideas, which derive from Hogarth's *Analysis of
Beauty*, provoke argument: in his own day Darwin was severely
criticized for his views on sexual attraction by Sheridan and by
Thomas Brown.[5] We can see why he made people uneasy: he
was taking a modern view of sex, with God ignored. So it is
appropriate that his remarks, though shocking in the 1790s,
enjoy currency through quotation in a book[6] that sold in millions
in the 1970s.

As well as explaining the fascination of curves, Darwin makes
good use of points: *Zoonomia* is apparently the first book to have
the numbered paragraph subdivisions now so widely used in

scientific textbooks and reports, for example, section 5.3.4. Darwin devised this system as a result of his long experience with Linnaean classification.

One serious gap in Darwin's armour was his ignorance of the important role of bacteria and viruses. In his day microscopic researches were despised as a triviality, and he did not react strongly enough against this folly: he failed to anticipate Pasteur by adopting the germ theory of disease. A few years later Darwin came near the germ theory when writing about smallpox inoculation: 'One grain of variolous matter, inserted by inoculation, shall in about seven days stimulate the system into unnatural action; which in about seven days more produces ten thousand times the quantity of a similar material thrown out on the skin in pustules!'[7] He also commended microscopic researches in a prescient sentence: 'I hope that microscopic researches may again excite the attention of philosophers, as unforeseen advantages may probably be derived from them, like the discovery of a new world.'[8] Fine sentiments; but it was a world that Darwin himself failed to discover. Still, his ignorance of the germ theory allowed him to avoid the error of thinking that people 'catch colds' through contact with germs, whereas it is low resistance that allows ever-present germs to get a grip.

Though we may think *Zoonomia* fallacious, it enjoyed immense success. The *European Magazine* quoted the opinion that *Zoonomia* 'bids fair to do for Medicine what Sir Isaac Newton's *Principia* has done for Natural Philosophy'; and the *Monthly Magazine* thought it 'one of the most important productions of the age'. There was a second edition to go with Volume II in 1796, and a third in 1801, of four volumes with 2100 octavo pages. There were at least five American editions, and German, Italian and French translations. In Charles Darwin's witty phrase, the book 'was honoured by the Pope by being placed in the Index Expurgatorius'. Beddoes, who was not unbiased, thought *Zoonomia* 'perhaps the most original work ever composed by mortal man', which would 'place the Author amongst the greatest of mankind, the founders of sciences'.[9]

[3]

Beddoes's praise, though scarcely valid for the whole volume, is not far from the mark when applied to the chapter on evolution. The ancient Greeks had the idea that the species now seen on earth evolved gradually from primitive forms, and in the next two thousand years the idea was revived from time to time. But it made little headway in seventeenth- and eighteenth-century Europe, for two reasons. First and foremost, the Christian Church decreed that species were created by God and immutable. Second, even the men of science found themselves subconsciously favouring the fixity of species, because of the great success of Linnaeus in classifying species of plants. Anyone wishing to propound evolutionary ideas had not only to find the correct intellectual path but also to leap over these two invisible psychological barriers.

Erasmus Darwin cared little for conventional wisdom or the Church (though he was careful now not to be too outspoken in his published work), and he succeeded in propounding a theory of evolution much better and more complete than any previous version. He begins his exposition badly, with a male bias: he suggests that in the foetus the male provides the active nucleus and the female merely the food on which it grows. This view would have sabotaged his evolutionary theory, and fortunately he discards it a few pages later (I 501) when, after pondering over mules, he admits that the female contributes almost equally to the make-up of the progeny. He believes that the embryo begins as a 'simple living filament' which, 'whatever form it may be, whether sphere, cube or cylinder', is capable of being excited, perhaps by 'the surrounding fluid', to bend into a ring, and 'by degrees the living ring may become a living tube' (I 496).

Darwin then draws attention to the great changes which occur in animals. First, there are the changes during the life of an individual animal 'as in the production of the butterfly with painted wings from the crawling caterpillar; or of the respiring frog from the subnatant tadpole' (I 504). Second, he points to the great changes which have, down the centuries, been produced by animals 'by artificial or accidental cultivation, as in horses, which we have exercised for the different purposes of strength or swiftness, in carrying burthens or in running races' (I 504); or in the various breeds of dog, the bulldog for strength and courage, the greyhound for speed; and so on, with many further examples, including cattle, pigeons, sheep and camels, Third, he notes that monstrosities, or mutations as we should now say, may be inherited: 'Many of these enormities of shape are propagated, and continued as a variety at least, if not as a new species of animal. I have seen a breed of cats with an additional claw on every foot; of poultry also with an additional claw, and with wings to their feet' (I 505). All these anatomical changes and the similar structure of the warm-blooded animals lead him

> to conclude that they have alike been produced from a similar living filament. In some this filament in its advance to maturity has acquired hands and fingers, with a fine sense of touch, as in mankind. In others it has acquired claws or talons, as in tygers and eagles. In others, toes with an intervening web, or membrane, as in seals and geese.... [I 506]

All animals, then, 'undergo perpetual transformations', and, if adequate air and water are available, the 'three great objects of desire, which have changed the forms of many animals by their exertions to gratify them, are those of lust, hunger and security'. The first, lust, leads Darwin to an account of sexual selection:

> A great want of one part of the animal world has consisted in the desire of the exclusive possession of the females; and these have acquired weapons to combat each other for this purpose. . . . So the horns of the stag are sharp to offend his adversary, but are branched for the purpose of parrying or receiving the thrusts of horns similar to his own, and have therefore been formed for the purpose of combating other stags for the exclusive possession of the females; who are observed, like the ladies in the times of chivalry, to attend the car of the victor. [I 507]

Other examples are boars and polygamous birds, such as the cock and the quail. Darwin concludes:

> The final cause of this contest amongst the males seems to be, that the strongest and most active animal should propagate the species, which should thence become improved. [I 507]

Although his statement is too bald to be entirely true, Darwin seizes on the essential point—the central tautology of evolution —that the species is improved through the 'fitter' animals tending to have more (and fitter) progeny than the weaker ones.

The second of the controlling forces is 'the means of procuring food, which has diversified the forms of all species of animals'. Darwin explains how each animal has become adapted to its method of acquiring food, citing the hard nose of the swine, the elephant's trunk, the rough tongues of cattle, and the peculiarities of birds, which were later to impress Charles Darwin in the Galapagos Islands.

> Some birds have acquired harder beaks to crack nuts, as the parrot. Others have acquired beaks adapted to break the harder seeds, as sparrows. Others for the softer seeds of flowers, or the buds of trees, as the finches. Other birds have acquired long beaks to penetrate the moister soils in search of insects or roots, as woodcocks; and others broad ones to filtrate the water of lakes, and to retain aquatic insects. All which seem to have been gradually produced during many generations by the perpetual endeavour of the creatures to supply the want of food.   [I 508]

The third of the controlling forces, the want of security, or the means of escaping other more powerful animals, 'seems much to have diversified the forms of their bodies and the colour of them'. Some animals, he says,

> have acquired wings instead of legs, as the smaller birds, for the purpose of escape. Others great length of fin, or of membrane, as the flying fish, and the bat. Others great swiftness of foot, as the hare. Others have acquired hard or armed shells, as the tortoise and the echinus marinus. . . . The colours of many animals seem adapted to their purposes of concealing themselves either to avoid danger, or to spring upon their prey.   [I 508, 513]

He identifies the use of mimicry as well as camouflage, mentioning the

> frog-fish, Lophius Histrio, which inhabits the large floating islands of sea-weed about the Cape of Good Hope, and has fulcra resembling leaves, that the fishes of prey may mistake it for the sea-weed, which it inhabits.   [I 508]

After mulling over all these mechanisms, Darwin concludes:

> Would it be too bold to imagine, that in the great length of time since the earth began to exist, perhaps millions of ages before the commencement of the history of mankind, would it be too bold to imagine, that all warm-blooded animals have arisen from one living filament, which THE GREAT FIRST CAUSE endued with animality, with the power of acquiring new parts, attended with new propensities, directed by irritations, sensations, volitions, and associations; and thus possessing the faculty of continuing to improve by its own inherent activity, and of delivering down those improvements by generation to its posterity, world without end!   [I 509]

This is more a declaration of faith in evolution than a question, and, appropriately, there is no question mark at the end. Four comments are needed, however.

First, Darwin treats religious susceptibilities very tenderly. It was 1794, not 1789, and tact was imperative. So he salutes the 'GREAT FIRST CAUSE'; this was not too difficult, since he had sympathy with deism. But he wishes to deprive God of his traditional role as officer-in-charge of evolution and to say that evolution proceeds naturally, *without divine intervention.* This is the meaning of the phrase 'by its own inherent activity': he is *not* proposing the absurd idea that animals consciously control their own evolution, as some have suggested.

Second, the vague remark about all creatures arising from 'one living filament' is clarified a few years later in *The Temple of Nature*: 'all vegetables and animals now existing were originally derived from the smallest microscopic ones, formed by spontaneous vitality' in primeval oceans.[10] This is in accord with the modern view of life's origins, that amino-acids were compounded from simpler molecules in primeval waters.

The third notable feature of Darwin's summary is the time scale. In his day good Christians accepted that the world was formed in 4004 B.C., but Darwin realized that this was most unlikely, and specified 'millions of ages', which, if we take an age as roughly a century, means 'hundreds of millions of years'. This is just right: evolution from small and simple sea-creatures to humans has taken about 500 million years.

My fourth comment is a warning not to be misled by the phrase 'directed by irritations, sensations, volitions and associations'. This phrase is repeated *ad nauseam* in *Zoonomia* and really means nothing, since everything is 'directed by irritations, etc'. We can best avoid irritation by ignoring the phrase.

Darwin rounded off his view of evolution in the third edition of *Zoonomia*, where he states that if species are evolving, some will become extinct.

> This idea is shown to our senses by contemplating the petrifactions of shells, and of vegetables, which may be said, like busts and medals, to record the history of remote times. Of the myriads of belemnites, cornua ammonis, and numerous other petrified shells, which are found in the masses of limestone which have been produced by them, none now are ever found in our seas.[11]

Darwin's exposition of evolution in the first (and second)

editions of *Zoonomia* is an important advance in biology.[12] In the
last few years of his life he was to develop his ideas further.


[4]


Returning from biological theory to real life at Derby in 1794–5
we find Darwin hard at work on Volume II of *Zoonomia*. Knowing he could pop unusual cases into the book gave him an added
zest in his medical work. His family seemed to be doing well.
Erasmus junior was growing quite wealthy and told his brother
Robert: 'I am not afraid of being rich, as our father used to say
at Lichfield he was, for fear of growing covetous; to avoid which
misfortune, as you know, he used to dig a certain number of duck
puddles every spring, that he might fill them up in the autumn.'[13]
The symbolism is obscure, though Robert presumably understood it. Robert himself was very busy with his medical practice
at Shrewsbury. Now twenty-eight, he was thinking of getting
married, and the signs were that Susannah Wedgwood would be
his wife. Josiah and Erasmus were both delighted at the prospect
of their families being united in this way.

At home, besides contending with the six younger children,
now aged between twelve and four, Darwin and Elizabeth quite
often entertained visitors, especially young admirers of Darwin's
books. One such disciple and a frequent caller was Dewhurst
Bilsborrow, a Cambridge undergraduate who was to become a
clergyman. Bilsborrow later began writing a biography of
Darwin, but it was never published. Another visitor in 1794 was
Thomas Young, then twenty-one, who seven years later pro-
pounded the wave theory of light, and became as wide-ranging
as Darwin in his talents and knowledge. Darwin and Young took
to each other at once. Young wrote: 'I was highly gratified with
the remainder of the day, which I spent almost entirely with
Darwin. He gave me my choice of looking over three cabinets, of
cameos, of minerals and of plants.'[14] And Darwin wrote a letter
of introduction which pleased Young: 'He unites the scholar
with the philosopher, and the cultivation of modern arts with
the simplicity of ancient manners.'[15]

Darwin's fame as a doctor was becoming rather excessive,
though he took no notice of it and continued normally in his

profession. Patients often came to him from London, and one of these (probably in the mid 1790s, but possibly earlier) was Miss Fielding, a grand-daughter of Lady Charlotte Finch, governess to the Royal Household. Miss Fielding was restored to health after staying for some time at his house. When King George III heard of Darwin's fame through Lady Charlotte, he said: ' "Why does not Dr Darwin come to London? He shall be my physician if he comes"; and he repeated this over and over again in his usual manner.'[16] But Darwin and Elizabeth did not like the idea of living in London, so the royal request was in vain.

[5]

With one of his most difficult patients, Tom Wedgwood, Darwin made what seems in retrospect a tragic mistake. In his day doctors dispensed opium nonchalantly, and Darwin was particularly keen on the drug because it did have some effect, unlike most medicines of the time. He recommends opium for hundreds of the diseases covered in *Zoonomia*, some quite trivial. A few escalating examples will suffice, chosen just from pages 300–350 of Volume II:

*Anorexia*. Want of appetite . . . Opium half a grain twice a day. . . .
Impotency . . . he was advised to take a grain of opium before he went to bed. . . .
Gallstones . . . Opium a grain and a half. . . .
Painful epilepsy . . . Opium a grain every half hour. . . .
Sleepwalking . . . Opium in large doses. . . .
*Tetanus trismus* . . . Opium in very large doses. . . .

Although Darwin knew of opium addiction, described in Canto II of *The Loves of the Plants*, he did not realize the danger of his treatments.

The crucial letter to Tom Wedgwood was written on 10 August 1794. Darwin first says he is glad to hear that Tom is feeling better, as a result of 'the climate of Devon, and the chearfulness of your companions'. The most congenial of the companions was S. T. Coleridge, and Darwin's letter is addressed to 'Ottery St. Mary, Devonshire', where Tom was staying to be near the Coleridges. Though improved in health. Tom was still complaining of numerous debilities, which Darwin patiently deals with, one by one. For the first, a feverishness at night which kept him awake, Darwin recommends regular meals, and not too much 'potation'. The second, a swelling of the tonsils, he blames on a decayed tooth, to be treated either by extracting the tooth or by 'extract of Bark twice a day', or both. Tom's third complaint, a change in skin texture, Darwin welcomes as indicating a 'degree of plumpness' instead of his usual emaciation. Finally, Tom asked about suitable medicines to take, and Darwin replies: 'I have no great opinion of the cicuta. . . . About five grains of rhubarb, and ¾ of a grain, or a grain, of opium, taken every night for many months, perhaps during the whole winter, I think a medecine of much greater value in your situation.'[17] So Tom Wedgwood, and by implication his close friend Coleridge, whose opium addiction started at about this time, began a six-month course of opium prescribed by Darwin as a 'suitable medicine': it was an experience from which neither recovered. (In his letter Darwin originally wrote 'five grains of opium', but fortunately crossed out the opium and replaced it by rhubarb.)

[6]

Another Tom, far more energetic and surnamed Beddoes, was very active in 1794. He read the proofs of Volume I of *Zoonomia* and contested Darwin's views on how our fibres are stimulated to give us the idea of squareness, solidity and other tactual qualities. Darwin's reply ends: 'I can readily have an idea of an idea . . . but I believe I am got into that sublime figure of rhetoric called the Profound. Adieu.'[18] Beddoes went on worrying at the subject like a terrier, but Darwin grew tired of it: 'I do not enter the inane dispute about the inanity of the universe, I leave that to the disciples of Berkeley and Hume. . . . The other observations in your letter are all good and ingenious, but I am too idle to write about them.'[19] Although Beddoes's energy was sometimes overpowering, Darwin usually approved of the pamphlets he received so often from his friend. After reading one of them, 'On the art of self-preservation', Darwin wrote: 'You deserve a civic crown for saving the lives of your fellow-citizens.'[20] When Beddoes agreed to revise Brown's *Elements of Medicine*, Darwin gave him some advice on this difficult task:

'All you can do will be to white-wash the old building as it stands, and to put a neat portico to it by way of preface commendatory, and cover the irregularities by shrubberies of myrtle and orange flower.'[21]

For Beddoes, 1794 was a year of decision. He married Edgeworth's daughter Anna and began planning his 'Pneumatic Institution' at Clifton. The idea was to try to cure diseases by administering gases to patients, with oxygen as the first candidate. Most current medicines were either desperate or ineffective, and Beddoes's idea was at least logical and novel, even if it proved less effective than he hoped. Four years later, after considerable help from Edgeworth, Darwin, Watt and Tom Wedgwood, Beddoes eventually opened the Pneumatic Institution. In 1794 Darwin organized a subscription for it at Derby and raised thirty-two guineas, including five guineas he contributed himself and ten guineas from the Strutts. These details appear in a letter of 30 November 1794 from Darwin to Watt,[22] who was apparently arranging for a subscription in Birmingham.

Being a friend of Beddoes in the 1790s carried penalties that Darwin did not appreciate until later. Darwin had lived most of his life in a free-thinking era, when unorthodox opinions raised a few eyebrows in polite society, but did not provoke vendettas. After the excesses of the French Revolution in 1792, the climate changed: Pitt began his repression of the radicals, which led to the trial of the twelve reformers in 1794. Darwin was well aware of the trend, and he was careful not to say anything explicit against God or King in *Zoonomia*. What he did not realize soon enough was that a new crime had been created—guilt by association. Darwin was guilty of associating with Beddoes, a notorious radical whose pamphlet about the French Revolution refers to France being 'purged not only from *Ecclesiastical Drones* . . . but also from the monstrous debauchery of the richer, and the beggarly insolence of the poorer Noblesse'. Some of Beddoes's extreme opinions were also rather silly: for example, in his 'Observations on calculus . . .' he suggests that we might, by chemical arts, 'teach our Woods and Hedges to supply us with butter and tallow'. Darwin was already publicly linked with Beddoes through the 'Letter to Dr Darwin on pulmonary consumption' which Beddoes published in 1793.

Beddoes was intensely irritating to the Establishment, and wide open to parody, through his sillier ideas; equally irritating

was the continued popularity of Darwin's *Botanic Garden*, with
its obvious sympathy for the French Revolution. Why not deflate
this dynamic duo 'at a stroke' with a parody, written in rhyming
couplets, as if by Darwin? The outcome of this idea was *The
Golden Age*, said to be 'a poetical epistle from Erasmus D——n
M.D. to Thomas Beddoes M.D.', published by Rivington in
1794, and running to 202 lines. The anonymous author seriously
damaged Beddoes's credibility by ridiculing his extreme ideas;
Darwin was injured too, by association and by a few side-swipes.
(Darwin had a notice inserted in the *Derby Mercury* to say he
was not the author, but this was only a local anaesthetic for the
wound he received.)

The main target of *The Golden Age* is Beddoes's idea that
vegetables may be adapted to grow animal products. The author
(taken as Darwin by the casual reader) begins with fulsome
praise of Beddoes as the Bigot's Scourge and the Pride of
Democrats, and asks us to listen

> While in Rhyme's Galligaskins I enclose
> The broad posteriors of thy brawny prose.  [9–10]

In the golden age the trees will grow beef and the hedges butter:

> No more the lazy Ox shall gormandize,
> And swell with fattening grass his monstrous size;
> No more trot round and round the groaning field,
> But tons of Beef our loaded Thickets yield!  [45–8]

This opens the way for a kick at Darwin:

> See plants, susceptible of joy and woe,
> Feel all we feel, and know whate'er we know!  [73–4]

Then, in a curious foretaste of Shelley's *Queen Mab*, Darwin is
made to praise the 'pious Atheists',

> Who, foes to Power Despotic, dare defy
> The Kings of Kings, that Bugbear of the sky.  [143–4]

This takes us to a golden era, free of priests, of kings and of the
King of Kings, a time when all the plants and trees will join in
the rejoicing,

> And ye, oh! Swine, lift up your little Eyes,
> With rapture riot round your rotten Styes.  [199–200]

Darwin had only been dipping a tentative finger in the river of radicalism: he did not wish to abolish either the King or the King of Kings. Now the author of this brilliant parody had stolen up behind, pushed him right into the river, and walked off incognito. It gave him a nasty shock, and warned him that the spirit of the age was beginning to turn against him. Another sign was the publication in 1794 of T. J. Mathias's satirical verses *The Pursuits of Literature*, though Darwin is only one of many poets there lampooned.

The year 1794 marked the zenith of his popularity, with the *Botanic Garden* still enjoying its great fame and *Zoonomia* acclaimed as a medical wonder. But 1794 was also the year of Paley's *Evidences of Christianity*, and with Britain fighting for survival against Napoleon in the next decade, a comfortable faith in God was required, not atheistic evolutionism. In the years of repression that followed, the time was out of joint for Darwin, who was a prime example of an unrepressed mind, inquiring and free-thinking. His reputation suffered death by a thousand pinpricks.[23]

[7]

The bouncing Beddoes did not oust Darwin's 'antient friends', Boulton, Watt, Wedgwood and Edgeworth: there is correspondence with all four during 1794. During November a medical call took Darwin to Birmingham; but it also prevented him from calling on Watt, much to his chagrin, as appears from his letter of 30 November to Watt, in which he also says: 'I have been so much engaged in common business, and in finishing the second vol. of my book, that I have not thought much about airs.'[24]

Edgeworth's letters to Darwin in 1794 are among his friendliest. He is very flattering about *Zoonomia*, thanking Darwin for 'your immortal present'. Edgeworth foresees that one 'of my Great Great grandchildren will with laudable vanity shew the *ex dono* to his envying contemporaries and exult in the friendship of his Ancestor'. Edgeworth was not deceived by Darwin's deistic cover-up: 'Your Ens Entium is the same as your living filament—your God of God!' Edgeworth ends this letter, dated 7 September 1794, by offering his 'best Services to Mrs D, whom I admire as much as a man ought to admire the wife of his friend'.[25] In his letter of 11 December Edgeworth says that 'Anna seems happy with Dr Beddoes' and, more ominously, that his wife Elizabeth is rather ill.

Josiah Wedgwood, now sixty-four, was also ill in 1794, with familiar symptoms, of pain in the right jaw and in what Darwin called his 'no leg'. But he was very much better after a visit to Buxton, and Darwin wrote cheerfully on 9 December:

> Your letter gives me great pleasure in assuring me . . . that you have become free from your complaint—the ceasing of the palpitation of your heart and of the intermission of your pulse is another proof of your increase of strength. . . . As you are *so* well, I advise you to leave off the bark and to take no medicine at present.[26]

Unfortunately Darwin's optimism was misjudged: within a few days Wedgwood's face began to swell and there were signs of mortification. Darwin hurried to Etruria and stayed there for some days. But nothing could be done. Wedgwood gradually sank, in pain and fever, and died on 3 January 1795. It was a sad end for Darwin's closest friend, whose achievement in simultaneously advancing art, technology and industry has never since been equalled.

Two months after Wedgwood's death, on 15 March, Darwin wrote a long letter to Edgeworth, which shows he was depressed by the loss of his friend and dismayed about the feeling against French sympathizers:

> The death of Mr Wedgwood grieves me very much. He is a public as well as private loss—we all grow old but you!—when I think of dying it is always without pain or fear—this world was made for the demon you speak of, who seems daily to gain ground upon the *other gentleman*, by the assistance of Mr Pitt and our gracious ———
> I dare not mention his name for fear that high treason may be in the sound; and I have a professed spy shoulders us on the right, and another on the opposite side of the street, both attornies! and I hear every name supposed to think different from the minister is put in alphabetical order in Mr Reeve's doomsday book, and that if the French should land, these recorded gentlemen are to be all imprison'd to prevent them from committing crimes of a deeper dye. Poor Wedgwood told me he heard his name stood high in the list.[27]

The repressive atmosphere in England made Darwin think of emigrating to his favourite land across the sea, America, where

George Washington was in his second term as President, and Dr Small's protégé Thomas Jefferson had until recently been Secretary of State. Darwin told Edgeworth: 'America is the only place of safety—and what does a man past 50 (I don't mean you) want? Potatoes and milk—nothing else. These may be had in America untax'd by Kings and priests.'[28] This shows how deeply Darwin was perturbed at the turn of events; from now on, his published views are often milder than his real ones—a situation familiar today, but unfamiliar to the Darwin of previous years.

Darwin commends Edgeworth's plan for a telegraph system for the defence of Ireland—'it would be like a giant wielding his arms and talking with his fingers'—and sends Edgeworth a receipt for £104, apparently interest on a loan Darwin had made to him. Since Erasmus junior was away, Darwin didn't know how to send a legal receipt—'Mr Burns, the Quaker, once let me a lease, which began with "Friend Darwin, Honest men need no Lawyer. I hereby let thee &c".'[29] So Darwin sent Edgeworth an informal receipt. He also mentions that the *European Magazine* has a feature about him, probably by William Seward, a distant relation of Anna.

This article, in the February 1795 issue, has an engraved portrait and begins with the remark that 'the annals of literature scarcely produce a single instance', apart from Darwin, of so high a poetical talent being hidden until the age of nearly sixty. The poem on Prince Frederick is then quoted in full, followed by a summary of Darwin's life; the article ends with the hope that his writings will provide 'much future entertainment and instruction'.

Entertainment is not the best word for Darwin's correspondence with Tom Wedgwood in 1795, but at least the letters are *not* primarily about Tom's health. Instead they concentrate on eye operations to combat cataract. On 24 February 1795, going straight to the point as usual, Darwin suggests that a steel wire having a sharp point and a screw should 'be suddenly put into the center of the cornea, which will steady the eye'; then a small piece should be cut from the cornea with 'a fine circular saw made of hollow wire' serrated at the end and slipped over the other wire. 'The operation is nice', Darwin rightly says—and nasty too, we might add. In his next letter (9 March) Darwin advises Tom to practise on calves' or sheep's eyes before risking the treatment of humans, and gives another drawing of his proposed surgical instrument. He also suggests that 'a bit of glass ground into a shape like a shirt-sleeve stud be put in the hole made in the center of the cornea, and left there', so that it 'would stay and become a glass eye': the 'future scar would not signify'. Almost as if he knew that you might think his ideas horrific, Darwin sets them nicely in perspective, telling Tom: 'If you can make these people see by such glass eyes, you will gain immortal honour, and serve the human animal.'[30]

Darwin also has some medical advice for Tom: 'If your digestion is not good, half a grain of opium may be taken, or a second glass of wine.'[31] It is scarcely an ideal treatment for indigestion, in the light of modern knowledge.

Darwin's next letter to Tom Wedgwood (23 January 1796) is a reply to Tom's comments on Volume I of *Zoonomia*. The discussion ranges over images of ideas, the lymphatic system, surprise, vertigo, nest-building by birds, prismatic colours, and sleep; Darwin defers other topics 'till we happen to meet', and he says Volume II should be published in March or April 1796.

[8]

With the publication of Volume II of *Zoonomia*, Darwin's medical reputation reached its highest point. Volume II has 300,000 words, extends to 772 pages and weighs five pounds: it is a work of reference rather than a readable book. Darwin begins with a a catalogue of diseases, divided into Classes, Orders, Genera and Species, then gives details of each disease (sometimes with case histories) and the recommended treatments. Two examples are enough to indicate the form and scope of the catalogue:

CLASS I: *Diseases of Irritation*
ORDO I: Increased irritation
GENUS I: With increased actions of the sanguiferous system
SPECIES

| | |
|---|---|
| 1. *Febris irritativa* | Irritative fever |
| 2. *Ebrietas* | Drunkenness |
| 3. *Haemorrhagia arteriosa* | Arterial haemorrhage |
| 4. *Haemoptoe arteriosa* | Spitting of arterial blood |
| 5. *Haemorrhagia narium* | Bleeding from the nose . . . |

CLASS III: *Diseases of Volition*
ORDO I. Increased volition
GENUS II: With increased actions of the organs of sense

SPECIES

| | |
|---|---|
| 1. *Mania mutabilis* | Mutable madness |
| 2. *Studium inane* | Reverie |
| 3. *Vigilia* | Watchfulness |
| 4. *Erotomania* | Sentimental love |
| 5. *Amor sui* | Vanity . . . [II 3; II 317] |

And so it goes on, numbers 6 to 18 being desire of home, superstitious hope, pride of family, ambition, grief, irksomeness of life, desire of beauty, lust, anger, rage, and the triple fears of poverty, death and hell.

Darwin's treatments of the diseases of irritation and sensation are generally unimpressive. Take measles, a disease of sensation (Ordo I, Genus III, Species 10):

> The measles are usually attended with inflammatory fever with strong pulse, and bear the lancet in every stage of the disease. . . .
>
> [II 242]

Like most eighteenth-century doctors, Darwin was far too ready to bare the lancet and begin bleeding. On childbirth, however, he cuts through the fog of current error:

> As parturition is a natural, not a morbid process, no medicine should be given, where there is no appearance of disease. The absurd custom of giving a powerful opiate without indication to all women, as soon as they are delivered, is, I make no doubt, frequently attended with injurious, and sometimes with fatal consequences.
>
> [II 189]

The description of scarlet fever is compelling:

> *Scarlatina maligna.* The malignant scarlet fever begins with inflamed tonsils; which are succeeded by dark drab-coloured sloughs from three to five lines in diameter, flat, or beneath the surrounding surface; and which conceal beneath them spreading gangrenous ulcers. . . . [II 245]

This is one of many diseases in which 'the patient generally dies in a few days'; so we cannot blame Darwin for trying everything in his M.M.—which stands for *materia medica*, not *memento mori*:

> M.M. A vomit once. Wine. Beer. Cyder. Opium. Bark. . . . Broth. Custards. Milk. Jellies. Bread pudding. Chicken. . . .

It sounds like the contents of the larder; but this is only the first course, for the complete treatment occupies two pages. Darwin suggests giving oxygen, passing electric shocks through the tonsils, and seeking a method of inoculation—'no one could do an act more beneficial to society, or glorious to himself' (II 246).

Darwin is at his best on the diseases of volition. He knows that bodily ailments are often of mental origin, and that many obsessions will have to be recognized as diseases before they can be cured. For example, *spes religiosa*, superstitious hope, is a 'maniacal hallucination' that in mild form produces merely 'an agreeable reverie', but when given public support has 'occasioned many enormities' : 'What cruelties, murders, massacres, has not this insanity introduced into the world!' Then there is *orci timor*, the fear of hell:

> Many theatric preachers among the Methodists successfully inspire this terror, and live comfortably upon the folly of their hearers. In this kind of madness the poor patients frequently commit suicide; although they believe they run headlong into the hell which they dread! Such is the power of oratory, and such the debility of the human understanding! [II 379]

Next, in curious juxtaposition, comes *Satyriasis* or 'ungovernable desire of venereal indulgence', for which Darwin specifies four smart shocks: 'M.M. Venesection. Cathartics. Torpentia. Marriage' (II 380). Three pages later those who fear 'the supposed ill consequences of self pollution' receive similar treatment: 'M.M. . . . Marry them . . . a certain cure.'

Credulity is a most deplorable disease, Darwin thinks, endemic in 'the bulk of mankind', who 'have thus been the dupes of priests and politicians in all countries and in all ages of the world' (II 410). 'Credulity is made an indispensable virtue' by religious sects, and is best cured by increasing 'our knowledge of the laws of nature' and setting 'the faculty of reason above that of imagination'.

Darwin's kindness to the mentally ill emerges in a case of hallucination:

> Miss G——— . . . said, as I once sat by her, 'My head is fallen off, see it is rolled to that corner of the room, and the little black dog is nibbling the nose off'. On my walking to the place which she looked at, and returning, and assuring her that her nose was unhurt, she became pacified, though I was doubtful whether she attended to me. [II 361–2]

Another unrecognized disease is 'loss of beauty', often 'painfully felt by Ladies'; but some of the usual remedies, particularly cosmetics containing white lead, have 'destroyed the health of thousands'. Darwin advises removing unwanted sun tan with concentrated lemon juice or dilute hydrochloric acid; but fashions change and this whitening operation, so likely to be 'painfully felt', would have few takers today.

After discussing the diseases of Association, Darwin adds a ninety-page supplement on 'Sympathetic Theory of Fever', which was very influential in its day. Two of his suggestions have since proved their worth. The first is blood transfusion, a revival of an old idea. The second, deriving from Brindley's experiences with mill-stones, is the idea of whirling patients in a centrifuge, or rotative couch, as Darwin calls it. Watt made a detailed engineering design to Darwin's specification, shown in Plate 12A. As W. J. White remarks in his history of the centrifuge in aerospace medicine, 'Darwin's analysis marked the beginning of the therapeutic use of centrifugation'.[32] It is a subject with far-reaching future applications in creating artificial gravity in space stations.

Volume II of *Zoonomia* ends with 118 pages of Materia Medica, defined as 'all substances which may contribute to the restoration of health'—and *may* is the right word. They fall into seven classes, of which the first, Nutrientia, is most important because it includes food. Digressing, Darwin notes that population is sparse 'where men lived solely by hunting' and that agriculture allows a great increase. 'But pasturage cannot exist without property both in the soil and the herds', and 'an inequality of the ranks of society must succeed', an inequality which he thinks is too great. To secure 'the greatest sum of human happiness', he says, 'there should be no slavery . . . and no despotism.' As well as food, he includes oxygen and blood transfusion in the Nutrientia. His second class of restoratives, which 'increase the irritative motions', include opium, alcohol, love and joy. Those in the third class increase secretion, and range from ginger to hopeless distress; those in the fourth, which increase absorption, include acid of vitriol and electric sparks. And so on: the medicines are classified as thoroughly, and fruitlessly, as the diseases.

[9]

For Erasmus one of the happiest events of 1796 was the marriage in April of his son Robert to Susannah Wedgwood, Josiah's eldest daughter. It is not often that a son marries the woman his father would have chosen, but in this, as in so many other matters, Robert seems to have fallen in with his father's wishes. The conformity was probably subconscious, but none the less significant for that. Susannah was one year older than Robert, whom she had known since early childhood. She often stayed with the Darwins at Derby, and was a great favourite with Erasmus: she gave him lessons in music, one of the few subjects of which he was ignorant.

Although ten of Erasmus's fourteen children were alive and healthy, it is curious that at the age of sixty-five he still had no grandchildren. Elizabeth outdid him by becoming a grandmother in 1797 with the birth of Reginald Pole, son of her eldest son Sacheverel. Reginald later became rector of Radburn for forty-two years, after the death of his half-uncle Edward Pole.

Every Christmas Erasmus, Elizabeth and their family would go to Elston to visit Erasmus's mother, now in her nineties, but still healthy and active. The Christmas visit in 1796 proved to be the last, for his mother died in April 1797 at the age of ninety-five.

Though his own health remained good, Darwin was now beginning to cut down his regular medical practice. In February 1796 he wrote to Thomas Greene asking for details of the medicines he had prescribed in the previous year or two for a Mr Garick, whose will was being contested. Darwin was 'subpoena'd on a tryal, which is to take place at Stafford'.[33] This was typical of the tasks he was beginning to wish he could avoid.

Darwin's fame as a physician was now almost legendary, and during 1797 a gentleman arrived from London asking Darwin to examine him: 'I am come from London to consult you, as the greatest physician in the world, to hear from you if there is any hope in my case. . . . It is of the utmost importance for me to settle my worldly affairs immediately; therefore I trust that you will not deceive me, but tell me without hesitation your candid opinion.'[34] After examining him, Darwin had to say there was no hope; he could not expect to live more than a fortnight. The man seized Darwin's hand and said: 'Thank you, doctor, I thank you; my mind is satisfied; I now know there is no hope for me.' Darwin asked him: 'But as you come from London, why did you not consult Dr Warren, so celebrated a physician?' He replied: 'Alas! doctor, I *am* Dr Warren.' He died a week or two later.

Not all his patients were so dramatic, and with Tom Wedgwood it was back to square one. Darwin's letter of 7 February 1797 records the return of the worms—'the ascarides are a dreadful enemy. . . .'[35] Tom was continuing his mechanical inventions, and Darwin compliments him on an ingenious inkstand. In a longer letter on 27 March, Darwin says 'ascarides are so nearly transparent and so hair-like' that he never believes in their existence unless they are seen to move: 'your enemas would probably kill them'—and half-kill Tom as well, we might add, with the easy arrogance of hindsight.

Though Darwin was curtailing his medical practice, there was no let-up in his literary work. During 1797 his book on female education was published, and he wrote a smooth elegy on the poet William Mason, author of *The English Garden*, who died in April. But Darwin's main work was on his next book, the treatise on vegetable life *Phytologia*, which was to occupy him for three years.

[10]

In January 1796 Darwin received a visit from a loquacious young man with a slight Devonshire accent, a great friend of Tom Wedgwood: it was S. T. Coleridge. For Darwin the visit was of no special import, but for Coleridge it was crucial: in Darwin he found someone to admire and emulate, and, eventually, to hate. Why the final hatred? Because Coleridge tried to rival Darwin's immense breadth of expert knowledge, and failed; and the bitter irony was that he failed as a result of his opium addiction, for which he probably held Darwin responsible. To Coleridge in his later years, Darwin must sometimes have seemed like a Borgia who had poisoned his chief rival.

In 1796, Coleridge was twenty-three and still at the stage of admiring Darwin. His enthusiastic letters show how Darwin appeared to one of the leading intellects of the young generation. His first letter, to Josiah Wade on 27 January 1796, has a phrase

already quoted in Chapter 1: 'Derby is full of curiosities, the
cotton, the silk mills, Wright, the painter, and Dr Darwin, the
everything, except the Christian! Dr Darwin possesses, perhaps,
a greater range of knowledge than any other man in Europe,
and is the most inventive of philosophical men. He thinks in a
*new* train on all subjects except religion.'[36]

Two days later Coleridge wrote to John Edwards: 'Dr
Darwin is an extraordinary man, and received me very courteously—He had heard that I was a Unitarian and bantered
incessantly on the subject of Religion. . . . He is an Atheist—but
has no new arguments. . . . When he talks on any other subject
he is a wonderfully entertaining and instructive old man.'[37]
Though Coleridge was unshaken in his Unitarianism, he probably flinched a little when Darwin called it 'a feather-bed to
catch a falling Christian'.

A year later, when John Thelwall was about to visit Derby,
Coleridge offered his most famous tribute: 'Dr Darwin will no
doubt excite your respectful curiosity. On the whole, I think, he
is the first *literary* character in Europe, and the most original-
minded Man.'[38]

Coleridge was now very much under Darwin's spell, and his
poems written or published in 1796 have strong Darwinian
echoes. In the *Religious Musings* Coleridge's reference to the
stifling desert wind—'through the tainted noon the Simoom
sails [in] purple pomp'—is very like Darwin's picture of the
Simoom in *The Economy of Vegetation*: 'Fierce on blue streams
he rides the tainted air'. As a note on the Simoom, Darwin has a
long excerpt from Bruce's *Travels*, which Coleridge also quotes.
At the end of his 'Lines written at Shurton Bars', Coleridge has
a 200-word note on 'Light from plants', which is an exact copy,
apart from some misprints, of a note in *The Loves of the Plants*
(pp. 182-3). Neither of these borrowings is acknowledged.
Coleridge's *Destiny of Nations* is riddled with Darwinian echoes:
for example, in *The Economy of Vegetation* Darwin asks the
Ethereal Powers to 'yoke the vollied lightnings to your cars',
while Coleridge sees his involvèd Monads 'yoke the red
lightnings to their volleying car'.[39]

But Coleridge's Darwinism was never entirely uncritical.
From the first, he was doubtful about Darwin's verse form. His
'Monody on a Tea Kettle', written in 1790 when he was
eighteen, is a skit on Darwin: the tea kettle damaged by over-

heating becomes '*the sooty swain* has felt the fire's fierce rage'.
Two months after meeting Darwin, Coleridge published a
friendly mock-Darwinian sonnet in *The Watchman*. Then, in May
1796, he suddenly ends a letter to Thelwall with the isolated
sentence, 'I absolutely nauseate Darwin's poem.'[40] So here is a
date when Coleridge broke free from Darwin's stylistic influence.
But Coleridge was still addicted to the ideas—and the opium—
prescribed by Darwin. *The Ancient Mariner* and 'Kubla Khan'
were germinating in a doubly Darwinian nutrient.

## [11]

The centre of gravity of Darwin's friendships was changing,
especially after the death of Josiah Wedgwood. The old Lunar
circle was in eclipse after the Birmingham riots, and Darwin
was moving towards a new group which included Beddoes,
Edgeworth and Tom Wedgwood, with Coleridge and William
Godwin on the fringes. His old friends Keir, Boulton and Watt
remained, but largely in the background.

Of Darwin's old friends, Edgeworth was now the closest,
despite being away in Ireland. Six letters from Edgeworth to
Darwin in 1796–7 have survived in manuscript, though Darwin's
replies have not. On 27 February 1796 Edgeworth wrote about
the Irish elections, in which he was a candidate, and asked if
Darwin had seen the sketches of Lady Hamilton in several
different attitudes—'one or two of them put me in mind of Mrs
Darwin'.[41] On 11 April Edgeworth reported having met a man
from New York who said Darwin was in the highest repute
there, the poetry of *The Botanic Garden* being 'placed above that
of any of our former English classics'. Edgeworth's letter of 31
May is chiefly concerned with the state of Ireland, which was
parlous; this theme recurs in his letter of 18 December, where
he also mentions the book he and his daughter Maria had been
writing, *Practical Education*. On 5 July 1797 Edgeworth reports
the burning of houses and the progress of the book, but on 11
September he had an old and sad story to tell: 'My dear Doctor,
I wish you could infuse a fresh portion of health into the constitution of my poor wife.—But I fear, alas! that is impossible. . . .'[42] The dreaded consumption had seized Elizabeth

Edgeworth as it seized her sister Honora seventeen years before, and her step-daughter Honora seven years before. In his seventeen years of marriage to Elizabeth, Edgeworth 'never once saw her out of temper, and never received from her an unkind word, or an angry look'.[43] She died in November 1797.

Darwin probably wrote quite often to Beddoes in 1796–7, but only one letter is recorded, acknowledging the receipt of Beddoes's 'Essay on the public merits of Mr Pitt'. This essay is rich in irony, and Darwin suggests that an inverted exclamation mark should be used to warn the casual reader of lurking irony amidst Beddoes's apparent praise of Pitt. Since one aim of irony is to give the discerning reader the pleasure of discerning it, Darwin's idea of labelling it may seem ironical. But if he had sprinkled *The Botanic Garden* with ¡ signs, he might have saved himself from the sneers of many stupid critics over the years. Beddoes's essay is not exclusively about Pitt: he has plenty of other ideas to air, for example on additives to make food more nourishing: 'Could opium be used?', he asks. The idea of lacing bread and gruel with opium deserves an exclamation mark both ways up, the irony lying in Beddoes's unawareness of it.

To include Coleridge and Godwin on the fringe of Darwin's circle of friends may seem strange, because he probably met Coleridge only once or twice, and never met Godwin at all. But he knew of them through Tom Wedgwood, who was soon to pay pensions to both; and Darwin was linked with them intellectually, as a mentor of Coleridge and as a fellow radical with Godwin. In June 1796 Godwin called at Darwin's house, but unfortunately found him away at Shrewsbury. Godwin later regretted he did not wait a day or two for the return of Darwin, 'so extraordinary a man, so truly a phenomenon'. Godwin continues: 'We paid our respects, however, to his wife, who is still a fine woman and cannot be more than 50. She is perfectly unembarrassed and tolerably well-bred.'[44] Unembarrassed at his own condescension, Godwin has the temerity to add that she put 'an improper construction' on his visit, saying he was 'probably come to see the lions'. It looks as though the serious and parsonical Godwin was a victim of Elizabeth's 'sportive humour'.

For Coleridge the years 1796–7 were critical. Soon after meeting Darwin in January 1796, he started *The Watchman*; but it failed in May, and in July he came with his wife Sara to stay with Mrs Evans of Darley near Derby for five weeks. Possibly

he saw Darwin again, and certainly he thought of opening a
school in Derby: but this, like so many of his projects, came to
nothing; instead he moved to Nether Stowey in Somerset, where
he met Wordsworth in the autumn. Their creative collaboration
in the next two years—when most of Coleridge's best poems
were written—changed the face of English poetry, and left
Darwin's verse style like a stranded whale on the sands of time.

# TWELVE

# Wounded but Undaunted

## 1798–1802

DARWIN'S REPUTATION had been suffering surface scratches for several years, but 1798 brought three serious wounds that were all the more disconcerting for being unconcerted. One was medical, one was politically inspired and the third was literary. These attacks damaged his prestige, but not his spirit: the two books yet to come were his best.

The weightiest attack, from Edinburgh, took the form of a 560-page book, *Observations on the Zoonomia of Erasmus Darwin* by Thomas Brown, who severely criticizes Darwin's materialism, his evolutionary ideas, and his fourfold division of the sensorium. Though Brown's own ideas are often silly, Darwin felt the wounds keenly, because Brown was only eighteen when he wrote his comments, and just starting as a medical student at Edinburgh. It was not pleasant for Darwin to see his life work mangled by an unqualified boy. What is worse, Brown had sent his manuscript to Darwin asking for an opinion and had remained unmoved by Darwin's arguments in the ensuing metaphysical correspondence in 1796–7.[1] Brown's attack was damaging, yet it also gave *Zoonomia* an added reputation: probably no other serious scientific book has evoked so solid a riposte so promptly.

The most effective attack on Darwin in 1798, which transformed him from a fashionable author almost to a laughing-stock within a few weeks, was government-inspired, the originator being George Canning, Under-Secretary for Foreign Affairs in Pitt's Government. The *Anti-Jacobin* periodical had been founded in the previous year with the aim of combating all ideas subversive of the established government or religion. Canning controlled the magazine, and he was no fool: he saw that Darwin's evolutionary ideas were deeply subversive of established religion, because Darwin denied God the guiding role he was designed to fill. Canning also wished to attack Godwin, whose *Political Justice* was subversive of all government. So, with two collaborators, Hookham Frere and George Ellis, Canning set out to destroy Darwin's reputation with a parody, *The Loves of the Triangles*, written in Darwinian verse, and to damage Godwin by implying that he (under the name 'Higgins') was the author. The 294 lines of *The Loves of the Triangles* were published serially in three numbers of the *Anti-Jacobin* for 16 April, 23 April and 7 May 1798.

Today this parody seems a feeble squib, with none of the brilliance of *The Golden Age*: it was trivial and ephemeral, but perfectly timed. Darwin's fame as a poet had become over-inflated, and now, seven years after *The Botanic Garden*, people were ready to turn against him. Canning presented them with a pin to puncture the balloon of his fame, and they used it.

*The Loves of the Triangles* is as silly as its title suggests: a parabola, a hyperbola ('blue-eyed wanton') and an ellipse are made to sigh for the love of a rectangle. The authors score off Darwin by imitating his style and applying it to trivial or inept subjects. A sharper sting comes in the sarcastic notes, where Canning accuses Godwin of teaching that 'whatever is, is wrong', and ridicules three of Darwin's ideas: that human beings have evolved from lower forms of life; that electricity will have important practical applications; and that the mountains are older than the Bible says (six thousand years in the orthodox interpretation). Since all three of Darwin's ideas have proved correct, Canning's weapon was a boomerang which returned to flatten him—many years after everyone had forgotten about it. In the fracas created by *The Loves of the Triangles* the long-term casualties are Canning and the literary historians who have accepted the potency of the parody: so Darwin has the last laugh. But his laugh is hollow, because the parody deeply dented his double reputation as a poet and as a thinker.

The third attack on Darwin in 1798, far less obvious but the most important in the long run, came from rural Somerset, in the form of Wordsworth and Coleridge's *Lyrical Ballads*. Both these young poets had been influenced by Darwin, as we have seen. Wordsworth particularly liked Darwin's enthusiasm for the French Revolution, his keen appreciation of mountain scenery, and his belief that plants experience emotions, which is the very basis of Wordsworth's credo,

> 'Tis my faith that every flower
> Enjoys the air it breathes.

In the early 1790s, as Wordsworth recalled fifty years later, 'my taste and natural tendencies were under an injurious influence from the dazzling manner of Darwin'.[2] By 1798 both Wordsworth and Coleridge realized that Darwin's 'dazzling manner' was a disastrous dead end, which they must avoid if they were to blaze a new trail for English poetry.

In the Advertisement to *Lyrical Ballads*, Wordsworth has Darwin in mind when he says that 'readers accustomed to the gaudiness and inane phraseology of many modern writers' may find the ballads strange and awkward. And in the preface to the second edition Wordsworth says he wishes to 'write about incidents and situations from common life' (not sylphs and gnomes) 'in the real language of men in a state of vivid sensation' (not in the unreal glitter of Darwinian couplets). Wordsworth rejects 'poetic diction' and asserts that 'all good poetry is the spontaneous overflow of powerful feelings', in obvious contrast to the 'manufactured' Darwinian verse.

The *Lyrical Ballads* announced a new age of poetry, and put paid to Darwin's popularity as a poet; but his spirit broods over Wordsworth and Coleridge in a strange and commanding way. His influence over two of the brightest minds of the new generation is the most striking example of his magnetism.

[2]

Darwin's grip is evident in three of their best poems, Wordsworth's *Tintern Abbey* and Coleridge's *Ancient Mariner* and 'Kubla Khan'. The first two were published in 1798; the third was written between 1797 and 1799, but not published till 1816.

Wordsworth was very keen on *Zoonomia*. He read it when it came out, and early in 1798 he was desperately anxious to see it again: 'I write merely to request (which I have very particular reasons for doing) that you would contrive to send me Dr Darwin's Zoonomia *by the first carrier*', he wrote to Cottle.[3] One

of the lyrical ballads, 'Goody Blake and Harry Gill', is a para-
phrase of the story in *Zoonomia* (II 359) of a farmer cursed by
an old woman who was stealing sticks. *Zoonomia* also throws its
shadow over *Tintern Abbey*, giving Wordsworth the central idea
of uniting animal pleasure in nature (the 'glad animal movements') with tranquil recollection of images of natural objects,
to create 'a sense sublime of something far more deeply inter-
fused'. In *Zoonomia* (I 23) Darwin remarks that it is rare for the
organ of vision to be entirely destroyed; but he had met two
blind men in this condition, and they never dreamt of visible
objects. This is the origin of the curious phrase at the beginning
of Wordsworth's reverie, that the forms of nature have *not* been
to him 'as is a landscape to a blind man's eye'; he means that he
*has* remembered them, and owed to them his 'sensations sweet'.
Darwin's general theme is that 'our ideas are animal motions of
the organs of sense'. Wordsworth seizes on this mechanistic
idea and transforms it into an organic vision by linking images of
nature with both bodily sensations, 'felt in the blood and felt
along the heart', and mental insights, when 'the burthen of the
mystery' of the world is lightened, and 'we see into the life of
things'.

Coleridge wrote *The Ancient Mariner* the year after his long
talk with Darwin, who was then starting work on *Phytologia*.
Darwin had probably explained to Coleridge his philosophy of
organic happiness, foreshadowed in *Zoonomia*, but best expressed
in *Phytologia*. Briefly, his idea is that the evolutionary struggle
for survival, despite its apparent savagery, serves to maximize
the 'sum total of terrestrial happiness', which includes the
happiness of all animals and, in a lesser degree, plants. When an
aged or unhealthy animal dies, the amount of happiness lost is
small; while much happiness is gained by the insects (and other
creatures or plants) that feed on its remains. And many geological strata, such as limestone and coal, are formed from the
remains of once happy creatures or plants; whence the idea that
mountains are 'mighty monuments of past delight'. In *The
Temple of Nature* Darwin emphasizes that instincts 'link the
reasoning reptile to mankind', and in his concern for general
organic happiness he thinks we 'should eye with tenderness all
living forms'.

In *The Ancient Mariner* the climax comes when the Mariner
looks at the luminous creatures in the wake of the ship and

suddenly feels a universal sympathy with all living things, however humble:

> O happy living things! . . .
> And I blessed them unaware.

Immediately the Albatross falls from his neck and he sheds his guilt. The Mariner's sympathy with the whole of organic nature is indistinguishable from Darwin's concern to 'eye with tenderness all living forms', and the ending of *The Ancient Mariner* is Darwin with godly trimmings:

> He prayeth well, who loveth well
> Both man and bird and beast.
> He prayeth best, who loveth best
> All things both great and small.

The scene that triggered the Mariner's revelation, the luminous trail of the ship, is taken straight from Darwin. In *The Economy of Vegetation* he tells us how the Nymphs of Fire

> . . . gild the surge with insect-sparks, that swarm
> Round the bright car, the kindling prow alarm, [I 199–200]

to which he adds a note:

> In some seas, as particularly about the coast of Malabar, as a ship floats along, it seems during the night to be surrounded with fire, and to leave a long tract of light behind it. Whenever the sea is gently agitated it seems converted into little stars, every drop as it breaks emits light, like bodies electrified in the dark. [Note IX]

These shining snake-like 'tracts of light' behind a ship attracted Coleridge and fascinated his Mariner:

> Beyond the shadow of the ship,
> I watched the water-snakes:
> They moved in tracks of shining white,
> And when they reared, the elfish light
> Fell off in hoary flakes.

(The proximity to Darwin's wording shows that Coleridge is describing a genuine phenomenon, not manufacturing supernatural snakes, as some critics have thought.)

Soon after his revelation, the Mariner hears a roaring wind:

> The upper air burst into life . . .
> And to and fro, and in and out,
> The wan stars danced between.

This picture of a pulsating aurora with the stars shining through derives from Darwin's line, 'The wan stars glimmering through its silver train', and its footnote telling us that 'small stars are seen undiminished through both the light of the tails of comets, and of the aurora borealis'.[4]

So Coleridge is deeply indebted to Darwin for the main theme, the climax, and several of the key images of *The Ancient Mariner*. Many other verbal echoes have been noted,[5] which we need not pursue here.

'Kubla Khan' is even more Darwinian: underground rivers, caverns, domes and blossomy lawns are Darwin's stock-in-trade as a poet. He was deeply impressed by his visit to the Derbyshire caverns in 1767: underground water flow fascinated him and led him to his explanation of artesian wells—which are really subterranean streams. In *The Loves of the Plants* (III 85–130) he tells us of the 'spacious cavern' and 'massy dome' at Wetton in the Peak District, and the 'extensive and romantic common' below 'where the rivers Hamps and Manifold sink into the earth' and flow three miles underground before emerging at Ilam and joining the Dove near Ashbourne:

> Where Hamps and Manifold, their cliffs among,
> Each in his flinty channel winds along.

From here it is but a short step to Coleridge's land of Xanadu,

> Where Alph, the sacred river, ran
> Through caverns measureless to man,

near a 'pleasure dome' and a 'romantic chasm'. Darwin sees the Manifold flowing in 'gaping gulphs' among 'rocks rear'd on rocks in huge disjointed piles', and refers to 'the numerous large stones which seem to have been thrown over the land by volcanic explosions'. This easily transforms into Coleridge's 'deep romantic chasm', from which 'a mighty fountain momently was forced' amid 'dancing rocks'. Equally close is Darwin's image of the Cracow mines, with their 'crystal walls', 'white towers', 'glittering domes' and 'bright steeps', down which 'impetuous fountains burst their headlong way'.[6]

Darwin tells us how the Liffey flows from 'secret caves' with 'bright meandering waves' and how nymphs guide 'rills along their sinuous course' or pour their 'bright treasure in a thousand rills', while nereids 'weave the mazy dance' amid 'blossomed orchards'. All this is like Coleridge's sacred river,

> ... meandering with a mazy motion ...
> [through] gardens bright with sinuous rills,
> Where blossomed many an incense-bearing tree.

Even the most notorious line in 'Kubla Khan', 'As if this Earth in fast thick pants were breathing', has its parallels in Darwin's

> Now o'er their head the whizzing whirlwinds breathe,
> And the live desert pants, and heaves beneath.[7]

There is more breathing and panting, and a damsel too, in the lines (page 194) in *The Loves of the Plants* about the Sorceress, who 'circles thrice in air her ebon wand', as if to match Coleridge's 'damsel with a dulcimer' who is asked to 'weave a circle round him thrice'.

These examples are enough to show that Darwin's phrases and images are the building bricks of 'Kubla Khan': but Coleridge put them together with a magic beyond Darwin's powers.

[3]

We now return from the damsel with a dulcimer to the Darwins in Derby. At the end of 1798 Edward was sixteen, and had just about reached his final height of six feet two inches; Violetta (fifteen) and Emma (fourteen) had both been pupils at the Ashbourne school. Francis was twelve, John eleven and Harriot eight. Darwin's elder children seemed firmly set in their careers in 1798. Susan and Mary Parker were doing well with the school at Ashbourne. Erasmus junior was busy with his legal work at Derby. Robert's medical practice at Shrewsbury was now very extensive and lucrative. His marriage with Susannah seemed happy, and in 1798 their daughter Marianne was born—their first child and Erasmus's first grandchild.

In the years 1798–9 Erasmus did not see many of his friends, but there was a visit from Edgeworth in the spring of 1799. After the death of his wife Elizabeth in the autumn of 1797, Edgeworth had not taken long to decide he would marry again, as he told Darwin in a letter on 21 May 1798: 'I am going to be married to a lady of small fortune and large accomplishments ... liked by my family, loved by me.'[8] Since Ireland was on the brink of rebellion, Edgeworth wasted no time, and ten days later he married the lady, Miss Frances Beaufort. This fourth marriage seems to have been just as happy as the second and third. During 1798 Edgeworth also became a member of the Irish Parliament and was surprised to find the Irish politicians 'very harmless creatures', though Darwin had predicted they would be savage. As inventive as ever, he offers Darwin the idea of warming hot-houses by air pipes laid through dunghills, which he says will ensure a supply of air at 95° Fahrenheit. He also mentions a speaking-machine just announced from France, which was not as good as Darwin's machine of 1771. Soon Edgeworth had other preoccupations, for in the autumn the French landed at Killala on the west coast, and Edgeworthstown was on their road to Dublin. But the invaders were defeated in a battle nearby, and the Edgeworth family escaped unscathed after a hazardous week.

On 12 March 1799, before his visit, Edgeworth wrote to Darwin sending 'half a year's interest—same as before, viz 6% on £5100 amounting to £153-0-0'.[9] This confirms other signs that Darwin was growing quite wealthy during the 1790s. In the early 1780s he had been pressed for money when maintaining Radburn Hall and the house in Derby. But in 1793 he was able to buy the house at Ashbourne, and soon afterwards made this substantial loan to Edgeworth.

When Edgeworth visited Derby in 1799, he had with him his daughter Maria, now thirty-two, who was about to become the most celebrated novelist of the day in England, after the success of *Castle Rackrent* the next year. Maria liked Darwin very much and said he was 'not only a first-rate genius, but one of the most benevolent, as well as wittiest of men. He stuttered, but far from lessening the charm of his conversation . . . the slowness with which his words came forth, added to the effect of his humour and shrewd good sense.'[10]

Darwin's zest for friendship declined after the death of his closest friend Josiah Wedgwood in 1795. Friendships are rather like a juggler keeping a number of plates spinning on the top of flexible poles—they need continual spinning-up. But Darwin's spinning-up was becoming half-hearted: he was hard at work writing books, and authors are poor letter-writers; he was not so young now, being sixty-eight in 1799; he was occupied more with his large and growing family; and he was becoming reluctant to travel, though he did go to treat Samuel Galton at Bath in 1799, and charged forty guineas.[11]

Though slacker, the bonds between Darwin and his old Lunar

friends, Keir, Boulton and Watt, were still strong. The most sprightly letter between them at this time is one from Keir to Darwin, imagining a French invasion, presumably in 1798 or 1799: 'I suppose, like Archimedes when Syracuse was taken and soldiers rushed into his house, you will tell the French, *when* they come to Derby, not to disturb your meditations; and that you are just on the point of catching the *matter* of electricity by the tail, and the *matter* of heat by its whiskers.'[12]

Darwin's newer friendships with Beddoes and Tom Wedgwood were tending to evaporate. Tom Wedgwood had begun the final nomadic phase of his life, when he bought houses in the south of England in a vain search for a settled home where his perplexed mind might find peace. Darwin lost track of him during these wanderings. As for Beddoes, he was fully occupied with his Pneumatic Institution, where he had taken on as his assistant a nineteen-year-old Cornishman called Humphry Davy. Within a year Davy vindicated Beddoes's faith in the medical use of gases by discovering the anaesthetic effects of nitrous oxide ('laughing gas'). But, amazing as it now seems, no one—not even Beddoes or Darwin—took notice of his immediate suggestion that it could serve as an anaesthetic in medical operations. Not until forty-five years later was nitrous oxide used as a dental anaesthetic, a role it filled for more than a century.

Darwin wrote to Beddoes on 29 December 1799 about Tom Wedgwood's health. After the usual references to the dreaded ascarides, Darwin says, 'If he will pass 2 or 3 days at my house, I shall be glad of a visit from him, and will study both his body and mind.'[13]

Though some of his friendships were faltering, Darwin had new disciples, such as Dr R. J. Thornton, who was beginning to publish his botanical illustrations gathered in *The Temple of Flora*, the finest of all books of botanical drawings. Thornton was a devout Darwinian, who treated *The Botanic Garden* almost as a bible, and Darwin returned the compliment by commending Thornton's plates as having '*no equal*'.[14]

During 1799 Darwin himself was finishing his three years' work on *Phytologia*, the book about vegetable life. The agriculture filters into his letters: for example, on 13 October he wrote to Samuel Moore, Secretary of the Society of Arts, commending a drill plough designed by Mr Swanwick of Derby.[15]

In 1799 the war against Napoleon was not going well, and

Pitt brought in a temporary new financial measure—income tax. Darwin was puzzled to know what income he should declare to the commissioners. He told Robert: 'I kept no book, but believed my business to be £1000 a year, and deduct £200 for travelling expenses and chaise hire, and £200 for a livery-servant, four horses and a day labourer.'[16] This was accepted by the authorities. Charles Darwin was surprised that the figure was so low, and concluded that his income must have been higher in the 1780s and earlier 1790s, but had fallen off by 1799. This seems very likely.

[4]

In 1798 Erasmus junior presented the image of a successful solicitor; but inwardly, deep neuroses were festering. His debility showed itself as a reluctance to deal with business, a fairly common fault, which his father thought annoying rather than serious. In January 1798, when he had failed to perform some small task for his brother Robert, his father had written in apology to Robert (on 8 January):

> His neglect of small businesses (as he thinks them, I suppose) is a constitutional disease. I learnt yesterday that he had like to have been arrested for a small candle bill of 3 or 4 pounds in London, which had been due 4 or 5 years, and they had repeatedly written to him! and that a tradesman in this town has repeatedly complained to a friend of his that he owes Mr. D £70, and cannot get him to settle his account . . . he procrastinates for ever![17]

During 1799 Erasmus junior tried to solve his problems by retiring from business, although he was only forty. He had the idea of building a cottage in the botanic garden at Lichfield. But his father was against it and in a letter to Robert on 8 August referred to the idea as one 'which I much disapprove. Therefore you will please not to mention it, and I hope it will fall through.'[18] It did; but in November Erasmus junior bought Breadsall Priory, four miles north-north-east of Derby, to which he hoped to retire before long, or, as his father despairingly put it on 28 November, 'to sleep away the remainder of his life'.[19] At the end of 1799 Erasmus junior made a final attempt to settle his neglected accounts, but the effort proved beyond him:

Mr Darwin had been working for two nights, and when urged in the evening of December 29th to take some rest and food, he answered with a most distressed expression, holding his head, 'I cannot, for I promised if I'm alive that the accounts should be sent in tomorrow'. Early in the night of the same day he could bear his misery no longer, and seems to have rushed out of the house, and leaving his hat on the bank, to have thrown himself into the water.[20]

The next day, 30 December 1799, his father told Robert:

> I write in great anguish of mind to acquaint you with a dreadful event—your poor brother Erasmus fell into the water last night at the bottom of his garden, and was drowned.[21]

One of his clerks, Mr Parsons, brought the news that his body had been found. Emma and Violetta were with their father at the time, and five years later Emma (wishing to refute a calumny by Anna Seward) recalled the scene:

> He immediately got up, but staggered so much that Violetta and I begged of him to sit down, which he did, and leaned his head upon his hand . . . he was exceedingly agitated, and did not speak for many minutes . . . he soon after said that this was the greatest shock he had felt since the death of his poor Charles.

Anna Seward had dared 'to accuse my dear papa of want of affection and feeling towards his son', Emma continues, with growing indignation: 'I want to scratch a pen over all the lies, and send the book back to Miss Seward . . . and to swear the truth of what I have said before both houses of Parliament.'[22] Emma's indignant reaction confirms other indications that her father felt his son's suicide very deeply. Four years later Robert said that his father had found it a constant exertion to obtain relief from the thought of his son's death.

During 1800 Erasmus spent a long time trying to sort out his son's accounts. On 8 February he wrote to Robert: 'I am obliged as executor daily to study his accounts, which is both a laborious and painful business to me.'[23] Six months later he was still at work, and on 18 August he wrote to Thomas Byerley at Etruria: 'I have examined the books of my late Son, and believe the account you have sent me to be right, and have herein transmitted you a note for the money, 148-10-0.'[24] There is no suggestion that Erasmus junior was in debt when he died: it is just that his accounts were not up to date.

Darwin's anguish over his son's death was sharpened by the feeling that he ought to have foreseen and prevented the tragedy. He was supposed to be a doctor of great sympathy, insight, sagacity and benevolence; yet he had failed to fathom the distress of his own son. On 29 December 1799, a few hours before his son walked out to die, Darwin had calmly written the letter to Beddoes already quoted, saying he was 'truly sorry to hear Mr T. Wedgwood is in so indifferent a stage of health', and little realizing that his son was in much more desperate a state.

Darwin had a monument erected in memory of his son, and he wrote to Robert on 22 February 1800: 'Mrs Darwin and I intend to lie in Breadsall church by his side.'[25] Their intention was fulfilled.

[5]

As some relief from the gloom, a new plant came out in the spring of 1800: *Phytologia, or the Philosophy of Agriculture and Gardening*. Another bulky volume, a quarter of a million words compressed into 612 quarto pages, *Phytologia* is the best of Darwin's prose works: it is free of the basic fallacies that mar *Zoonomia* and is solidly grounded in the good earth; it has many new ideas and some major discoveries, notably the specification of photosynthesis and of plant nutrients. Darwin says in the introduction that with the aid of 'the modern improvements in chemistry' he hopes he may be able to develop 'a true theory of vegetation', and this hope is at least partly fulfilled. The book is dedicated to Sir John Sinclair, President of the Board of Agriculture in the 1790s, who suggested to Darwin that he should write it.

*Phytologia* is in three parts: the first is on the 'physiology of vegetation', covering plant structure and functioning; the second part is entitled 'the economy of vegetation', and deals with seed growth, photosynthesis, nutrition, manures, drainage, aeration and diseases; the third part is on 'agriculture and horticulture', with the accent on productivity of fruits, seeds, root crops, trees and flowers.

Darwin starts by reminding us that, although we associate life with 'palpable warmth and visible motion', the 'cold and motionless fibres of plants' are also alive, and that 'vegetables are in reality an inferior order of animals'. He stresses the individuality of buds:

> If a bud be torn from the branch of a tree, or cut out and planted in the earth with a glass cup inverted over it . . . it will grow, and become a plant in every respect like its parent. This evinces that every bud of a tree is an individual vegetable being; and that a tree therefore is a family or swarm of individual plants. [pp. 1–2]

Charles Darwin states that his grandfather was the originator of this idea, 'now universally adopted'.[26]

Erasmus sees the advantages of sexual generation in providing variety for evolution to work with. The 'paternal progeny of vegetables in buds, or bulbs, or wires', he says, 'exactly resemble their parents'. Without 'new blood', deterioration sets in after many generations. What they need is sex:

> From the sexual, or amatorial, generation of plants new varieties, or improvements, are frequently obtained; as many of the young plants from seeds are dissimilar to the parent, and some of them superior to the parent in the qualities we wish to possess. . . . Sexual reproduction is the chef d'œuvre, the master-piece of nature.
> [pp. 115, 103]

Darwin tells us how ingeniously plants disperse their seeds, some using plumes to fly in the wind, others being sticky to be carried by animals, and so on. Digressing into animal life, he suggests artificial insemination to breed 'new kinds of mules', using 'the method of Spallanzani, who diluted the seminal fluid of a dog with much warm water, and by injecting it fecundated a bitch, and produced puppies like the dog' (p. 119).

Darwin explains that leaves are the lungs of plants and, like animal lungs, have a huge surface area for interaction with atmospheric gases. He believed plant leaves 'breathed' through minute pores (which were discovered thirty years later, and called stomata); in 1783 he tested this idea by carefully covering the surfaces of several leaves with oil, which killed the leaves. Darwin's worst mistake in his plant physiology is to carry his analogy with animals too far by suggesting a circulation of sap in what he calls the 'aortal arteries and veins' of plants.

Darwin's greatest insight in this part of the book is to recognize the vital role of sugar, and its conversion into starch (or vice versa). The value of sugar as food is shown by the fact that the slaves in Jamaica grow fat in the sugar-harvest, though they endure at that time much more labour. . . . Great God of Justice! grant that it may soon be cultivated only by the hands of freedom, and may thence give happiness to the labourer, as well as to the merchant and consumer. [p. 77]

As a step towards this humane goal, he suggests growing sugar beet in Britain:

In many plants sugar is found ready prepared . . . thus in the beet-root, the crystals of it may be discerned by a microscope. . . . [Sugar] may some time or other be economically procured from the vegetables of this climate, as Margraff extracted it from the beet-root. [pp. 77, 588]

Darwin's discussion of the 'muscles, nerves and brain' of vegetables is biased towards insectivorous and sensitive plants: the Venus fly-trap closes when it feels an insect on it; a whole stem of mimosa collapses when one leaflet is cut with scissors. He concludes that each individual bud of a plant possesses muscles (used in the Venus fly-trap), nerves (to feel the insect) and brain (to direct the nerves and muscles). Thus he persuades himself that plants feel, 'though in a much inferior degree even than the cold-blooded animals' (p. 133).

In Part II of *Phytologia* the most important chapter is entitled 'Manures, or the food of plants'. It runs to seventy-two pages and covers everything needed to make a plant flourish, from carbon dioxide and water to phosphorus and nitrates. Sugar (or starch), he reminds us, is the main product of 'digestion' in plants, as shown by 'the great product of the sugar-cane, and of the maple-tree in America' (p. 189). Darwin recognizes that carbonic gas (carbon dioxide) and water provide the main food of plants:

This carbonic gas . . . is the principal food of plants. . . . Next to carbonic acid the aqueous acid, if it may be so called, or water, seems to afford the principal food of vegetables . . . when vegetable leaves are exposed to the sun's light, they seem to give up oxygen gas. [pp. 193, 194]

The process of photosynthesis that is the basis of all vegetable life may be summed up as:

carbon dioxide + water + light energy → sugar + oxygen,

in the presence of chlorophyll. Although he never wrote this explicit equation, Darwin recognized all the components in it, and he enjoys the credit for first specifying the full process of photosynthesis, going much further than Ingenhousz (1779), who showed that plants absorb carbon dioxide and give out oxygen in sunlight. Darwin anticipates by forty years much of Liebig's work on photosynthesis. He nearly writes the equation when he says: 'by the decomposition of water in the vegetable system, when the hydrogen unites with carbon and produces oil, the oxygen becomes superfluous, and is in part exhaled' (p. 194). The only item wrong is 'oil', a carbon-hydrogen compound, when it should be 'sugar', a carbon-hydrogen-oxygen compound; this error is a mere mental lapse, because Darwin says a few pages before that sugar is the end product of the process.

Though photosynthesis is the main source of nutriment for plants, Darwin's recognition of other essential elements is even more remarkable, for many of the processes he expounds were not elucidated until fifty years later. He begins with nitrogen: 'The azote, or nitrogen . . . seems much to contribute to the food or sustenance of vegetables . . . and is given out by their putre-faction . . . forming volatile alkali [ammonia]' (p. 195). Darwin received credit in his own day for recognizing that nitro-gen was vital, and was possibly absorbed through trapping in the soil or the formation of ammonia. But today the credit usually goes to Liebig, born three years after *Phytologia* was published.

Amazingly enough, Darwin also manages to hit on the importance of nitrates: he suggests that 'the acid of nitre', from which nitrates form, 'probably may contribute much to promote vegetation' (p. 232).

Carbon is next on Darwin's menu for vegetables, and then phosphorus:

> Another material which exists, I believe, universally in vegetables, and has not yet been sufficiently attended to, is phosphorus. This like the carbon, nitrogen, hydrogen, and sulphur, is probably a simple substance, as our present chemistry has not yet certainly analysed any of them. [p. 207]

Darwin's faith in phosphorus sprang from his observation of phosphorescence in all decaying matter, from wood and putre-scent veal to more picturesque examples:

> in the streets of Edinburgh, where the heads of the fish called

whitings or haddies are frequently thrown out by the people, I have on a dark night easily seen the hour by holding one of them to my watch. [p. 208]

According to Sir John Russell, in his *History of Agricultural Science in Great Britain*,[27] Darwin was the first to state that nitrogen and phosphate are essential for the growth of plants.

Calcium is another vital element, Darwin believes, and he suggests a search for calcium phosphate, hoping that we might 'discover a mountain of phosphate of lime in our own country'. This was a most intelligent precognition of the widespread search for phosphates later in the century.

Nothing that can help the fertility of the soil should be wasted, Darwin insists: the Chinese say that 'a wise man saves even the parings of his nails and the clippings of his hair'. He proposes sewage farms: 'The manures of towns and cities, which are all now left buried in deep wells, or carried away by soughs into the rivers, should be . . . carried out of towns . . . for the purposes of agriculture' (p. 242). Darwin's concern for manure reaches its logical conclusion in his injunction: 'Burn nothing which may nourish vegetables by its slow decomposition beneath the soil.' The needless burning of 'a hair or a straw', he says, 'should therefore give some compunction to a mind of universal sympathy'. What would he have thought of the annual burning of two million tons of straw in British fields?

In this chapter on manures Darwin comes very near to defining the carbon and nitrogen cycles—the two fundamental chemical processes in nature, discovered much later according to orthodox histories of science.

The draining, watering and aeration of soil are the next topics, and they are covered just as fully. Darwin recommends the boring of artesian wells and also tells us how to find natural springs, for example, in places where mists begin earliest, or frosts melt earliest. He explains how to drain valleys and marshes, for which he recommends his horizontal windmill, giving the diagram shown in Fig. 8 and an elaborate water pump of his own design, which requires two pages of explanation and a diagram too detailed to reproduce here. He discusses the advantages of flooding meadows and aerating the soil, and describes at length one of his most carefully thought-out inventions, a drill-plough, with ten drawings and fourteen pages of instructions.

Part II of *Phytologia* ends with a long discourse on diseases of plants—mildew, ergot, canker and insects, particularly the aphis.

> The most ingenious manner of destroying the aphis would be effected by the propagation of its greatest enemy, the larva of the aphidivorous fly. . . . This plague of the aphis might be counteracted by the natural means of devouring one insect by another.     [p. 356]

This biological warfare is indeed 'ingenious': Darwin deserves and receives recognition as a pioneer in the biological control of insects.[28]

But he doesn't stop there; he wonders about biological control of rats and other vermin that harm plants:

> American . . . water-rats . . . are so liable to be affected with tape-worm as is supposed much to diminish their numbers. . . . Could some of these diseased American rats be imported into this country, and propagate their malady amongst the native rats of this climate?
> [pp. 583–4]

So Darwin was a pioneer in germ warfare, or at least worm warfare, and in the 1950s his idea was paralleled half-intentionally by myxomatosis and rabbits.

Part III of *Phytologia* is a practical handbook on food production. Darwin devotes fifty pages to fruits, full of ripe wisdom about pruning, grafting, preservation, and so forth. He goes into great detail, and even bursts into verse:

> Behead new-grafted trees in spring,
> Ere the first cuckoo tries to sing;
> But leave four swelling buds to grow
> With wide-diverging arms below. . . .     [p. 429]

He is just as keen on seeds, because land provides more food per acre under grain than under animal pasturage. But Darwin is not a vegetarian: he believes we should eat both animal and vegetable food, because human teeth and intestines are structurally midway between 'those of the carnivorous and phytivorous animals'.

When he delves into the ins and outs of root crops, Darwin comes up with a very radical specimen, an aerial potato from the odorous garden of a well-named military friend: 'I was this day shown by my friend Major Trowel of Derby a new variety of the potato in his excellent new-made garden, the soil of which consists of marl mixed with lime and stable-manure' (p. 474). Apparently the ground was so rich that the potatoes burst out into the air on stalks.

Returning to earth, Darwin offers many useful ideas on the bark, leaves and wood of trees. To grow trees straight, he says, you should plant them close, because their 'contest with each other for light and air propels them upwards'. With the threat of French invasion in the offing, he considers where timber should be grown. 'In the present insane state of human society', he says, when 'war and its preparations employ the ingenuity and labour of almost all nations; and mankind destroy or enslave each other with as little mercy as they destroy and enslave the bestial world', farmland should be reserved for growing food. But 'all those unfertile mountains from the extremity of Cornwall to the extremity of Scotland, should be covered with extensive forests of such kinds of wood as experience has shewn them to be capable to sustain' (pp. 527–8). On barren mountains 'pines, as Scotch fir', he says, might 'succeed astonishingly'. So Darwin specifies (a century early) the Forestry Commission's twentieth-century planting programme.

Finally, after telling us how to grow a beautiful flower garden, Darwin propounds his philosophy of organic happiness. He first draws a doleful picture of vegetables being eaten by animals, and weak animals by stronger ones:

> Such is the condition of organic nature! whose first law might be expressed in the words, 'Eat or be eaten!' and which would seem to be one great slaughter-house, one universal scene of rapacity and injustice!
>
> Where shall we find a benevolent idea to console us amid so much apparent misery? [p. 556]

He offers a cheerful answer: the more active animals have a greater capacity for pleasure, and these are the animals most likely to survive. So the evolutionary struggle for existence is really a maximization of organic pleasure. Since so many geological strata, such as limestone and coal, are the remains of animal or vegetable life, these strata can be regarded as 'monuments of the past felicity of organized Nature'.

Darwin concludes his own monumental book by adding to our organic happiness with a long and amusing mock-heroic poem on broccoli-growing:

This boon I ask of Fate, where'er I dine,
O, be the Proteus-form of cabbage mine! ... [p. 560]

This is a happy note on which to end our sampling of *Phytologia*, a book that deserves more recognition than it has yet received as a classic in the advancement of plant nutrition and agricultural chemistry.

## [6]

In 1800 Darwin continued hard at work: he extensively revised *Zoonomia* for the third edition, and began his last poem, *The Temple of Nature*. He wrote twice to Boulton about the enclosure of Needwood Forest, signing off as 'your *old* and affectionate friend'. Edgeworth wrote on 31 March to 'my dear and excellent friend', and told Darwin that these words 'really express my feelings'.[29]

In August Darwin had a letter from Gilbert Wakefield, an enterprising clergyman who was in Dorchester gaol, serving a two-year sentence after writing a pamphlet attacking Bishop Watson. Wakefield sent Darwin a poem he had written, 'Imitation of Juvenal', and Darwin replied on 19 August:

I am much obliged to you for your severe and elegant satire, which you have so good cause to write, who so long have felt the persecution of these flagitious times! When one considers the folly of one great part of mankind, and the villany of another great part of them, the whole race seems to sink into contempt.[30]

Darwin was horrified at the mean-minded persecution of nearly everyone who dared to criticize the Establishment. War or no war, he saw the persecution as a sad erosion of British liberty.

Wakefield read *The Botanic Garden* for the first time in gaol: 'I have read his first volume . . . with extraordinary delight and admiration.' He thought it 'a poem destined for immortality'. Wakefield sent some detailed criticisms to Darwin, who received them kindly, complimenting Wakefield on his 'very great sensibility to the elegancies of language'.[31] Darwin invites Wakefield to visit him 'if you are ever released from the harpy-claws of power'. But Wakefield died soon after leaving prison, at the age of forty-five.

The year 1801 began badly for Darwin. In the spring he was seriously ill with pneumonia, and although he seemed to recover, he never regained his former energy. On 6 May he told Robert: 'I am I think perfectly recover'd, but am like other corpulent old men soon fatigued with walking, especially up hill or up stairs.'[32] From now on, his work as a doctor was limited to irregular consultations. But his mental energy was undiminished, and he was hard at work on *The Temple of Nature*, which, far from showing any decline, is in nearly all respects better than *The Botanic Garden*. He finished the poem towards the end of the year.

The third and revised edition of *Zoonomia* appeared in 1801. Though the fundamental fallacies remain, most of the revisions are improvements. In the chapter on evolution Darwin adds a section about vegetables, which had not been mentioned in the earlier editions. He explains how changes in vegetables have arisen 'by their perpetual contest for light and air above ground, and for food or moisture beneath the soil'. For example, plants too slender to rise by their own strength become climbers, adhering to stronger trees. Darwin also produces a new theory of heredity in sexual reproduction, very close to the modern view if his 'fibrils or molecules' (really 'small particles') are read as DNA molecules. 'Collected separately by appropriated glands of the male or female', he says, these 'molecules' when mixed generate the new embryon, 'resembling in some parts the form of the father, and in other parts the form of the mother, according to the quantity or activity of the fibrils or molecules at the time of their conjunction'.[33]

Having virtually retired from medical practice, Darwin was no longer so keen to live in the centre of Derby, especially since the River Derwent at the bottom of the garden was now a perpetual reminder of his son's suicide. Elizabeth also wished to escape to a more rural environment. Radburn Hall was ruled out, because her son Sacheverel Pole was installed there. But an alternative was available: Breadsall Priory, which Erasmus junior had bought a month before his death, was a pleasant country house four miles from Derby (Plate 9c). Darwin and Elizabeth both liked the Priory, and they would probably have moved there in 1801 but for his illness.

Darwin was seventy in December 1801, yet his flair for innovation remained strong. The introduction of vaccination by Jenner in 1798 had come too late to affect Darwin's career. But he welcomed the discovery and immediately foresaw the situa-

tion eventually reached in 1976, when the first virtual eradication
of smallpox occurred. Darwin also saw how to use current
religious imperatives to promote compulsory-voluntary vaccination, as he explains in a letter to Jenner on 24 February 1802:

> Your discovery of preventing the dreadful havoc made among
> mankind by the smallpox . . . may in time eradicate the smallpox
> from all civilized countries, and this especially: as by the testimony
> of innumerable instances the vaccine disease is so favourable to
> young children, that in a little time it may occur that the christening
> and vaccination of children may always be performed on the same
> day.[34]

The Darwins moved from Derby to Breadsall Priory, or 'The
Priory' as it was more often known, on 25 March 1802. The
move appeared to be a great success, as Erasmus told Edgeworth
on 17 April:

> . . . all of us like our change of situation. We have a pleasant house,
> a good garden, ponds full of fish, and a pleasing valley somewhat
> like Shenstone's—deep, umbrageous, and with a talkative stream
> running down it. Our house is near the top of the valley, well
> screened by hills from the east, and north, and open to the south,
> where, at four miles distance, we see Derby tower.
> Four or more strong springs rise near the house, and have formed
> the valley, which, like that of Petrarch, may be called *Val chiusa*, as
> it begins, or is shut, at the situation of the house. I hope you like the
> description, and hope farther, that yourself and any part of your
> family will sometime do us the pleasure of a visit.[35]

But it was not to be: before he had finished writing this letter
to Edgeworth, Erasmus died, apparently of a heart attack, at
9 a.m. on the morning of Sunday 18 April 1802.

A letter from Robert Darwin to Edgeworth on 1 May
describes the events leading up to his father's death:

> On the 10 April, he was attacked with a severe cold fit of fever,
> followed with a proportionate hot fit, and with feelings and
> symptoms that threatened an inflammation of the lungs, from which
> he had suffered so much last spring. In this state, he was bled twice
> during that day, and lost 25 ounces of blood; the pulse became soft
> and slow, he got well in two days and remained so, to all appearance.
> On Saturday, the 17th, walking in his garden with Mrs Darwin and
> Mrs Mainwaring, a lady of his own age, the conversation turned
> on the extent of his alterations, when Mrs M remarked that he
> would not finish in less than 10 years. 'Mrs Mainwaring, 10 years is

a long time for me to look forward. 5 years since, I thought, perhaps my chance of life better than yours; it is now otherwise.' Mrs Darwin expressed some surprise, to hear him speak in this manner, and complimented him on his good colour, his spirits etc. 'I am always flushed in this manner just before I become ill.'[36]

He slept well that night until nearly 7 a.m., but soon after rising,

> he was seized with a violent shivering fit, and went into the kitchen to warm himself; he returned to his study, lay on the sofa, became faint and cold, and was moved into an arm-chair, where without pain or emotion of any kind he expired a little before nine o'clock.[37]

This is Charles Darwin's account, and he adds that although Erasmus's medical attendants, Dr Fox and Mr Hadley, differed about the cause of his death, Robert was sure it was 'an affection of the heart'. When Charles visited Elizabeth at the Priory many years later, she 'showed me the sofa and chair, still preserved in the same place, where he had lain and expired'.[38]

Erasmus was buried in Breadsall Church, with the following memorial inscription:

> Of the rare union of Talents which so eminently distinguished him as a Physician, a Poet and Philosopher, his writings remain a public and unfading testimony. His Widow has erected this monument in memory of the zealous benevolence of his disposition, the active humanity of his conduct, and the many private virtues which adorned his character.[39]

The church was burnt down on 4 June 1914 'by a dastardly act of incendiarism'[40] and, when it was rebuilt, the memorial inscription was replaced in the wall. Darwin's house and grounds at Breadsall Priory were converted into a golf club in 1976.

## [7]

In the last years of his life Darwin had many detractors, and many champions too: although his literary fame had declined from the dizzy heights of the early 1790s, his scientific standing was very high, and quite recently boosted by *Phytologia*. But his evolutionary ideas, in *Zoonomia*, and his open praise of the early years of the French Revolution, in *The Botanic Garden*, made him many enemies among those who thought themselves pillars of Church and Government.

Darwin's death gave his enemies the chance to slander him. Many of the obituaries were laudatory or at least respectful, but there were several baseless slanders which Robert Darwin and Edgeworth spent time and effort in refuting.

By far the most important notice was in the *Monthly Magazine* for 1 June 1802, entitled 'Biographical Memoirs of the late Dr Darwin' and running to seven pages of small print. The author promises to describe the life of 'this far-celebrated man' quite 'without fear, favour or affection'. Darwin ,we are told, had 'two natural daughters'; was in youth 'fond of sacrificing to both Bacchus and Venus'; ate 'a large quantity of food'; and had a stomach that 'possessed a strong power of digestion'. All this, though snide, is not far from the truth, and the comments on Darwin's books are generous and perceptive. The author calls *Zoonomia* 'unquestionably, a noble effort of human labour or of human wit', and *The Botanic Garden* provokes the comment: 'No man, perhaps, was ever happier in the selection and composition of his epithets, had a more imperial command of words, or could elucidate with such accuracy and elegance the most complex and intricate machinery.' Finally, and ominously, we are told: 'There are reasons for suspecting that Dr Darwin was not a believer in Divine Revelation. . . . A few days before his death . . . the Doctor was observed to speak with a considerable degree of sedateness on the subject and . . . added "let us not hear anything about hell".'[41]

Four slanders mar this biography. First, Darwin is said to have 'frequently walked with his tongue hanging out of his mouth': even Anna Seward was indignant at this 'idiot-seeming indelicacy', and expressed 'her entire disbelief of its truth'.[42] The second slander, which upset his family most, is that Darwin was irascible and that his death was brought on by 'a violent fit of passion'. This was immediately refuted by Dewhurst Bilsborrow, who refers to Darwin's 'mild and good humoured benevolence' and says, 'I have the *concurrent testimony*' of the servants and others that '*not a single angry word passed on that day*'.[43] Edgeworth also refuted this and the third slander, that Darwin wrote merely for money, saying that once, when needing £1000, he asked Darwin for a loan, and he sent it 'by return of the post'.[44] The fourth slander is that flattery was the 'most successful means of gaining his notice and favour': on the contrary, all the indications are that Darwin was almost immune to either fame or flattery. 'Throughout his letters I have been struck with his indifference to fame', Charles Darwin remarked.[45]

This sniping at Darwin as soon as he was in his grave needs to be noticed, but it is more than balanced by the praise from his friends, which was generous and characteristic.

James Watt was a man of few words, and his tributes to Darwin are short and to the point: 'For my part, it will be my pride, while I live, that I have enjoyed the friendship of such a man. . . . He was almost my most ancient acquaintance and friend in England, I having been intimate with him for thirty-four years, and on many occasions much indebted to his good offices.'[46]

James Keir, Darwin's oldest friend, wrote to Robert on 12 May 1802, giving what is in my view the best short summary of his friend's qualities. Keir begins by emphasizing his sympathy and benevolence, in the passage already quoted on page 46. Then he comments on Erasmus's independence and originality:

> Your father did indeed retain more of his original character than almost any man I have known, excepting, perhaps, Mr Day. Indeed the originality of character in both these men was too strong to give way to the example of others. . . . Your father paid little regard to authority, and he quickly perceived the analogies on which a new theory could be founded. This penetration or sagacity by which he was able to discover very remote causes and distant effects, was the characteristic of his understanding. . . . If to this quality you add an uncommon activity of mind and facility of exertion . . . you will have, I believe, his principal features.[47]

Of his books, Keir says: 'The works of your father are a more faithful monument and more true mirror of his mind than can be said of those of most authors.'[48] He wrote not for gain or fame, but solely from 'ardent love of the subject'. It is worth amplifying one phrase of Keir's, when he refers to Darwin's 'uncommon activity of mind and facility of exertion'. Between 1783 and 1803 Darwin produced books running to one and a half million words, often on abstruse subjects and embodying new discoveries or original ideas—equivalent to a book the length of this one every fifteen months for twenty years. When you consider how much hard work goes into a book, and remember that Darwin was very busy as a doctor during the first fifteen years and quite elderly during the last five, his productivity is staggering.

THIRTEEN

# The Pageant of Life
## 1803-1832

THOUGH DARWIN's life was over, his best poem was yet to come—*The Temple of Nature*, portraying the pageant of life, from the beginnings to the arrival of human beings. The couplets are as skilful and polished as ever, but Darwin's really amazing achievement is to present a picture of life's development that is very largely correct when seen in the light of modern knowledge. He believed that life originated as microscopic specks in primeval seas and gradually evolved under environmental pressures (without assistance from any deity), through fishes, amphibians and reptiles to the forms we now see on Earth.

Darwin intended the title of the poem to be *The Origin of Society*: this title appears as the running head at the top of every even-numbered page, and in the subtitles, for example, on page 1: 'ORIGIN OF SOCIETY. CANTO 1. PRODUCTION OF LIFE'. *The Temple of Nature* appears as the title only once—on the title page, where *The Origin of Society* is given in smaller type as an alternative. A pre-publication announcement in the *Monthly Magazine* for December 1802 refers to the poem as *The Origin of Society*, but someone presumably thought this title too provocative: readers might object to having a microscopic speck as an ancestor. So the neutral title was slipped in just before publication, which was in April 1803. To avoid confusion, I shall continue to use *The Temple of Nature*; but remember that Darwin intended it to be *The Origin of Society*.

Darwin says in the preface that he aims 'simply to amuse' by presenting the pageant of life in the order in which, as he believes, it unfolded. The machinery—to him as vital for a poem as for a steam engine—derives from the Eleusinian mysteries: a Hierophant teaches neophytes about the origin and progress of society. Most of the story is told (in four cantos) by the Priestess of Nature, Urania, who lives in the luxurious Temple of Nature: its 'ponderous domes' extend for 'many a league', and it also sports 'bowers of pleasure' where,

> Pleas'd, their light limbs on beds of roses press'd,
> In slight undress recumbent Beauties rest;
> On tiptoe steps surrounding Graces move,
> And gay Desires expand their wings above.   [I 93–6]

After these pleasantries Darwin embarks on his main theme, and in a few quick couplets takes us through the formation of the Earth and the evolution of microscopic life:

> Ere Time began, from flaming chaos hurl'd
> Rose the bright spheres, which form the circling world;
> Earths from each sun with quick explosions burst,
> And second planets issued from the first.
> Then, whilst the sea at their coeval birth,
> Surge over surge, involv'd the shoreless earth,
> Nurs'd by warm sun-beams in primeval caves
> Organic Life began beneath the waves. . . .
> Hence without parent by spontaneous birth
> Rise the first specks of animated earth.   [I 227–34, 247–8]

Today most biologists believe that life arose 'spontaneously' on Earth, through the formation of amino-acids from simple organic molecules in the atmosphere or oceans under the action of solar ultra-violet radiation, lightning or other energy sources. So Darwin's picture fits in with modern ideas, though his calm certainty proceeds from an erroneous belief that spontaneous generation was quite common. His belief was reasonable, because many experiments had claimed to demonstrate spontaneous generation: all of them must have failed to eliminate contamination, but this seemed an unlikely explanation at the time. So Darwin arrived at the right starting point for evolution via an incorrect belief—quite a common mode of advance in science.

Darwin's belief that the primeval oceans were 'shoreless' may also be wrong, but if so it is of no consequence. Again he gave a good reason: what are now 'some of the highest mountains' are composed of 'limestone rocks' formed beneath the sea.

Darwin needs only three close-packed couplets to summarize evolution:

First forms minute, unseen by spheric glass,
Move on the mud, or pierce the watery mass;
These, as successive generations bloom,
New powers acquire, and larger limbs assume;
Whence countless groups of vegetation spring,
And breathing realms of fin, and feet, and wing.     [I 297–302]

In life's early stages, he says, there were 'vast shoals' of tiny creatures with shells, which on their death formed the strata of coral, chalk and limestone:

Age after age expands the peopled plain,
The tenants perish, but their cells remain.     [I 317–18]

His view of the subsequent course of evolution is very similar to modern ideas:

> After islands or continents were raised above the primeval ocean, great numbers of the most simple animals would attempt to seek food at the edges or shores of the new land, and might thence gradually become amphibious; as is now seen in the frog, who changes from an aquatic animal to an amphibious one; and in the gnat, which changes from a natant to a volant state.     [I 327 note]

Or, to put it in verse, the host of sea creatures

Leaves the cold caverns of the deep, and creeps
On shelving shores, or climbs on rocky steeps.
As in dry air the sea-born stranger roves,
Each muscle quickens, and each sense improves;
Cold gills aquatic form respiring lungs,
And sounds aerial flow from slimy tongues.     [I 329–34]

In support of these ideas on amphibia, Darwin refers to modern examples of creatures having both gills and lungs, and points out how the evolutionary progress from water to land is paralleled by the growth of the human embryo:

Thus in the womb the nascent infant laves
Its natant form in the circumfluent waves ...
With gills placental seeks the arterial flood,
And drinks pure ether from its Mother's blood.     [I 389–90, 393–4]

Finally, the infant 'bursts his way' into the light of day, 'tries his tender lungs and rolls his dazzled eyes'.

Canto II is devoted to 'the Reproduction of Life'. Though individual lives are short,

... REPRODUCTION with ethereal fires
New Life rekindles, ere the first expires.   [II 13–14]

Darwin believes that asexual reproduction came first:

The Reproductions of the living Ens
From sires to sons, unknown to sex, commence. . . .
Unknown to sex the pregnant oyster swells,
And coral-insects build their radiate shells . . .
Birth after birth the line unchanging runs,
And fathers live transmitted in their sons;
Each passing year beholds the unvarying kinds,
The same their manners, and the same their minds.
                    [II 63–4, 89–90, 107–10]

As explained in *Phytologia*, asexual reproduction has its
defects:

The feeble births acquired diseases chase,
Till Death extinguish the degenerate race.   [II 165–6]

The remedy is sex, which Darwin very much approves of, because
it improves the species and adds to organic happiness. Sexual
rivalry does provoke battles among males in some species:

There the hoarse stag his croaking rival scorns,
And butts and parries with his branching horns.   [II 321–2]

On the other hand, there may be married bliss, which gives
Darwin a chance 'simply to amuse':

The Lion-King forgets his savage pride,
And courts with playful paws his tawny bride;
The listening Tiger hears with kindling flame
The love-lorn night-call of his brinded dame. . . .
High o'er their heads on pinions broad display'd
The feather'd nations shed a floating shade;
Pair after pair enamour'd shoot along,
And trill in air the gay impassion'd song.   [II 357–60, 375–8]

All these and many more, fishes, insects and plants, follow
behind Love's flower-decked car.

The physical bias of Canto II is balanced by Canto III, on the
'Progress of the Mind'. Urania and the Muse begin with a world
tour, and their chemically alert eyes

... mark how Oxygen with Azote-Gas
Plays round the globe in one aerial mass,

Or fused with Hydrogen in ceaseless flow
Forms the wide waves, which foam and roll below.   [III 13–16]

Then Urania tells the Muse, and the attendant squads of nymphs, virgins and naiads, how human powers of reason developed. Most animals, she says, have weapons or armour, citing bulls, stags, boars, eagles, electric eels and snakes; but humans rely on hand, eye and brain:

Proud Man alone in wailing weakness born,
No horns protect him, and no plumes adorn . . . .   [III 117–8]

The forms learnt by touch in infancy are reinforced by the eye,

Symbol of solid forms is colour'd light,
And the mute language of the touch is sight.   [III 143–4]

This leads on to Darwin's theory of ideal beauty from 'the nice curves which swell the female breast' and an erotic tale of Eros wooing Dione, with a full-page drawing of the happy pair by Fuseli.

Then Darwin moves back to a more abstract theme, a philosophy of art and science. The key, he believes, is 'the fine power of IMITATION', which

. . . apes the outlines of external things;
With ceaseless action to the world imparts
All moral virtues, languages, and arts.   [III 286–8]

His idea is that we merely imitate what we see, or what others have done; occasionally, in the hands of a creative artist or scientist, the imitations lead on to a new synthesis.

Hence to clear images of form belong
The sculptor's statue, and the poet's song,
The painter's landscape, and the builder's plan,
And IMITATION marks the mind of Man.   [III 331–4]

By imitation too we gradually learnt speech and language, by which we express thoughts and weave them into a culture by memory:

As the soft lips and pliant tongue are taught
With other minds to interchange the thought;
And sound, the symbol of the sense, explains
In parted links the long ideal trains;
From clear conceptions of external things
The facile power of Recollection springs.   [III 395–400]

After a long tribute to Reason, basis of 'all human science worth
the name', Darwin warns us that our vaunted wisdom is not so
different from the instinctive wisdom of the wasp, bee or spider,
which links 'the reasoning reptile to mankind'.

Though he disliked many religious practices, Darwin was
much in favour of the sympathy and benevolence inculcated in
the New Testament morality. 'The seraph, Sympathy', he says,
'charms the world with universal love', and the following motto
is inscribed over the Temple of Nature:

> IN LIFE'S DISASTROUS SCENES TO OTHERS DO,
> WHAT YOU WOULD WISH BY OTHERS DONE TO YOU. [III 487–8]

This precept, 'if sincerely obeyed by all nations, would a
thousand-fold multiply the present happiness of mankind', Darwin remarks in a note. His theory of the progress of the mind,
expressed in this canto, is complex and ingenious; it deserves
further study by philosophers.

In Canto IV of the poem, 'Of Good and Evil', Darwin brilliantly versifies his evolutionary theory and philosophy of
organic happiness. His picture of the web of slaughter in the
struggle for existence has an unrivalled freshness and force. At
the very start Darwin ranges between a wolf and a seed:

> The wolf, escorted by his milk-drawn dam,
> Unknown to mercy, tears the guiltless lamb;
> The towering eagle, darting from above,
> Unfeeling rends the inoffensive dove;
> The lamb and dove on living nature feed,
> Crop the young herb, or crush the embryon seed.    [IV 17–22]

The owl kills small creatures, which themselves prey on others;
insects like the gadfly and ichneumon fly lay eggs in animals or
other insects. Even the plants are at war:

> Yes! smiling Flora drives her armèd car
> Through the thick ranks of vegetable war;
> Herb, shrub, and tree, with strong emotions rise
> For light and air, and battle in the skies;
> Whose roots diverging with opposing toil
> Contend below for moisture and for soil;
> Round the tall Elm the flattering Ivies bend,
> And strangle, as they clasp, their struggling friend . . .
> And insect hordes with restless tooth devour
> The unfolded bud, and pierce the ravell'd flower.    [IV 41–8, 53–4]

Vicious combat pervades the oceans too:

> In ocean's pearly haunts, the waves beneath
> Sits the grim monarch of insatiate Death. . . .
> —Air, earth, and ocean, to astonish'd day
> One scene of blood, one mighty tomb display!
> From Hunger's arm the shafts of Death are hurl'd,
> And one great Slaughter-house the warring world!
>
> [IV 55–6, 63–6]

The roster of evils continues with a depressing list of human ills, from the 'iron hand' of Slavery and the pains of Disease to writhing Mania, ragged Avarice, earthquake, pestilence, hunger and 'the curst spells of Superstition', which fetter 'the tortured mind' (IV 84–5).

Is there nothing but woe, then? On the contrary, Urania replies, good and evil are nicely balanced. Human beings enjoy the pleasure of consciousness, the delights of natural scenery, the warmth of sunshine, the fragrance of flowers, the taste of fruits, the charms of music, painting and all the imaginative arts; and above all they may 'drink the raptures of delirious love'. There are also the satisfactions of philanthropy, the triumphs of science, and the heroic endeavours of those who fight against the suppression of knowledge by governments:

> Oh save, oh save, in this eventful hour
> The tree of knowledge from the axe of power;
> With fostering peace the suffering nations bless,
> And guard the freedom of the immortal Press!    [IV 283–6]

With the advance of knowledge and science, Darwin foresees tower blocks, piped water and traffic jams:

> Bid raised in air the ponderous structure stand,
> Or pour obedient rivers through the land;
> With cars unnumber'd crowd the living streets,
> Or people oceans with triumphant fleets.    [IV 315–18]

Next Darwin propounds his philosophy of organic happiness. Tennyson's 'nature, red in tooth and claw' came as a shock to the Victorians, but Darwin had the answer fifty years before. The ideas of over-population and 'limits to growth' have come as a nasty shock to our era, but Darwin dealt with them 150 years earlier:

Each pregnant Oak ten thousand acorns forms
Profusely scatter'd by autumnal storms. . . .
The countless Aphides, prolific tribe,
With greedy trunks the honey'd sap imbibe. . . .
—All these, increasing by successive birth,
Would each o'erpeople ocean, air, and earth.

So human progenies, if unrestrain'd,
By climate friended, and by food sustain'd,
O'er seas and soils, prolific hordes! would spread
Erelong, and deluge their terraqueous bed;
But war, and pestilence, disease, and dearth,
Sweep the superfluous myriads from the earth.
[IV 347–8, 351–2, 367–74]

Darwin is pleased that 'every pore of Nature teems with life',
for the proliferating life all contributes to the sum total of organic
happiness:

Hence when a Monarch or a mushroom dies,
Awhile extinct the organic matter lies;
But, as a few short hours or years revolve,
Alchemic powers the changing mass dissolve [IV 383–6]

—and new life burgeons. So, even when 'earthquakes swallow
half a realm alive', we should not grieve too much, because 'the
wrecks of Death' are only a change in form. The 'restless atoms
pass from life to life',

Whence drew the enlighten'd Sage the moral plan,
That man should ever be the friend of man;
Should eye with tenderness all living forms,
His brother-emmets, and his sister worms. [IV 425–8]

Finally Darwin salutes the mountains of limestone as the
remains of creatures that once enjoyed life:

Thus the tall mountains, that emboss the lands,
Huge isles of rock, and continents of sands,
Whose dim extent eludes the inquiring sight,
ARE MIGHTY MONUMENTS OF PAST DELIGHT;
Shout round the globe, how Reproduction strives
With vanquish'd Death—and Happiness survives;
How Life increasing peoples every clime,
And young renascent Nature conquers Time. [IV 447–54]

There is no more to be said. The nymphs and naiads, astonished at the discourse, troop silently into the Temple for a ceremonial finale.

[2]

The Additional Notes to *The Temple of Nature* extend to 120 pages, and cover a wide variety of subjects. As usual, Darwin's ideas press on the boundaries of knowledge, and often step over. He begins with eleven pages on spontaneous vitality, listing the experiments which, not unreasonably, led him to believe in it, and commending microscopic researches. The other end of life, old age and death, is covered in a ten-page note. Reproduction, and the advantages of sex, generate a six-page note, and hereditary diseases receive three pages with a sting in the tail: 'As many families become gradually extinct by hereditary diseases, as by scrofula, consumption, epilepsy, mania, it is often hazardous to marry an heiress, as she is not unfrequently the last of a diseased family' (Note XI). This injunction against marrying heiresses was reproduced in a weaker form by Darwin's grandson Francis Galton in his book *Hereditary Genius*[1]—a title that seems rather ironic since he failed to mention his grandfather's priority.

The longest note, of thirty-four pages, is an electromagnetic theory of chemistry. Darwin is groping towards the idea that the electrical and magnetic 'ethers', as he calls them, control chemical reactions on an atomic scale: 'electric and magnetic attractions and repulsions', he says, 'may be applied to explain the invisible attractions and repulsions of the minute particles of bodies in chemical combinations and decompositions' (p. 75). Now that all students of chemistry learn about chemical reactions in terms of electron interchanges, we have to acclaim Darwin as a pioneer of electrochemistry—but only just, because his ideas are vague, though basically correct.

Quickly changing from electrical to aesthetic attraction, Darwin offers a thirteen-page 'Analysis of Taste'. 'Four sources of pleasure', he says, arise from 'the excitation of the nerves of vision by light and colours': novelty, repetition, colour melody and association. This ingenious theory has been discussed in detail by Logan.[2] The next note runs to fifteen pages, on the theory and structure of language; it is an impressive survey, starting from the premise that words are the symbols of ideas, and proceeding to complex languages. The final note, fourteen pages on the analysis of articulate sounds, has already been quoted in discussing the speaking machine (p. 88). Other notes range from volcanoes and mosquitoes to Egyptian hieroglyphics. With *The Temple of Nature* Darwin neatly rounds off his life's work. Most of his life had been devoted to the science of life, first as a doctor, then as a botanist and theoretical biologist. Now he had welded animal biology and botany into a satisfying synthesis with his concept of evolution, which only won acceptance after the publication of his grandson's *Origin of Species* fifty-six years later.

The *Temple of Nature* did not enjoy the great popular success of *The Botanic Garden*. There was nothing new in the style, and, with Napoleon poised to strike across the Channel in 1803, people were not too interested in the broad philosophical sweep of the poem, especially since the evolutionary theme was thought to be an insult to both Christianity and human dignity, as well as seeming wildly unlikely to most readers. The reviews were mostly unfavourable: the *Monthly Magazine* was appreciative, but the *Anti-Jacobin Review* condemned Darwin for his 'total denial of any interference of a Deity', and the *Critical Review* attacked him for trying 'to substitute the religion of nature for the religion of the Bible'.[3] Though there was a second edition in 1806, and a third in 1825, these were only published as part of Darwin's collected poetical works.

So *The Temple of Nature* remained a biological time-bomb reclining on the library shelves, looked at with suspicion or not at all by most readers. And when the bomb exploded, it attracted little notice.

[3]

Though Darwin himself enjoyed life at the Priory for only a few weeks, he saw enough to know that the move was a success for Elizabeth. She continued to live there for thirty years, and the house became known as 'Happiness Hall' to her Galton grandchildren because they enjoyed their visits so much.

But that lay ahead. At the time of her husband's death Elizabeth was fifty-four, and their six children, aged between eleven and twenty, needed much of her attention in the next few years. Their fortunes were mixed, and only two of them outlived their mother. The eldest, Edward, became a cavalry officer and after retiring lived at Mackworth, near Derby. In his forties he was an invalid and could not walk: he weighed over twenty-five stone and was unable to get out of his carriage when he visited the Priory. He died at the age of forty-seven in 1829.

The healthiest and most talented of the children was their eldest daughter Violetta, who married Samuel Galton's son Tertius in 1807 and went to live at Leamington. Violetta, who lived to be ninety, had seven children: the eldest, Elizabeth Anne, lived to the age of ninety-eight; the second, Lucy, married James Moilliet, son of Keir's daughter Amelia, so that the Moilliets are a triply Lunar family, descended from Darwin, Galton and Keir. Violetta had three sons, Darwin, Erasmus and Francis Galton, the last of whom had much in common with his grandfather Erasmus Darwin.

The third child of Erasmus and Elizabeth was Emma, who was so indignant about Anna Seward's slanders of her father. Her niece Elizabeth Anne Galton said 'she was very beautiful, agreeable and amiable, and most kind-hearted';[4] but her health was poor, and she died in 1818 at the age of thirty-four after a long and painful illness. For a few years before that she ran a small charity school started by her younger sister Harriot.

The fourth child, Francis, grew up to be more like his father than any other of Erasmus's sons. He became a doctor and was very enterprising and energetic, but he lacked his father's intellectual penetration. In 1808 he went on a voyage to Turkey with four companions, and was the only one of the five who returned alive. He married in 1815 and after his mother's death lived at Breadsall Priory: he was Deputy Lieutenant of Derbyshire, was knighted in 1820 and died in 1859, aged seventy-three.

The fifth child, John, graduated at Cambridge University, like Francis, but was of a quieter temperament. He chose the Church as his profession, and in 1815 he became rector of Elston; but he died three years later, at the age of thirty-one.

The youngest child, Harriot, started a school in Derby before she was twenty. At twenty-one she married Captain, later Admiral, T. J. Maling, and afterwards travelled widely with him. She died of dysentery at Valparaiso in 1825 when she was thirty-five.

Of Elizabeth's other children, her eldest son Sacheverel died in 1813, aged forty-four; her eldest daughter, Elizabeth, who married Colonel Bromley, died in 1821; her second daughter Millicent, whose illness had first brought Erasmus and her mother together, lived to be over eighty. Milly was happily married to John Gisborne, author of the poem *The Vales of Wever* and a good friend of Erasmus.

Elizabeth herself retained her humour and energy to a ripe old age. Even in her eighties she closely supervised the gardeners at the Priory and would spend all day outdoors. At her death in 1832, aged eighty-five, Elizabeth had had eleven children, forty-one grandchildren and twenty-eight great-grandchildren; three of the children and fifty-seven of the others survived her.[5]

Inevitably, the years 1803–32 saw the deaths of all Erasmus's old friends and relatives. His brother John, the conscientious clergyman, died in 1805, and his sister Ann in 1813. The longest-lived of his brothers was the eldest, Robert the naturalist, who died at Elston in 1816 at the age of ninety-two. Of Darwin's friends, the youngest died soonest: Tom Wedgwood finally succumbed to his debilities in 1805 at the age of thirty-four; Tom's medical adviser Dr Beddoes died in 1808, aged forty-eight; and Anna Seward in 1809, aged sixty-six. Darwin's old Lunar friends died between 1809 and 1820: his 'most antient' friend in Birmingham, Matthew Boulton in 1809 at eighty-one, honoured as 'the father of Birmingham'; Edgeworth in 1817 at seventy-three, inventive to the last, designing what we call 'macadamized' roads; James Watt in 1819 at eighty-three, full of honours and recognized, then and now, as the greatest of British engineers; and finally, James Keir, Darwin's oldest friend, in 1820 aged eighty-five.

To recover from this dismal list of obituaries we may turn to the thriving school at Ashbourne, where Susan and Mary Parker continued to follow their father's advice, and to maintain their school's high reputation. Susan retired in 1817 after her marriage to Mr Hadley, the Derby surgeon who had attended Erasmus in his last illnesses. Mary continued the school until 1827, when she too retired.

Finally, we must visit Shrewsbury, where a new Darwinian patriarchy was arising. As the years passed, Robert Darwin became a commanding figure in the town: he was extremely successful in his medical practice and was said to have the highest income of any provincial doctor. He was six feet two inches tall, and he gave up weighing himself when he reached twenty-four stone. His burly coachman had to test the floorboards for him before he entered a new patient's house. Robert and his wife Susannah had two sons and four daughters, all long-lived. After Susannah died in 1817, aged fifty-two, Robert maintained close links with the family of her brother Josiah Wedgwood II, who lived at Maer, only twenty miles from Shrewsbury.

Robert's second son Charles, born in 1809, proved rather a disappointment to his father. At Shrewsbury School Charles gave the impression that he learnt almost nothing: 'The school as a means of education to me was simply a blank.'[6] So his father sent him to Edinburgh in 1825, when he was sixteen, to learn medicine; but Charles found the course distasteful, so he left Edinburgh after two years and went on to Cambridge University, with the idea of becoming a country clergyman like his uncle and great-uncle John. At Cambridge, Charles said, 'my time was wasted, as far as the academical studies were concerned':[7] in this harsh judgement he is unfair to himself, however, for he emerged with a good pass degree and became skilled as a naturalist and geologist.

Robert was a formidable figure, psychologically as well as physically; his children stood in awe of him, and never deviated from complete obedience. Charles in particular was sure that whatever his father did or said was 'absolutely true, right, and wise'. Yet this formidable man had once been equally dominated by his own father, Erasmus: he had become a doctor because Erasmus wanted him to, though he always hated his profession; he had married in conformity with his father's wishes and had adopted nearly all Erasmus's ideas, including evolution, temperance, treating patients by psychological methods, and scepticism in religion, where he went beyond his father and became a complete atheist (though he did not publicize the fact).

In 1831 Charles was dutifully preparing for a career as a country clergyman. Then in August he was offered the chance of going as naturalist on the round-the-world voyage of H.M.S. *Beagle*. The Hydrographer of the Navy recommended him to Captain FitzRoy as 'a Mr Darwin grandson of the well known philosopher and poet'.[8] Charles was very keen to accept, but his father said no, because he thought it unsuitable for a clergyman;

so Charles obediently refused the offer. But Robert did say he would think again if Charles could find 'a man of sense' to speak in favour. At the time Charles was staying with his uncle Josiah Wedgwood II, who was strongly in favour. Faced with such a formidable man of sense, Robert gave way, and on 27 December 1831 Charles sailed away on the *Beagle* to begin his illustrious career.

[4]

Erasmus was still influential as a 'well-known philosopher and poet' for twenty years after his death, despite the blows to his prestige in the late 1790s. His poems remained popular, and *Beauties of the Botanic Garden*, a volume of selections, was published in 1805, followed by his collected poetical works (that is, *The Botanic Garden* and *The Temple of Nature*) in 1806, republished in 1824–5. American editions of *Zoonomia* appeared in 1803, 1809 and 1818, and an Italian translation came out in 1803–6. Two American editions of *The Temple of Nature* were published in 1804 and a German translation in 1808. Darwin's medical reputation remained very high, too, and his granddaughter Elizabeth Anne Galton remembered family consultations with doctors in the 1820s: 'When they heard that my mother was daughter to Dr Erasmus Darwin it was with difficulty my father could make them take a fee. Sir Astley Cooper almost embraced my Mother, he was so pleased to see a daughter of Dr Darwin.'[9]

Not everyone was so appreciative of Darwin: Coleridge remained under Darwin's spell, both intellectually and physically (via the opium), but he continually chafed against both. Though Coleridge wrote few good poems after 1800, his dramatic criticism and philosophical writings have subsequently been much admired. But in his psychological theory Coleridge draws heavily on *Zoonomia*; in particular, Coleridge's theory of dramatic illusion comes straight from Darwin's chapter on Sleep.[10] Coleridge deeply resented his need to borrow from Darwin, but opium addiction had destroyed his ability to achieve much on his own, as surely as it destroyed his truthfulness—'truth and drugs do not keep company'.[11] Coleridge expressed his resentment by projecting his own debilities on to Darwin, whom he accused of being 'a great plagiarist' and of writing letters to himself; but both practices were Coleridge's own,[12] rather than Darwin's.

Coleridge did not like Darwin's evolutionary views, and referred to his 'Orang Outang theology of the human race, substituted for the first chapters of the book of Genesis'.[13] Coleridge is scornful of the possibility that 'a male and female ounce' might produce 'in course of generations a cat, or a cat a lion. This is *Darwinizing* with a vengeance.'[14] This condemnation of evolutionary thinking as 'Darwinizing' came fifty years before *The Origin of Species*, and apparently the word stuck. At a scientific house party in September 1856, three years before *The Origin of Species* appeared, the engineer Thomas Sopwith gave a talk on evolution, and the Revd. J. B. Reade commented, 'That is rank Darwinism.'[15]

Darwin still held some sway too over Wordsworth, whose sonnet on Westminster Bridge, written soon after Darwin's death, has the famous line, 'All bright and glittering in the smokeless air', which is distinctly Darwinian, being sharp and bright and reminiscent of several lines in *The Loves of the Plants*, such as:

All wan and shivering in the leafless glade . . .
And all the glittering pageant melts in air.

Wordsworth must also have been deeply impressed by Darwin's picture of Cambyses's army being buried in the sand,

. . . awhile the living hill
Heaved with convulsive throes—and all was still,

because Wordsworth reproduced it nearly twenty years after Darwin's death in the poem 'To Enterprise', where he wrote:

An Army now, and now a living hill
That a brief while heaves with convulsive throes—
Then all is still.[16]

Darwin's successor as a popular poet was Walter Scott, whose *Lay of the Last Minstrel* (1805) had an even greater success than *The Botanic Garden*. Scott gives his opinion of Darwin in a letter to Edgeworth on 10 February 1812, saying that some passages in *The Botanic Garden*, such as 'the march of Cambyses' and 'the descent of Juno' ensure Darwin a 'ranking among British poets of the highest class'.[17]

[5]

Darwin's important influence on the younger generation of Romantic poets, Keats, Shelley and Byron, during the years 1810–24 is a long story that must be kept short.[18]
Of the three, Keats might seem likely to be closest to Darwin: 'trained as a doctor and later turned to poetry' would fit both. Bernard Blackstone in his book *The Consecrated Urn* has suggested that Keats's entire career as a poet parallels Darwin's. To show this is not all moonshine, here are two verbal parallels. In *The Eve of St Agnes*, the Beadsman moves

> Along the chapel aisle by slow degrees:
> The sculptur'd dead, on each side, seem to freeze;

and later the moonbeams shine through a stained-glass window on the sleeping Madeline: this resembles the lines in *The Loves of the Plants* (III 23–6) quoted on page 195. The second parallel is the image of virgins round flowered altars, in *The Temple of Nature*:

> Long trains of virgins from the sacred grove . . .
> With flower-fill'd baskets round the altar throng,
> Or swing their censers, as they wind along.

This is very like the censer-swinging virgins in Keats's 'Ode to Psyche':

> Nor altar heap'd with flowers;
> Nor virgin-choir to make delicious moan . . .
> From swingèd censer teeming:
> Thy shrine, thy grove, thy oracle. . . .[19]

These and other echoes show that Keats breathed the atmosphere of Darwin's poems, though he rejected their stiff couplets.
Of all the Romantic poets, Shelley was Darwin's keenest follower. From Darwin he had the idea of combining science and poetry, and in such poems as 'The Cloud' Shelley eventually achieved a fusion of poetry and science which went far beyond Darwin's more mechanical skills. Shelley, like Darwin, was a sceptic in religion, a keen radical in politics, an enthusiast for science and a fighter against tyranny and oppression in all its forms. Darwin's philosophy of organic happiness also appealed

to Shelley, partly because he liked the idea of plants having 'feelings'.

Shelley became familiar with Darwin's poems while he was at Eton (1804–10), not because Darwin was on the curriculum, but through his privately chosen mentor Dr James Lind, physician to the Royal Household at Windsor, who was a cousin of Keir and one of Watt's closest friends in the 1760s. In much of his life's work Shelley followed Lind's guidance,[20] and Darwin was among Dr Lind's prescriptions. Several echoes of Darwin can be heard in Shelley's juvenile poems, and many more in his first long poem, *Queen Mab* (1813). In this tirade against present evils, Shelley closely follows Darwin's attacks in *The Temple of Nature* on superstition, tyrants, slavery, war, alcohol, avarice and luxury, as well as using the machinery of a goddess in a 'magic car'. Darwin's attack on war,

> While mad with foolish fame, or drunk with power,
> Ambition slays his thousands in an hour,

is paralleled by Shelley's

> When merciless ambition, or mad zeal,
> Has led two hosts of dupes to battlefield.

Darwin's line about the struggle for existence,

> And one great Slaughter-house the warring world!,

reverberates in Shelley's

> Making the earth a slaughter-house!

Darwin's line about 'a Monarch or a mushroom' is turned by Shelley into

> Yon monarch, in his solitary pomp,
> Was but the mushroom of a summer day.[21]

In Shelley's greatest poem, *Prometheus Unbound* (1819), the main theme is regeneration of the world through universal love; it is no coincidence that in *The Temple of Nature* the seraph Sympathy 'charms the world with universal love'. The many individual echoes include the climactic line that ends Act III of *Prometheus Unbound*,

> Pinnacled dim in the intense inane,

which derives from Darwin's memorable line,

Hung with gold tresses o'er the vast inane.[22]

Shelley's 'Sensitive Plant', with its personified flowers, obviously owes much to *The Loves of the Plants*, and Shelley's lyrics of the sky abound in phrases from Darwin. For example, Darwin's phrase, 'each nice pore of ocean, earth, and air', inspired Shelley's summary of water circulation in 'The Cloud': 'I pass through the pores of the ocean and shores.' Shelley's *Adonais* has striking affinities with Canto II of *The Temple of Nature*, for in both Urania grieves over human wrongs. In Shelley's *Witch of Atlas*, the Witch would

Ride singing through the shoreless air . . .
And laughed to hear the fire-balls roar behind,

just as Darwin's nymphs would

Ride, with broad eye and scintillating hair,
The rapid Fire-ball through the midnight air.[23]

The famous lovers' voyage in *Epipsychidion* has its scenery taken from the lines about the 'brooding halcyons' in *The Loves of the Plants* quoted on page 196.

Shelley's friend Byron, though fond of rhyming couplets, was not very sympathetic to Darwin. In *English Bards and Scotch Reviewers* (1809) he calls Darwin

That mighty master of unmeaning rhyme,
Whose gilded cymbals, more adorn'd than clear,
The eye delighted, but fatigued the ear.    [lines 800–2]

A few lines later Byron refers to 'vulgar Wordsworth', the 'meanest object of the lowly group', so he is relatively kind to Darwin.

More by accident than by design, Byron pushed Darwin into the driving seat of the band-wagon of science fiction, via Mary Shelley's *Frankenstein*. In the preface she says that the book was suggested by a long discussion between Byron and Shelley in 1816 about 'the nature of the principle of life, and . . . the experiments of Dr Darwin' on the subject. This discussion sprang from a mixed-up remembrance of the note on Spontaneous Generation in *The Temple of Nature*. Afterwards Mary could not sleep: 'My imagination, unbidden, possessed and guided me. . . .' And so *Frankenstein*, the seminal work of science fiction, was born. Brian Aldiss[24] sees Darwin as the chief father-figure of science fiction, not only imaginatively, through his biological speculations and *Frankenstein,* but also through his technological forecasts in the spirit of Jules Verne.

So, even though Darwin's poems fell out of favour by the 1820s, his ideas were influencing the intellectual climate through being ground fine in the minds of greater poets, then disseminated like the 'ten thousand seeds each pregnant poppy sheds', by Wordsworth, Coleridge, Shelley and Keats—and even Pushkin.[25] Not all the poets of the time were under Darwin's spell: Crabbe altered his poem *The Library* in 1807 to remove resemblances to Darwin;[26] Blake detested the technology celebrated in *The Economy of Vegetation,* and was probably none too pleased that his superb engravings contributed to the poem's success. But Blake approved of—and acted on—Darwin's views about painting, expressed in a note in *The Economy of Vegetation* (I 358): 'Why should not painting as well as poetry express itself in metaphor, or in indistinct allegory?'[27]

Darwin was often criticized for being a painter in words, a purveyor of glittering images rather than a true poet. His main appeal was to the eye, and among the eyes he appealed to were those of England's greatest painter, Turner, who accepted Darwin's idea that poetry was, as it were, painting in words. Turner began writing verse in 1793 and his sketch-books 'contain on the whole even more poetry than drawings',[28] mainly visual Darwinian-type verse. After 1809, Turner usually 'illustrated' his paintings with verse quotations said to be taken from his long poem *The Fallacies of Hope.* Turner was influenced more by Thomson[29] than by Darwin, but there are many parallels between Turner's verse and Darwin's, because both are so intensely visual. Darwin often word-paints Turnerian scenes: the start of Canto IV of *The Loves of the Plants,*

> Now the broad Sun his golden orb unshrouds,
> Flames in the west, and paints the parted clouds,

is a real Turner skyscape, reminiscent of Turner's own line, 'Yon angry setting sun and fierce-edged clouds,'[30] appended to his painting of *Slavers throwing overboard the dead and dying.*

So Darwin stands as a leading progenitor of the Romantic movement in poetry, and as a fellow word-painter with the leader of a new era in art.

# FOURTEEN

# The Darwinian Legacy
## 1833-1977

In JANUARY 1833 Charles Darwin in the *Beagle* was being battered by storms off Tierra del Fuego, but eventually he arrived back safely from his world voyage, in 1836. He began writing about his observations and discoveries on the voyage, and then in 1839 he married his cousin Emma Wedgwood. Charles's father had married a Wedgwood, and his elder sister Caroline, who had taken him under her wing after his mother died, married Josiah Wedgwood III in 1837. So it is no surprise to find Charles marrying a Wedgwood; and he even reproduced almost exactly the scenario of his father's marriage. Each married, about a month before his thirtieth birthday, a woman one year older than himself whom he had known since childhood and whose father was named Josiah Wedgwood.

Having thus flouted the laws of probability, Charles retired to Down House in 1842 to remake the laws of biology. At Down, a semi-invalid with a rigid routine, devotedly attended by Emma and surrounded by a large family, Charles took a forty-year voyage through the seas of biology: he worked and thought, and wrought the Darwinian revolution.

Authors of books on Charles Darwin often suggest that Charles and his grandfather were quite different in temperament. Erasmus, so they say, was speculative and superficial, with an eighteenth-century exuberance; Charles factual, thorough and hardworking, with a Victorian reticence. But I see Erasmus and Charles as very similar. Charles certainly worked hard, within the limits set by his invalidism. But Erasmus, with his tiring medical practice and his lengthy books, worked even harder. Charles was not at heart a Victorian gentleman, though he conformed to that pattern for the sake of a quiet life: he grew up in the reign of George IV and harboured Georgian thoughts; and as his life progressed, he inclined ever more strongly towards the evolutionary thinking and religious scepticism of his grand-father and father. Charles may seem to have been more timid in his speculations than Erasmus. But Charles's major triumph in establishing evolution was one of the greatest speculations science has known: he could not answer the objections, and 'maintained his faith in his position regardless of the valid arguments that could be brought against it'.[1] The family faith in evolution sustained him.

The few differences between Erasmus and Charles arose from the different climates of opinion in which they lived; from Charles's ill-health and consequent diffidence; and from Erasmus's greater range of talents, particularly as a poet and inventor. Otherwise the two seem to offer an excellent example of hereditary likeness between a man and his grandfather.

The intellectual similarities are easy enough to see. For Charles, as for Erasmus, the books he wrote are 'a faithful monument and true mirror of his mind'. So we only need to look through the books. Charles's *Voyage of the Beagle*, with its first-hand naturalist's reports, would have been sheer wish-fulfilment for Erasmus, who stuffed the notes to his poems with second-hand descriptions of exotic plants and animals, but never left Britain. Charles made striking discoveries in geology in the 1840s, recorded in his books on *Coral Reefs* (1842), *Volcanic Islands* (1844) and the geology of South America (1846). Erasmus was just as keen on geology, the subject of hundreds of lines in his poems and seventy pages in the Notes, or in *Phytologia*; and he specially liked the 'living rocks of worm-built coral' which may well have given him the idea of the 'mighty monuments of past delight'. Both Erasmus and Charles had a taxonomic tendency: Erasmus's eight-year botanic apprenticeship translating and rewording Linnaeus produced the four volumes of the *System of Vegetables* and *Families of Plants*; Charles's eight-year biological apprenticeship, spent acquiring a deep understanding of species through an intensive study of barnacles, produced the four volumes of his treatise on *Cirripedia* (1854).

Both Darwins were fascinated by the fertilization processes in plants—'nothing in my life has ever interested me more', Charles said.[2] Erasmus declared his interest with *The Loves of the Plants*; Charles with his *Contrivances by which Orchids are*

*Fertilized* (1862), *Cross- and Self-Fertilization in the Vegetable Kingdom* (1876) and *Different Forms of Flowers on Plants* (1877).

Both were attracted by signs of sensibility in plants: 'he could not help personifying natural things', and 'it has always pleased me to exalt plants in the scale of organized beings',[3] are quotations that could apply to either; actually, both the 'he' and the 'me' are Charles, and to prove it there are his books on *Insectivorous Plants* (1875), *Climbing Plants* (1875) and *Power of Movement in Plants* (1880)—the very subjects Erasmus drags in to justify his theory of sensibility in plants, in *The Botanic Garden* and *Phytologia*.

Erasmus and Charles also shared a strange-seeming pair of interests—facial expressions and worms. Erasmus has a long note on 'External signs of passions' in *The Temple of Nature*, to go with the comic lines:

When strong desires or soft sensations move
The astonish'd Intellect to rage or love;
Associate tribes of fibrous motions rise,
Flush the red cheek, or light the laughing eyes.   [III 335–8]

Charles found the subject fascinating, and wrote his book *Expression of the Emotions in Man and Animals* (1872). The worms come on the scene when Erasmus asks us to 'eye with tenderness' our 'sister-worms' in *The Temple of Nature*; and in *Phytologia* he comments on the rise in soil level caused by animal and vegetable decay. So he would have relished Charles's book, *Formation of Vegetable Mould through the Action of Worms* (1881), especially the sentence: 'Worms have played a more important part in the history of the world than most persons would at first suppose' (p. 145).

If we omit Charles's delightful *Life of Erasmus Darwin* as too obvious, the only books left for comparison are those on evolution, *The Origin of Species* (1859), *Variations of Animals and Plants under Domestication* (1868) and *The Descent of Man and Selection in Relation to Sex* (1871). Here the obvious parallel is Erasmus's *Zoonomia*, together with *Phytologia* and *The Temple of Nature*, but the link is stronger than a mere parallel, for Charles grew up dominated by his father, a silent believer in evolution. Then, at Edinburgh in 1827, the eighteen-year-old Charles was treated to a tirade in favour of evolution from Dr Robert Grant:

I listened in silent astonishment, and as far as I can judge, without

any effect on my mind. I had previously read the *Zoonomia* of my
grandfather in which similar views are maintained, but without
producing any effect on me. Nevertheless it is probable that the
hearing rather early in life such views maintained and praised may
have favoured my upholding them under a different form in my
*Origin of Species*. At this time I admired greatly the *Zoonomia*. . . .[4]

A book whose evolutionary theories he 'admired greatly' at the
age of eighteen could scarcely fail to influence him when he
began developing such theories for himself ten years later:
though he was unconscious of it, his mind was prepared. Charles
says that when he next read *Zoonomia*, 'after an interval of ten
or fifteen years, I was much disappointed, the proportion of
speculation being so large to the facts given'.[5] He thought
*Zoonomia* weak on facts (a fair criticism), but he did not think it
wrong. About this time (1842) Charles began his notebooks on
'the species question': the heading 'Zoonomia' appears on the
first page, because he was taking notes on the book.

Charles Darwin's copy of *Zoonomia*, Volume I, is in the Cambridge University Library, and he has written in thirty-three
comments, mostly appreciative, ranging in length between one
word and forty. The most vigorous comment, beside the paragraph about the beaks of birds (quoted on page 244), is
'Lamarck!!', and Charles adds, 'Lamarck concisely forestalled by
my grandfather.' Charles also read *Phytologia* carefully: there
are fifteen annotations and about fifty marked passages in his
copy. There are several markings against Erasmus's account of
the happiness of organic life on page 557, and a double marking,
with the word 'good', stands beside Erasmus's reference to 'the
plan of Mr Bakewell in England in respect to quadrupeds, who
continued to improve his flocks and herds by the marriages of
those in which the properties he wished to produce were most
conspicuous' (p. 451). Charles's copy of *The Botanic Garden*,
which has the date 1826 written in, is also heavily marked, and
has eight comments, mainly botanical, mostly in one group
dated 'Dec. 1857'. So Charles read his grandfather's books quite
carefully.

After *Zoonomia*, statements of the principle of evolution by
natural selection came fairly thick and fast, from Hutton (1797),
Wells (1813), Prichard (1813), Lawrence (1819), Matthew
(1831), Chambers (1844), and finally Darwin and Wallace
in 1858. Some of these expositions of evolution were cogent and

comprehensive,[6] but none of them succeeded in convincing the world. (Indeed none was so well known as Lamarck's 1809 theory of purposive evolution.) At the end of 1858, *after* the presentation of Darwin's paper to the Linnaean Society, the Society's president said that the year had not been marked by any striking discoveries.

After the short paper of 1858 Charles summarized his long years of thought about evolution in what he called an abstract of a proposed major work on the subject, published in November 1859 as *On the Origin of Species by means of Natural Selection . . .* The book eventually persuaded the world that evolution by natural selection was the key to understanding the past and present pageant of life.

How did Charles Darwin succeed when so many other statements of natural selection had fallen on deaf ears? First, the time was ripe: intellectual opinion had been 'softened up' by the earlier announcements of evolution, including Erasmus's, which was still remembered. Second, Charles presents modestly and honestly a mass of evidence he had been collecting for twenty years. Third, he states a number of objections, and answers them —a masterstroke that floored many critics. Fourth, he never mentions human origins, except in one cryptic sentence— another diplomatic coup. Detractors may say that Charles was merely restating an unoriginal theory and failing to mention its most pungent conclusion. That is true, but he still brought about the greatest intellectual revolution of the nineteenth century, and his fame will shine undimmed for as long as human culture endures. Although the obvious links between Erasmus and Charles need to be stated, I should like to make it clear that I have the highest admiration for Charles, and believe his fame to be well deserved.

In the first edition of *The Origin of Species* Charles says very little about previous expositions of evolution, because he was not conscious of having benefited from them. But the evolutionary chapter in his grandfather's *Zoonomia* had an immense subconscious influence on him. Of many examples, I give three. First, Charles's account of sexual selection:

> This form of selection depends . . . on a struggle between the individuals of one sex, generally the males, for the possession of the other sex. . . . Generally, the most vigorous males, those which are best fitted for their places in nature, will leave most progeny. But in

many cases, victory depends not so much on general vigour, as on having special weapons, confined to the male sex. A hornless stag or spurless cock would have a poor chance of leaving numerous offspring. . . .[7]

This is very similar to Erasmus's account, quoted on page 243. The second resemblance is stylistic. One of Erasmus's mannerisms is to write very long sentences of the form: 'When we consider example 1; when we compare x with y; when we think over example 2; we cannot but conclude that . . .' Charles also often uses the same grammatical form.[8] The third parallel is the famous finale of *The Origin of Species* (p. 463):

> Thus, from the war of nature, from famine and death, the most exalted object which we are capable of conceiving, namely, the production of the higher animals, directly follows. There is grandeur in this view of life, with its several powers, having been originally breathed by the Creator into a few forms or into one; and that, whilst this planet has gone cycling on according to the fixed law of gravity, from so simple a beginning endless forms most beautiful and wonderful have been, and are being evolved.

In substance and in some of its wording, this is close to Erasmus's rhetorical summary of evolution, quoted on page 244, and his account of the war of nature in *The Temple of Nature*. Charles also takes heed of the markings he made in *Phytologia* where Erasmus emphasizes that the more vigorous and happier animals survive. In *The Origin of Species* Charles says: 'The war of nature is not incessant . . . the vigorous, the healthy, and the happy survive and multiply' (p. 79).

The title of Charles's book offers another possible subconscious link. Erasmus chose *The Origin of Society* as the title for his poem on the evolution and development of life. Change the three letters *o-ty* to *pe-s* and you have: *The Origin of Species*.

When the Darwins differ in their evolutionary theory, Erasmus is (partly by luck) often nearer the modern view. For example, Erasmus specified 'millions of ages' for the time scale of evolution, while Charles was pressed into too short a time scale by the (mistaken) arguments of Victorian physicists. A second example is the inheritance of acquired characters, which Charles was forced into adopting in later editions of *The Origin of Species*, where he suggests that we should 'look at the inheritance of every character whatever as the rule, and non-inheritance as the anomaly' (p. 26). Erasmus suggested, more cautiously, that 'many of these acquired forms or propensities are transmitted to their posterity' (*Zoonomia* I 503). But it is unfair to press such comparisons too far, because Charles goes into much more detail than Erasmus and is therefore more prone to error.

Ironically, Charles could have solved one of his major evolutionary problems—geographical dispersal, especially through seeds carried by ocean currents—simply by consulting *The Loves of the Plants*. 'Until I tried, with Mr Berkeley's aid, a few experiments,' Charles remarks, 'it was not even known how far seeds could resist the injurious action of sea water.'[9] Even after these careful experiments, he could only tentatively conclude that seeds *might* travel hundreds of miles. Yet Erasmus in his note on *cassia* in *The Loves of the Plants* (pp. 124–5) had given details of seeds carried from America to Norway and still capable of germination. Besides *cassia* he mentions 'the fruit of the anacardium, cashew-nut; of cucurbita lagenaria, bottlegourd; of the mimosa scandens, cocoons; of the piscidia erythrina, logwood tree; and cocoa-nuts', and several seeds carried from the West Indies to Scotland and Ireland. Charles came very near to spotting this clue, because he read *The Loves of the Plants* in December 1857, less than two years before *The Origin of Species* was published, and the last three lines of the note on *cassia* are marked with a pencil line in his copy.

Despite his strong affinity with his grandfather, Charles was forced to disown him, because reviews of *The Origin of Species*, particularly Bishop Wilberforce's offensive essay in the *Quarterly Review*, accused him of merely reviving the ideas of his 'grandsire'. So Charles had to emphasize his independence; and the female members of Charles's family persuaded him to sever the links more brutally, because they were good Victorian Christians and did not approve of the free-thinking Erasmus. Strangely enough, Charles himself and his elder brother Erasmus—and their revered father—were all more atheistic than Charles's grandfather; but, by a curious logic, that proved old Erasmus to be even more deplorable, in having such a bad hereditary influence.

Charles was uneasy about his forced renunciation of Erasmus, and wanted to make amends. At the age of seventy, after thirty-seven years of rigid routine at Down, Charles made the startling decision to write a biography of his grandfather. It was a brave gesture: he had written nothing like it before; he felt completely at sea, and feared he would make a fool of himself. But he persevered and produced an excellent book. Then diffidence took over, and he allowed the biography to be published in a book with the title page, 'Erasmus Darwin, by Ernst Krause', followed in smaller type by 'with a preliminary notice by Charles Darwin'. In fact the 127-page 'preliminary notice' is longer and far more valuable than the 86-page essay which it prefaces. This injustice was repaired in the second edition, in 1887, after Charles's death, where the title page reads, 'The Life of Erasmus Darwin, by Charles Darwin', and then, lower on the page, 'being an introduction, etc'. Yet the author of the book is still listed as Krause in most library catalogues.

This is strange enough, but it is even stranger that Charles, having written down his opinions of his grandfather, allowed his family, in practice his daughter Henrietta, to censor the book. Henrietta disapproved of Erasmus, and, as a good Christian herself, she did not wish to damage the Darwin family image by allowing her father to praise him. So her censorship took the form of removing nearly everything favourable to Erasmus; consequently, the published version is very different in tone from the first set of proofs, giving a false impression of her father's views. (She also chopped the book up in a most confusing way, and reduced its length by 12 per cent.)

Charles submitted to the cuts, as appears from a letter to his cousin Francis Galton on 14 November 1879: 'I am *extremely* glad that you approve the little life of our grandfather, for I have been repenting that I ever undertook it as work quite beyond my tether. The first set of proof-sheets was a good deal fuller, but I followed my family's advice and struck out much.'[10]

My review of the affinities between Erasmus and Charles can appropriately end with Charles's generous tribute to his grandfather's qualities:

His energy was unbounded. In his day he was esteemed a great poet. As a physician he was eminent in the noble art of alleviating human suffering. He was in advance of his time in urging sanitary arrangements and in inculcating temperance. He was opposed to any restraint of the insane, excepting as far as was absolutely necessary. He strongly advised a tender system of education. With his prophetic spirit, he anticipated many new and now admitted scientific truths, as well as some mechanical inventions. He seems to have been the first man who urged the use of phosphate of lime in agriculture, which has proved of great importance to the country. He was highly benevolent and retained the friendship of many distinguished men during his whole life. He strongly insisted on humanity to the lower animals. He earnestly admired philanthropy, and abhorred slavery. But he was unorthodox; and as soon as the grave closed over him he was grossly calumniated. Such was the state of Christian feeling at the beginning of the present century; we may at least hope that nothing of the kind now prevails.[11]

His hope was vain. Henrietta presumably disapproved, and a thick blue pencil line is drawn through the whole of Charles's long tribute, which is here published for the first time.

[2]

Charles Darwin and evolution were Erasmus's most important legacies, but others demand a mention. In 1833 five of Erasmus's children were still alive—Robert, Susan Hadley and Mary Parker, Violetta Galton and Francis. Robert continued his thriving medical practice at Shrewsbury, and he was still practising in 1846 when Charles remembered him saying, 'This day, sixty years ago, I received my first fee in Shrewsbury.'[12] Robert died in 1848, aged eighty-two, unaware of his son's future fame. Susan Hadley and Mary Parker both often visited their half-sister Violetta, and when Susan died in 1856, aged eighty-three, Violetta's daughter Elizabeth Anne said 'it was a great grief to my mother and all the family'.[13] Mary Parker, 'who was much respected by the Darwin family', died in 1859 at eighty-five. Sir Francis Darwin also died in 1859, while the high-spirited Violetta lived on until 1874.

Erasmus's hereditary influence was even stronger in Violetta's son Francis Galton than in Charles Darwin. Galton inherited the inventiveness and many-sidedness of Erasmus: at Cambridge, where he began by reading medicine before turning to mathematics, he seems to have shared many of Erasmus's interests. Today Galton is remembered particularly for the idea of eugenics, and for three practical innovations that would have pleased Erasmus: identification by fingerprints; the pioneering in anthropometry, with many applications, such as 'identikit' pictures; and the work in meteorology that led to weather maps and the starting of the Meteorological Office. Galton was interested in his grandfather's work, and in 1886 he arranged for a bust of Erasmus to be placed in Lichfield Cathedral with an inscription describing him as:

> A skilful observer of Nature, vivid in imagination, indefatigable in research, original and far-sighted in his views. His speculations were mainly directed to problems which were afterwards more successfully solved by his grandson Charles Darwin, an inheritor of many of his characteristics.

The hereditary influence continues strongly into the next generation. Erasmus's scientific and inventive talents seem to have been distributed among three distinguished sons of Charles Darwin: George, Francis and Horace. Of these three, the most famous is Sir George Darwin (1845–1912), now known as 'the father of geophysics', whose classical researches into the dynamical evolution of the Earth-Moon system in the 1880s are not only admired but actually used by geophysicists today.[14] Erasmus's scientific interests were directed towards the Earth and all that lives on it, and his chief contributions to physical science—for example, artesian wells and cloud formation—were in the realms of geophysics. Erasmus believed that the moon was born by fission from the Earth, a theory that George Darwin turned into a plausible mathematical form by invoking the phenomenon of resonance between the free period of oscillation of the primitive Earth and its rotation period, both of which might have been about two hours, he thought, thus making the Earth 'shake itself apart'. The theory has its supporters today.[15]

George's brother Sir Francis Darwin (1848–1925) was a leading botanist who helped with his father's researches, and Sir Horace Darwin (1851–1928) was an eminent engineer. George, Francis and Horace between them encompass Erasmus's talents in geophysics, botany and invention, and Francis also had some of his skill in writing verse. Charles Darwin's family was also plagued by apparently hereditary illness, which affected George and Horace.[16]

Hereditary resemblances to Erasmus have continued into later generations. I shall only mention one, however: the bust of Erasmus in Plate 1 is very much like Ralph Vaughan Williams, who was a grandson of Charles's sister Caroline and Josiah Wedgwood III.

[3]

In the half-century after his death many of Erasmus's scientific ideas were confirmed and established by others. I shall not try to list them, because there are so many and because it is usually impossible to say whether his ideas influenced the rediscoverers and re-inventors. Any topic in *The Botanic Garden* is liable to have come to the notice of budding inventors, because thousands of copies were distributed round the libraries of affluent Victorian households. For example, Darwin's prophecies about air travel inspired the inventor of the aeroplane, Sir George Cayley, who first became interested in the subject in 1792 and quoted Darwin's verses in one of his papers on aerial navigation.[17] On the other hand, when a canal lift like Darwin's was built in 1875, his influence was probably nil, because his design was buried in the Commonplace Book, where very few would have seen it. The same conclusion applies to his meteorological ideas—for example, on the airglow and the importance of fronts—because these were rediscovered early in the twentieth century, when Erasmus was in obscurity. The effect of his biological ideas was equally hit-or-miss: Lamarck's evolutionary theories in his *Philosophie Zoologique* (1809) were almost certainly influenced by *Zoonomia*; but no one has suggested that sewage farms began as a result of Darwin's proposal in *Phytologia*.

In the Victorian era, when many of his scientific ideas were coming to fruition, his literary fame was fading. The process took a long time, however, because literary reputations are passed down from teacher to pupil, and can last for several generations—especially if the author's books are widely available in libraries. Charles Darwin said, 'I have myself met with old men who spoke with a degree of enthusiasm about his poetry, quite incomprehensible at the present day.'[18]

A revealing guide to Darwin's literary status in Victorian times is G. L. Craik's popular two-volume *History of English Literature*, of which the third edition was published in 1866. Craik feels bound to include Darwin among 'the great poets of the era', but attacks him quite fiercely: 'Nothing is done in passion and power. . . . Every line is as elaborately polished and sharpened as a lancet.' Darwin's verse, he says, 'has no divine soul. . . . Its very life is galvanic and artificial.' This is fair comment, but then Craik seems to disqualify himself by saying 'there is not a trace of humour' in anything Darwin wrote. Even Craik finds it difficult not to praise Darwin a little, and says that 'no writer has surpassed him in the luminous representation of visible objects in verse'.[19] Most impressively of all, Craik gives Byron three pages, Shakespeare nine, Milton twelve, and Darwin eighteen.

Literary reputations do take a long time to fade, but once dead they take even longer to revive, because the teacher-pupil time-lag persists, and at first only a few teachers will be evangelizing. So it has been with Darwin. Once he had been fully deflated, he was open to uncontradicted misrepresentation from detractors who read the literary historians, but did not read Darwin's own books.

Erasmus remained in limbo between 1900 and 1950, in the sense that he was generally either ignored or belittled: none of his books was republished, most general references were unfavourable, many were unfair and some were malicious. Signs of malice abound in The Stuffed Owl (1930), an 'anthology of bad verse', where Darwin is singled out as a target:

Hear DARWIN, whom no scand'lous detail ruffles,
Record the love-lorn loneliness of truffles. . . .

The compilers of the anthology, trying to be witty, showed their nitwittedness by failing to see Darwin's own playfulness. Not so malicious, just unfair, is E. V. Lucas's chapter on Erasmus in his book A Swan and Her Friends (1907). Lucas says: 'His methods I intend to display by a burlesque.' He then quotes all 284 lines of The Loves of the Triangles and not one of Darwin's own. So Erasmus is condemned unheard. Another way of being unfair to Erasmus was to misquote his verse and then scoff at it. The refloating of Darwin's reputation as a poet was thwarted by an epidemic of misquotation, which has persisted beyond 1950: to give one surprising example, there are six misprints fatal or damaging to the sense in the twenty-two lines quoted on pages 206, 207 and 253 of R. E. Schofield's scholarly book about the Lunar Society (1963).

Scientists and historians of science have been rather shy of Erasmus: they saw the label 'speculative' pinned on him, and turned away as if fearful of infection. Their shyness showed itself clearly in some of the books celebrating the centenary of The

*Origin of Species* in 1959. One of these, *Forerunners of Darwin: 1745–1859*, has whole chapters on Maupertuis, Buffon, Diderot, Kant and Herder; but Erasmus receives nothing more than a chancy reference in a chapter on fossils, and a denigratory footnote elsewhere. In another centenary volume, *A Century of Darwin* (1958), the chapter on 'theories of evolution' by the eminent biologist C. H. Waddington, dismisses *Zoonomia* as 'a long and unfortunately remarkably boring poem'. The most widely read books about Charles Darwin still propagate the myth that *Zoonomia* is a poem: for example, Julian Huxley and H. B. Kettlewell, in *Charles Darwin and His World* (1965), say that Erasmus 'left to posterity two books recording his views in verse—*The Botanic Garden* and *Zoonomia*'; and Alan Moorehead, in *Darwin and the Beagle* (1969), refers to 'the famous poem *Zoonomia*'.

There were some exceptions to the general neglect of Erasmus between 1900 and 1950. First, between 1902 and 1909, there were several detailed German studies of Darwin's poems, by Brandl and Eckhardt.[20] Then in 1930, as a complete contrast, came Hesketh Pearson's witty biography, *Doctor Darwin*. This is most entertaining, and was widely read; but it tends to reduce Erasmus to an amusing lightweight, with little mention of his real achievements. Two other bright spots in this Darwinian 'dark age' are Alfred Noyes's sympathetic portrayal of Erasmus in *The Torchbearers* (1922–30) and J. V. Logan's study of *The Poetry and Aesthetics of Erasmus Darwin* (1936), still the best commentary on Erasmus's aesthetics and psychology. Logan also appreciates the comic intent of his poems, particularly *The Loves of the Plants*, 'the fine flowering of Darwin's bent to write light and humorous verse'.[21]

The real revival of interest in Erasmus Darwin began in the 1950s and has steadily gained strength. In 1954 a new annotated edition of *The Temple of Nature* was published, and proved so popular that a second edition followed in 1960; but it would be unfair to conceal the fact that these editions were of a Russian translation, by N. A. Kholodkovskii, with long notes by E. N. Pavlovsky.[22] The prophet began to be honoured in his own language too in the 1950s, in papers by Eric Robinson and Nora Barlow,[23] and in C. D. Darlington's important book *Darwin's Place in History* (1959). Erasmus's work also began to attract attention again among literary critics and historians, such as

Elizabeth Schneider (*Coleridge, Opium and Kubla Khan*, 1953), Bernard Blackstone (*The Consecrated Urn*, 1959), Elizabeth Sewell, who calls *The Temple of Nature* a 'noble poem' in her book *The Orphic Voice* (1960), and H. W. Piper (*The Active Universe*, 1962). The authoritative study of the Lunar group, R. E. Schofield's *Lunar Society of Birmingham*, was published in 1963, and so was my own introductory book *Erasmus Darwin*.

In the past ten years Erasmus's own writings have been coming back into circulation. In 1968 his book on female education was reprinted in facsimile, and selections from his books and letters were published as *The Essential Writings of Erasmus Darwin*. In 1973 the Scolar Press produced a beautiful facsimile reprint of *The Botanic Garden*, quickly followed by *The Temple of Nature*. In the same year the B.B.C. broadcast a fifty-minute dramatized documentary on Darwin, 'A Mind of Universal Sympathy', with Freddie Jones giving a convincing impersonation of Erasmus. The new appreciation of Darwin in the literary world has been greatly enhanced by Donald Hassler's books, *The Comedian as the Letter D* (1973), a study of Darwin's 'comic materialism', and *Erasmus Darwin* (1973) in the Twayne English series. The flow of specialized articles in journals has been increasing, and, if the momentum continues, we may yet see Darwin receiving the kind of scholarly attention that has been lavished on lesser figures like Boswell or Horace Walpole.

[4]

To conclude, I should try to summarize Erasmus's human qualities and intellectual achievements. His talents were diverse, and all of a high order: as a doctor, as an inventor, as a scientist, as a poet and as a writer of scientific books on the frontiers of knowledge, he was among the most original and expert of practitioners. He was famous for his benevolence and sympathy, and his immense energy. He was extremely successful socially, in both literary and scientific circles, and was a lifelong friend of many eminent men, Matthew Boulton, Benjamin Franklin, James Keir, James Watt, Josiah Wedgwood and others. He seems to have been a great success as a family man, especially with his second marriage, and he was particularly kind to Susan and Mary Parker.

What are the flaws in this perfection? First, there is his stammer, which everyone noticed. He himself said that stammering is due to a deep-seated wish to make an impression. Did this mean that he was at root insecure? After reading so many of his exuberant letters, I find this suggestion difficult to accept. But he was certainly sensitive. Charles Darwin remarked that Erasmus disliked any display of emotion; he 'wished to conceal his own feelings, and perhaps did so too effectually'.[24] His son Robert said 'he never would allow any common acquaintance to converse with him upon any subject that he felt poignantly. . . . It was his maxim, that in order to feel cheerful you must appear to be so.'[25] His sensitivity often breaks through the outward *bonhomie*, for example in his long-felt grief at the death of his son Charles, in the delicacy of his verses, in his 'hopeless love' of Mrs Pole, in his deep feeling for the plight of the slaves and in his general 'sympathy and benevolence'. Usually, however, he hid his sensibility behind a mask of cheerfulness and social grace. Though he allowed many of his feelings to overflow into his books and poems, there are some we cannot see. As Charles Darwin truly said: 'There was, moreover, a vein of reserve in him.'[26]

The only way to summarize Darwin's achievements quickly is to list them. On the next page there is a list of seventy-five subjects in which he was a pioneer, in the sense that he advanced valid new ideas, developed relevant new inventions or scientific methods, supported lines of action subsequently adopted or seized on the significance of existing facts. The subjects are listed alphabetically to emphasize their variety.

1. abolition of slavery
2. adiabatic expansion
3. aesthetics
4. afforestation
5. air travel
6. animal camouflage
7. artesian wells
8. artificial insemination
9. aurorae
10. biological adaptation
11. biological pest control
12. canal lifts
13. carriage springs
14. carriage steering
15. centrifugation
16. clouds
17. compressed-air actuators
18. copying-machines
19. cosmology
20. educational reform
21. electrical machines
22. electrochemistry
23. electrotherapy
24. evolutionary theory
25. exercise for children
26. fertilizers
27. formation of coal
28. geological strata
29. hereditary diseases
30. ideal gas law
31. individuality of buds
32. language
33. limestone deposits
34. manures
35. mental illness
36. microscopy
37. mimicry
38. moon's origin
39. nerve impulses
40. night airglow
41. nitrogen cycle
42. ocular spectra
43. oil drilling
44. organic happiness
45. origin of life
46. outer atmosphere
47. phosphorus
48. photosynthesis
49. Portland Vase
50. rocket motors
51. rotary pumps
52. secular morality
53. seed-drills
54. sewage farms
55. sexual reproduction
56. speaking-machines
57. squinting
58. steam carriages
59. steam turbines
60. struggle for existence
61. submarines
62. survival of the fittest
63. telescopes
64. temperance
65. travel of seeds
66. treatment of dropsy
67. ventilation
68. warm and cold fronts
69. water as $H_2O$
70. water closets
71. water machines
72. wind-gauges
73. windmills
74. winds
75. women's lib.

The pages where these subjects are mentioned can be found in the index.

To this factual list we must add the less tangible intellectual achievements: that Darwin was perhaps the finest physician of his time, famous both for his skill and for his kindness to poor patients; that he helped to forward the Industrial Revolution, by assisting and urging on his close friends Boulton, Watt, Keir and Wedgwood, and by his own inventiveness; that he deeply influenced the leading English poets of the next generations, particularly Wordsworth, Coleridge and Shelley.

Though I may be biased, I regard Erasmus Darwin as the greatest Englishman of the eighteenth century. If you disagree, can you name anyone else in the past 250 years with a list of accomplishments so numerous, so notable and so varied?

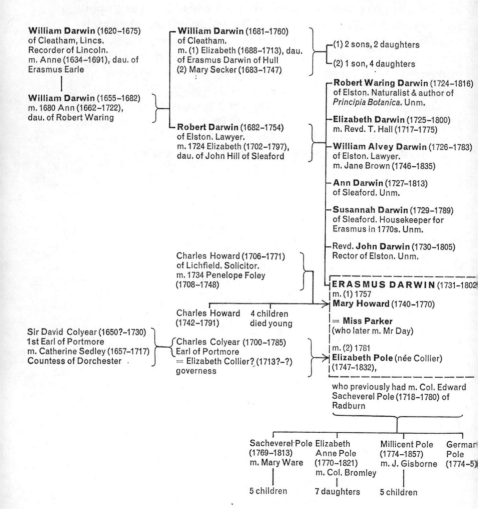

William Darwin (1620–1675)
of Cleatham, Lincs.
Recorder of Lincoln.
m. Anne (1634–1691), dau. of
Erasmus Earle

William Darwin (1655–1682)
m. 1680 Ann (1662–1722),
dau. of Robert Waring

William Darwin (1681–1760)
of Cleatham.
m. (1) Elizabeth (1688–1713), dau.
of Erasmus Darwin of Hull
(2) Mary Secker (1683–1747)

(1) 2 sons, 2 daughters
(2) 1 son, 4 daughters

Robert Darwin (1682–1754)
of Elston. Lawyer.
m. 1724 Elizabeth (1702–1797),
dau. of John Hill of Sleaford

Robert Waring Darwin (1724–1816)
of Elston. Naturalist & author of
*Principia Botanica*. Unm.

Elizabeth Darwin (1725–1800)
m. Revd. T. Hall (1717–1775)

William Alvey Darwin (1726–1783)
of Elston. Lawyer.
m. Jane Brown (1746–1835)

Ann Darwin (1727–1813)
of Sleaford. Unm.

Susannah Darwin (1729–1789)
of Sleaford. Housekeeper for
Erasmus in 1770s. Unm.

Revd. John Darwin (1730–1805)
Rector of Elston. Unm.

Charles Howard (1706–1771)
of Lichfield. Solicitor.
m. 1734 Penelope Foley
(1708–1748)

Charles Howard      4 children
(1742–1791)            died young

ERASMUS DARWIN (1731–1802)
m. (1) 1757
Mary Howard (1740–1770)

= Miss Parker
(who later m. Mr Day)

Sir David Colyear (1650?–1730)
1st Earl of Portmore
m. Catherine Sedley (1657–1717)
Countess of Dorchester .

Charles Colyear (1700–1785)
Earl of Portmore
= Elizabeth Collier? (1713?–?)
governess

m. (2) 1781
Elizabeth Pole (née Collier)
(1747–1832),

who previously had m. Col. Edward
Sacheverel Pole (1718–1780) of
Radburn

Sacheverel Pole
(1769–1813)
m. Mary Ware

5 children

Elizabeth
Anne Pole
(1770–1821)
m. Col. Bromley

7 daughters

Millicent Pole
(1774–1857)
m. J. Gisborne

5 children

German
Pole
(1774–5?)

# FIVE GENERATIONS
# OF THE DARWIN FAMILY,
# CENTRED ON ERASMUS

—3 sons, 2 daughters

—3 sons, 3 daughters

┌ **Charles Darwin** (1758–1778)
│ Medical student. Unm.

├ **Erasmus Darwin** (1759–1799)
│ Lawyer. Unm.

├ **Elizabeth Darwin** (1763–1764)

├ **Robert Waring Darwin** (1766–1848)
│ of Shrewsbury. Doctor.
│ m. 1796 Susannah (1765–1817),
│ dau. of Josiah Wedgwood

└ **William Alvey Darwin** (1767–1767)

┌ **Susan Parker** (1772–1856)
│ Schoolteacher, m. Mr Hadley

└ **Mary Parker** (1774–1859)
  of Ashbourne. Schoolteacher. Unm.

┌ **Edward Darwin** (1782–1829)
│ of Mackworth. Army officer. Unm.

├ **Frances Anne Violetta Darwin**
│ (1783–1874) m. 1807 Samuel
│ Tertius Galton (1783–1844)

├ **Emma Georgina Elizabeth**
│ **Darwin** (1784–1818). Teacher. Unm.

├ Sir **Francis Sacheverel Darwin**
│ (1786–1859). Doctor & traveller.
│ m. Jane Ryle (1794–1866)

├ Revd. **John Darwin** (1787–1818)
│ Rector of Elston. Unm.

├ **Henry Darwin** (1789–1790)

└ **Harriot Darwin** (1790–1825)
  m. 1811 Adm. T. J. Maling

┌ **Marianne Darwin** (1798–1858)
│ m. 1829 Henry Parker

├ **Caroline Darwin** (1800–1888)
│ m. 1836 Josiah Wedgwood III
│ (1795–1880)

├ **Susan Elizabeth Darwin**
│ (1803–1866). Unm.

├ **Erasmus Alvey Darwin**
│ (1804–1881). Unm.

├ **Charles Robert Darwin**
│ (1809–1882)
│ m. 1839 Emma Wedgwood
│ (1808–1896)

└ **Emily Catherine Darwin**
  (1810–1866) m. 1863 C. Langton

┌ **Henry Hadley**, surgeon

└ **Eliza Hadley**. Unm.

┌ **Elizabeth Anne Galton**
│ (1808–1906) m. E. Wheler

├ **Lucy Harriot Galton**
│ (1809–1848) m. J. Moilliet

├ **Millicent Adèle Galton**
│ (1810–1883) m. R. Bunbury

├ **Darwin Galton** (1814–1903)

├ **Erasmus Galton** (1815–1909)

└ Sir **Francis Galton** (1822–1911)

┌ 3 sons (Reginald, Edward, John)

└ 7 daughters (Mary, Emma, Frances,
  Georgina, Violetta, Ann, Millicent)

# REFERENCES

The place of publication of books is London, unless otherwise stated.

The following abbreviations are used in these references:

Baron: J. Baron, *Life of Edward Jenner*. 2 vols. Colburn, 1838.

Birm. Ref. Lib.: Birmingham Reference Library.

Camb. Univ. Lib.: Cambridge University Library.

Commonplace Book: Erasmus Darwin's manuscript Commonplace Book, kept at Down House, Kent.

Darlington: C. D. Darlington, *Darwin's Place in History*. Oxford: Blackwell, 1959.

C. Darwin, *Autobiog.*: Charles Darwin, *Autobiography* (ed. N. Barlow). Collins, 1958.

C. Darwin, *Life*: Charles Darwin, *The Life of Erasmus Darwin*, with an essay on his scientific works by Ernst Krause. Murray, 1879 (2nd ed. 1887). Passages appearing in the proofs but not the final version are given as: 'C. Darwin, *Life*, p. 5 (deleted)'.

*Ec. Veg.*: E. Darwin, *The Economy of Vegetation* (see p. 339).

Edgeworth: R. L. and Maria Edgeworth, *Memoirs of R. L. Edgeworth*. 2 vols. Hunter, 1820. (Reprinted, Irish University Press, Shannon, Ireland, 1969.)

*Gent. Mag.*: *Gentleman's Magazine*.

Gignilliat: G. W. Gignilliat, *The Author of Sandford and Merton*. New York: Columbia University Press, 1932.

Hutton: *The Life of William Hutton* (ed. L. Jewitt). Warne, 1872.

Keele Univ. Lib.: Keele University Library, Wedgwood archive.

Logan: J. V. Logan, *The Poetry and Aesthetics of Erasmus Darwin*. Princeton, N.J.: Princeton University Press, 1936.

*Lov. Pl.*: E. Darwin, *The Loves of the Plants* (see p. 339).

Meteyard: E. Meteyard, *The Life of Josiah Wedgwood*. 2 vols. Hurst & Blackett, 1865–6.

Moilliet: J. K. Moilliet (ed.), *Life and Correspondence of James Keir*. Privately printed, 1868.

Muirhead: J. P. Muirhead, *The Origin and Progress of the Mechanical Inventions of James Watt*. 3 vols. Murray, 1854.

H. Pearson: H. Pearson, *Doctor Darwin*. Dent, 1930.

K. Pearson: K. Pearson, *The Life, Letters and Labours of Francis Galton*. 4 vols. Cambridge: C.U.P., 1914–30.

*Phil. Trans.*: *Philosophical Transactions of the Royal Society of London* (1666 to present).

*Phytologia*: E. Darwin, *Phytologia* (see p. 340).

*Pus and Mucus*: C. Darwin, *Experiments establishing a criterion between mucaginous and purulent matter*. Cadell, 1780.

Salt. Lib.: William Salt Library, Stafford.

Schofield: R. E. Schofield, *The Lunar Society of Birmingham*. Oxford: O.U.P., 1963.

Seward: Anna Seward, *Memoirs of the Life of Dr Darwin*. Johnson, 1804.

Seward, *Letters*: Anna Seward, *Letters*. 6 vols. Edinburgh: Constable, 1811.

Stock: J. E. Stock, *Memoirs of the Life of Thomas Beddoes*. Murray, 1811.

*Tem.Nat.*: E. Darwin, *The Temple of Nature* (see p. 340).

Wedgwood: *Letters of Josiah Wedgwood* (ed. K. E. Farrer). 3 vols. Manchester: E. J. Morton, 1974. (My quotations from Wedgwood's letters are from the MSS at Keele University Library. But I refer to the published version because it is more accessible, gives all the MS reference numbers and differs only trivially from the MSS.)

Wheler: Elizabeth Anne Wheler, 'Memorials of my Life'. (Unpublished typescript in possession of Dr J. L. Moilliet.)

*Zoonomia*: E. Darwin, *Zoonomia* (1796) (see p. 340).

Other major sources are given in the book list on pages 342–3.

The following styles of numeration are used:
for volume and page numbers in multi-volume books (except *Zoonomia*): ii 439–56;
for volume and page numbers in periodicals: *23*, 246–51;
for canto and line numbers in Darwin's poems: III 47–53

Chapter 1 (*pages* 13–19)

1. H. Williams, *Great Biologists*, p. 80.
2. Muirhead, ii 279.
3. Darlington, p. 12.
4. From *Monthly Mag. 13*, 462 (1802) to P. Porter, *The Listener 90*, 386 (1973).
5. *Ec. Veg.* I 289–96.
6. *Lov. Pl.* I 115–16.
7. L. T. C. Rolt, *Thomas Telford* (Longman, 1958), p. 29.
8. *Phil. Trans. 78*, 43–52 (1788).

## Chapter 2 (*pages* 20–36)

1. S. T. Bindoff, *Tudor England* (Penguin, 1950), p. 48.
2. C. Brown, *The Annals of Newark-upon-Trent* (Sotheran, 1879), pp. 33–6.
3. *Phil. Trans. 30*, 963–8 (1719).
4. W. Moore, *The Gentlemen's Society at Spalding* (Pickering, 1851), p. 30.
5. *Phil. Trans. 30*, 963–8 (1719).
6. Lincoln's Inn *Black Books* iii 256–7.
7. *Gent. Mag. 78*, 869 (1808).
8. C. Darwin, *Life*, p. 53 (deleted).
9. C. Darwin, *Life*, p. 6.
10. Commonplace Book, after p. 174.
11. J. C. V. Kendall and M. P. Jackson, *A History of the Free Grammar School, Chesterfield* (privately printed, 1965), p. 9.
12. C. Darwin, *Life*, p. 5 (deleted).
13. C. Darwin, *Life*, p. 6.
14. *Ec. Veg.* I 349–56.
15. R. W. Dixon, letter to C. Darwin, 20 December 1879. MS in Camb. Univ. Lib.
16. C. Darwin, *Life*, p. 7.
17. Ibid. pp. 7–8.
18. Ibid. pp. 9–10.
19. Ibid. p. 11.
20. R. F. Scott, *Admissions to the College of St John* ... Part III (Cambridge: Deighton Bell, 1903), p. 601.
21. C. Darwin, *Life*, p. 12.
22. T. Newte, *A Tour in England and Scotland in 1785* (Robinson, 1788), p. 4.
23. S. Ayling, *George the Third* (Collins, 1972), p. 25.
24. *European Mag. 27*, 75–6 (1795).
25. T. Gurney, *Brachygraphy* (3rd ed., 1752), p. 7.
26. MS at Wellcome Institute Library, London.
27. Ibid.
28. From MS in St John's College Library, Cambridge. See also C. Wordsworth, *Scholae Academicae* (Cambridge: C.U.P., 1877), pp. 179–81.
29. R. F. Scott, *Admissions*, p. 601.
30. Commonplace Book, after p. 164.
31. C. Darwin, *Life*, p. 13.
32. See B. Smith and J. L. Moilliet, *Notes & Rec. Roy. Soc. 22*, 144–54 (1967).
33. C. Darwin, *Life*, pp. 13–14.
34. *Gent. Mag. 78*, 869 (1808).
35. *European Mag. 27*, 75 (1795).
36. See *Fragments from Reimarus*, ed. C. Voysey (Williams & Norgate, 1879).
37. From MS at Historical Society of Pennsylvania, Philadelphia.
38. See C. Darwin, *Life*, p. 119, and A. Hope, *New Scientist 57*, 309 (1973).
39. *Monthly Mag. 13*, 458 (1802).
40. C. P. Moritz, *Journeys of a German in England in 1782* (Cape, 1965), p. 176.
41. J. Kobler, *The Reluctant Surgeon* (Heinemann, 1960), pp. 68–72.
42. S. Tuke, *Description of the Retreat* (York, 1813).

## Chapter 3 (*pages* 37–56)

1. See H. Clayton, *Coaching City*.
2. See F. Swinnerton, *A Galaxy of Fathers* (Hutchinson, 1966), pp. 35–47.
3. Seward, pp. 8–9.
4. Commonplace Book, after p. 174.
5. *Phil. Trans. 50*, 241 (1757).
6. Ibid., pp. 250–1.
7. Seward, p. 10.
8. C. Darwin, *Life*, pp. 21–4.
9. S. Thiele and T. K. With, *Scand. Journ. Clin. Lab. Invest. 16*, 465–9 (1964).
10. Seward, p. 15.
11. See A. Geikie, *Memoir of John Michell* (Cambridge: C.U.P., 1918); C. L. Hardin, *Annals of Science 22*, 27–47 (1966); and R. E. Schofield, *Mechanism and Materialism* (Princeton, N.J.:

Princeton University Press, 1970), pp. 241–9.
12. *Phytologia*, p. 383.
13. *Ec. Veg.* II 193–4, 199–200.
14. Ibid. II 355–60.
15. Hutton, pp. 171–2.
16. Ibid.
17. Seward, p. 2.
18. C. Darwin, *Life*, pp. 35–6.
19. Seward, pp. 5–6.
20. Ibid., p. 2.
21. C. Darwin, *Life*, p. 40.
22. G. L'E. Turner, *Notes & Rec. Roy. Soc. 29*, 53–79 (1974).
23. Edgeworth, *Memoirs* (3rd ed., 1844), p. 299.
24. C. Darwin, *Life*, p. 40.
25. Seward, pp. 2–3.
26. Seward, *Letters* ii 309.
27. Darwin, *Life*, p. 40.
28. Ibid., p. 42.
29. *Phil. Trans. 51*, 526–9 (1760).
30. Schofield, p. 28.
31. J. A. Langford, *A Century of Birmingham Life* (Birmingham: Osborne, 1868), i 148.
32. Seward, p. 4.
33. From MS at Birm. Ref. Lib.
34. *The Swan of Lichfield*, ed. H. Pearson (Hamilton, 1936), p. 49.
35. Seward, pp. 64–5.
36. Schofield, p. 28.
37. From MS at Birm. Ref. Lib.
38. Ibid.
39. Ibid.
40. Ibid.
41. See L. T. C. Rolt, *Horseless Carriage* (Constable, 1950), ch. 1.
42. Stringer Collection, Bodleian Library.
43. From MS at Salt Lib.
44. Ibid.
45. Lichfield Record Office, Minute Books of Lichfield and Staffordshire Turnpike, D.15.

## Chapter 4 (*pages* 57–83)

1. H. Bode, *James Brindley*, pp. 11–14.
2. In Burton-on-Trent Public Library, dated 1760.
3. Wedgwood, iii 233–4.
4. Ibid., iii 251.
5. From MS at Birm. Ref. Lib.
6. Wedgwood, iii 273–312 has the pamphlet and Darwin's amendments.
7. Wedgwood, i 58.
8. Ibid., i 68.
9. Edgeworth, i 185.
10. T. Jefferson, *Autobiography* (New York: Putnam, 1914), pp. 5–6.
11. From MS at Birm. Ref. Lib.
12. C. Darwin, *Life*, pp. 28–9.
13. G. de Beer, *Jean-Jacques Rousseau* (Thames and Hudson, 1972), p. 91.
14. H. Pearson, p. 39.
15. From MS at the Royal Society of Arts (Guard Book Vol. 12, Collection 'A').
16. Ibid.
17. R. Strauss, *Carriages and Coaches* (Secker, 1912), p. 26.
18. Edgeworth, i 162.
19. Ibid., i 162.
20. Ibid., i 163–4.
21. Ibid., i 165–7.
22. Seward, p. 17.
23. From MS at Birm. Ref. Lib.
24. From MS at Camb. Univ. Lib.
25. From MS at the Royal Society of Arts (Guard Book A).
26. Schofield, p. 48.
27. From MS at Camb. Univ. Lib.
28. From MS at Birm. Ref. Lib.
29. Ibid.
30. Muirhead, i 4.
31. Ibid., i cxx.
32. Ibid., i 15.
33. *Partners in Science*, ed. E. Robinson and D. McKie (Constable, 1970), p. 13.
34. Meteyard, ii 207.
35. Muirhead, i 32.
36. See Hutton, pp. 170–2; and *Godwin and Mary*, ed. R. Wardle (Constable, 1967), pp. 100–1.
37. From MS at Birm. Ref. Lib.
38. C. Darwin, *Life*, pp. 28–9.
39. *Pus and Mucus*, p. 127.

40. Ibid., pp. 127–8.
41. C. Darwin, *Life*, p. 41.
42. J. Boswell, *The Life of Samuel Johnson* (Dent, 1906), i 628.
43. Ibid., ii 113.
44. Seward, pp. 75–6.
45. From MS at Keele Univ. Lib.
46. From MS at Birm. Ref. Lib.
47. From MS at Salt Lib. See also *Gent. Mag. 54*, 87 (1784) and Seward, *Letters*, vi 136.
48. Edgeworth, i 197.
49. Ibid., i 183.
50. From MS at Birm. Ref. Lib.
51. From MS at Historical Society of Pennsylvania, Philadelphia.

52. M. A. Hopkins, *Dr Johsonn's Lichfield*, p. 96.
53. Ibid.
54. Wedgwood, i 209.
55. Meteyard, ii 30.
56. Wedgwood, i 207.
57. From MS at Keele Univ. Lib.
58. From MS at the Royal Society of Arts (Guard Book A).
59. Meteyard, ii 31.
60. Wedgwood, i 324.
61. Seward, pp. 12–14.
62. Ibid., p. 13.
63. *Pus and Mucus*, pp. 130–1.
64. C. Darwin, *Autobiog.*, pp. 224–5.
65. See P. V. Tobias ,*Trans. Roy. Soc. S. Africa 40*, 239–60 (1972).

## Chapter 5 (*pages* 84–104)

1. C. Darwin, *Life*, p. 6.
2. A. Seward, *Poetical Works*, ii 89–102.
3. Schofield, p. 56.
4. Meteyard, ii 210.
5. Ibid.
6. From MS at Birm. Ref. Lib.
7. *Tem. Nat.*, Add. Note XV, pp. 107–20.
8. From MS at Down House.
9. C. Darwin, *Autobiog.*, p. 224.
10. Wedgwood, ii 66, 73, 92–5.
11. Ibid., ii 105.
12. C. Darwin, *Life*, p. 57.
13. Wedgwood, ii 109–32.
14. *Zoonomia*, ii 162.
15. Wedgwood, ii 100–1.
16. C. Darwin, *Life*, pp. 30–1.
17. Moilliet, p. 50.
18. See W. Burton, *Wedgwood and His Pottery* (Cassell, 1922), pp. 67–76.
19. American Philosophical Society MS Franklin papers III 112.
20. Ibid.
21. Wedgwood, ii 124.
22. Gignilliat, pp. 77–8.

23. American Philosophical Society MS Franklin papers IV 5.
24. *Phil. Trans. 64*, 344–9 (1774).
25. Commonplace Book, p. 162.
26. See L. T. C. Rolt, *James Watt*, pp. 50–5.
27. Muirhead, ii 84.
28. Ibid., ii 81.
29. Ibid., ii 82.
30. Schofield, p. 116.
31. J. Dos Passos, *Jefferson* (Hale, 1955), p. 287.
32. Muirhead, i clviii.
33. Royal Society archives : Letters and papers, Decade VII, No. 2.
34. Muirhead, i clvi–clviii.
35. *Papers of Thomas Jefferson* (Princeton, 1950), i 165.
36. From MS at Birm. Ref. Lib.
37. Schofield, p. 125.
38. W. T. Stearn, *Endeavour 27*, 3–10 (1968) gives some of the drawings in colour.
39. J. Cradock, *Literary and Miscellaneous Memoirs* (Nichols, 1828), iv 143–4.

## Chapter 6 (*pages* 105–138)

1. *Pus and Mucus*, p. 131.
2. H. S. Torrens, *Newsletter of Geolog. Curators Group* No. 1, pp. 5–10 (1974).

3. Boswell, *Life of Johnson*, i 630.
4. Ibid., i 625–9.
5. D. Clarke, *The Ingenious Mr Edgeworth*, p. 85.

6. B. Boothby, *Sorrows Sacred to the Memory of Penelope* (Cadell, 1796), p. 71.
7. Wedgwood, ii 281.
8. Schofield, p. 141.
9. Ibid., p. 142.
10. Commonplace Book, p. 8.
11. F. N. C. Mundy, *Needwood Forest* (Lichfield: Jackson, 1776), p. 4.
12. Ibid., pp. 45–6.
13. Seward, *Letters*, iii 154.
14. See *European Mag.* 37, 226 (1800); *Phytologia*, pp. 528–9; Logan, pp. 99–100; and *Notes and Queries*, 13 Feb. 1875, pp. 122–4.
15. Seward, pp. 125–6.
16. Ibid., pp. 126–7.
17. Ibid., pp. 128–9.
18. Ibid., pp. 130–1.
19. *Gent. Mag.* 53, 428 (1783).
20. Commonplace Book, p. 72.
21. Seward, pp. 99–100.
22. Ibid., p. 99.
23. *Zoonomia* i 352; Commonplace Book, p. 27.
24. Commonplace Book, p. 66.
25. Ibid., p. 51.
26. Ibid.
27. Ibid., p. 34.
28. Ibid., p. 51.
29. Ibid., p. 65.
30. Ibid., pp. 58–9.
31. For further details of canal lifts, see C. R. Weaver, *Discovery*, July 1965, p. 57; C. Hadfield, *Canals of the West Midlands* (David and Charles, 1966); D. H. Tew, *Trans. Newcomen Soc.* 28, 35–58 (1951–2); H. S. Torrens, *Bristol Ind. Arch. Soc. Jnl.* 8, 4–10 (1976); and R. Atthill, *Old Mendip* (David and Charles, 1964), p. 173.
32. Commonplace Book, pp. 33, 38.
33. Muirhead, ii 115.
34. S. P. Thompson, *Journ. Soc. Telegraph Eng.* 17, 576 (1888); Schofield, p. 166.
35. A. Bennet, *New Experiments in Electricity* (Derby: Drewry, 1789), p. 81.
36. Commonplace Book, p. 46.
37. See Varro, *Rerum Rusticarum* III v 17. (Translation: Varro's *On Agriculture* (Heinemann, 1934), p. 457.)
38. Commonplace Book, p. 45.
39. From MS at Birm. Ref. Lib.
40. Schofield, p. 143.
41. From MS at Birm. Ref. Lib.
42. Ibid.
43. Ibid.
44. Commonplace Book, pp. 56–7.
45. Seward, p. 104.
46. Ibid., pp. 104–5.
47. Ibid., pp. 105–6.
48. *Pus and Mucus*, p. 132.
49. *An Elegy on the much-lamented death of a most ingenious Young Gentleman* (Robinson, 1778).
50. From MS in Fitzwilliam Museum, Cambridge.
51. C. Darwin, *Life*, p. 82.
52. Seward, pp. 108–15.
53. Ibid., p. 114.
54. Wedgwood, ii 443.
55. Seward, p. 107.
56. Ibid., p. 117.
57. Bodleian Library MS Eng. poet d.10 fol. 82.
58. C. Darwin, *Life*, p. 26 (deleted).
59. *Phil. Trans.* 68, 94–5 (1778).
60. British Library Add. MS 42071, ff. 48–52.
61. Ibid.
62. Edgeworth, i 363–5.
63. Commonplace Book, p. 87.
64. Schofield, p. 74.
65. Wedgwood, ii 542–3.
66. From MS at Keele Univ. Lib.
67. Wedgwood, ii 541–52.
68. See R. Reilly and G. Savage, *Wedgwood: The Portrait Medallions* (Barrie and Jenkins, 1973).
69. See B. Tattersall, *Stubbs and Wedgwood* (Tate Gallery, 1974).
70. Commonplace Book, p. 85.
71. Ibid., p. 89.
72. See W. Bemrose, *Life of Joseph Wright* (Bemrose, 1885), p. 87.
73. Commonplace Book, p. 80.
74. Ibid., pp. 98–100.
75. *Pus and Mucus*, pp. 127–35.
76. From MS at Down House.
77. Seward, p. 144.
78. Edgeworth, ii 268.
79. A. Seward, *Elegy on Captain Cook* (3rd ed., Dodsley, 1781), p. 10.
80. C. Darwin, *Life*, pp. 31–2.
81. Ibid., pp. 32–3.

## Chapter 7 (pages 139–155)

1. Seward, pp. 148–9.
2. Ibid., p. 150.
3. Ibid., p. 151.
4. T. Lowndes, *Tracts* (1827), ii 322–5.
5. Muirhead, ii 123.
6. Ibid., ii 124 (and i clx).
7. *Ec. Veg.* III 201–4, 209–10. For details of the water controversy, see, e.g., *Correspondence of . . . Watt on . . . the Composition of Water*, ed. J. Muirhead (Murray, 1846); D. McKie, *Lavoisier* (Constable, 1952), ch. 15; and Muirhead, i clx–clxiii.
8. From British Museum (Natural History) MS Banks Correspondence, Vol. 2, pp. 31–56.
9. American Philosophical Society Misc. MSS.
10. Ibid.
11. From MS Banks Corresp., see note 8.
12. From MS in Fitzwilliam Museum, Cambridge (Perceval Bequest).
13. Ibid.
14. Ibid.
15. From MS Banks Corresp., see note 8.
16. *System of Vegetables*, pp. i–ii
17. Ibid.
18. *Monthly Review* 72, 401–10; 73, 1–13 (1785).
19. Commonplace Book, p. 110.
20. From MS at Birm. Ref. Lib.
21. Ibid.
22. T. Lowndes, *Tracts* (1827), ii 322–5.
23. Gignilliat, p. 253.
24. T. Lowndes, *Tracts* (1827), ii 322–5.
25. C. Darwin, *Life*, p. 45.
26. From MS at Down House.
27. From MS at Birm. Ref. Lib.
28. *Lov. Pl.* II 25–8, 31–2, 45–6, 47–54.
29. From MS at Birm. Ref. Lib.
30. E. Robinson, *Annals of Science 9*, 360 (1953).
31. Ibid., p. 361.
32. From MS at Keele Univ. Lib.
33. F. Galton, *Memories of My Life* (Methuen, 1908), p. 10.
34. *Phil. Trans.* 74, 201 (1784).
35. Royal Society archives: Letters and papers, Decade VIII, No. 102.

## Chapter 8 (pages 156–180)

1. Bodleian Library MS Eng. poet. d.10 fol. 82.
2. *Phil. Trans.* 75, 1–7 (1785).
3. Ibid.
4. From MS at Birm. Ref. Lib.
5. From MS at Down House.
6. Ibid.
7. From papers in Derby Central Library.
8. Ibid.
9. Ibid.
10. E. Robinson, *Annals of Science 9*, 359–67 (1953).
11. C. Darwin, *Life*, p. 54.
12. *Notes and Queries 12*, 449 (9 June 1923).
13. Ibid.
14. From MS at Birm. Ref. Lib.
15. Ibid.
16. Gignilliat, p. 239.
17. C. Darwin, *Life*, p. 101.
18. Seward, *Letters*, i 33.
19. Ibid., i 14–15.
20. *Lov. Pl.* II 85–6.
21. From MS at Birm. Ref. Lib.
22. *Lov. Pl.* II 87, note; and 93–104.
23. F. D. Klingender, *Art and the Industrial Revolution*, pp. 35–6.
24. Ibid.
25. *Poetry of the Anti-Jacobin*, ed. L. Rice-Oxley (Oxford: Blackwell, 1924), p. 95.
26. *Lov. Pl.* II 87, note.
27. From MS at Birm. Ref. Lib.
28. Commonplace Book, p. 45.
29. Commonplace Book, p. 157.
30. Bodleian Library MS Montagu d.2.
31. *Medical Transactions 3*, 285 (1785).
32. From MS 'Withering letters' at Royal Society of Medicine.

33. Ibid.
34. Royal Society archives BLA.d.
35. From MS at Camb. Univ. Lib.
36. Ibid.
37. Ibid.
38. Seward, *Letters*, i 34.
39. Edgeworth, ii 83.
40. C. Darwin, *Life*, pp. 64–5.
41. Commonplace Book, p. 89.
42. *Families of Plants*, p. 8.
43. D. W. Forrest, *Francis Galton* (Elek, 1974), p. 2.
44. C. Darwin, *Life*, p. 87 (deleted).
45. American Philosophical Society MS Franklin papers XXXV 70.
46. *Phil. Trans. 76*, 313–48 (1786).
47. C. Darwin, *Life*, p. 84.

48. American Philosophical Society MS Franklin papers IV 5.
49. Schofield, pp. 271–2.
50. Meteyard, *A Group of Englishmen* (Longman, 1871), pp. 253–4.
51. From MS Dryander Correspondence, No. 43, British Museum (Natural History).
52. Royal Society archives.
53. American Philosophical Society MS Franklin papers XXXV 70.
54. See W. Herschel, *Phil. Trans.* 77, 231 (1787); P. Moore, *Phil. Trans.* A *285*, 481 (1977).
55. American Philosophical Society MS Franklin papers XXXV 70.

## Chapter 9 (*pages* 181–208)

1. Moilliet, pp. 78–81.
2. C. Darwin, *Life*, p. 92.
3. *Phil. Trans.* 78, 43–52 (1788).
4. D. S. L. Cardwell, *From Watt to Clausius* (Heinemann, 1971), ch. 2.
5. *Phil. Trans.* 78, 43–52 (1788).
6. Ibid.
7. R. W. Darwin, *Appeal to the Faculty Concerning the Case of Mrs Houlston* (Shrewsbury, 1789).
8. From MS 'Withering letters' at Royal Society of Medicine.
9. From MS at Birm. Ref. Lib.
10. From MS 'Withering letters'.
11. From MS at Birm. Ref. Lib.
12. Wheler i 14.
13. From MS at Camb. Univ. Lib.
14. Ibid.
15. *Life of Mary Anne SchimmelPenninck* (Longman, 1858), i 151–3.
16. From MS at Birm. Ref. Lib.
17. *Ec. Veg.* II 315–16.
18. C. Darwin, *Life*, p. 46.
19. A Keith, *Darwin Revalued* (Watts, 1955), p. 103.
20. H. Walpole, *Letters*, ed. P. Toynbee (Oxford, 1905), xiv 124, 125, 126, 141.
21. *Analytical Review 4*, 29–36 (1789).
22. From MS at Camb. Univ. Lib.
23. Seward, pp. 361, 296, 376.
24. Seward, *Letters*, i 333.
25. Seward, pp. 169–70.

26. J. Pilkington, *View of . . . Derbyshire* (Derby: Drewry, 1789), i 263, 275.
27. From MS at Birm. Ref. Lib.
28. Moilliet, pp. 95–6.
29. Ibid., pp. 110–11.
30. From MS at Down House.
31. Wedgwood, iii 77.
32. *Ec. Veg.* II 315–16, note.
33. *European Mag. 16*, 462 (1789). Also in later ed. of *Ec. Veg.*
34. Rylands Library, Manchester, English MS 1110, p. 49.
35. Wedgwood, iii 88.
36. Ibid., iii 92–3.
37. Meteyard, ii 581.
38. Wedgwood, iii 101.
39. See W. Mankowitz, *The Portland Vase and the Wedgwood Copies* (Deutsch, 1952), pp. 58–9.
40. From MS at Birm. Ref. Lib.
41. Ibid.
42. *Ec. Veg.* I 281, note.
43. Ibid. I 281–8.
44. Muirhead, ii 230–1.
45. Ibid., ii 232.
46. *Ec. Veg.* I 254, note.
47. Ibid. I 271–8.
48. From MS at Birm. Ref. Lib.
49. Ibid.
50. From MS at Camb. Univ. Lib.
51. Ibid. The contract with Johnson is in Liverpool City Library.

52. E. Dowden, *The French Revolution and English Literature* (New York: Scribner, 1897), p. 20.
53. C. Darwin, *Life*, p. 30..

54. Stock, App. 6, pp. xxxvii–xxxviii.
55. Ibid.
56. C. Darwin, *Life*, p. 37.
57. Ibid., pp. 37–9.

## Chapter 10 (*pages* 209–233)

1. From MS at St John's College Library, Cambridge.
2. See G. Keynes, *Blake Studies* (O.U.P., 1971), pp. 59–61.
3. See J. Frazier, *The Ecologist 4*, 176–80 (1974).
4. Seward, p. 395.
5. From MS at Camb. Univ. Lib.
6. C. Darwin, *Autobiog.*, p. 225 (with year changed to 1791).
7. B. Boothby, *Sonnets Sacred to the Memory of Penelope* (Cadell, 1796), p. 10.
8. Schofield, p. 359.
9. Ibid.
10. Hutton, p. 255.
11. E. Robinson, *Annals of Science 9*, 359–67 (1953).
12. Broadsheet dated 10 October 1791, at Derby Central Library.
13. H. Walpole, *Letters*, xv 110.
14. Seward, p. 193.
15. G. H. Darwin, papers in *Phil. Trans.*, 1879–82; and *The Tides* (Murray, 1901), ch. 16.
16. E. Halley, *Phil. Trans. 16*, 104 (1686).
17. See D. G. King-Hele, *Phil. Trans.* A 278, 67–109 (1975).
18. See D. G. King-Hele, *The Observatory 95*, 1–12 (1975).
19. See J. T. Wilson, *IGY, the Year of the New Moons* (Joseph, 1961), p. 28.

20. *Lov. Pl.* IV 45, note.
21. See Baron, i 22–4.
22. *Analytical Review 15*, 287–93 (1793). See also *Monthly Review 11*, 182–7 (1793) and *Critical Review 6*, 162–71 (1792).
23. W. Cowper, *Poetical Works* (O.U.P., 1911), 0p. 418.
24. From MS in Fitzwilliam Museum, Cambridge.
25. R. N. Ringler, *Eng. Lang. Notes 5*, 27–32 (1967).
26. *Descriptive Sketches*, line 34, note; *Ec. Veg.*, Add. Note VIII.
27. See C. Wordsworth, *Social Life at the English Universities in the Eighteenth Century* (Cambridge, 1874), p. 589.
28. From MS at Camb. Univ. Lib.
29. Ibid.
30. C. A. Lubbock, *The Herschel Chronicle* (C.U.P., 1933), p. 237.
31. *Life and Letters of Maria Edgeworth*, ed. A. J. C. Hare (Arnold, 1894), i 21.
32. C. Darwin, *Life*, p. 51.
33. Moilliet, p. 128.
34. C. Darwin, *Life*, p. 52.
35. Ibid., p. 64.
36. Ibid.
37. From MS at Historical Society of Pennsylvania, Philadelphia.
38. From MS at Keele Univ. Lib.
39. Ibid.

## Chapter 11 (*pages* 234–263)

1. R. C. Smith, *Derbyshire Miscellany 4*, 17–23 (1967).
2. Ibid.
3. Ibid.
4. See D. Gardiner, *English Girlhood at School* (O.U.P., 1929), pp. 347–56; B. Simon, *Studies in the*

*History of Education* (Lawrence and Wishart, 1960), pp. 50–6; J. Kamm, *Hope Deferred* (Methuen, 1965), *passim*; and *Encyclopaedia Britannica*, Vol. 23, article on 'Women, Education of'.
5. See G. H. Lewes, *History of*

*Philosophy* (3rd ed., Longman, 1867), ii 364; T. Brown, *Observations on the Zoonomia* (Edinburgh, 1798), pp. 294–302.

6. A. Comfort, *The Joy of Sex* (Quartet Books, 1974), p. 67.
7. *Tem. Nat.* Add. Note VIII.
8. Ibid., Add. Note I, p. 11.
9. *European Mag.* 27, 77 (1795); *Monthly Mag.* 2, 485 (1796); C. Darwin, *Life*, p. 102; Stock, pp. 131, 133.
10. *Tem. Nat.* Add. Note VIII
11. *Zoonomia* (3rd ed., 1801), ii 244.
12. See J. Harrison, *Journ. Hist. Ideas* 32, 247–64 (1971).
13. C. Darwin, *Life*, p. 66.
14. G. Peacock, *Life of Thomas Young* (Murray, 1855), p. 49.
15. Ibid.
16. C. Darwin, *Life*, p. 69.
17. From MS at Keele Univ. Lib.
18. Stock, p. xliii.
19. Ibid., p. xlv.
20. Ibid., p. 102.
21. Ibid., p. 106.
22. From MS at Birm. Ref. Lib.
23. See N. Garfinkle, *Journ. Hist. Ideas* 16, 376–88 (1955).
24. From MS at Birm. Ref. Lib.

25. From MS at Camb. Univ. Lib.
26. Meteyard, ii 610.
27. From MS at Camb. Univ. Lib.
28. Ibid.
29. Ibid.
30. From MS at Keele Univ. Lib.
31. Ibid.
32. W. J. White, *A History of the Centrifuge in Aerospace Medicine* (Santa Monica, Calif.: Douglas Aircraft Co., 1964), ch. 1.
33. From MS at Salt Lib.
34. C. Darwin, *Life*, pp. 105–6.
35. From MS at Keele Univ. Lib.
36. S. T. Coleridge, *Collected Letters*, ed. F. L. Griggs (O.U.P., 1956), i 177.
37. Ibid., i 178–9.
38. Ibid., i 305.
39. *Rel. Mus.* 268; *Ec. Veg.* IV 67, I 116; *Dest. Nat.* 54. Also Coleridge, *Happiness*, 42–65, and *Lov. Pl.* III 357–70.
40. Coleridge, *Collected Letters*, i 216.
41. From MS at Camb. Univ. Lib.
42. Edgeworth, ii 178.
43. Ibid. ii 179.
44. C. K. Paul, *William Godwin* (King, 1876), i 261.

## Chapter 12 (*pages* 264–287)

1. See D. Welsh, *Life and Writings of Thomas Brown* (Edinburgh: Tait, 1825), pp. 42–61.
2. W. Wordsworth, *Poetical Works* (2nd ed., O.U.P., 1954), iii 442.
3. *The Letters of William and Dorothy Wordsworth* (2nd ed., O.U.P., 1967), i 199.
4. *Ancient Mariner*, 313, 316–17. *Ec. Veg.* I 134 and Note IV.
5. See J. L. Lowes, *The Road to Xanadu* (New York: Vintage Books, 1959), *passim; Notebooks of S. T. Coleridge*, ed. K. Coburn (Routledge, 1957), Vol. I, *Notes*, no. 174, and *Text*, no. 132.
6. *Ec. Veg.* II 130.
7. *Ec. Veg.* III 459–60, 26, 520, 468. *Lov. Pl.* IV 184. *Ec. Veg.* II 473–4.

8. From MS at Camb. Univ. Lib.
9. Ibid.
10. M. Butler, *Maria Edgeworth* (O.U.P., 1972), p. 32.
11. K. Pearson, i 46.
12. Moilliet, p. 145.
13. From MS at Keele Univ. Lib.
14. See C. Bush, *18th Cent. Stud.* 7, 295–320 (1974); *Temple of Flora* (Collins, 1972), p. 4; R. J. Thornton, *Botanical Extracts* (Bensley, 1810), *passim*.
15. From MS at Royal Society of Arts.
16. C. Darwin, *Life*, pp. 25–6.
17. Ibid., p. 75.
18. C. Darwin, *Life*, p. 84 (deleted).
19. C. Darwin, *Life*, p. 76.
20. C. Darwin, *Life*, p. 75 (deleted).
21. C. Darwin, *Life*, p. 72.

22. Ibid., pp. 73–4.
23. Ibid., p. 74.
24. From MS at Keele Univ. Lib.
25. C. Darwin, *Life*, p. 74.
26. Ibid., p. 111.
27. J. Russell, op. cit., p. 63.
28. See *Encyclopaedia Britannica*, Vol. 12, article on 'Insect'; Rachel Carson, *Silent Spring* (Penguin, 1965), p. 252.
29. From MS at Camb. Univ. Lib.
30. G. Wakefield, *Memoirs* (Johnson, 1804) ii 229–32.
31. Ibid.
32. From MS at St John's College Library, Cambridge.
33. *Zoonomia* (3rd ed., 1801), ii 295.

34. Baron, i 541.
35. Edgeworth, ii 264.
36. From MS at Camb. Univ. Lib.
37. C. Darwin, *Life*, p. 126.
38. Ibid., pp. 126–7.
39. Ibid., p. 127.
40. J. C. Cox, *Journ. Derby Arch. & Nat. Hist. Soc.* 37, 91–6 (1915).
41. *Monthly Mag.* 13, 457–63 (1802).
42. Seward, p. 424.
43. *Monthly Mag.* 13, 548–9 (1802).
44. Ibid., *14*, 115–16 (1802).
45. C. Darwin, *Life*, p. 68.
46. Muirhead, ii 279.
47. C. Darwin, *Life*, p. 49.
48. Ibid., p. 68.

## Chapter 13 (*pages* 288–306)

1. F. Galton, *Hereditary Genius* (Watts, 1950), pp. 124–33.
2. Logan, pp. 67–77.
3. See N. Garfinkle, *Journ. Hist. Ideas 16*, 386 (1955), and *Monthly Mag. 15*, 632–6 (1803).
4. Wheler, i 45.
5. For the family biography, I rely mainly on Wheler and K. Pearson.
6. C. Darwin, *Autobiog.*, p. 27.
7. Ibid., p. 58.
8. G. de Beer, *Charles Darwin* (Nelson, 1963), p. 23.
9. Wheler, i 62.
10. See E. Schneider, *Coleridge, Opium and Kubla Khan*, pp. 91–101.
11. M. Lefebure, *S. T. Coleridge: A Bondage of Opium*, p. 44.
12. See N. Fruman, *Coleridge: The Damaged Archangel* (Allen & Unwin, 1972), pp. 93–4.
13. See *The Athenaeum*, no. 2474, p. 423 (1875).
14. Ibid.
15. B. W. Richardson, *Thomas Sopwith* (Longman 1891), p. 256.
16. *Lov. Pl.* I 317, II 346; *Ec. Veg.* II 497–8; *To Enterprise*, 114–16.
17. From MS in Salt Lib. (HM 37/54).
18. For further details, see D. King-Hele, in *Le Romantisme Anglo-Americain* (Paris: Didier, 1971),
pp. 147–63, and D. M. Hassler, *Erasmus Darwin*, ch. 5.
19. *Eve of St. Agnes*, 13–14; *Tem. Nat.* I 159–62; 'Ode to Psyche', 29–30, 47–8.
20. See D. King-Hele, *Shelley: His Thought and Work* (Macmillan, 1971), p. 5.
21. *Tem. Nat.* IV 103–4, 66, 383; *Queen Mab*, VI 178–9, VII 48, IX 31–2.
22. *Ec. Veg.* I 98; *Prometheus Unbound*, III 204.
23. *Ec. Veg.* I 85, 127–8; 'The Cloud', 75; *Witch of Atlas*, 485, 488.
24. B. W. Aldiss, *Billion-Year Spree* (Weidenfeld and Nicolson, 1973), ch. 1.
25. See R. F. Gustafson, *Pub. Mod. Lang. Ass. 75*, 101–9 (1960).
26. See R. L. Chamberlain, *Journ. Eng. Germ. Phil. 61*, 833–52 (1962).
27. See A. S. Roe, in *William Blake*, ed. A. H. Rosenfeld (Providence, R.I.: Brown University Press, 1969), pp. 158–95.
28. A. J. Finberg, *Turner's Sketches and Drawings* (Methuen, 1910), p. 69.
29. J. Lindsey, *Turner* (Panther, 1973). ch. 5, ch. 10.
30. Ibid., p. 249.

## Chapter 14 (*pages* 307–323)

1. P. J. Vorzimmer, *Charles Darwin: The Years of Controversy* (University of London Press, 1972), p. xv. For Charles's affinity with Erasmus, see H. E. Gruber, *Darwin on Man* (Wildwood, 1974), pp. 46–72.
2. *More Letters of Charles Darwin* (Murray, 1903), ii 419.
3. *Life and Letters of Charles Darwin* (1887), i 117; C. Darwin, *Autobiog.*, p. 135.
4. C. Darwin, *Autobiog.*, p. 49.
5. Ibid.
6. See Darlington, pp. 14–24.
7. C. Darwin, *The Origin of Species* (Dent, 1928), pp. 87–8.
8. Ibid., pp. 38–9, 168, 391.
9. Ibid., p. 355.
10. K. Pearson, ii 194.
11. C. Darwin, *Life*, p. 124 (deleted).
12. Ibid., p. 86 (deleted).
13. Wheler, ii 430.
14. See, for example, D. P. Rubincam, *Journ. Geophys. Res. 80*, 1537–48 (1974).

15. A. B. Binder, *The Moon 11*, 53–76 (1974); *13*, 431–73 (1975).
16. See G. Raverat, *Period Piece* (Faber, 1960), ch. X.
17. See J. L. Pritchard, *Sir George Cayley* (Parrish, 1961), pp. 233, 93.
18. C. Darwin, *Life*, p. 92.
19. G. L. Craik, *History of English Literature*, ii 382–97.
20. L. Brandl, *Erasmus Darwins Temple of Nature* and *Erasmus Darwins Botanic Garden* (Vienna: Braumüller, 1902 and 1909); E. Eckhardt, *Beobachtungen uber den Stil in Erasmus Darwins poetischen Werken* (Greifswald, 1907).
21. Logan, p. 99.
22. *Khram Prirody* (Moscow: Academi Nauk SSSR, 1960).
23. E. Robinson, *Annals of Science 9*, 359–67 (1953): *10*, 314–20 (1954). N. Barlow, *Notes & Rec. Roy. Soc. 14*, 85–98 (1959).
24. C. Darwin, *Life*, p. 76.
25. Ibid.
26. Ibid., pp. 76–7.

# ERASMUS DARWIN'S MAIN WRITINGS

1. Poem on the death of Prince Frederick. In *Academiae Cantabrigiensis Luctus in obitum Frederici celsissimi Walliae Principis*. Cambridge: Bentham, 1751. Republished in *European Magazine 27*, 75–6 (1795).
2. 'Remarks on the Opinion of Henry Eeles, Esq., concerning the Ascent of Vapour'. *Philosophical Transactions of the Royal Society 50*, 240–54 (1757).
3. 'An uncommon Case of an Haemoptysis'. *Phil. Trans. 51*, 526–9 (1760).
4. 'Experiments on Animal Fluids in the exhausted Receiver'. *Phil. Trans. 64*, 344–9 (1774).
5. 'A New Case in Squinting'. *Phil. Trans. 68*, 86–96 (1778).
6. *A System of Vegetables* . . . translated from the thirteenth edition of the Systema Vegetabilium of Linneus by a Botanical Society at Lichfield. 2 vols. Lichfield: J. Jackson, for Leigh and Sotheby, London, 1783.
7. 'An Account of an artificial Spring of Water'. *Phil. Trans. 75*, 1–7 (1785).
8. 'An Account of the successful use of Foxglove in some Dropsies, and in the pulmonary Consumption'. *Medical Transactions 3*, 255–86 (1785).
9. *The Families of Plants* . . . translated from the last edition of the Genera Plantarum . . . by a Botanical Society at Lichfield. 2 vols. Lichfield: J. Jackson, for J. Johnson, London, 1787.
10. 'Frigorific Experiments on the mechanical Expansion of Air'. *Phil. Trans. 78*, 43–52 (1788).
11. 'Of the Medicinal Waters of Buxton and Matlock', in J. Pilkington's *A View of the Present State of Derbyshire* (Derby: Drewry, 1789), pp. 256–75.
12. *The Botanic Garden: a Poem, in Two Parts.*
    Part I, *The Economy of Vegetation*. London: J. Johnson, 1791.
    Part II, *The Loves of the Plants*. London: J. Johnson, 1789.

Later English editions: *Part I.* 2nd edition, 1791. 3rd, 1795. 4th, 1799. 5th, 1806. 6th, 1824. *Part II.* 2nd, 1790. 3rd, 1791. 4th, 1794. 5th, 1799. 6th, 1806, 7th, 1824.

IRISH EDITIONS. Dublin: Moore, 1793–6.

AMERICAN EDITIONS. New York: Swords, 1798. 2nd ed., 1807.

TRANSLATIONS. French: Paris, 1800. Portuguese: Lisbon, 1803–4. Italian: Milan, 1805; Naples, 1817.

*Beauties of the Botanic Garden* (selections). London: Cadell, 1805. New York: Longworth, 1805.

Facsimile reprint of the complete *Botanic Garden* (1st ed. of both Parts) by Scolar Press, Menston, 1973.

13. *Zoonomia; or, The Laws of Organic Life.*

Part I. London: J. Johnson, 1794.

Parts I–III. London: J. Johnson, 1796 (2nd ed. of Part I, corrected). 2 vols.

Third edition (revised): London: J. Johnson, 1801. 4 vols.

IRISH EDITIONS. Dublin: Byrne, 1794–6; Dugdale, 1800. 2 vols.

AMERICAN EDITIONS. Part I. New York: Swords, 1796. Parts II and III. Philadelphia: Dobson. 1797. 2 vols. Later editions: Boston, 1803 and 1809; Philadelphia, 1818; A.M.S. Press, New York, 1975.

TRANSLATIONS. German: Hanover, 1795–7. Italian: Milan, 1803–5. Also French edition.

14. *A Plan for the Conduct of Female Education in Boarding Schools.* London: J. Johnson, 1797. Later editions: Dublin: Chambers, 1798; Philadelphia: Ormond, 1798; facsimile reprint by Johnson Reprint Corp., New York, 1968.

15. *Phytologia; or, The Philosophy of Agriculture and Gardening.* London: J. Johnson, 1800.

IRISH EDITION. Dublin: Byrne, 1800.

GERMAN TRANSLATION. Leipzig, 1801. 2 vols.

16. *The Temple of Nature; or, The Origin of Society.* London: J. Johnson, 1803. 2nd ed., 1806. 3rd ed., London: Jones, 1825.

AMERICAN EDITIONS. New York: Swords, 1804; Baltimore: Bonsal and Niles, 1804.

TRANSLATIONS. German: Brunswick, 1808. Russian: 1911, in *Journ. Min. National Education*; in book form, Moscow: Acad. Sci., 1954; 2nd ed., 1960.

Facsimile reprint by Scolar Press, Menston, 1973.

There are also many short poems published in magazines, etc.: Logan (pp. 152–4) lists seventeen; two others are the poem on shorthand in Gurney's *Brachygraphy* (see p. 28), and 'Idyllium: the Prison', in *Monthly Magazine 1,* 54 (1796). Many manuscript verses may be found in the Commonplace Book at Down House (see p. 341). Anna

Seward printed several of his short poems (with her own alterations) in her *Memoirs*.

## MANUSCRIPT SOURCES

Darwin's most important unpublished book, the 200-page Common-place Book, is in the Darwin Museum at Down House, Downe, Kent, together with many other MSS, family portraits, and mementoes. Numerous MSS, at present largely uncatalogued, have in recent years been deposited at the Cambridge University Library by Mr George Darwin and other members of the family: the material includes many letters to and from Edgeworth. Also at Cambridge, St John's College Library has a medical notebook and two letters: the Fitzwilliam Museum Library has 14 letters, to Banks, Cadell, Hayley, Hutton and others; and Darwin College has many family portraits, on loan from Mr George Darwin. The largest single collection of letters—about 50, to Boulton and Watt—is at the Birmingham Reference Library. The Wedgwood archive at Keele University Library has the 11 letters to Tom Wedgwood, a few to and from Josiah, and hundreds from Josiah to Bentley, in which Darwin is often mentioned. The John Rylands Library at Manchester has 1600 pages of MS copies of Wedgwood letters. The William Salt Library at Stafford has the letters to Barker about the early canal project and other material. The Lichfield Record Office has the canal agreement, the leases of Darwin's house, and other material. The Derby Central Library has MS records of the Derby Philosophical Society. The Bodleian Library has a number of MS poems and one letter. Liverpool City Libraries have one letter and the contract for *The Botanic Garden*.

The Royal Society of London has the MSS of the papers published in *Phil. Trans.*, the paper on the meteor of 1783, and other material. Also in London, the Royal Society of Arts has the important letters about carriages and windmills; the British Library has the letters to Greville about the polygrapher; the Royal Society of Medicine has the MS 'Withering letters', including one of Darwin's; the Wellcome Institute Library has the shorthand notebooks of medical lectures; the Botany Library of the British Museum (Natural History) has letters to Dryander and MS copies of letters to Banks. In the U.S.A., the American Philosophical Society, Philadelphia, has Darwin's three extant letters to Franklin, and others; and the Historical Society of Pennsylvania has a number of letters, including one to Reimarus.

# SELECTED BOOK LIST

In preparing this biography, I have utilized more than 400 books and 100 articles in periodicals which mention Darwin or his work. The selection below is confined to (a) books in which he plays a major part, (b) biographies of his close friends, and (c) a few 'background books'. The place of publication is London, unless otherwise stated.

Blackstone, B. *The Consecrated Urn*. Longman, 1959.

Bode, H. *James Brindley*. Aylesbury: Shire Publications, 1973.

Brown, T. *Observations on the Zoonomia of Erasmus Darwin*. Edinburgh, 1798.

Burke, H. F. *Pedigree of the Family of Darwin*. Privately printed, 1888.

Burton, A. *Josiah Wedgwood*. Deutsch, 1976.

Clarke, D. *The Ingenious Mr Edgeworth*. Oldbourne, 1965.

Clayton, H. *Coaching City*. Bala: Dragon Books, 1971.

Craik, G. L. *History of English Literature*. 3rd ed. Griffin, 1866.

Crowther, J. G. *Scientists of the Industrial Revolution*. Cresset Press, 1962.

Darlington, C. D. *Darwin's Place in History*. Oxford: Blackwell, 1959.

Darwin, Charles. *The Life of Erasmus Darwin*, together with an essay on his scientific works by Ernst Krause. Murray, 1879. 2nd ed., 1887. I have relied a great deal on this excellent short life. (Reprinted by Gregg International, 1971.)

———. *Autobiography*. Ed. Nora Barlow. Collins, 1958.

Dickinson, H. W. *Matthew Boulton*. Cambridge University Press, 1936.

Edgeworth, R. L. and Maria. *Memoirs of Richard Lovell Edgeworth*. 2 vols. Hunter, 1820. (Reprinted by Irish University Press, Shannon, 1969.)

Gibbs, F. W. *Joseph Priestley*. Nelson, 1965.

Gignilliat, G. W. *The Author of Sandford and Merton*. New York: Columbia University Press, 1932.

Hassler, D. M. *The Comedian as the Letter D: Erasmus Darwin's Comic Materialism*. The Hague: Nijhoff, 1973.

———. *Erasmus Darwin*. New York: Twayne, 1973. Establishes Darwin's status as a literary figure.

Hopkins, Mary, A. *Dr Johnson's Lichfield*. Owen, 1956.

King-Hele, D. *Erasmus Darwin*. Macmillan, 1963. Introduction to his work and ideas.

King-Hele, D., ed. *The Essential Writings of Erasmus Darwin*. MacGibbon and Kee, 1968. Selection from his books, letters, etc.

Klingender, F. D. *Art and the Industrial Revolution*. Paladin, 1972.

Lefebure, M. *Samuel Taylor Coleridge: A Bondage of Opium*. Gollancz, 1974.

Logan, J. V. *The Poetry and Aesthetics of Erasmus Darwin*. Princeton, N.J.: Princeton University Press, 1936. The best study of Darwin's aesthetics and psychology.

Lowes, J. L. *The Road to Xanadu*. First published 1927; reprinted by Vintage Books, New York, 1959.

Meteyard, E. *The Life of Josiah Wedgwood*. 2 vols. Hurst & Blackett, 1865–6. (Reprinted by Cornmarket Press, 1970.)

Moilliet, J. K. *Life and Correspondence of James Keir*. Privately printed, 1868.

Muirhead, J. P. *The Origin and Progress of the Mechanical Inventions of James Watt*. 3 vols. Murray, 1854.

Nicolson, B. *Joseph Wright of Derby*. 2 vols. Routledge & Kegan Paul, 1968.

Pearson, H. *Doctor Darwin*. Dent, 1930; Penguin, 1943. An entertaining picture of Darwin and his friends.

———. *Extraordinary People*. Heinemann, 1965.

Pearson, K. *The Life, Letters and Labours of Francis Galton*. 4 vols. Cambridge University Press, 1914–30.

Peck, T. W., and Wilkinson, K. D. *William Withering of Birmingham*. Bristol: Wright, 1950.

Piper, H. W. *The Active Universe*. Athlone Press, 1962.

Rolt, L. T. C. *James Watt*. Batsford, 1962.

Schneider, E. *Coleridge, Opium and Kubla Khan*. Chicago: University of Chicago Press, 1953.

Schofield, R. E. *The Lunar Society of Birmingham*. Oxford University Press, 1963. The standard work on the Lunar Society.

Seward, Anna. *Letters*. 6 vols. Edinburgh: Constable, 1811.

———. *Memoirs of the Life of Dr Darwin*. Johnson, 1804. Essential for Darwin's life at Lichfield.

Sewell, E. *The Orphic Voice*. New Haven, Conn.: Yale University Press, 1960.

Stock, J. E. *Memoirs of the Life of Thomas Beddoes*. Murray, 1811.

Wedgwood, Josiah. *Letters*. 3 vols. Manchester: E. J. Morten, 1974.

Williams, H. *Great Biologists*. Bell, 1961.

Wolf, A. *A History of Science, Technology and Philosophy in the Eighteenth Century*. 1938; 2nd ed., Allen and Unwin, 1952.

# ACKNOWLEDGEMENTS

In writing this book and searching for manuscripts and other material, I have left a trail of debts of gratitude, and I first wish to thank all those who know they helped me but are *not* named in the lists below. I have already thanked them individually, and I can assure them that their collective assistance has exceeded that from all other sources. My greatest single debt is to Dr Sydney Smith of St Catherine's College, Cambridge, who so kindly gave me the benefit of his unrivalled knowledge of the Darwinian manuscripts, and selected much interesting uncatalogued material for me at the Cambridge University Library. I also particularly thank Sir Hedley Atkins and Mr Philip Titheradge for their special efforts to enable me to make the fullest use of the unique collection at Down House; and I am very grateful to Dr Hugh Torrens and Mr Ian Fraser of Keele University for their enterprise in finding relevant manuscripts in the Wedgwood archive at the University Library.

For their courtesy in allowing me to quote excerpts from manuscripts in their possession, I am glad to make acknowledgements to: Down House and the Royal College of Surgeons of England, for the Commonplace Book and other MSS; Mr George Darwin and the Cambridge University Library; the Bodleian Library, Oxford; Messrs. Josiah Wedgwood and Sons of Barlaston and the Keele University Library where the Wedgwood papers are deposited; the Royal Society; the Royal Society of Arts; the Royal Society of Medicine; Dr John Moilliet; the Matthew Boulton Trust; Birmingham Public Libraries; Derby Central Library; Lichfield Record Office; the Trustees of the William Salt Library, and Messrs. Hand, Morgan and Owen, Stafford; the John Rylands Library, Manchester; the Syndics of the Fitzwilliam Museum, Cambridge; the Master and Fellows of St John's College, Cambridge; the Trustees of the British Library and of the British Museum (Natural History); the Wellcome Historical Library; the American Philosophical Society; and the Historical Society of Pennsylvania.

For permission to reproduce the photographs specified, I am pleased to make acknowledgements to: Down House and the Royal College of Surgeons of England (Plates 7A, 7B, 8A, 8B, 9C, 12B, Figs. 5, 6 and 7); the late Sir Robin Darwin (Plate 1); Mr George Darwin and the Master and Fellows of Darwin College, Cambridge (Plates 2A, 2B and 3A); the Royal Society (Plates 4B, 5B, 6B and 6C); the National Portrait Gallery (Plates 4C, 5A, 5C and 5D); the *Birmingham Post* (Plate 3B); the Science Museum (Plate 4A); Josiah Wedgwood and Sons, Barlaston (Plate 4D); the Tate Gallery (Plate 6A); Major J. W. Chandos-Pole and *Derbyshire Countryside* (Plate 9A); Derby Central Library (Plate 9B); Dr John Moilliet (Plate 10B); Birmingham Public Libraries (Plate 11 and Fig. 2); and the Royal Society of Arts (Figs. 3 and 4).

Finally, I express my sincere thanks to Giles de la Mare, of Faber and Faber, for his kind interest, continual encouragement and valuable comments throughout the process of writing and publication of this book.

# Index

Figures in *italics* indicate leading references on a subject. Books and poems (other than Erasmus Darwin's) are indexed under their authors' names. In the Darwin entries the relation to Erasmus is given in brackets.